Francophone Literature as World Literature

Literatures as World Literature

Can the literature of a specific country, author, or genre be used to approach the elusive concept of "world literature"? **Literatures as World Literature** takes a novel approach to world literature by analyzing specific constellations—according to language, nation, form, or theme—of literary texts and authors in their own world-literary dimensions. World literature is obviously so vast that any view of it cannot help but be partial; the question then becomes how to reduce the complex task of understanding and describing world literature. Most treatments of world literature so far either have been theoretical and thus abstract, or else have made broad use of exemplary texts from a variety of languages and epochs. The majority of critical work, the filling in of what has been traced, lies ahead of us. **Literatures as World Literature** fills in the devilish details by allowing scholars to move outward from their own areas of specialization, fostering scholarly writing that approaches more closely the polyphonic, multiperspectival nature of world literature.

Series Editor
Thomas O. Beebee

Editorial Board
Eduardo Coutinho, Federal University of Rio de Janeiro, Brazil
Hsinya Huang, National Sun-yat Sen University, Taiwan
Meg Samuelson, University of Cape Town, South Africa
Ken Seigneurie, Simon Fraser University, Canada
Mads Rosendahl Thomsen, Aarhus University, Denmark

Volumes in the Series
German Literature as World Literature, Edited by Thomas O. Beebee
Roberto Bolaño as World Literature, Edited by Nicholas Birns and Juan E. De Castro
Crime Fiction as World Literature, Edited by David Damrosch, Theo D'haen, and Louise Nilsson
Danish Literature as World Literature, Edited by Dan Ringgaard and Mads Rosendahl Thomsen
From Paris to Tlön: Surrealism as World Literature, By Delia Ungureanu
American Literature as World Literature, Edited by Jeffrey R. Di Leo
Romanian Literature as World Literature, Edited by Mircea Martin, Christian Moraru, and Andrei Terian
Brazilian Literature as World Literature, Edited by Eduardo F. Coutinho
Dutch and Flemish Literature as World Literature, Edited by Theo D'haen
Afropolitan Literature as World Literature, Edited by James Hodapp
Francophone Literature as World Literature, Edited by Christian Moraru, Nicole Simek, and Bertrand Westphal
Samuel Beckett as World Literature (forthcoming), Edited by Thirthankar Chakraborty and Juan Luis Toribio Vazquez
Bulgarian Literature as World Literature (forthcoming), Edited by Mihaela P. Harper and Dimitar Kambourov
Philosophy as World Literature (forthcoming), Edited by Jeffrey R. Di Leo

Francophone Literature as World Literature

Edited by
Christian Moraru, Nicole Simek,
and Bertrand Westphal

BLOOMSBURY ACADEMIC
NEW YORK • LONDON • OXFORD • NEW DELHI • SYDNEY

BLOOMSBURY ACADEMIC
Bloomsbury Publishing Inc
1385 Broadway, New York, NY 10018, USA
50 Bedford Square, London, WC1B 3DP, UK
29 Earlsfort Terrace, Dublin 2, Ireland

BLOOMSBURY, BLOOMSBURY ACADEMIC and the Diana logo are trademarks of Bloomsbury Publishing Plc

First published in the United States of America 2020
This paperback edition published in 2022

Volume Editor's Part of the Work © Christian Moraru, Nicole Simek, and Bertrand Westphal

Each chapter © Contributors

Cover design by Simon Levy

For legal purposes the Acknowledgments on p. ix–xi constitute an extension of this copyright page.

All rights reserved. No part of this publication may be reproduced or transmitted in any form or by any means, electronic or mechanical, including photocopying, recording, or any information storage or retrieval system, without prior permission in writing from the publishers.

Bloomsbury Publishing Inc does not have any control over, or responsibility for, any third-party websites referred to or in this book. All Internet addresses given in this book were correct at the time of going to press. The author and publisher regret any inconvenience caused if addresses have changed or sites have ceased to exist, but can accept no responsibility for any such changes.

Library of Congress Cataloging-in-Publication Data

Names: Moraru, Christian, editor. | Simek, Nicole Jenette, 1976- editor. | Westphal, Bertrand, editor.
Title: Francophone literature as world literature / edited by Christian Moraru, Nicole Simek, and Bertrand Westphal.
Description: New York: Bloomsbury Academic, 2020. | Series: Literatures as world literature | Includes bibliographical references and index.
Identifiers: LCCN 2020000821 (print) | LCCN 2020000822 (ebook) | ISBN 9781501347146 (hardback) | ISBN 9781501347160 (pdf) | ISBN 9781501347153 (ebook)
Subjects: LCSH: French literature–French-speaking countries–History and criticism. | French literature–20th century–History and criticism. | French literature–Appreciation.
Classification: LCC PQ3809 .F7325 2020 (print) | LCC PQ3809 (ebook) | DDC 860.9–dc23

LC record available at https://lccn.loc.gov/2020000821
LC ebook record available at https://lccn.loc.gov/2020000822

ISBN: HB: 978-1-5013-4714-6
PB: 978-1-5013-7111-0
ePDF: 978-1-5013-4716-0
eBook: 978-1-5013-4715-3

Series: Literatures as World Literature

Typeset by Deanta Global Publishing Services, Chennai, India

To find out more about our authors and books visit www.bloomsbury.com and sign up for our newsletters.

To Bi Kacou Parfait Diandué (1973–2019), in memoriam.

Contents

Preface and Acknowledgments ix

Introduction: Reading Francophone Literature with the World *Christian Moraru, Nicole Simek, and Bertrand Westphal* 1

Part I Systems and Institutions of Literary Francophonie: Language, Written Culture, and the Publishing World

1 African Literature, World Literature, and Francophonie *Bertrand Westphal* 49

2 Francophone African Publishing and the Misconceptions of World Literature *Raphaël Thierry* 66

3 Malinke, French, Francophonie: African Languages in World Literature *Bi Kacou Parfait Diandué* 83

4 Globalizing the Spiritual and the Mythological: Indian Writing in French from Pondicherry *Vijaya Rao* 93

Part II Francophone Spatialities: Cities, Landscapes, Environments

5 Mapping World Literature from Below: Tierno Monénembo and City Writing *Eric Prieto* 107

6 Questions of Diversity in the Global Literary Ecology and *banlieue* Literature *Laura Reeck* 122

7 As the World Falls Apart: Living through the Apocalypse in Christian Guay-Poliquin's *Le poids de la neige* and Catherine Mavrikakis's *Oscar de Profundis* *Vincent Gélinas-Lemaire* 136

8 Poetry in the World: Aimé Césaire, Édouard Glissant, and the Language of Landscape *Jane Hiddleston* 151

Part III Relational Identities: Sex, Gender, and Class in Francophone World Arenas

9   World Literature, *littérature-monde*, and the Politics of Difference
    Thérèse Migraine-George   167

10 Queer Desire on the Move: Resistance to Homoglobalization in
    World Literature in French *Jarrod Hayes*   180

11 Locations of Identity: *Littérature-mondaine* and the Ethics of Class in
    Evelyne Trouillot's *Le Rond-point* *Régine Michelle Jean-Charles*   194

Part IV Francophone Literature and Planetary Intertexts

12 Writing French in the World: Transnational Identities and Transcultural
    Ideals in the Works of Michel Houellebecq and Boualem Sansal
    Jacqueline Dutton   209

13 Literature's Purchase: Remaking World Economic Relations in Crusoe's
    Footsteps *Nicole Simek*   227

14 Worlding *Négritude*, or Aimé Césaire's Global Caliban *Zahi Zalloua*   239

15 From Postmodern Intertextuality to "Decomposed Theater": Matei
    Vișniec between Romanian and Francophone Literatures *Emilia David*   252

Bibliography   267
Notes on Contributors   292
Index   297

Preface and Acknowledgments

"Are all literatures world literatures?" wonder the editors of a 2018 book published in the same series as ours.[1] They also point out that the issue seldom comes up with respect to "presumably 'major' literatures such as French or British."[2] They imply, and we too recognize here, that this question is still raised, *expressis verbis* or not, apropos of literary cultures perceived as less central to a world-system whose accounts, at least, are in turn still marked by some of the hierarchies and epistemological biases of the *littérature universelle* paradigm.

In pushing back against this model, *Francophone Literature as World Literature* does not skirt the question either. But, in asking it, our collection's chapters focus on Francophone writing from outside the Hexagon—from European countries like Luxembourg and from former French colonies—as well as from inside metropolitan France, with both *Beur* literature and highly acclaimed authors such as Michel Houellebecq as major examples. Thus, our contributors trace the ways in which Francophone writers from all over the world lay bare the "worldedness" of their roots and efforts. Uncovering the planetary inscription of the literary works and cultural traditions of a francosphere encompassing Asia, Africa, Canada, the Caribbean, and Europe, without forgetting, inside the latter, France itself is in fact one of this book's major tasks. For, as it will become readily apparent, Francophone writers—whether we talk about established figures or the recently arrived—make their cases for this world presence assiduously, time and over again. Particularly in the wake of the *littérature-monde* debate, however, French literature traditionally understood can neither claim nor afford anymore, we believe, the self-assigned exceptionalist position inside the world-system of writing of French expression. The Flauberts, the Rimbauds, the Célines, the Durases, and their metropolitan peers and successors must occupy, instead, a more democratically configured place within this system and participate in similar relays and processes of worlding, planetary negotiations, and "planetarizing" ("mondializing") relevance as any other voices of literary Francophonie no matter what their locations and backgrounds are—hence our World Literature approach to the immensely rich and variegated Francophone corpus.

Bringing together not only Francophone material but also scholars of literary Francophonies from Australia to Africa and Québec and from the Caribbean to Romania and India, this book would not have been possible without the unflagging support provided by the Bloomsbury staff, as well as by our institutions and colleagues. Thus, we want to recognize Editorial Director Haaris Naqvi, whose professional guidance and help overall has been unparalleled, as well as Editorial Assistant Amy Martin, the press's outside readers, and its marketing and production teams. We are also most grateful to Thomas Oliver Beebee, editor of the Literatures as World Literature series, for his generosity and interest in this project from the get-go.

At University of North Carolina, Greensboro, Beth Miller has helped editing the book and has done the index. Christian Moraru would also like to thank the following institutions, programs, and individuals: the Alexander von Humboldt Foundation, for its steady sponsorship over the years; UNCG chancellor Franklin D. Gilliam, Jr., and Provost Dana Dunn, for their support of advanced collaborative research bringing together faculty from UNCG and other universities; the College of Arts and Sciences, for travel grants awarded by Dean John Z. Kiss; UNCG's Class of 1949 Distinguished Professor in the Humanities Endowment; UNCG's Atlantic World Research Network and its director, Professor Christopher Hodgkins; UNCG's Office of Research and Economic Development and its vice chancellor, Dr. Terri L. Shelton, for well-targeted, dependable funding; UNCG's International Programs Center, for recent travel awards; the University's Walter Clinton Jackson Library and Information Technology Services specialists, for all their invaluable assistance; the UNCG English Department's Head, Professor Scott Romine, for his unique leadership and the English faculty for their collegiality and participation in the conversation about World Literature and its place in the department. Gratefully acknowledged are also the support, kindness, and friendship of Henry Sussman, Eileen Julien, Keith Cushman, Karen Kilcup, Stephen Yarbrough, Jean-Michel Rabaté, Alexandru Matei, Jeffrey R. Di Leo, and Radu Țurcanu. Camelia has helped, once again, in far more ways than can be described here.

Francophone Literature as World Literature features solely original work. Most contributions have been written in English. Three of them have been done in other languages and have been rendered into English: Bertrand Westphal's "African Literature, World Literature, and Francophonie" (translated from the French by Amy Wells); Bi Kacou Parfait Diandué's "Malinke, French, Francophonie: African Languages in World Literature" (translated from the French by N'Guessan Kouadio Germain); and Emilia David's "From Postmodern Intertextuality to 'Decomposed Theater': Matei Vișniec between Romanian and Francophone Literatures" (translated from the Italian by Elizabeth MacDonald). All translations have been thoroughly revised by the editors.

Finally, we should note that the bibliography compiled at the end lists, as consistently as possible, items the contributors both reference and use in their chapters. Here, "use" means, quasi invariably, engaging with the works in question in ways requiring more formal citation. In some cases, however, our critics mention in their respective chapters solely the author name, title, and possibly the publication year. In this category fall mostly primary material and some philosophy and literary-cultural scholarship. The bibliography includes texts of this sort because, while they are not fully referenced in their respective chapters and sometimes are mentioned only in endnotes, they are relevant to the overall discussion in those contributions.

Christian Moraru, Nicole Simek, and Bertrand Westphal

Notes

1 Mircea Martin, Christian Moraru, and Andrei Terian, eds., "Preface and Acknowledgments," in *Romanian Literature as World Literature* (New York, NY: Bloomsbury, 2018), xiv.
2 Martin, Moraru, and Terian, eds., "Preface and Acknowledgments," xiv.

Introduction: Reading Francophone Literature with the World

Christian Moraru, Nicole Simek, and Bertrand Westphal

> A comprehensive, all-embracing art, an art that joins together, a tissue-art, an art of links, a network-like art. An art that places thousands of points in relation to one another and explores the roads all these interconnected points entreat us to take.
> —Grégoire Polet, "L'atlas du monde"

"As far as poetry and politics go," Martinican writer Édouard Glissant declares in a 2003 interview given to Philippe Artières and reprinted in the collective volume *Pour une littérature-monde* coedited by Michel Le Bris and Jean Rouaud, "I think I have always listened to my instinct telling me that the utmost object of poetry is the world: the world of becoming, the world that jostles us, the world that defies understanding, ... the world as place of meeting, of cultural impact, and of the human in all its forms."[1] What ties the literary and the political together, Glissant goes on, is "this reference to the world." This world, he specifies, is not a "kind of abstract universal" but a concrete and immediate *totalité-monde*. However, this "world totality" is non-"totalist," and it is definitely non-totalitarian; in it, people, cultures, and histories stand "in relation to one another," worlded.[2] The French-Caribbean author further insists that being in relation in and with the world is a prerequisite to creating aesthetically and, by the same token, to *re*creating politically. Whether we talk about the making of poetic form or about the remaking of a socioeconomic system still undergirded, as Glissant reminds us, by hegemonic versions of relationality, either action is for him—as it is for the editors of *Francophone Literature as World Literature*—predicated on an awareness of the world-as-world or, as we shall see later on, of the world as *planet* and its *problématique-monde* or "planetary problematics": the world as a space of multiple and inevitable encounters, as an involved, simultaneously encouraging and troubling relational setup consisting structurally and thematically of links, interchanges, and frictions among individuals, groups, politics, places, and literary-cultural entities on scales ranging from the sub- to the transnational, the regional to the planetary, the human to the nonhuman, and the animate to the inanimate.

In focusing on Francophonie's literary production as World Literature, our book attends to works in a plethora of French varieties worldwide by treating those texts as literary practices fundamentally engaged with and molded, at distance and in situ, by this highly complex world structure and its issues.³ The chapters revisit key aspects, moments, and whereabouts of recent Francophone literatures so as to canvas and problematize these literatures' very *worldedness* at a time the latter is becoming geoculturally as well as theoretically impossible to ignore and requires, accordingly, systematic and *appositely world-minded* critical reflection—hence the plea we enter, with some qualifications, in the final section of this introduction and across the volume on behalf of a World Literature approach to this Francophone corpus.⁴ For, we contend, Glissant's world-relational ontology bears not only on writing and politics but also on making sense of the written word, political activism, and life generally in Francophone spaces—in brief, on critical interpretation. That is to say, the other face of this ontology is a reading model. Indeed, we discern a critical and critically worlded platform in Glissant's *Poetics of Relation*, in his poetics largely, and beyond it in much of Francophone literatures. This program, which we deem foundational to a World Literature-informed revisiting of these literary bodies, demands dealing with them, and not solely with their *littérature-monde* rebellious extension, as an art shaped by a world problematics—by conversations, transactions, clashes, overlaps, and cross-pollinations with a whole spectrum of worldly presences, influences, traditions, idioms, and so forth. Essentially on the same wavelength, we read post–Second World War Francophone literatures with the world-as-world. Not only do we not cast aside the "Francophone" category, as we will explain at greater length later on, but we also associate *littérature-monde* to it and read *for* the world in this entire literary domain as well as we do, conversely, for this body of work's own inscription into the world unfolding inside, across, and outside literary Francophonie's old and new abodes.

Thus, we ask, most basically, which world networks—and, more broadly, which kind of world—are Francophone writers part of? And, vice versa, which world or worlds, which networks of language, literature, race, ethnicity, gender, faith, material culture, and localities do these authors' works give voice to and power?⁵ These webs, we stress throughout, bring into play a plurality: not—by a long shot—an egalitarian one, but one fraught with asymmetries and injustices and surely tilted to certain hubs of political-economic leverage and cultural prestige. At the same time, centers and margins alike, former French colonies, today's multiethnic and multiracial France, as well as the other sites enmeshed in this networked aggregate, all reveal themselves as crossroads at once geohistorically situated and of the bigger world, worldly. Together, they stage a mundane diorama of loosely organized yet mobile multiplicities differing from one another according to place, imperial past, postimperial developments, and so on.

In line with the Bloomsbury series' title, our book's refers to *Francophone Literature*. But—and we want to make this absolutely clear—the singular form harbors and de facto means multitudes, and so "literature" should be read as "literatures." We attempt to capture this astonishing diversity and richness not just in the plural of our standard designation of the phenomenon at hand, "Francophone literatures," as we do later, but also in the notion, upheld throughout the following fifteen chapters, that metropolitan French literature itself as conventionally taught and written on has become, under the impact of the feedback loop generated by Francophonie's world literary apparatus, *no more and no less than just one of these Francophone literatures.*[6] In highlighting this plurality—one whose makeup is, to repeat, far from genuinely pluralist and democratic—we do not aim to disregard the continuities among those literatures conjoined by the "Francophone" common denominator, but to foreground, rather, a heterogeneous planetary reality, also acknowledging that the all-embracing Francophone perspective itself has not always done justice to such complexities either. As writing in a certain language and as a linguistically centered approach thereto, it can have and arguably has had unifying and even homogenizing repercussions insofar as it has lumped together the remarkably discrepant ethnocultural worlds both brought into being and into conversation by the dissemination of French across continents. That is why our introduction leads off with a brief and occasionally data-driven survey of what we would dub Francophonie's language *ecologies*, a concept meant to drive home the linguistic facet of the point we make apropos of Francophone literatures: the French-speaking world actually constitutes a world-system of "combined and uneven" worlds in which French and its users exist alongside and in interface with other tongues and dialects and those employing them within and across their own world-systems of language and culture.[7] In this sense, the idiom itself is "always already," and eminently, worlded, albeit in ways seldom equitable or widely beneficial. But worlded are also the prose, poetry, and drama done in it, an idea rehearsed in the second segment of these considerations. We also show there how multilingual and multiliterary-multicultural ecologies go hand in hand. This situation, this world reality, is characteristic of literary Francophonie and, more specifically, of the "littérature-monde en français"—in an approximate translation, "World Literature in French"—to whose controversial "manifesto" we turn thereafter. The discussion of *Pour une littérature-monde* serves as a segue into the case section four of this introduction makes for the world-as-world or the world *qua* planet as an epistemological model for grasping the *monde* and the *mode* of *littérature-monde* and, subsequently, for a planetary, World Literature-oriented critical engagement with Francophone literatures. We close with a rationale for the book's structure and a chart plotting succinctly the intersecting trajectories of the chapters across the world problematics taken up by some of the most representative Francophone writers after the Second World War.

1. Francophonie in the World, the Worlds of Francophonie: Linguistic, Legal, and Political Frameworks

Whether "Francophonie" is understood as referring to the world's population of French speakers or, more narrowly, to the Organisation Internationale de la Francophonie (OIF), which was founded in 1970 to foster cooperation among French-speaking countries, the notion has been deployed basically to designate political, economic, and cultural ties binding Francophones together as a collective whole distinct from its non-French-speaking "others." Born under nineteenth-century French colonial imperialism—an inheritance they would never quite be able to shake off—the terms "Francophone" and "Francophonie" became widely employed only after the dissolution of France's empire in the 1960s. Significantly, an internal tension marks this use in the postcolonial period. "Francophonie" shores up a linguistic connection between France and its former possessions—and, as such, it has come under scrutiny as a vehicle of neocolonial power—but the concept also calls to mind, through its very distinction from "French," the many lives the French language leads inside and outside the French nation-state. Michaël Oustinoff captures this duality well in the glossary to *Traduction et mondialisation*, where he writes that

> just like *arabophonie, hispanophonie, lusophonie*, and so on, Francophonie is a crucial, living feature of the contemporary world. In fact, it takes two forms. The first, belonging to the past, is a nostalgic Francophonie, more or less tinged with neocolonialism, that seeks to defend the French language in order to regain its former influence, against the tide of history. But there is a second, more resolutely modern form that is no longer centered only on France, a form that is fully open to the extreme diversity of Francophone worlds and is fully integrated into *globalization* and *cultural diversity*.[8]

To insist on the wide range of today's Francophone literatures, as we do here, is, then, both to forefront the worldedness of Francophonie and to make visible the variety and disjunctions that must be taken into account by any study of world networks, literary or otherwise. That said, if we are to understand the organization of these multiplicities, we cannot discount the world-shaping force and effects of the reality covered by the first meaning Oustinoff assigns to "Francophonie." Nor can we ignore that, strictly speaking, *arabophonie, hispanophonie*, and even *anglophonie* rarely occur as nouns in either French or English; Francophonie thus constitutes something of a *hapax legomenon*, pointing as it does to the world of worlds that it is part and parcel of *and* to the unique political history and institutional frameworks that have forged and bolstered it.

One path into this history takes us through the legislative management of French around the world. In France, we might begin our genealogy on October 5, 1958, with the adoption of the new Constitution inaugurating the Fifth Republic. While European countries such as the UK and Sweden have declined, like the United States at least at the federal level, to set an official language, France has done just that. The opening paragraph of Article 2 of the French Constitution, a segment devoted to "Sovereignty," stipulates that "the language of the Republic shall be French."[9] It bears noting that this passage did not appear in the 1958 text; it was proposed in a June 25, 1992, amendment to constitutional law. In the wake of this reform, the notorious Toubon Law, as it is known—it was named after the minister of culture and Francophonie who had pushed for it—was passed during the turbulent summer of 1994. A group of parliamentary deputies referred the act to the Conseil Constitutionnel. The council ruled that its Article 11, which addressed freedom of speech and communication, contravened the Declaration of the Rights of Man and of the Citizen.[10] Only two years later was an enforcement decree signed specifying how the law would be implemented. Officially, the new regulation concerned "the use of the French language" as well as the idiom's "enrichment." The legislature considered the latter indispensable given that the proposal formally prohibited all recourse to a foreign language (with English the implicit target here) in government and public-sector communications, as well as in the workplace, advertising, consumer-goods user manuals, and so forth. For instance, one would no longer speak of *e-mail* but of *courriel*—a Québécois contraction of "courrier électronique," the term is, one might say, "Francophone."

More importantly, the law's opening article is relevant to the matter at hand. If the article's first two paragraphs are unsurprising, the third quite unexpectedly references Francophonie. "[The French language] is," we learn, "the privileged link among the States constituting the Francophone community."[11] Here, "community" does not necessarily mean what it did for Charles de Gaulle in the late 1950s. Nevertheless, the term remains ambiguous, and yet it still appeared in the French Constitution at the time the Toubon Law was passed. This should have raised questions not only about the language of the law or about the place of the national language *in* the law but also outside the juridical context, namely, about Francophonie and its literary dimension. However, neither Francophonie nor the Francophone literary archive has been thoroughly examined from this legal perspective, even though such an angle is revealing, for the extent to which the language and its use have been regulated by the French legislature is truly striking. In the Constitution, language matters have repeatedly been the object of amendments reflecting the preoccupations of the moment, especially over the last decades. Taking all this into account, it is then less surprising that Francophonie makes for a major, passionately political issue, while, as remarked earlier, no equivalent situation can be said to exist for Anglophonie, Germanophonie, or Sinophonie.

The unique legal narrative delineated here reflects, no doubt, France's linguistic situation, one that has had its implications on various scales. Within the country's borders, the first and foremost consequence was that French became, by legislative fiat, the national language at the expense of all other tongues spoken in the Hexagon. This exclusive status is also markedly more restrictive than that of the official languages of most of France's neighbors. Although they have established one or more official languages—sometimes more indirectly, as in Italy—these countries recognize the existence and use of regional idioms.[12] In France, the 1951 Deixonne Law, which predated the Fifth Republic, allowed schools to teach a number of languages described as "regional," with Basque, Breton, Catalan, and Occitan among them. In July 2008, a new constitutional revision acknowledged these languages in Article 75, Paragraph 1 of the Constitution, which notes that "regional languages are part of France's heritage," even though, we should add, one might well question the actual institutional support of this "heritage."

In any event, French got to enjoy, under the law, the same official role on the mainland and off it, that is, in what is commonly called "Overseas France" or, in administrative parlance, the DROM-COM ("départements et régions d'outre-mer et collectivités d'outre-mer"), "overseas departments, regions, and collectivities" such as Martinique, Guadeloupe, and French Polynesia.[13] Local tongues, understood as regional, can be legally recognized here, though, as were, for example, Tahitian, in a 1981 decree extending the 1951 Deixonne Law, and four Melanesian languages in 1992. Tahitian is actually taught in schools and at the University of French Polynesia in Papeëte. However, in March 2006, France's Council of State annulled a provision of French Polynesia's Assembly bylaws authorizing speakers to use Tahitian or Polynesian tongues in addition to French.[14] The same holds in Martinique and Guadeloupe, where French is the official language, but Creole is accepted in schools without being official. Once more, given the high number of legislative actions targeting language, we can only conclude that the employment and function of the official idiom are in France, quite characteristically, subject to legal prescriptions. We should keep this in mind, for it reflects a certain French vision of Francophonie that oftentimes crosses the linguistic into the cultural.

It is also worth asking, along the same lines, how the October 4, 1958 Constitution viewed Francophonie. Interestingly, the text makes no mention of French or regional tongues, as it does not reference Francophonie either. Nonetheless, Title XIV of the Constitution's current version is jointly dedicated to "Francophonie" and "Association Agreements." It was the constitutional law of July 23, 2008 that brought about this recognition of Francophonie. Article 87 stipulates that "the Republic shall participate in the development of solidarity and cooperation between countries and peoples having the French language in common." This article existed previously in slightly different form: it was not "the Republic," an allegorical designation of "France," that was to take this initiative, but rather "the Republic and the Community." Promoted by de Gaulle, the "French Community" was designed to bring together the independent countries mushrooming on the ruins of the defunct French empire. Logically, after independence, said "Community" quietly faded away. The new version of Article 87 is based, then, on a belated revision of the original text. Also, Title XIV now comprises, in complete form, Article 88, which stipulates benevolently that "the Republic may enter into agreements with countries that wish to associate with it in order to develop their civilizations."[15] But, if Article 87 underlines the pivotal role of the French language for "the Republic," Article 88 raises a few unanswered questions: What are "civilizations" exactly? How can one "develop" them? What sorts of "associations" and "agreements" could encourage such a "development," and, more specifically, what would France's role be in it? We should note that these "reforms" were brought forward during the presidency of Nicolas Sarkozy (2007–12), in between two significant political events, one being a speech given by the French head of state in July 2007 at Cheikh Anta Diop University in Dakar, Senegal, a talk that triggered a heated argument over Sarkozy's vision of Africa and of the continent's presence in history and in the world today, and the other a highly controversial debate over French and French national identity.[16]

Sparked off in November 2009, the dispute extended into the world of Francophonie, so it is worth asking at this point how the same dynamic of idiom and nationhood plays out in the other twenty-eight officially Francophone countries on the planet.¹⁷ Some of these are plurilingual, while elsewhere there are no other official languages besides French. In Europe, to start with, Belgium, Luxembourg, Switzerland, and Monaco are Francophone, but only the last of the four is exclusively so, the others being at least trilingual, and Switzerland even quadrilingual given that German, French, Italian, and Romansh are recognized inside its borders.¹⁸ In Italy, French now plays a marginal role, but it has been the co-official language of the Aosta Valley since 1561. In North America, it has been the only official language of Québec since 1974, and in the province of New Brunswick and the Northwest, Yukon, and Nunavut Territories, it is a second official idiom—as is well known, at the federal level, Canada recognizes English and French. Haiti, in turn, is both Francophone and Creolophone. However, no Asian country is officially Francophone—and this includes a Middle Eastern state such as Lebanon—while in Oceania only Vanuatu is, even though it has adopted two other languages as well. By contrast, in sub-Saharan Africa, there are numerous Francophone countries. Here too, some of them—eleven, actually—are exclusively Francophone.¹⁹ One of them is the Democratic Republic of the Congo (DRC, formerly known as Zaire), the country, we are told, with the largest number of potential French speakers on the planet. In ten other African states, French is among the several official languages.²⁰ As to the Maghreb, there are no officially Francophone countries here despite their high number of users of French—nearly two-thirds of the population in Tunisia and one-third in Morocco speak French.²¹ Also, alongside French and one or more additional official languages, some countries promote what they call "national languages." In Djibouti, for instance, French and Arabic are official, while Somali and Afar are "national."

It also bears pointing out that the percentage of French speakers varies widely from one country to another across the Francophone world. Whether the language has official status or not is of relatively small consequence. What matters is its actual use. For example, unlike in Tunisia, in Burundi, where French is co-official, barely 8 percent of the population resorts to French, and in Mali, 16 percent, according to the OIF.²² Vietnam's situation is similar. Annexed by France in 1858, it was incorporated into French Indochina in 1887 before gaining its independence in 1954. Given its tumultuous history, Vietnam is sometimes viewed as partially Francophone in the collective French imaginary, and, revealingly, literature helps preserve this perception. However, less than 1 percent of today's Vietnamese population actually speaks the language of the former colonizer.²³ A very different case is illustrated by Mauritius, whose National Assembly communicates in English. Otherwise, the country has no official language, although it has the largest proportion of French speakers (73 percent) outside Europe and the DROM-COM.²⁴ In Europe, the prize goes to the Federation Wallonia-Brussels, where the percentage is 98 percent, ahead of France and Monaco (97 percent), which are followed by Luxembourg (92 percent).²⁵ The OIF estimates, in fact, that French is the fifth most spoken language in the world, after Mandarin, English, Spanish, and Arabic.²⁶ Many of these calculations are based on numbers that comprise the *entire* population of officially Francophone nation-states, but the reality is that, out of their 900 million residents, only one-third are speakers of French. We could expatiate at length on the interpretation of statistics, which, moreover, vary according to the weight one gives to different criteria, but we can still come quickly to a general conclusion: in the vast majority of countries described as Francophone, French has minority status, in the sense that less than half of the population uses it, if only because it is rarely the speakers' mother tongue.

For this and other reasons, and whether it is a (co-)official language or not, French rubs elbows with other languages all over the world. Sometimes these other languages were spread by colonialism, like English in Canada or Cameroon. Sometimes, and this is obviously the most common situation, they are national idioms. Burundi has made Kirundi official, and the same is true for Kinyarwanda and Swahili in Rwanda; Sango in the Central African Republic; Arabic in Chad, Comoros, and Djibouti; Malagasy in Madagascar; and Seychellois Creole in the Seychelles. As mentioned earlier, the DRC is supposed to be the most Francophone country in the world, but this claim must be put into context. The DRC indeed has 84 million inhabitants, but only 51 percent of them (42.5 million people) are Francophone, according to the OIF. While French is indeed its official language, the country also has four other national languages—Kikongo, Lingala, Swahili, and Tshiluba—not counting the approximately 200 idioms and dialects spoken locally, with Swahili rivaling French in terms of number of speakers as the former makes up for around 40 percent of the population, which is generally multilingual. Also, while French is hegemonic (at 70–97 percent) across the official channels of communication such as print media, radio, and television, as well as in literature, this is not the case with Congolese music, where Lingala reigns supreme.

Beyond Congo and Africa, multilingualism has been, indeed, a characteristic of the francosphere. There are several explanations for this. Here, we will touch, briefly, only on some of them. Thus, outside Europe, French was initially no more than a language imposed by the colonizer. Everywhere, its spread is checked by other languages, both European and non-European. At the time when they won their independence from France—and DRC and Ruanda-Urundi (later Rwanda and Burundi) from Belgium as well—the African countries that emerged from the former empire often retained French, and the motivations for such a decision had to do primarily either with the economy or with international affairs. Domestically, French has sometimes also served as a compromise between several competing languages. In today's globalizing world, adopting French is ordinarily perceived as stemming from a desire to ease the country's integration into the world-system of relations. But a nation such as Equatorial Guinea presents a more complicated situation. Once a Spanish colony, it adopted French as an official language alongside Spanish in 1998. Yet rather than representing a reaction to globalization, which, in turn, might have suggested a response to the expansion of French's reach, this measure was primarily motivated by local realities—surrounded by two Francophone countries (Cameroon and Gabon), Equatorial Guinea was actually already partly Francophone (in 2018, the number of French speakers stood at just under 30 percent of the population). Conversely, English has gained ground steadily in Francophone lands after the Second World War, and this has only added to their polyglot environment—as is well known, English exerts strong pressure in Canada, both in Québec and in bilingual provinces such as New Brunswick. What is more, nation-states that were never under English colonization are themselves becoming receptive to the world's twenty-first-century lingua franca, notably in Francophone Africa. In the aftermath of the massive Tutsi exodus to Uganda following the genocide and related policy decisions, English became one of the official languages in Rwanda in 2003. Today, Rwandans speak English more frequently than French, while Kinyarwanda is much more prevalent than either.[27] Also, in Burundi, an August 2014 decree, which has not yet been implemented, proposed making English the official language, alongside Kirundi, Swahili, and French, out of concern, according to the Burundian authorities, of becoming out of step with the standards of the East African Community.[28]

At any rate, it bears reminding ourselves that plurilingualism is part and parcel of Francophonie, namely, of those world territories set apart in the metropolitan public imagination, paradoxically enough, by the shared use of one idiom, French. The paradox is further compounded if we approach the problem of Francophonie's unifying language not through the lens of the countries where French is an (or the) official tongue but from the broader perspective of the OIF. Set up in 1967 as the Assemblée parlementaire de la francophonie, the OIF reunites countries where French is either a native or an administrative, cultural, or minority language. Eighty-eight states and governments belong to it, including former French colonies but also East European nations that have never been part of the French empire. The first members of the Assemblée parlementaire de la francophonie were all officially Francophone, but the organization expanded as soon as other membership principles (e.g., French as a language of culture) were adopted, and so Romania, Bulgaria, Albania, Moldova, and Armenia are now full OIF members, whereas the American state of Louisiana and Poland enjoy OIF observer status. This enlargement reflects the same logic as the creation of an international "Francophone space," which has continually opened up the new pathways and activity sectors listed on the organization's website. "Originally focused on cultural and educational cooperation," the OIF has acknowledged, "our mission has evolved over various summits and now includes politics (peace, democracy, and human rights), sustainable development, economics, and digital technology."[29] The shared language and its promotion have given rise to the creation of a common world sphere of operations that spans continents and is defined by the institutions listed in Article 2 of the charter adopted by the Conférence ministérielle de la Francophonie in Antananarivo, Madagascar, in November 2005.[30]

2. Multilingualism, Transnationalism, and the Literary Cultures of Francophonie

Derived from the heterogeneity of Francophone linguistic ecologies is the high number of other literatures thriving within them alongside French-language writing.

For the encounter and cross-pollination between Francophone and other traditions and, by the same token, the inscription of literary Francophonie into world aggregates, circuitries, and geographies of production, distribution, and recognition do not play out just at the outer borders of Francophonie. They occur *inside* the French-speaking world, too, from continental France itself, where Beur fiction is just one example, to Asia and the Caribbean. A salient case in point are the Francophone African countries, where, more than anywhere else on the planet, French is an official or co-official idiom. Most authors from this zone publish in French. Addressed by several chapters of our book, this situation raises a host of questions: these writers' relationship to French and their access to the publishing market in national languages; the reception of works written in French and the issue of audience more broadly; the coexistence of local literatures in different idioms, one of which may be standard French.

As diverse as the questions are the answers thereto, and it is noteworthy that the authors themselves have been rarely in agreement. Some, like Léopold Sédar Senghor, have extolled the use of French. Others, like Ahmadou Kourouma, the focus of another piece in our collection, adopt French also but view it and local languages such as Malinke as communicating vessels, working actively together through a process of intimate and mutual translation. There are, as well, authors inside and outside Francophonie who reject former colonial languages, thereby refuting Senghor's position, as did, most famously, Kenyan writer Ngũgĩ wa Thiong'o in another imperial context.[31] Finally, some claim that, through a long process of localizing appropriation, French has become a language of Africa, as Souleymane Bachir Diagne contends in *Penser et écrire l'Afrique aujourd'hui* (2017), a position another chapter of *Francophone Literature as World Literature* deals with.

Now, of course, the biggest hurdle for sub-Saharan African writers is most likely publication (especially in languages other than French), which would truly put linguistic diversity into practice. There are, unfortunately, few presses in Francophone Africa, and fewer still are those bringing out books in the national languages of their own parts of the world. Publishing a book in Wolof in Senegal or Fon in Benin, for instance, is possible but not easy. Even so, the volume in question, to be successful, would still need to be distributed under the right conditions and circulate effectively across the region's markets. A similar obstacle accounts for the low number of literary translations into African national languages beyond "a few bilingual texts (French into national languages) designed for educational purposes," as Lalbila A. Yoda describes the dire situation of Burkina Faso before concluding that "the language hierarchy, which places French front and center, does not allow a role for translation in the promotion of [Africa's] national languages or in the preservation of cultural diversity as recommended by most national, regional, and international guidelines and agreements."[32]

Adding to the stratification of the literary cultures of Francophone ecologies is the already noted presence of several former colonial languages. Cameroon's literature is, in this respect, just one instructive example among so many. The country boasts the widest linguistic gamut of Africa. French is among the 200-odd languages spoken there.

But so is English, which is employed in administrative subdivisions near the Nigerian border, and in which Imbolo Mbue, who was born in Limbe, one of Cameroon's partially Anglophone regions, has recently written and published her 2016 book *Behold the Dreamers*. We should point out that Mbue has been living in the United States since she was sixteen. Having immediately met with resounding success upon its publication, this PEN/Faulkner Award-winning novel was translated into French and in fact came out from Belfond the same year it was released by Random House. Nota bene, Mbue is not the exception here but the rule, which in turn bears out the multilingual condition of societies where French is an official or co-official language.

As one might expect, Canada makes for a great case study in this regard. If Québec has been vigorously defending a Francophone heritage striving for preeminence, New Brunswick has adopted a more moderate approach to the language issue, more specifically to the traditional clashes between French and English. On this topic, the final chapter of Acadian author Germaine Comeau's 2008 novel *Laville* presents, via its female narrator, a fascinating take on the idiom in which one expresses himself or herself. "Authors," writes Comeau, "always place themselves at the frontier between the word (their speech) and their thought. The structure of their speech is intimately connected to their way of telling reality. Perhaps we use an English structure with French words. Or perhaps we simply speak English with French words after all."[33] The title of the chapter is "Connivence," and there certainly is, we might gloss, connivance between the narrator and the character she addresses in a sort of concluding dialogue, but this mutual "support" or at least interaction also occurs between the two dominant languages that shape thought and the writing that gives it form in the novel. And such a reciprocal "reinforcement" is not the sole linguistic formula of this sort boosting the originality of New Brunswick's literature. Mixing up French, English, and even some Aboriginal Canadian languages, *chiac*, for example, is an Acadian vernacular worth mentioning here. Françoise Daigle's highly ambitious novel *Pour sûr*, which has won numerous literary prizes since it came out in Montreal in 2011, is only one of the remarkable texts in this idiom.[34]

But French-language bodies of work and even entire literatures in French have popped up and sometimes have been thriving in places that are not officially Francophone. We come across such a flipside of the Canadian setup, if you will, primarily in Asia and Africa. In the postcolonial era, several Southeast Asian countries formerly under French colonial rule illustrate this situation, in particular Vietnam (here, Anna Moï's name comes to mind first) and, to a lesser extent, Cambodia (Soth Polin, who mainly wrote in Khmer, published her novel *L'Anarchiste* in French in 1980).[35] To them, one should add India, on which Vijaya Rao, a contributor to our book, has done some groundbreaking research, bringing to light the literature in French that cropped up around Puducherry (Pondichery), a former French trading post on the Indian subcontinent.[36] Otherwise, it is surely a truism that some of the most substantial outcomes of literary Francophonie have historically clustered around the Mediterranean. For the recent past, one might adduce Egypt (and mention figures such as Edmond Jabès, René Cossery, and Joyce Mansour), and for today, four of the five countries of the Maghreb (Libya is the exception), where, we should recall, French is not an official language even though it serves as lingua franca, primarily in administration and cultural production. While Mauritania's literature still remains little known to outsiders, the rest of the region has for decades been alive with the output of some of the greatest and most successful Francophone writers ever: Kateb Yacine, Rachid Mimouni, and Assia Djebar in Algeria; Driss Chraïbi and Tahar Ben Jelloun in Morocco; and Albert Memmi, Hélé Béji, and Abdelwahab Meddeb in Tunisia. A similar case is presented by Lebanon, with Andrée Chedid, Vénus Khoury-Ghata, and Amin Maalouf, to name only a few of its most canonical writers, and even by Syria, with poet Adonis, who, like the three Franco-Lebanese authors just enumerated, divides his time between Beirut and Paris.

Whereas the contacts and creative synergies between Francophone (or, in Lebanon, Anglophone) languages and literary traditions, on one side, and, on the other, Arabic or Berber idioms and texts are sometimes weak in these areas of the francosphere, numerous writers make use here of two or more languages, as does Moroccan Abdelfattah Kilito, for instance. Some of his titles are as revealing as they are flippant, such as the 2008 *Tu ne parleras pas ma langue* (Thou Shalt Not Speak My Language), which was composed in Arabic and afterwards translated into French, and the 2013 *Je parle toutes les langues, mais en arabe* (I Speak All Languages, but in Arabic), written in French, and where Kilito comments on the French public's ignorance of Arabic-language literature.[37] In his 2007 story collection *Le Cheval de Nietzsche*, Kilito returns to the situation of the bilingual author in North Africa by asking:

> What language do you dream in? The bilingual person can't escape this rather silly question.... I'd be tempted to respond differently depending on who asks. Would I give, then, an Arabic speaker the same answer as I would a French speaker? I'd probably feel guilty—and for good reason—if, guided by my own interests at that moment, I cheated in my answer. At any rate, what is the point of saying that I dream in French or Arabic? I do indeed have an interest here, though: you don't favor one language without a reason.[38]

In *Je parle toutes les langues, mais en arabe*, he pursues this line of reflection, explaining in more detail the intricacies and challenges of the linguistic environment in which Moroccan authors cannot but operate:

> What is it like for those who write in Arabic? In a sense, they too have a forked tongue, not only because they generally know French, more or less, and French phrases and expressions slip into their texts, but also because, above all, their literary models are in French. As for the others, the "Francophones" (a word with multiple connotations), they insist on the fact that they speak Arabic and that this shows in their work; they write, of course, in French, but this doesn't mean Arabic is forgotten, they assure us. They invite us to read their texts as palimpsests, then: behind the French letters are Arabic letters—impure writing is met with muddled reading.[39]

To borrow some catchphrases from Kilito himself, one can say that it is in large part in its own, intrinsic linguistic "palimpsest" that Francophonie masks or reveals that it is "a word with multiple connotations," thus connecting directly with a broader, World Literature context. On the European side and particularly in France, the "masking" has been going on pretty well, unfortunately, for here a striking asymmetry bears noting, which has to do precisely with how Arabic-language writing has been treated by the book industry. That is, this literature is definitely the other literatures' poor cousin at all the major French publishing houses with the exception of Actes Sud/Sindbad and barely reaches fifteenth place among literatures translated into French, at 0.6 percent of the total number of works translated or about thirty fiction books yearly. Moreover, authors rendered into French are often Egyptian, Palestinian, or Lebanese, whereas Maghrebin Arabic-language writers are underrepresented, as if North African literature were essentially Francophone.[40] For instance, Ahlam Mosteghanemi, an Algerian novelist of resounding success across the Arabic-speaking world, gets little attention in the Francophone sphere, particularly in France, whereas she has been extensively translated into English in recent years.[41] Similarly, thanks to Paul Bowles's English version, Mohamed Choukri's *Le Pain nu* (*For Bread Alone*) garnered international accolades in 1973, while it was another seven years before this text was translated into French by Tahar Ben Jelloun.[42]

The back-and-forth across languages, the translation fervor, and the overall polyglossia of Francophone ecologies are more subdued in France than in other countries, given the relatively constrictive norms limiting access to linguistic alternatives. Nonetheless, the latter are not entirely absent even though, again, as *the* "language of the Republic," French should be, in principle at least, *the* language of French literature as well. Despite the impression most dictionaries, textbooks, and anthologies of French literature are wont to give, the *actual* literary environments historically developing inside metropolitan France have not lacked in plurilingualism.[43] But, if so, where should one place, one might ask, literatures written in languages today considered regional or in by- (or inter-)national idioms spoken in areas straddling the French border? Or, taking up a historical perspective now, what should one make of the poetry the troubadours wrote in Occitan? We might note that, oddly enough, these authors are better known in Italian schools than in French schools. Millions of Sicilian, Lombardian, and other Italian high school students are familiar with the names of twelfth-century poets from the French region between Périgord and Limousin such as Bertran de Born, Bernard de Ventadour, and Arnaut Daniel because Dante Alighieri mentions them in *The Divine Comedy*, which the same students read assiduously. In Brittany and Corsica, to take only two more examples from inside the Hexagon, the situation is similar. In 1975, journalist and writer Pierre-Jakez Hélias had great success with his semiautobiographical novel *Le Cheval d'orgueil* (The Horse of Pride). Originally written in Breton, the book was translated into French by the author himself, and it was in this language that it was distributed, not in the original. One might also mention here Marc/Marcu Biancarelli, who is, along with Jérôme Ferrari, without a doubt, among the best-known Corsican writers. Writing in Corsican, Biancarelli is published in Corsica's main city, Ajaccio. While Ferrari writes in French and won the Goncourt Prize in 2012 for *Le Sermon sur la chute de Rome*, Biancarelli has little chance of being awarded anything in Paris. True, he has been translated into French—by Jérôme Ferrari.

In other parts of continental France, literary cultures in languages other than French have been thriving in border zones on both sides of the French frontier. Roussillon, an area roughly corresponding to the Pyrénées-Orientales *département*, has been nurturing a Catalan literature that nearly a third of the local population could potentially access and among whose authors one might mention Jordi Pere Cerdà, a poet whose French name is Antoine Cayrol.[44] Showered in literary prizes across the border in Spanish Catalonia/Catalunya, Cerdà is not well known, however, in France beyond the Pyrénées-Orientales, or Northern Catalonia, as the Catalans call this French region. The situation in Alsace, whose linguistic history has swung back and forth from one language to another, is not the simplest either since literature from this small border region is trilingual: French, German, and Alsatian. On the one hand, it makes sense to cast, say, Strasbourg writer Sebastian Brant/Sébastien Brant out of the bosom of French literature, as it were. Published in Basel, Brant's 1494 *Das Narrenschiff* was one of the most widely read works of the late Middle Ages—in Brant's time, Strasbourg did not yet belong to the kingdom of France but only became part of it after the 1648 Treaty of Westphalia. On the other hand, dealing with a writer like René Schickele in a similar fashion proves tricky. Schickele was born in Obernai, 20 miles southwest of Strasbourg, in 1883, during the period when Alsace was annexed by the German Empire. Figurehead of literary Expressionism, major cultural go-between of his time, friend of Thomas Mann and Stefan Zweig, and longtime resident of the Black Forest, Schickele wrote mostly in German. A little before the rise of Nazism, he left Germany for Provence, where he died in 1940. After bringing out his last two German books in Amsterdam, he published his last novel in French in 1938.[45] Born German by force of circumstances, Schickele became a French national in 1918, after the Treaty of Versailles was signed. The description of his status varies from one critic to another, however. Schickele is alternately presented as a Franco-German writer, an Alsatian writer, a German-speaking Alsatian writer, and a German writer of French origins. In any event, he is no more acknowledged in French-literature anthologies than Bernard de Ventadour. It is nonetheless true that he saw himself as a "citoyen français *und deutscher Dichter*"—a "French citizen and German poet."[46]

While Schickele's case is rare in France, it is much less so in Europe and elsewhere in the world. Luxembourg is one European region where, like in Alsace, literature is done in three tongues: German (with Josiane Kartheiser as a prime example), French (we would mention here only Jean Portante, author of the 1997 novel *Mrs Haroy ou la mémoire de la baleine*), and *lëtzebuergesch* (a name familiar to some of us might be Roger Manderscheid). Moreover, Luxembourgian writer and singer Claudine Muno has achieved the feat of publishing fiction in four languages: the three mentioned earlier, as well as English, an idiom currently on the rise in predominantly Francophone areas of literary production. Outside Europe, this multilingualism—authors working in at least two idioms or different authors writing in different languages in a largely Francophone linguistic ecology—is even more widespread. And yet, to reiterate, holding the pride of place in the Francophone world-system as it does, France remains an exception, primarily on the mainland, but also, if to a lesser degree, in the DROM-COM. Truth be told, it must be said emphatically that France is one of the rare French-speaking countries where the employment of language is subject to such a prescriptive management. This situation is the result of both cultural tradition and a long-standing tendency toward political centralization, which, as we saw earlier, manifests itself in the legislation of norms surrounding language use.

The politics of language regulation has been undoubtedly conspicuous. Apropos of this politics, Louis-Jean Calvet speaks of "*politologie linguistique*,"[47] or linguistic politology, "for," observes Calvet, "behind every language policy is a politics in the broader sense."[48] More to the point, the politics in question here is national or, better still, nationalist. For, in a country like France, the notion of a unique language continues to serve as an emblem and conduit for national sentiment in an age where the tensions between the diversification of identity formation across the metropolitan territory and the Jacobin ideal of linguistic homogeneity are bound to soar. Against this constraining backdrop, the Franco-Greek Vassilis Alexakis—who, born in Greece, resides mainly in France and writes in both French and his native language—presents us with a fascinating exception. Alexakis decided to learn Sango, the co-official language of the Central African Republic, an experience he relates in his 2002 novel *Les Mots étrangers* (*Foreign Words*). Reviewing the book, *Libération* critic Jean-Baptiste Harang comments that "Sango is not an easy language. Its use in writing is limited. Besides, it is far outside our Indo-European linguistic habits (it really forces us to twist our vocabulary), and there's no shortage of reasons not to learn it. But, as [Alexakis's] narrator puts it, awakening suddenly one night, 'Having no reason to learn a language is no reason not to learn it,' and on the following page, after rubbing his eyes: 'I hope Sango will one day do me the courtesy of explaining to me why I learned it.'"[49]

3. "In the Midst of a Renaissance," or The Hexagon No Longer Holds

The persistence and even widening of economic and social inequalities between the North and the South, the acceleration in population migration triggered by such ever-exacerbating disparities, as well as other kinds of displacement, flow, and relocation of people, capital, goods, and information have over the last decades increasingly belied the Jacobin and other ideals of stability and homogeneity, linguistic and otherwise, pulling away, in the process, national territory, identity, and idiom from one another. Undeniably, this multilayered decoupling has been a global development and, as such, has also affected France, the French language, and the literature produced and published in it. The nation's "family romance"—in Marthe Robert's sense of *le roman familial*—has thus been taking a more and more pronounced planetary turn, for while France's literary and cultural romance with itself continues to express a "more or less primitive desire to recast life under ideal circumstances,"[50] these circumstances, even if they were to be brought together and successfully managed within a specifically national framework, would still have an inevitably macroscopic, indeed, worlded purview. For, nowadays and in the foreseeable future, every family romance of this sort, whether literally familial or ethnocultural, characterizing, that is, entire polities, is likely to inscribe itself into—to interpolate and interpellate—the world as a whole, precarious and ever-morphing as this whole is. At once instrument and effect of this inscription into the world-as-world, Francophone literatures are, we insist, part of a World Literature itself marked by fluidity, complexity, and promise as by worrisome proclivities, old and new.

Reading *this* world's literatures of French expression according to the narrow rationale of area studies is making, we think, less and less sense. At a time when, in keeping with human communities worldwide, aesthetic production grows more and more mobile, diasporic, multiethnic, and multiply connected economically, culturally, geographically, and politically, Francophone authors' passports and national affiliations furnish, of necessity, limited insights into these writers' works. In fact, separating authors into national categories no longer is in the twenty-first century—if it ever was—a straightforward operation. Such classification would not pay off, critically speaking, either, and this is precisely what Alain Mabanckou underscores in a 2006 article provocatively titled "La francophonie, oui; le ghetto, non. La littérature francophone n'appartient pas aux lettres françaises" (Francophonie, Yes; The Ghetto, No: Francophone Literature Does Not Belong to French Letters). In this chapter, Mabanckou confesses that "in my classroom in Michigan, I mix everything together. I don't care about the writers' nationalities. The question I ask is the following: 'Is this text written in French or not?' If it is, then it's a Francophone text. Consequently, when I'm dealing with a literary theme, I take care to avoid the French/Francophone distinction."[51]

Mabanckou's point is well taken. Moreover, if the old, colonial, and neocolonial logic that has made metropolitan French literature the axis on which "non-French" (but Francophone) literatures have hinged for a long time has always been fallacious, that logic is even more so today, in an era profoundly defined, despite bloated anti-immigration rhetoric and bureaucracy, by residential mobility, unstable or plural citizenship, competing political allegiances, and similar realities that have rendered inadequate the fixed and monistic identity rubrics to which legislatures are ordinarily partial and under which authors—and oftentimes the meanings of their works too—are chalked up. Born in 1955 in Hungary, residing in France since the late 1970s, and writing in the national language of her adoptive country, Eva Almassy, for example, projects herself in the "Emma la Magyare" chapter from *Pour une littérature-monde* onto the character of Emma, who "had to fight to get an exit visa [out of her native land]. Her world consisted of a single country: Hungary." In France, on the other hand, "she had to fight to get a residence permit."[52] Mabanckou himself was born in the Republic of the Congo, was naturalized in France, and has been teaching in the United States, at University of Michigan and then UCLA. Gao Xingjian, laureate of the 2000 Nobel Prize in Literature, has a similar profile. Born in China, he became a French citizen in 1988 and expresses himself in both French and Chinese. No wonder his biographical presentation shifts from one critic to another, and so does Wajdi Mouawad's. Described by commentators as a naturalized Canadian Lebanese dramatist, a Canadian of Lebanese descent, or a Lebanese-Canadian, Mouawad lives mainly, but not solely, in France. In fact, a large number of Francophone writers residing in France or elsewhere in the northern hemisphere hold two passports.

Indubitably, citizenship, national belonging, political loyalty, and idiom in the twenty-first-century Francophone world are as many-sided as anywhere on the planet. These elements may or may not mix—let alone match—and so they may run parallel, across, or counter to each other, as the case may be, giving birth to subjectivity aggregates not only hard to sort out critically but also often met with essentialist, ethnocentric, nationalist, chauvinistic, or racist reactions intent on "safeguarding" the "true" or "truly French" nature of France's official language and, in the final analysis, "true Frenchness" itself. This is basically the agenda behind the two mainstream concepts of Francophonie itself, which, much like the abovementioned identity ingredients, frequently reinforce and intermingle with one another even though there are situations when they operate, or are treated, rather, as distinct or even diametrically opposed. One is largely political, and in this particular context "Francophonie" is spelled with a capital F; the other is, roughly put, cultural and designated by lowercase "francophonie." If we do not adopt this dissociation here, that is because, in practice, the two are intimately bound up with each other. Joining them are, first, their shared concern to protect the "integrity" of French from actual or imaginary "external threats" and, second, a simplistically conceived center-periphery dynamic according to which the marginality of one pole—the formerly colonial terrain of today's linguistic and literary Francophonie—is construed "ambiguously" as suggestive of a political, neocolonial subordination to the other, as Mabanckou remarked in his 2006 piece and again a year later. "The notion of Francophonie," he reflects, "perpetuates ambiguity. [Francophonie] isn't necessarily something to denigrate, but, because of the term's unavoidably political undertones—and never has a notion been so fiercely contested—its most merciless prosecutors deem it an extension of France's foreign policy in its former colonies!"[53]

The commentary was occasioned by the publication of *Pour une littérature-monde* three months after the March 16, 2007 historic appearance in *Le Monde* of "Manifeste pour une littérature-monde en français" (Manifesto for a *littérature-monde* [World Literature] in French). Sponsored by Le Bris, a writer and organizer of the Étonnants Voyageurs festival in Saint-Malo, Brittany, and by Jean Rouaud, a novelist known in particular for the 1990 *Les Champs d'honneur* (*Fields of Glory*), the proclamation gained the support not only of Mabanckou but also of forty-three other cosigners, including Tahar Ben Jelloun, Maryse Condé, Édouard Glissant, Nancy Huston, J. M. G. Le Clézio, Anna Moï, Wajdi Mouawad, Boualem Sansal, Dai Sijie, and Abdourahman Waberi.[54] In the book, the goal of all these luminaries of French-language literature is to move away from what is commonly called Francophone literature and toward a "littérature-monde en français." In effect, they do not hesitate to pronounce literary Francophonie dead, considering it to be the obsolete manifestation of the very neocolonialism denounced by the "prosecutors" Mabanckou referred to the year before. "Let's be clear: the emergence of a consciously affirmed, transnational world literature in French, open to the world," the "Manifeste" states boldly, "signs the death certificate of so-called Francophone literature [*francophonie*]."[55] Now supposedly defunct, the latter is to be replaced by a hopefully more egalitarian literature model. This would do away with the historically hegemonic Hexagonal center, substituting it with a "heterarchically" set up *archipelago*, one redolent, of course, of Glissant's geocultural imaginary—after all, Glissant has also endorsed the manifesto. As the *littérature-monde* proclamation announces, rather buoyantly,

> It looks to us like we're in the midst of a renaissance, of a dialogue in a vast polyphonic ensemble, without concern for any battle for or against the preeminence of one language over the other or any sort of "cultural imperialism" whatsoever. With the center placed on equal footing with other centers, we're witnessing the birth of a new constellation, in which language, now freed from the burden of its exclusive pact with the nation, from every other power hereafter but those of poetry and the imaginary, will know no other frontiers but those of the spirit.[56]

"Now a world language that has permanently escaped from metropolitan control," French is at long last unyoked from France, and so is, more broadly, the Francophone world overall from the cultural authority of the French nation-state.[57] Following from these twin critical moves is the no less controversial "de-cent[erring of] a model of French studies that was focused exclusively on the [H]exagon."[58]

It is not the first time that such radically transformative operations have been proposed.[59] But it is in *Pour une littérature-monde* that they provide, more forcefully than anywhere in pre-2007 French and Francophone literature and scholarship, a steppingstone for an uncompromising, if at times problematic, rationale for "World Literature in French." This is a two-pronged argument aimed, in one direction, at emancipating literary Francophonie from French privilege, bias, patronizing attitude, and "ghettoizing" treatment of the former colonies, and, in another, at sanctioning and building on the incorporation of French *and* continental French literature into the bigger world, on the worlding of a language and even of a national literary patrimony, which, we are informed, can no longer be monopolized—understood, assessed, and even claimed—by or within metropolitan France.[60] In this sense, and responding to the critical mass of French-language literature accumulated across the world as well as to the sheer fact that the same "'world' has been creeping into the place occupied by the term 'French,'"[61] *Pour une littérature-monde* did "create," as a critical-theoretical manifesto, a "point of no return."[62] "What is clear," Jacqueline Dutton aptly maintains, "is that before the *littérature-monde* manifesto burst on to the literary scene, thrusting itself into academic discourse, contemporary understanding of world literature in French was evolving more calmly out of the various strands of postcolonial, francophone, transnational, transcultural, and world literature studies."[63] The manifesto put an end to this quiet evolution, advocating polemically for

> "world literature" . . . because literatures in French around the world today are demonstrably multiple, diverse, forming a vast ensemble, the ramifications of which link together several continents . . . [but] also because all around us these literatures depict the world that is emerging in front of us, and by doing so recover, after several decades, from what was "forbidden in fiction."[64]

It would be helpful to situate this endorsement and Le Bris and Rouaud's initiative in the context of French cultural politics—as well as French politics generally—of the second half of the third millennium's first decade. Symbolically enough, the "archipelagic" or worlded rethinking of Francophone literatures was spearheaded by the *littérature-monde* group between two major, extremely controversial political events entailing the reassessment of France's colonial past. One was the February 2005 law regulating the approach to the "French presence" in North Africa in school textbooks; the other, the July 2007 speech given by President Sarkozy in Dakar. Note, too, that, predating by a mere few months the 2008 constitutional reform mentioned earlier, Le Bris and Rouaud's undertaking was also prompted by the literary prizes given out in Paris in the fall of 2006. As they write,

> In due course it will perhaps be said that this was a historic moment: in autumn 2006, five of the seven French literary prizes—the Goncourt, the Grand Prize for Novels of the Académie Française, the Renaudot, the Femina, and the Goncourt for High School Students—were awarded to foreign-born writers. A random coincidence, among publishers' fall catalogs, uniquely concentrating talent from the "peripheries," a random detour before the straying channel returns to the riverbed? A Copernican revolution, rather, in our opinion.[65]

While the awards may signal a sea change, the way the manifesto handles this mutation has met with varying degrees of enthusiasm, ranging from flat-out dismissals by critics who saw in *Pour une littérature-monde* a sort of "retro," "Anglophile," and romantic move itself dismissive of postcolonial and postmodern political-aesthetic concerns and accomplishments to more favorable reactions that would, nonetheless, involve important reservations and queries.[66] Sympathetic as we surely are to Le Bris, Rouaud, and their group's intervention, we, too, think that it invites a whole spectrum of questions. Here, we will limit ourselves to a few that strike us as both intertwined and more significant in light of our book's focus. In posing them, as well as in offering some answers, we hope to ford the gap between Francophone literatures and studies, on one side, and, on the other, a *littérature-monde* mode of writing and reading critical of the colonial, postcolonial, Gallocentric, and French nation-state-beholden legacies of Francophonie but also of itself and, not in the least, of its natural ally, the World Literature approach.

The first question pertains to the sometimes crude opposition between the presumed "center" (mainland France) and its "periphery" (France's former colonies and other Francophone countries), with the former judged as depleted and sterile and the latter as thriving and moving dynamically in step with the world. This is because the disjunction can end up, quite paradoxically, reinforcing the divide *littérature-monde* strives to bridge and legitimizing an essentialist view of various cultural regions, much though the signatories' intention is to leave this reductive vision behind. In the same vein, Le Bris places a lot of stock on travel, which is, one might say, his "specialty" and which, to his mind, allows for contact with others, as if the self/other, here/elsewhere, and Hexagon (France)/overseas France (planet) dichotomies that had underpinned earlier travel notions and accounts had the same meanings and played the same culturally stabilizing roles in our intensively diasporic and multiply connected times. While very much invested in questioning traditional Francophonie, Camille de Toledo refutes, besides the manifesto's lyricism, which borders on grandiloquence, precisely this surprisingly polarized worldview. As he writes in his 2008 book *Visiter le Flurkistan ou les illusions de la littérature monde* (Visiting Flurkistan, or The Illusions of World Literature), "It is not against the 'center' that the 'periphery' must be defended but *with* it," that is, with another, authentic insight into what this center has actually been and is, an understanding that will become more powerful and clearer "by making [the center] implode, by relying on immoderation, on cultural mixing, on Rabelais's creoleness, on the inventiveness of Du Bellay, on the original 'bastard' character of French and against the language's congealment, classical beauty, whiteness, [and] purity."[67] Called for, believe critics like Toledo, as did Glissant already more than two decades ago, is "disrespecting" the French language to the point where writers boldly refine and adapt it to a capacious planetary vision whose expressive needs bring together all participants to political, cultural, and linguistic Francophonie no matter who and where they are in a world of which the Hexagon is neither the center nor the linguistic and literary benchmark any more.[68]

But—and this is the second question we would ask apropos of the "Copernican" claims of the manifesto—why speak of World Literature *in French* as though there existed a world apart, set aside as such solely by the use of a common language, be it supranational? Why would language—and why would French alone—remain a, or *the*, dominant unifying factor at a time when increased border porousness and transregional, intercontinental, indeed, planetary scalarity have become characteristic not only of literary forms but also of our most basic ways of being-in-the-world? After all, Maryse Condé is adamant about "reiterating" in her piece for *Pour une littérature-monde* that "I write neither in French nor in Creole. I write in Maryse Condé."[69] The manifesto authors do not really address these problems even though they approvingly invoke the postcolonial paradigm, which is inherently hostile to the idea of a hegemonic language. Is then "World Literature in French," we also wonder, not just another name for a Francophonie defined less by its openness to the world and more by its detachment from Paris, a Francophonie more generous in its aims and yet still confined to a linguistic perimeter?

Noteworthy is, along these lines, that the title of the Gallimard collection, *Pour une littérature-monde*, dropped the modifier of the *Le Monde* text's original title, *en français* ("in French"), an indication that the book's contributors mean to flesh out and perhaps extend the initial lines of thought the manifesto sketched out. It is not just that the "bastardization," *métissage*, or contamination in the world arena of the otherwise obsessively monitored and regulated national idiom has rendered French polymorphous, creolized, and multiply decentered already. But some of these authors, who made a point to situate literature in French in the world without making explicit reference to the idiom in question or setting it up as the only unifier of the world they were contemplating, were open, following Glissant and his *tout-monde* concept, to a brand-new space to come, beyond linguistically specific common denominators altogether.[70] This space is, according to Belgian writer Grégoire Polet, the globe itself, which he fancies as a stage for the world drama of "shared experience." "A space of traffic, communication, and telecommunication, an almost entirely interconnected space, the globe we see today," the novelist argues in "L'atlas du monde" (The World Atlas), his *Pour une littérature-monde* piece, "is aware of itself as a site of collective, synchronic life, as an integral structure both in itself as a whole and in the relationships between its parts."[71]

If this mundane spatiality smacks of utopianism, as we feel it does at least in part, that is because the world and the appositely world-embracing ("Magellanian") writing envisaged by Polet are redolent, in places, of the late twentieth-century "global" world picture and of the "globalist" or "global studies" epistemologies associated with it, hence the last and perhaps most inevitable question we pose here.[72] This is about the relationships between *littérature-monde* and other global or world-systemic takes on literature, particularly between a *littérature-monde* of French expression, and possibly of French theoretical bend as well, on the one hand, and, on the other, Goethean *Weltliteratur* and the largely English, US scholarship-influenced World Literature notion. This line of inquiry could of course be flipped around so that one might ask: What ties does World Literature itself, as both practice and concept, maintain with *littérature-monde* seen, similarly, as literature and theory thereof? This is another important question because, where *littérature-monde* relies for its coherence and recognizable contour on a language that for all intents and purposes functions as an established, quasi-official institution, the World Literature paradigm paints a somewhat different picture. Oddly enough, that is because there is no Anglophonie truly equivalent to Francophonie but also because the whole issue seems moot at a time English *has* become the dominant language of the contemporary world. English, then, holds a simultaneously less *and* more prominent role in World Literature than French does in *littérature-monde*. Aside from the controversial problem of translation—and it is not World Literature in (English) translation that primarily preoccupies us here— one cannot ignore that World Literature studies tends to pay special attention to works written in or rendered into English, to which the original idiom, languages other than English, and their specifically linguistic-stylistic participation in meaning-making ordinarily take a back seat except when, on occasion, earlier modes of analysis such as philologically inclined comparatism or postcolonial studies get hold of the topic.[73]

Critics have dwelled at length on the knotty relationships between, on one side, a literary Francophonie still furrowed by colonial, post-, and neocolonial legacies and conflicts, and, on the other, the rising paradigm of World Literature, particularly of a World Literature in French, penned within and without traditional Francophone locations and in dialogue with a World Literature that, epistemologically and sometimes in the socioeconomic praxis of literary production, distribution, and reception, tends to cluster around English and US hubs. Instead, we and most, if not all, of our contributors think that the *littérature-monde* debate has actually laid the groundwork for bringing to the fore and building more determinedly on the compatibilities and homologies between these two aesthetic and critical-theoretical domains. For it bears recognizing that Francophone literatures participate substantially in the greater ensemble of World Literature, attest to and are extensively worlded, shaped by the lattice-like material and cultural world of the post–Second World War epoch, and so, on these and other grounds, lend themselves to a nuanced, carefully contextualized approach that is discriminately germane to—rather than "aping"—World Literature.[74] Indeed, in our view, *littérature-monde* is hardly just a symptom of the "Anglo-Americanization" of Francophone and French postcolonial studies.[75] At the same time, we want to make clear that the World Literature-inflected reading model should be no license for sidelining past and present tensions and culturally granular realities, which less historically and politically attuned theorizations and applications of revived Goethean *Weltliteratur* to Francophone and other literary patrimonies have sometimes short shrifted. In other words, while we welcome the *weltliterarisch* aplomb of *Pour une littérature-monde*, we feel compelled to discard neither the Francophone as a literary field nor the postcolonial as a critical modality in which the field has been traditionally explored—albeit especially in North America and elsewhere outside France—*qua* political and cultural-historical formation.

Our position is not isolated either. "By putting forth the concept of 'littérature-monde *en français*,'" Françoise Lionnet explains in an article that came out two years after the manifesto, "the signatories decry two distinct moments and movements: first, they denounce the self-referential, highly intellectualized, and, as they see it, alienated approach of modernist and post-modernist writers; and second, they announce the 'death' of francophonie because it carries the stigma of the 'pittoresque' and the 'exotique' and is a linguistic category that is nothing but 'the language of a virtual country.'" 'The overall intention,' Lionnet concludes,

> is positive: the authors wish to advance a progressive and all[-]encompassing approach to literary identity in the age of globalization. The goal is to link changes in the literary field to a vast swath of political changes, from increased cultural creolization everywhere to the fall of the Berlin wall, all of which results, for them, in the collapse of grand ideologies and the concomitant "autonomisation de la langue." But the manifesto falls far short of that goal, and it would have been much more far-sighted to propose instead that the term *francophonies* (in the plural) be maintained in order to underscore the geographic and historical multiplicities that it conveys, thus enabling a more interesting dialogue with the Goetheian

concept of [W]*eltliteratur* and the English "world literature," both of which imply an understanding of the *world* of literature as fundamentally transnational and polyphonic.[76]

Key in Lionnet's critique of the *littérature-monde* platform is rescuing the Francophone not in spite of but *for* a World Literature-informed examination, a project to which our book is fully committed. But, we would add, aligning "Francophone" and "World Literature" is only a first step; the two, we submit, should also be brought in line at least with some components of the "postcolonial," as well as with other aesthetic, geocultural, and ontological models coming to the fore on the heels of the "global turn" in critical theory.[77]

To that effect, we would point up what is otherwise readily apparent: in taking her initial step, Lionnet does not retain Francophonie "as is" or, rather, "was"; she retools the hollow-sounding, old-fashioned "Francophone community," updates it by pluralizing or, as we say later, "planetarizing" it. Interestingly enough, this move is in the spirit of a more progressive World Literature that, having resurfaced in the context of post–Cold War globalization and of a global studies-triggered recalibration of 1980s comparative literature, must resist and ordinarily has resisted the leveling impetus of the global and its economic-profit-driven paradigm.[78] Further, subscribing to a contemporary or planetary concept of Francophone literatures no longer entails buying, intentionally or not, into notions of colonial or quasi-colonial subservience, exoticism, straightforward and one-directional (former) metropolis-(former) colony "influence," Hexagonal benevolence, French-literature privilege, disproportionate allocation of cultural capital at the (former) imperial center, and so on. For this very reason, a historically, politically, and ethno-racially sensitive World Literature approach to these bodies of literature should find still serviceable some tenets and protocols of postcolonial analysis. The critical operations brought into play by the two paradigms need then not be considered utterly incompatible. They overlap in some respects, and so they may be put to use as complementary rather than mutually exclusive modi operandi. That is why Francophone literatures thus understood would make in the twenty-first century, we contend, for a *world* whose critical cartography a World Literature methodology checked by postcolonial awareness of power asymmetries, local heritages, and present avatars of past injustices is well positioned to undertake.

4. *Monde*, Planet, and Francophone Literatures as World Literature

Some of the questions raised by *Pour une littérature-monde*'s critics concern the previous sentence's italicized word, and they still stand. We add them here to those posed earlier: What kind of world is this?[79] What do the signatories mean by *monde*? To what extent and how is it different from the Anglo-centered world of globalization/*mondialisation*—"globe" and/or *monde*—or from the worlds of the French empire and the *communauté de la francophonie* for that matter, whether we assign "community" a nostalgically Gaullist meaning or not? As has been noticed, the *littérature-monde* writers rarely address this issue head-on. But, in some cases, they do take it up, and this is helpful, as we shall see momentarily. If the final and more important question is how to *read* Francophone literatures—including *littérature-monde* in French, "Frenches," as Lionnet puts it, and other idioms—following the World Literature shift marked by Le Bris, Rouaud, & Co. in Francophone studies, then one must realize that one cannot give an answer unless one gets a grip, first, on these *littératures' monde* itself.[80]

Sum total of aforementioned Francophone ecologies, this world forms, as Pierre Halen has proposed, a system. More precisely, it is a world-system of a certain kind, a systemic geocultural assemblage of "institutions"[81] but also one of geographical expanse, individuals and groups, affect, idiom, expression, historical testimony, and material life, all of them in turn co-opted into the broader system of the one world—as Achille Mbembe declares emphatically in a piece from *Je est un autre. Pour une identité-monde* (I Is an Other: For a World-Identity), a 2010 volume also coedited by Le Bris and Rouaud and another episode in the *littérature-monde* campaign, "there is, then, just one world, at least for the time being, and this world is all there is."[82] This world naturally encompasses other institutions and organizations, national or international, other regions of the planet, and other people, with their own feelings, idioms, and traditions. But—and this is important for the kind of world post-*littérature-monde* Francophonie wants to be, for the wider world it seems poised to be in, as well as for how we might read it today—what is at stake here is more than agglutinating many worlds into one. In a *littérature-monde* in French inclined—as it should be, urges Lionnet—to "maintain"[83] the Francophonie designation, the new Francophone world-system would first and foremost have to overhaul the old one by decentering the French nation-state and otherwise "end[ing] the pact with the nation." The national contract, the manifesto signatories stress, has oriented Francophone literary production toward France rather than toward the bigger world and, by the same movement, has subordinated this output to "French literature."[84] Turning the table on the latter, a Francophone *littérature-monde* system would now *comprise* the Hexagon's literary patrimony, placing it alongside other Francophone literary subsystems (Martinican, Belgian, Algerian or, on another scale, Maghrebin, etc.) rather than humbly petitioning metropolitan French letters, time and time again, for recognition and inclusion. Thus, older imperial hierarchies for which the Francophone "commonwealth" and, later, Sarkozy's vociferous Francophonie rhetoric failed to provide anything other than a facade, would also be replaced by less vertical, ideally horizontal, level, more balanced, and pluridirectional concatenations, associations, and exchanges. Likewise, the presumed "universality" exuded by Paris and, writes Le Bris, by its "self-proclaimed bureaucrats of the universal"[85] throughout the hierarchically organized French-speaking world would be superseded by local, heterogenous, and "impure" articulations of "multiversality." This would obtain not by doing the aesthetic bidding of the former metropolis and answering its mimetic appeal to sameness but in response to the kaleidoscopic world of others, Francophone or not, nearby or remote, as Juan Goytisolo suggests in "Défense de la hybridité ou La pureté, mère de tous les vices" (In Defense of Hybridity, or Purity, Mother of All Evils), the closing chapter of *Je est un autre*.[86]

Highly networked across political borders and functioning concurrently on local, national, regional, continental, and intercontinental scales; increasingly multicentric and "multitudinal"; a "constellation"-like world of interlinked worlds, not a system of satellites orbiting on foreordained trajectories around, and getting their light from, a central "star" (France);[87] spreading, with a kindred metaphor, across an "archipelago," not hemmed in by the shorelines of various isolated islands; variegated and diversity-friendly; multicultural in a "sharing," co-participatory rather than separatist kind of way, which vision ties, sometimes explicitly, Le Bris, Goytisolo, and Mbembe's *monde* ideal into the non-globalist, "communalist" world ontologies of Jean-Luc Nancy and Jacques Derrida;[88] not an ominous totality but an ever-provisional, shifting, and open geo-assemblage of real and potential interconnectedness: these are some of the traits and tropes of the Francophone world and literary world system, much though not all these particular terms feature *expressis verbis* or consistently in its proponents' accounts. Entwining an acute perception of an evolving reality in the territory with an aspirational, or, as we said previously, utopian image of what that territory may and perhaps should look like one day, the *littérature-monde* world picture, whether it insists on the Francophone classification or not, reminds one of the recent attempts to offer up the *planet* as a critical corrective, rather than outright antinomy, to the "globe" and calls, accordingly, for a World Literature analysis capable of placing the world *qua* planet at the center of its inquiries.

Some of those efforts predate the conversation around *littérature-monde*—if not the phrase itself, which, as Le Bris says in "Pour une littérature-monde en français," his contribution to *Pour une littérature-monde*, he "had launched" in the 1992 collective volume *Pour une littérature voyageuse*.[89] Gayatri Chakravorti Spivak's 2003 influential book, *Death of a Discipline*, which elaborates on an insight she advanced four years before in the chapter "Imperative to Re-imagine the Planet," is probably the first that pops to mind.[90] Since Spivak's 1999 piece, Masao Miyoshi's 2001 article "Turn to the Planet: Literature, Diversity, and Totality," and other groundbreaking works of the early 2000s, "planet," "planetary," and their lexical-methodological relatives have made inroads into fields, specialties, and debates, old and new, most of them already marked by global discourses and epistemologies.[91] An incomplete list and its mountainous bibliography would include world-systems analysis in the classical Immanuel Wallerstein line but also attempts to update Wallerstein's aging world model for the post–Cold War epoch; globalization studies with various foci and political-theoretical leanings from pro and contra neoliberalism to anti-globalization and *altermondialité*; trans- and post-nationalism in the "hemispheric" and "oceanic" context (Ralph Bauer, Robert Levine, Hester Blum, Yunte Hwang, Paul Jay, Paul Giles); ecocriticism, (neo)cosmopolitanism (Amanda Anderson, Bruce Robbins, Anthony K. Appiah, Rebecca Walkowitz, Jessica

Berman, Seyla Benhabib), and their explicitly planetary "eco-cosmopolitan" cross (Ursula K. Heise); larger topo-interpretive units, fields, and topics in comparative cultural studies and, chiefly with Bertrand Westphal, the advent of geocriticism; "world risk society sociology" also with a cosmopolitan twist (Ulrich Beck) and "network society" economics and communication-aesthetic theory (Manuel Castells, Steven Shaviro, Eugene Thacker, Alexander R. Galloway, Patrick Jagoda); human rights, ethics, and world governance; the "empire"/"new commons" critique of Deleuzian-Guattarian persuasion in the Michael Hardt and Antonio Negri vein; studies of (post)ethnicity and "voluntary affiliation" à la David Hollinger; new comparatism, World Literature (David Damrosch, Pascale Casanova, Emily Apter, Eric Hayot, etc.), "planetary literary history" (Frances Ferguson), "deep-time" literary history, analysis of genre as world-system, and planetary poetics (Wai Chee Dimock, Franco Moretti, Philip Leonard), as well as New Modernist Studies and inquiries into "planetary modernisms" (Susan Stanford Friedman) and "global modernism(s)" (Mark Wollaeger and Matt Eatough); spurred by the global studies-initiated challenge a planetary vision poses to the old colony/metropolis binary (Paul Gilroy), some areas of postcolonialism, including those covering Francophone literatures and cultures; and finally, but in energizing conversation with the critical-theoretical trends already enumerated here, first steps taken to rethink literary Francophonie internal or external to continental France as a *global* issue—to "read it with the globe: as world, as sphere, as a space of encounter with others and with the idea of otherness," as Susan Rubin Suleiman and Christie McDonald announce in the introduction to the landmark 2010 collective volume, *French Global: A New Approach to Literary History*.[92] Suleiman and McDonald also acknowledge that their main objective is to work out a non-"teleological" literary history by tracing the latter's constitutive routes beyond, outside, and even against the sometimes hierarchical binaries putatively coarticulating nation and language, France and *les Outre-mer* of today or yesteryear, Paris and a "rest" waiting for its approving nod, and so on. As the critics underscore, these antinomies have been both queried (Damrosch) and propped (Casanova) by a World Literature analytic algorithm otherwise rightly sensitive to transnational genesis, circulation, and canonicity of literary material.[93] Nadège Veldwachter's 2012 *Littérature francophone et mondialisation* and Thérèse Migraine-George's 2013 *From Francophonie to World Literature in French: Ethics, Poetics, & Politics* are among the first monographs to assign themselves the arduous task of examining, after *Pour une littérature-monde*, Francophone "literature as a borderless or worldly practice," while Mbembe and Felwine Sarr's 2017 coedited *Écrire l'Afrique-Monde* tests out the *littérature-monde* concept in African context.[94]

Historically bound up with the global lexicon and thematics as it has been, "planet" seems at this juncture well positioned to fulfill Spivak's dream of "interrupting" or "overwriting" not only "globe" but also highly centralized, and effectively centralizing, geo-entities of the colonial, postcolonial, and national/nationalist sort such as the former French empire, the Francophone "commonwealth," and France as a self-interested Francophonie sponsor, of which Le Bris, Rouaud, and their supporters are justifiably weary. If successful, the Spivakian maneuver would supplant "globalization" and "globality" by "planetarization" and "planetarity"; the global world-system by the planet's own system; "global agents" by "planetary subjects";[95] and globalism's rationality by "planet-thought"[96] or planetary "relationality,"[97] with similar replacements, displacements, and multiplications affecting the French and Francophone geocultural and literary systems. Developed by Christian Moraru and others across a series of books and articles during the second decade of the new millennium, the critical episteme of relatedness, of *ethical* relatedness in particular and its materially and culturally concrete play within the horizon of the planet bespeak a world logic akin both to the defining ontological dynamic of Glissant's *tout-monde* and to the *mondanéité* embedded in *littérature-monde*.[98] What we have called "worldedness" fundamentally bodies forth this relationality, this being-in-the-world on which both planetary theorists and the manifesto's editors and authors appear to be keen. Before we get into the suitability of a certain World Literature reading mode to Francophone literatures, then, and in order to get to it, a succinct overview of the planetarity world model and of its basic "geoaesthetic" bearings on the present discussion is in order.[99]

An attribute of the Heideggerian Da-sein, to begin with, being in this world and with its others has been enhanced by the unprecedented de-distancing of the world's places, peoples, and sociocultural practices after the fall of the Berlin Wall, a historical watershed, according to the *Pour une littérature-monde* writers, too. Brought closer and closer together in the post-1989, Internet era, the world's worlding inside and outside France and its former possessions and colonies has picked up speed, splicing them more intimately into worldwide circuitries of idiom, values, and goods, as Le Bris himself keeps noting. More than ever, one writes today by plugging oneself, and in turn further galvanizing, this planetary motherboard of roving themes, styles, and aesthetic energies; one writes to "recover the world" (*retrouver le monde*), as Le Bris avers, but one also writes *by* joining this world and those already there, in it.[100] Thus, being present in it, presence tout court, plays out as *co-presence* and adjacency, for better or worse, as the new planetary order is one of great opportunities and huge risks alike. So characteristic of our age, this *world condition of vicinity* marks the unparalleled, ever-expanding contiguity and codependency of actors, discourses, and settings previously imagined to be more discrete and autonomous. What worlds this world and what welds its independent clauses into an archipelago-like mundane syntax of subordinating and coordinating geo-ontology is a *Weltbild* (world picture). This, once more, must be grasped objectively, as what the existing world is like, and ethically or politically, as what it *ought* to become, what we would want it to be some day.

A certain World Literature version of comparative analysis could be, in our judgment, instrumental to this change, to this overwriting or rewriting of a world inherited from imperial histories that, understandably, many Francophone writers are not too happy about. In this sense, the chapters in *Francophone Literature as World Literature* are, we would like to think, both descriptive and "tran-scriptive," normative. For these comparative sites and protocols in and through which we "compare" the world's artifacts by "placing them together," side by side (as in the Latin *comparō*), are isomorphic to the world itself, to the juxtapositions (*comparationes*) its worlding sets off. So, again, it is important to ask, what kind of world are we contemplating in "World Literature in French"? Now, the usual answers have taken us into the problematics of globalization. What is not so clear is to what degree the hegemonic rhetoric of "globe" and "globalism," irrespective of its pro- or anti-neoliberal inflections, *already* construes the world's worlding processes in a certain fashion, thus ending up, ironically enough, further homogenizing the world, making it into a conquerable and commodifiable place, and adding descriptive insult to the world's real injuries rather than making this work anew. In this rhetoric, globalization is routinely dealt with—approvingly or not—as the sole fashion in which a worlding scenario has unfolded or as the only sort of globalization possible.

Yet "globe" is neither "world" nor all the world can be; it is the mainstream discourse of globalization that often gives the ideological illusion of this equivalence. It is helpful, then, to view this discourse as a Nietzschean "army of tropes" because of its tendency to naturalize itself as the default modality and thus "globalize" itself across and at the expense of other kinds of talking about and behaving in our world, but also because, more basically, "world," "globe," "planet," "earth," and the like are scarcely synonymous and therefore *should not be used interchangeably*. Instead, the distinctions among them would pave the way to meaningful action about and in the world. This action, this critical "overwriting," stands front and center both in the geoaesthetic outlook of Francophone *littérature-monde* and in a World Literature approach to Francophone literatures that would pride itself of being, as we said earlier, apposite to its object. Let us explain.

Following Martin Heidegger, critics across disciplines have tackled "worlding" as the world's *fuite en avant* toward worldedness, as an innate tendency of the world to piece together its parts and thereby morph into the world-as-world. This worlded setup has a history in which the Cold War marks an earlier stage. A new world worlded into being in the aftermath of the eventful late 1980s-early 1990s, into a new system all of a sudden more integrated than ever. This system has been called the earth's *netosphere* (from "network").[101] An increasingly world-systemic assemblage, it weaves together the economic-communicational sites, forms, channels, links, and technologies of data storage of the hyperwebbed era. Throughout the world, this geosystemic novelty was so sharply felt that many concluded that, to get a handle on it, we would have to come up with fresh methodologies, foci, and vocabularies. These turned out, eventually, to revolve around "global," "globalization," and the rest of the "globe" family. Before long, the discourse coalescing around them sent shock waves across the human sciences, which underwent a shift comparable to other, "linguistic," "postmodern," "ethical," and "cultural" *Paradigmenwechsel* of decades past.

As most globalization critics would point out, the world process "globe," "globalization," and its affiliates boil down to can be summed up as *totalization*. Rhetorically "perfect" for the ideological purposes of globalism, "globe" and "global" hint at a frictionless, complete, and perfect world.[102] The large-scale multiplication and strengthening of ties, connections, and barterings among individuals, communities, and cultures reinscribe the world as globe by "rounding off" its body, fashioning the polymorphic world into a sphere-like totality whose "smooth surface . . . allow[s] the unimpeded flow of capital, information[,] and language."[103] When *represented as* "globe," assumed to be *one* as in most versions of globalization, "world" is neither an open biocultural system nor our "natural" environment/ground (the "earth") demoted to the instrumental status of usable resource, "standing-reserve," nor is it our cosmic address ("Earth"), but a mundane whole that flaunts its totality—its "totalist" totality, we would add, to distinguish it from Glissant's ontological construct. The global world purports to be a well-rounded, integrated existentially and politically definitive closed system, a teleology enforced from a few centers of power by feedback loops, symmetries, parallels, and exchange procedures across a web of links progressively overlapping with the entire world itself. The world worlds into globe, goes global, once the infinite and multitudinous potentiality of worldly ontology has been repurposed materially and conceptually as domains of the one, the homogeneous, the circular, the repetitive, and the selfsame.

Topologically, both the empirical world and the globe are measurable, even though the actual world or *monde* remains a resilient trope and space of the variegated, mysterious, and illimitable and thus considerably more complex as structure and harder to manage and "tame" than the globe. The main differences between them do not lie in volume, scope, or geometry but in ontology, culture, and politics. Redolent of the "centering" and "smoothing" technology of command, monitoring, and exploitation that went into its making, the globe is a controlled *and* controlling system. A containment fantasy, an ominous panopticon, and a limit, it is a terminus to what the world can be. The globe is or rather becomes, sometimes *through the very rhetoric presuming to critique it*, a multitude, a multiplicity, and a potentiality shrunk down to the measurable and the measured. The world and the globe are both immensities. Both boggle the mind quantitatively. But, unlike the world and insofar as it results from relationally totalizing reinscriptions of the world, the globe is no longer an open-ended boundlessness, a project. Once it has been brought under the regime of rational calculability as globe, largely on economic-managerial, and technological grounds—whether through neoimperialist geopolitics and unification of markets or through rhetorical over-adjudication—it is reduced ontologically and does not operate as an endless space of qualitative leaps, as a playground of being any more. This ontological reduction has left its imprint on the entire paradigm of globality, be it "real" (the globe "as is" today) or realized rhetorically (the globe as ordinarily theorized).

"Planet" and the planetary component of *littérature-monde* theorizations set out to supply an alternative to this paradigm, a "corrective," as argued above. A terminological hub of the planetarity paradigm, "planet" lies behind yet another cross-disciplinary epoch-making "turn."[104] Planetarity is central to recent scholars' efforts to envisage a world increasingly at odds with the mainstream definitions of the "globe." Granted, there are many overlaps between the two. It is also true that "planet" constitutes, in some ways, a subcategory of "global," and, if there is something like planetary studies these days, it would not have been possible without the arrival of global studies in the early 1990s. And yet the world in or *qua* "planet" wants to be a different kettle of fish. As has been proposed, planet is not an accomplished oneness, a structured, coherently administered, and measured geopolitical expanse. Therefore, this system is characterized, both geoculturally and epistemologically, by multiplicity, open-endedness, and sociocultural and political potentialities. There is, both in the world's Francophone literatures and *in their own world*, imagined and "actually existing," overwhelming evidence suggesting that the planet need not be thought of as a closed system historically, politically, and otherwise. Neither an attained finitude nor a teleology, the planet is a *soft system*: young, evolving, and growing, a world but not *the* world, a webbed interrelatedness covering most of the world but not coterminous with it. The planet is not and "is intent" on not being a globality even though there is overwhelming evidence that it lives and acts like a system, or a system of systems, rather. For the same reason, again, it cannot be a totality, at least not in a monistic, centripetal, "strong" sense.

Ontologically and philosophically, the planet is not coextensive with our existential and cognitional gamut as humans, with all we can be and envisage, let alone that the *human world* is just one domain and way of being in and knowing the world. The planetary system is, then, "relative," that is to say, approximate, partially systematic in its extensity and loosely systematic in its intensity or functioning. Because it is not a totalist whole, the planet geomodel can be, geographically, culturally, and philosophically, many worlds or parts of worlds, nested inside each other at once rather than organized vertically. This spatial deployment of the planetary entails a geometry quite different from the global. Correspondingly, the individual committed to a planetary *Weltanschauung* may see himself or herself, not unlike the Greek and Roman Stoics, as participating in a number of worlds and world orders while physically located in a particular community, *polis*, or country. The planet functions as a geodiscursive projection across, astride, and sometimes against the one fixed on modern world maps by the spatiality of the nation-state, empire, and its successor, the global world-system in its standard accounts. In fact, spearheading as it does a cultural-imaginary remapping of the empirical world, the cartographic logos of planetarity messes deliberately with officially recognized distributions of space, bodies, and discourse on our road atlases, charts, and GPSs so as to challenge the worldviews of such neatly delineated topocultural encodings, inserting gaps, barriers, and silences where they were not before and replacing them with bridges, give-and-take, and contacts where one might not expect.

Whether analytically or ethically, as a sober assessment of what the world is or as the blueprint of a world to achieve, planet-thought and the thinking that has gone into the world of *littérature-monde*, Francophone or otherwise, seem cut from the same cloth. To literalize the metaphor and pursue its suggestions in the world of literature alone: "planet" and *monde* unfold the same world fabric, the same geo-*textum* of material life and cultural-aesthetic practices. Woven around countless knots or nodes rather than one (France, Paris, etc.), as before, this rich texture's warps and wefts are poised to unravel intertextually, and endlessly so, in any number of directions, revealing a profusion of many-faceted understandings as soon as one pulls whatever yarn of theme, ploy, influence, or tradition. Capable of tracking meaning over this mundane textuality by setting up linkages defiant of older categorizations, ethno-political territorializations, and jurisdictions of critical authority, national literary historiography, comparatism, imperial influence, and cultural capital, World Literature critics aware of the historical-political inscription of literary works and of the "unevenness" of their world playing field in terms of production, circulation, and appreciation are well equipped to tackle the literary *monde* of *littérature-monde* and of Francophone literatures at large. More than scholars of generations past, this new breed of comparatists—and there are quite a few in our book—*read for the network-world*, for that which the world of literary Francophonie quintessentially *is*. Nor do they lose sight of what earlier we identified as the "granularity" of the Francophone netosphere, to wit, of the "situational" modulation of at-distance connections, itineraries, and affiliations—of the "micro" nuancing of "macro" phenomena.

This deontological imperative of nuance and careful differentiations extends into critical practice methodological, epistemological, and disciplinary distinctions, some of them already addressed but worth reaffirming here—as they are throughout *Francophone Literature as World Literature*—so that our readers remain mindful both of the overlaps and dissimilarities between pivotal terms such as (prevailingly) Anglophone World Literature; World Literature in translation (as chiefly theorized, but also critiqued, by US comparatists); *littérature-monde* as identical neither with the previous two literary domains nor with Francophone literature (as Le Bris would have it), even though, as indicated already, *littérature-monde* is treated in our book under the broader and plural rubric of Francophone literatures; *littérature-monde en français* and *littérature-monde* not necessarily in, or only in, French and written, as specified above, in traditional and nontraditional Francophone sites, inside and outside today's France; postcolonial literatures in French as distinct from all of the above and complete with their by now classical interpretive modality, one both resistant and compatible with World Literature.

5. Canvassing the Worlds of Francophone Literatures: Modalities, Pathways, Foci

As mentioned upfront, we bring into focus Francophone writing since the Second World War, a period within which our contributors dwell mostly on post-1980s texts and authors. There are literary-cultural as well as geopolitical reasons for narrowing such a huge field down to several decades. Here, we would only reemphasize that it is especially in the context of the fast-enlarging world network society that Francophone literatures showcase the intensifying and often sternly articulated concern for the robust if sometimes self-conflicted worldedness of the francosphere and the world at large. And it is, accordingly, apropos of *this* corpus that the defining questions of our project are most effectively and most illuminatingly asked: How do these literatures limn and perhaps foster this worldedness? How do they "say" the world? How do the new, world-systemic and otherwise world-attuned modes of reading this world's planetarity—the very relationality fashioning our time—reshape the way we deal with other literary and cultural-material worldings before and during this interval? And, if Francophone literatures *are* in the world, then what do we mean—and what exactly do we *do* as critics—when we read them *with* it?

In response to the *problématique-monde* of the Francophone archive, *Francophone Literature as World Literature* is not organized geographically, by country or continent, for example. Nor does it aim at providing a literary history of contemporary Francophone literatures. Needless to say, the picture *en miettes* we draw of the latter is not exhaustive either, whether you look at it topologically or chronologically. But, if the picture is not the entire territory of literary Francophonie, it surely means to be its *heuristic map* and so offer a model of knowing and of understanding this whole cultural-linguistic domain as part and parcel of World Literature. To that effect, the volume's chapters work from particular material, themes, and contexts to bring out the broader, quintessential planetary interrelatedness variously subtending and concretely worlding recent Francophone writing. In so doing, the essays account both for the latter's inner intricacies *as* worlds and for their various articulations with other worlds and with those worlds' idioms and traditions.

Thus, the book's Part I, "Systems and Institutions of Literary Francophonie: Language, Written Culture, and the Publishing World," sets in train the discussion of a major theme of our project, namely, the connections and tensions among literary Francophonie, Francophone studies, and World Literature as aesthetic, academic, and publishing phenomena following Goethean *Weltliteratur*'s comeback and the polemics set off by the "Pour une littérature-monde" manifesto. Specifically, the contributors home in on institutional formations and Francophonie's interface, across and beyond them, with other idioms, literatures, canons, with pedagogical instruments such as anthologies, as well as with the national, regional, continental, and world industry. In "African Literature, World Literature, and Francophonie," our collection's first chapter, Bertrand Westphal takes his cue from Mbembe and what the Cameroonian critic identifies as the "shif[t] away from the human condition to the planetary condition." Westphal asks what this refocus on the world scale exactly means for Francophone African literatures. To answer the question, he looks first at the circumstances under which Africa's literatures can be said to break out of what Congolese thinker V. Y. Mudimbe has dubbed "the colonial library" and thus reposition themselves internationally. To take stock of the actual situation derived from such emancipatory moves, Westphal weighs the presence of African writers in a range of literature anthologies and competitions, addressing, after that, the role of French in African literatures commonly called "Francophone." In concluding, Westphal turns to the circulation of Francophone African books inside and outside Africa, examining the ways in which such a dissemination can be improved so as to bolster the planetary presence of an essential sector of the world's literary production.

In Chapter 2, "Francophone African Publishing and the Misconceptions of World Literature," Raphaël Thierry reviews contemporary developments in Francophone publishing, with particular focus on the book trade built around African literatures of French expression. While our time has seen an increase in critics' appreciation for literary diversity, it has also brought about, argues Thierry, a book industry that contributes to the centralization and homogenization of literary markets as well as to African-located publishing's decline. The latter, Thierry observes, is a paradox, given that it occurs at a juncture when both the recognition of certain African authors and the overall interest in African writing are rising. No realistic account of World Literature, Thierry concludes, can afford to ignore the extent to which the world publishing system, which is still organized "vertically," with Western presses at the top, fashions and even limits the meaning and impact of Africa's literary Francophonie.

The dynamic of idiom, colonization, and World Literature is the focus of this section's third intervention, Bi Kacou Parfait Diandué's "Malinke, French, Francophonie: African Languages in World Literature." In his discussion of Ahmadou Kourouma, the critic turns to geocriticism and linguistic analysis to examine how the Ivorian writer's novels unfold discursive spaces where the language of the former empire and indigenous idioms cross-pollinate to give birth to composite forms of expression. Bearing witness to a history of clashes, exchanges, and multidirectional influences, these forms, Diandué concludes, leave their imprint on the community and the individual alike, with artists like Kourouma serving as an illustration for how the two come together in literary practice.

In this segment's fourth contribution, "Globalizing the Spiritual and the Mythological: Indian Writing in French from Pondicherry," Vijaya Rao pays close attention to the colonial backdrop and modes of worldwide dissemination of this corpus. In response to Damrosch's "circulation" model of World Literature, Rao leans on Satya Mohanty's work to refine our understanding of how readership networks form and to argue for a definition of World Literature grounded in critical practice and cross-cultural conversation. The latter should take place today around Indian Francophone literature, too, as Rao shows in her reading of works by Sri Aurobindo and his disciples (Nolini Kanta Gupta, Prithwindra Mukherjee, and Ranajit Sarkar), as well as of K. Madavane's *The Mahabharata of Women*.

Grouped under the rubric of "Francophone Spatialities: Cities, Landscapes, Environments," *Francophone Literature as World Literature*'s second cluster of chapters foregrounds, perhaps more decidedly than elsewhere in the book, an emblematic modus operandi of this collection's essays: rather than proceeding top-down and extrapolating from existing World Literature definitions and approaches, they work outward from specific sites and texts. This approach is keyed to a consideration of the geolinguistic formations, material locations, and milieus of Francophone literatures such as nation-states, cities, banlieues, and islands, along with their socioethnic and literary-cultural and natural environs. Thus, in "Mapping World Literature from Below: Tierno Monénembo and City Writing," this segment's first chapter, Eric Prieto offers a bottom-up view of Francophone literatures. Instead of generalizing from World Literature and literary Francophonie notions marked by their academic articulations and agendas, Prieto draws from Guinean writer Tierno Monénembo's urban fictions and their eloquent entanglement in wider, Francophone, African, and planetary networks of culture and "city writing." If a defining transnational phenomenon of the current era has been the increasing pace of urbanization, particularly in the Global South, where 90 percent of global urban growth is now occurring, Prieto's intervention attempts to show how *bas-fonds* literature can contribute to this process of reconfiguration, one that brings the localized concerns of certain urban places into contact with the larger *problématique-monde* of global modernity.

In dialogue with Alexander Beecroft's 2014 book *An Ecology of World Literature*, Laura Reeck's chapter, "Questions of Diversity in the Global Literary Ecology and *banlieue* Literature," takes, next, a hard look at issues pertaining to the variety and multiplicity of idiom and literary expression in the French language. Her particular focus is the growing body of *banlieue* literature. One question she asks is whether the literary-cultural and linguistic innovations characterizing this corpus might strengthen or undermine the position of French as the only world idiom, according to Beecroft, to stand alongside English as a "super-central" language in the global literary ecology. Reeck shows that, despite their substantial contributions, *banlieue* writers still have to receive full recognition in the French literary system. She wonders, therefore, if containing and restricting diversity *within* this system might not lead, *outside* it, to French's being less sustainable over time as a core world language and to French-language literature's becoming less present on the planet's literary scene.

This part's third piece, Vincent Gélinas-Lemaire's "As the World Falls Apart: Living through the Apocalypse in Christian Guay-Poliquin's *Le poids de la neige* and Catherine Mavrikakis's *Oscar de Profundis*," scrutinizes the response to global trends in recent apocalyptic and postapocalyptic fiction from Francophone Québec. Noting that Québécois literature has long been marked by a tension between national tradition and globalization, Gélinas-Lemaire draws out the new spatialities and the negotiations with the bigger world obtaining in the contemporary novel of this Canadian province. His examples are two speculative novels by Christian Guay-Poliquin and Catherine Mavrikakis, respectively. In his analysis, the critic dwells on the writers' cloistral imaginary and its dialogue with the "idyllic" tradition of Québec literature, on one side, and with vaster archive and resonances of a world in turmoil, on the other.

Bringing up the rear in this portion of the book is Jane Hiddleston's contribution "Poetry in the World: Aimé Césaire, Édouard Glissant, and the Language of Landscape." The critic takes up the ecological predicament of the Caribbean world under modern-era globalization. In spirited conversation with critics and theorists who have recently intervened in the debate around world ecologies and post-Heideggerian notions of worldliness (Beecroft, Pheng Cheah, and Michael Niblett among others), Hiddleston attends not so much to environmental damage in the Caribbean as to how World Literature in general and, more specifically, Francophone poetic form from the region contest assumptions of human sovereignty and forge alternative relationships to the nonhuman world. Through syntactical, lexical, and rhythmic experimentation, she argues, Césaire's and Glissant's poetic works enter into dialogue with landscape, allowing its materiality, temporality, and nonhuman expressiveness to come forth in an aesthetics of resistance.

Part III, "Relational Identities: Sex, Gender, and Class in Francophone World Arenas," turns more insistently to the logic of literary-cultural relatedness of Francophone literary formations that have been obtaining over the past decades in conjunction with social group or class, capital, sex, gender, and other cognate individual and communal identity parameters. This section's chapters explore the forms relationality takes in literary structures and socioeconomic arrangements across the francosphere. Here, too, the contributions work from specific cases and sociocultural circumstances so as not to lose sight of the issue of specificity in a discussion often running the risk of grandiose and abstract elaborations. To the same effect, the critics pose questions of genre, device, style, as well as of form generally and of how writers deploy it to yoke together self and other, here and there, central and marginal, and particular and general across various world networks. All three essays of this section share a characteristic move that bespeaks their critical attitude toward existing models and "applications" of comparatism, World Literature, *littérature-monde*-inspired analysis, and postcolonial inquiry. That is, their authors, too, prefer to operate, as mentioned earlier, largely inductively, so as to avoid abusive impositions of critical-theoretical paradigms on such a diverse material. As they do so, they ask: What are the politics of difference playing out across the world domains of Francophonie? How can these politics be reframed in the wake of recent debates around *littérature-monde* and World Literature? How have queer Francophone worlds resisted globalizing pressures exerted across them on sexual imaginaries and practices? What challenges has literary Francophonie faced in asserting itself in the world against old and new, metropolitan and Western, economical-political and cultural-academic hegemonies and attempts at ordering this world?

In an effort to answer some of these questions, Thérèse Migraine-George contends in this part's first chapter, "World Literature, *littérature-monde*, and the Politics of Difference," that *littérature-monde* can sidestep some of the pitfalls inherent in the globalizing impetus of World Literature in English and in the potentially homogenizing thrust of translation. The workings of difference/*différance* at stake within *littérature-monde* can break away, the critic argues, from the narrow identity politics of multiculturalism by forging what the authors of "Pour une littérature-monde en français" view as a "constellation" loosely constituted around multiple, shifting, and interacting centers. More specifically, *littérature-monde* fosters, Migraine-George explains, a politics of hospitality susceptible to further diversity and inclusion within and beyond the French Republic. To examine this possibility, she turns to same-sex rights in the francosphere and to former French minister of justice Christiane Taubira's oratory, in particular to the literary references with which Taubira peppered the speeches she delivered during the *mariage pour tous* debates of 2012 and 2013.

Approaching queer writing from Québec, the Maghreb, sub-Saharan Africa, and the Caribbean from a perspective that is both comparative in method and global in scope, Jarrod Hayes examines local oppositions to and complications of homoglobalization in this part's second chapter, including the tendency to generalize Western assumptions about same-sex desire. To draw out the shape of these resistances and alternatives, his contribution "Queer Desire on the Move: Resistance to Homoglobalization in World Literature in French" takes stock of the main developments in queer Francophone studies and engages with works by Michel Tremblay, Mohamed Leftah, Frieda Ekotto, Jean-Euphèle Milcé, and Nicole Brossard, among others. Hayes's readings trace new ways to conceptualize and teach Francophone literatures at the intersections of post-*littérature-monde* World Literature and sexuality studies.

In the last contribution to Part III, "Locations of Identity: *Littérature-mondaine* and the Ethics of Class in Evelyne Trouillot's *Le Rond-point*," Régine Michelle Jean-Charles builds on Martin Munro's notion of "literature of the everyday"—*littérature-mondaine*—to investigate the quotidian investment through which Haitian literature pushes the boundaries of *littérature-monde* and forces us to imagine a more markedly class-oriented version of World Literature. Attending with particular acumen to the social stratification of Haitian society as portrayed and critiqued in Haitian author Evelyne Trouillot's novel *Le Rond-point*, Jean-Charles's analysis illuminates the ethical thrust of the narrative as well as the latter's ability to reframe the local and global dimensions of class asymmetries.

Finally, Part IV, "Francophone Literature and Planetary Intertexts," carries on the discussion of world relationality by turning to textual travels, encounters, and re-creative metamorphoses in Francophone world literatures across oceans and continents. In this section, our contributors show how writers of Francophonie participate actively in critical and original recirculation of literary and cultural materials across the planet's history, national traditions, and geopolitical boundaries. Consisting of individual acts of literary "worlding," this is, we learn, a concrete redistributive process that consolidates, alongside worldwide flows of demographic and commercial nature, world trajectories of multilingualism, intertextuality, cultural leverage, and canonicity and whose impact is as literary as it is economic and political.

As Jacqueline Dutton reminds us in the beginning of this part's first chapter, "Writing French in the World: Transnational Identities and Transcultural Ideals in the Works of Michel Houellebecq and Boualem Sansal," French-language literatures have never been entirely confined to a Francophone bubble even though declining translations over the past fifty years have reduced the range and reach of many authors writing in French. In the world today, the critic adds, writing in this idiom presents new challenges and new opportunities to develop identities, ideals, and practices that traverse national, cultural, and linguistic boundaries. Less constrained by national networks, more influenced by global, social, and virtual realities, the relative impact of writers today can be traced to their capacity not only to *dire le monde*, as Le Bris has suggested in his *littérature-monde* manifesto, but also to *prédire le monde*. In her chapter, Dutton sets out to explore the transnational identities, transcultural ideals, and translingual practices of Michel Houellebecq and Boualem Sansal as writers of World literature in French, focusing on their 2015 novels *Soumission* and *2084* respectively. Specifically, she seeks to uncover the intratextual, intertextual, and extratextual factors that, she submits, enhance the planetary appeal and mobility of these works as they "tell the world" to audiences themselves located in a world that extends far beyond nation-states.

This section's second piece, Nicole Simek's "Literature's Purchase: Remaking World Economic Relations in Crusoe's Footsteps," looks at a 2012 retelling of Daniel Defoe's *The Life and Strange Surprising Adventures of Robinson Crusoe* by Martinican writer and anti-capitalist critic Patrick Chamoiseau. In her analysis, Simek demonstrates that this Francophone rewriting of a novel so often taken to be an emblematic modern portrait of *homo economicus* constitutes, in reality, a more complex worlding operation. The critic concludes that the rewriting protocols in play here offer, through their own dynamic, an alternative mode of being-in-the-world, a way out of the dominant economic strictures of contemporary life.

In "Worlding *Négritude*, or Aimé Césaire's Global Caliban," this segment's penultimate chapter, Zahi Zalloua takes up a key problem of the complex, literary-cultural and political intertextuality undergirding the Martinican writer's celebrated retelling of *The Tempest*. Asking how we might negotiate the tensions between the play's particularist appeal and its universalizing dimension, Zalloua argues that Césaire's engagement with the Shakespearian tutor text both discloses and incites us to invent imaginings of subjectivity, language, and relationality distinct from those marking Shakespeare's colonial world as well as from today's racialized and racializing world. Revealingly, the critic spotlights acts of worlding that operate intertextually, as they relate Césaire to his precursor critically, and politically—and geopolitically as well—as they project a *négritude* that throws bridges between struggles as diverse as those of Free Palestine, Black Lives Matter, and anti-colonial Creole resistance.

Our book closes with Emilia David's chapter on Romanian-born Francophone writer Matei Vişniec. In "From Postmodern Intertextuality to 'Decomposed Theater': Matei Vişniec between Romanian and Francophone Literatures," David argues that Vişniec's widely acclaimed plays in French speak to a systematic and original attempt to join thematically, formally, and intertextually Francophone and literary-cultural world networks. However, David also shows that, as with other authors whose country of birth is Romania, such as Tristan Tzara, Panaït Istrati, E. M. Cioran, and Eugène Ionesco, Vişniec's early, Romanian work cannot be overlooked when one tries to come to grips with his French writings. After briefly sketching out the tradition Vişniec comes from— including his involvement in the Romanian postmodernism of the 1980s—David moves on to a discussion of how his drama relates to his illustrious predecessor and Romanian Francophone writer Ionesco and to other, Romanian as well as French authors.

Notes

1 Édouard Glissant, "Solitaire et solidaire. Entretien avec Édouard Glissant." With Philippe Artières, in *Pour une littérature-monde*, ed. Michel Le Bris and Jean Rouaud (Paris, France: Gallimard, 2007). Unless otherwise indicated, all translations of French texts are ours. The title of Le Bris and Rouaud's essay collection could be,

and has been, translated into English as "Toward a World Literature," sometimes with the help of a hyphen in the main phrase ("World-Literature"), reversing the order of the terms in the main phrase ("Literature-World"), making the capitalized words lowercase, and so on.

2 Le Bris and Rouaud, *Pour une littérature-monde*, 77–8.

3 The introduction to *Francophone Literature as World Literature* and some of the contributions to this book differentiate between "World Literature" (uppercase initials) and "world literature" (lowercase). While the distinction is not always clear-cut, the former designates: a discipline update or successor of comparative literature; an approach; a field of human expression or worldwide phenomenon largely speaking, one whose understanding may be and usually is informed by said discipline and methodology. The latter, less frequently used in our introductory chapter, stands for the *world*'s literature in a more general, unspecialized sense.

4 The notion that the approach to a body of work understood as world literature should be analogously "worlded" and therefore "apposite" to this approach's object has been articulated in detail apropos of other literatures as well. See, for instance, Christian Moraru and Andrei Terian, "Introduction: The Worlds of Romanian Literature and the Geopolitics of Reading," in *Romanian Literature as World Literature*, ed. Mircea Martin, Christian Moraru, and Andrei Terian (New York, NY: Bloomsbury, 2018), 1, 17.

5 An "apposite" take on a postcolonial, Francophone, or any national literature for that matter as *world* literature calls for reading that particular literature as part of vast, multiple, and themselves "worlded" networks. See, for a detailed theorization of this position, Moraru and Terian, "Introduction," 21, passim.

6 On "Francophonies," "Francophone literatures," "Frenches," and the "non-metropolitan," "de-center[ing]" thrusts of the plural involved in such designations, see, among others, Françoise Lionnet, "Universalisms and Francophonies," a 2009 article reproduced in *World Literature in Theory*, ed. David Damrosch (Malden, MA: Wiley Blackwell, 2014), 300, 306, 308.

7 The expression has been used by Franco Moretti to discuss *A Hundred Years of Solitude* in chapter 9 of *Modern Epic: The World-System from Goethe to García Márquez*, trans. Quintin Hoare (London, UK: Verso, 1996), 243, and has since become a catchphrase. As such, it has been recently taken up by the Warwick Research Collective in *Combined and Uneven Development: Towards a New Theory of World-Literature* (Liverpool, UK: Liverpool University Press, 2015).

8 Michaël Oustinoff, "Glossaire," in *Traduction et mondialisation*, ed. Michaël Oustinoff (Paris, France: CNRS Editions, 2011), 151.

9 English translations of the Constitution here and elsewhere are taken from the version provided on the Conseil Constitutionnel's website, https://www.conseil-constitutionnel.fr/en/constitution-of-4-october-1958.

10 Decision n° 94-345 DC of July 29, 1994. Recital 6 recalls that "the French language, like all living languages, evolves by integrating terms into its vocabulary from diverse sources, such as regional languages, popular expressions, or foreign words." Our translation. Conseil Constitutionnel, "Décision n° 94-345 DC du 29 juillet 1994," https://www.conseil-constitutionnel.fr/decision/1994/94345DC.htm.

11 See paragraph 1, "By virtue of the Constitution, the French language is a fundamental element of France's personality and heritage," and paragraph 2: "It is

Introduction: Reading Francophone Literature with the World   39

the language of education, the workplace, commerce, and public services." Editors' translation.

12   This dictate stems from the Autonomy Statute of Trentino–South Tyrol (Trentino-Alto Adige) adopted in 1972, which has the force of constitutional law. Italian and German are the region's co-official languages.

13   There are thirteen DROM-COM, including the uninhabited Clipperton Island, located in the Eastern Pacific, southwest of Mexico.

14   "CEDH, 39426/06 Exposé des faits et Questions aux Parties, 13 octobre 2008, 39426/06," Doctrine, https://www.doctrine.fr/d/CEDH/HFCOMOLD/CASELAW/2008/CEDH003-2503232-2701349 (accessed December 8, 2018).

15   The version in force from October 5, 1958, to August 5, 1995, reads: "The Republic and the Community may enter into agreements with States which wish to associate with it in order to develop their civilizations."

16   "Le discours de Dakar de Nicolas Sarkozy de 2007: L'intégralité du discours du président de la République, prononcé le 26 juillet 2007," LeMonde.fr, November 9, 2007, last modified October 12, 2012, https://www.lemonde.fr/afrique/article/2007/11/09/le-discours-de-dakar-de-nicolas-sarkozy_1774758_3212.html (accessed December 8, 2018).

17   This debate was launched in a November 2, 2009 circular signed by Eric Besson, the minister responsible for "immigration and national identity." On the linguistic implications of the discussion, see, for example, Céline Jeannot, Sandra Tomc, and Marine Totozani, "Retour sur le débat autour de l'identité nationale en France: quelles places pour quelle(s) langue(s)?" *Revue de Linguistique et de Didactique des Langues* 44 (2011): 63–78.

18   Although 70 percent of its population has good command of French, Andorra is officially a Catalan-speaking state (see Article 2 of the 1993 Andorran Constitution).

19   Benin, Burkina Faso, Republic of the Congo, Democratic Republic of the Congo, Côte d'Ivoire, Gabon, Guinea, Mali, Niger, Senegal, and Togo.

20   Burundi, Cameroon, Central African Republic, Comoros, Djibouti, Equatorial Guinea, Madagascar, Rwanda, Seychelles, and Chad.

21   The 2011 Moroccan Constitution stipulates: "Arabic is [demeure] the official language of the State. The State works for the protection and for the development of the Arabic language, as well as the promotion of its use. Likewise, Tamazight [Berber/amazighe] is an official language of the State, being common patrimony of all Moroccans without exception" (translated by Jefri J. Ruchti, Constitute.org, https://www.constituteproject.org/constitution/Morocco_2011.pdf?lang=en). The situation is comparable in Algeria, where Tamazight has had official status alongside Arabic since the 2016 constitutional reform. In Tunisia, Arabic is the sole official language.

22   Organisation Internationale de la Francophonie, *La Francophonie dans le monde 2006-2007*, ed. Christian Valentin (Paris, France: Nathan, 2007), 16–19, https://www.francophonie.org/IMG/pdf/La_francophonie_dans_le_monde_2006-2007.pdf (accessed December 10, 2018). These statistics are often estimates. In 2018, according to the Observatoire de la langue française de l'OIF (Organisation Internationale de la francophonie), Francophones represented 35 percent of the population in Morocco, 52 percent in Tunisia, 17 percent in Mali, 8 percent in Burundi, and less than 1 percent in Vietnam ("Estimation du nombre de

francophones [2018]," http://observatoire.francophonie.org/wp-content/uploads/2018/09/Francophones-Statistiques-par-pays.pdf [accessed December 10, 2018]).

23 Observatoire de la langue française de l'OIF, "Estimation du nombre de francophones (2018)."
24 Observatoire de la langue française de l'OIF, "Estimation du nombre de francophones (2018)."
25 Observatoire de la langue française de l'OIF, "Estimation du nombre de francophones (2018)."
26 Determining the hierarchical classification of a language on the basis of number of speakers is of little use. According to Pascale Casanova, "A language is globally dominant if it is a second language used by bilingual speakers throughout the world. And thus it is not the number of speakers that determines whether it is dominant (in that case, Chinese would be the dominant language): it is the number of plurilingual speakers who 'choose' it" (*La langue mondiale. Traduction et domination* [Paris, France: Seuil, 2015], 17).
27 National Institute of Statistics of Rwanda (NISR), Ministry of Finance and Economic Planning (MINECOFIN), *Rwanda Fourth Population and Housing Census, 2012. Thematic Report: Education Characteristics of the Population* (2012), 43. Between 5 percent and 6 percent of Rwandans speak French.
28 Radio France Internationale, "Burundi: l'anglais officialisé aux côtés du français et du kirundi," August 29, 2014, http://www.rfi.fr/afrique/20140829-le-burundi-met-ordre-politique-linguistique/ (accessed December 14, 2018).
29 Organisation Internationale de la Francophonie, "Une histoire de la francophonie," https://www.francophonie.org/Une-histoire-de-la-Francophonie.html (accessed December 15, 2018). Our translation. The first "Francophonie Summit" was held at the Palace of Versailles in 1986 and has met every two years since.
30 See the *Charte de la Francophonie* of 2005, Article 2, concerning the "institutions and actors" of Francophonie, which include conferences of Heads of state, ministerial conferences, the OIF, a mayoral association, educational associations, and the TV5 network, among others (https://www.francophonie.org/IMG/pdf/charte_francophonie_antananarivo_2005.pdf).
31 See Ngũgĩ wa Thiong'o, *Decolonising the Mind: The Politics of Language in African Literature*, 1986 (Oxford, Nairobi, and Portsmouth, NH: James Currey-EAEP-Heinemann, 2008), 18–19, 32n17.
32 Lalbila Aristide Yoda, "Traduction et plurilinguisme au Burkina Faso," *Hermès, La Revue* 56, no. 1 (2010): 39, 40, https://www.cairn.info/revue-hermes-la-revue-2010-1-page-35.htm (accessed February 24, 2019). Our translation.
33 Germaine Comeau, *Laville* (Moncton, Canada: Perce-Neige, 2008), 269. Two pages later, she illustrates this, adding: "Dans ma perspective des choses, ces citations *fitent seamlessly* dans mon texte, dans mon message, dans ma création et dans ma vie, comme la langue anglaise elle-même a réussi à *fiter* dans ma vie, à se mêler au flot de mes mots, à façonner ma réalité et mes valeurs . . . Si les jeunes d'astheure ont quelque chose à dire et qu'ils choisissent de l'écrire en anglais parce qu'ils ont les mots pour le dire, s'ils n'ont pas peur de 'mal dire' les choses, je leur dois un respect inconditionnel. L'anglais n'est plus la langue du conquérant, c'est la langue de la mondialisation. *Why should meaningful sentence structures be the same for everybody?*"

34 In her novel, Françoise Daigle humorously summarizes—or deplores—Chiac's reception: "No matter how logical it is grammatically, Chiac is usually denounced as the supreme example of mediocrity, a masterful deviation from normative French, which is taken to be superior, a form of language that's right (Freudian slip: a uniform that's tight). Grin and bear/wear it" ("Aussi grammaticalement logique qu'il puisse être, le chiac est la plupart du temps dénoncé comme modèle suprême de médiocrité, une déviation magistrale par rapport au français normatif, une forme langagière [lapsus : uniforme bandagière] supposée supérieure. Prendre/perdre son mal en patience"). In *Pour sûr* (Montreal, Canada: Les Editions du Boréal, 2013), 240. Our translation.

35 See Nguyen Phuong Ngoc, "Anna Moï ou la langue migrante comme liberté," in *Littératures migrantes et traduction*, ed. Alexis Nouss, Crystel Pinçonnat, and Fridrun Rinner (Aix-en-Provence, France: Publications de l'Université de Provence, coll. Textuelles, 2017), 55–64.

36 See Vijaya Rao's anthology, *Ecriture indienne d'expression française* (New Delhi, India, and La Réunion: Yoda Press and Le Germ, 2008).

37 Abdelfattah Kilito, *Tu ne parleras pas ma langue*, trans. Francis Gouin (Arles, France: Actes Sud-Sindbad, 2008). In *Je parle toutes les langues, mais en arabe* (Arles, France: Actes Sud-Sindbad, 2013), 34, Abdelfattah Kilito specifies: "I speak all languages, but in Arabic.... Unfortunately, I am not the author of this beautiful expression, not really, not exactly; it's a quote adapted from a passage from Kafka's diary that itself refers to an artist from Prague: 'You see, I speak all languages, but in Yiddish.'" Our translation.

38 Abdelfattah Kilito, *Le Cheval de Nietzsche. Récits* (Casablanca, Morocco: Le Fennec, 2007), 156–7. Our translation.

39 Kilito, *Je parle toutes les langues, mais en arabe*, 20.

40 See Délégation générale à la langue française et aux langues de France, "Références 2013: Langue française et traduction en Méditerranée," a survey conducted between 2010 and 2011 by the journal *Transeuropéennes* and the Euro-Mediterranean foundation Anna Lindh pour le dialogue entre les cultures, http://www.culture.gouv.fr/Espace-documentation/Documentation-administrative/References-2013-langue-francaise-et-traduction-en-Mediterranee (accessed January 9, 2019). For a precise sociological study, see Richard Jacquemond, "Les flux de traduction entre le français et l'arabe depuis les années 1980 : un reflet des relations culturelles," in *Translatio. Le marché de la traduction en France à l'heure de la mondialisation*, ed. Gisèle Sapiro (Paris, France: CNRS Editions, 2016), 347–70.

41 A couple of her novels have nonetheless been translated into French with Albin Michel, *Mémoire de la chair* (Paris, France: Albin Michel, 2002) and *Le Chaos des sens* (Paris, France: Albin Michel, 2006). In both cases the translations appeared nine years after the Arabic originals.

42 On the translation of Francophone Maghrebin authors into Arabic, see Richard Jacquemond, "Le retour du texte. Jalons pour l'histoire de la traduction arabe de la littérature maghrébine d'expression française," in *Littératures migrantes et traduction*, ed. Nouss, Pinçonnat, and Rinner, 175–86.

43 We should, however, mention here the third volume of the *Encyclopédie de la Pléiade*, with a preface by Raymond Queneau, which was dedicated to "Littératures françaises, connexes, marginales," or "French, marginal, and related literatures" (*Histoire des*

littératures, III. Littératures françaises, connexes, marginales, ed. Raymond Queneau [Paris, France: Gallimard, 1958]).

44 See Josep Samuel Marquès Meseguer, "Espai i identitat en l'obra de Jordi Pere Cerdà. Una geografia literària cerdaniana" (doctoral thesis, Université de Perpignan-Via Domitia, France, and Universitat Jaume I de Castelló de la Plana, Spain, defended in Perpignan, France, September 5, 2018).

45 Of the three post-1933 books he published while alive, the first two came out in Amsterdam (*Liebe und Ärgernis des D. H. Lawrence*, 1934; *Die Flaschenpost*, 1937); the third, in French, was published in Paris with Fayard in 1938, bearing an emblematic title: *Le Retour*, or The Return.

46 Eric Robertson, *Writing between the Lines: René Schickele, "Citoyen français, deutscher Dichter" 1883-1940* (Amsterdam, Netherlands, and Atlanta, Georgia: Rodopi, 1995). In 1997, Robertson published an essay on another great figure of French/German bilingualism, Yvan Goll, who was born in the Vosges in 1891 and who was forced to flee to the United States with his wife Claire (a poet like himself) in 1939 to escape Nazi persecution. See *Yvan Goll–Claire Goll: Texts and Contexts* (Amsterdam, Netherlands, and Atlanta, Georgia: Rodopi, 1997).

47 Louis-Jean Calvet, "Introduction à la politologie linguistique," 2002, in *Les langues: quel avenir?, Les effets linguistiques de la mondialisation* (Paris, France: CNRS Editions, 2017), 15–40.

48 Calvet, *Les langues: quel avenir?*, 63.

49 Jean-Baptiste Harang, "Le dernier sango à Paris," *Libération*, September 12, 2002, quoting Vassilis Alexakis, *Les Mots étrangers* (Paris, France: Stock, 2002), 92, 93. Translations of the two quotations from the novel are taken from Vassilis Alexakis, *Foreign Words*, trans. Alyson Waters (Iowa City, IA: Autumn Hill Books, 2006).

50 Marthe Robert, *Origins of the Novel*, 1972, trans. Sacha Rabinovitch (Bloomington, IN: Indiana University Press, 1980), 34.

51 Alain Mabanckou, "La francophonie, oui; le ghetto, non. La littérature francophone n'appartient pas aux lettres françaises," *Le Monde*, March 18, 2006, https://www.lemonde.fr/idees/article/2006/03/18/la-francophonie-oui-le-ghetto-non_752169_3232.html (accessed July 2, 2019).

52 Eva Almassy, "Emma la Magyare," in Le Bris and Rouaud, *Pour une littérature-monde*, 262.

53 Alain Mabanckou, "Le chant de l'oiseau migrateur," in Le Bris and Rouaud, *Pour une littérature-monde*, 55.

54 Muriel Barbery et al., "Pour une 'littérature-monde' en français," *Le Monde des Livres*, March 15, 2007, https://www.lemonde.fr/livres/article/2007/03/15/des-ecrivains-plaident-pour-un-roman-en-francais-ouvert-sur-le-monde_883572_3260.html (accessed January 17, 2019).

55 Muriel Barbery et al., "Toward a 'World Literature' in French," trans. Daniel Simon, *Contemporary French & Francophone Studies* 14, no. 1 (2010): 115.

56 Barbery et al., "Toward a 'World Literature' in French," 116.

57 Alec G. Hargreaves, Charles Forsdick, and David Murphy, "Introduction: What Does *Littérature-monde* Mean for French, Francophone and Postcolonial Studies?" in *Transnational French Studies: Postcolonialism and* Littérature-monde, ed. Alec G. Hargreaves, Charles Forsdick, and David Murphy (Liverpool, UK: Liverpool University Press, 2012), 2–3.

58 Hargreaves, Forsdick, and Murphy, "Introduction," 2.
59 Hargreaves, Forsdick, and Murphy, "Introduction," 2.
60 On "ghettoization," see, among others, Typhaine Leservot, "From *Weltliteratur* to World Literature to *Littérature-monde*: The History of a Controversial Concept," in Hargreaves, Forsdick, and Murphy, *Transnational French Studies: Postcolonialism and Littérature-monde*, 43.
61 Deborah Jenson, "Francophone World Literature (*Littérature-monde*), Cosmopolitanism and Decadence: 'Citizen of the World' without the Citizen?" in Hargreaves, Forsdick, and Murphy, *Transnational French Studies: Postcolonialism and Littérature-monde*, 16.
62 David Murphy, "The Postcolonial Manifesto: Partisanship, Criticism and the Performance of Change," in Hargreaves, Forsdick, and Murphy, *Transnational French Studies: Postcolonialism and Littérature-monde*, 71.
63 Jacqueline Dutton, "*État present*: World Literature in French, *Littérature-monde*, and the Translingual Turn," *French Studies* 70, no. 3 (2016): 418.
64 Barbery et al., "Toward a 'World Literature' in French," 116.
65 Barbery et al., "Toward a 'World Literature' in French," 113. The laureates of these various prizes were Nancy Huston (*Lignes de faille*), Alain Mabanckou (*Mémoires de porc-épic*), and Jonathan Littell (*Les Bienveillantes*).
66 For a comprehensive rebuttal of the manifesto from a postcolonial perspective that deems *Pour une littérature-monde* an aesthetically and politically questionable step backwards, see Charles J. Sugnet, "*Pour une littérature-monde en français*: Manifesto Retro?" *International Journal of Francophone Studies* 12, nos. 2–3 (2009): 237–52.
67 Camille de Toledo, *Visiter le Flurkistan ou les illusions de la littérature monde* (Paris, France: PUF, 2008), 83. Our translation.
68 Édouard Glissant, *Introduction à une poétique du divers* (Paris, France: Gallimard, 2013), 52.
69 Maryse Condé, "Liaison dangereuse," in Le Bris and Rouaud, *Pour une littérature-monde*, 215.
70 In *Traité du Tout-monde. Poétique IV*, Édouard Glissant writes: "J'appelle Tout-monde notre univers tel qu'il change et perdure en échangeant et, en même temps, la 'vision' que nous en avons. La totalité-monde dans sa diversité physique et dans la représentation qu'elle nous inspire. . . . La mondialité, si elle se vérifie dans les oppressions et les exploitations des faibles par les puissants, se devine aussi et se vit par les poétiques, loin de toute généralisation" (I call Whole-World our universe as defined by its capacity to change and persist while it is changing, as well as our "vision" of this universe. The totality-world in its physical diversity and in how we represent this world. . . . While globalization shows its true nature in the oppression and exploitation of the weak by the powerful, it also reveals itself through poetics, apart from all generalizations) (Paris, France: Gallimard, 1997), 176.
71 Grégoire Polet, "L'atlas du monde," in Le Bris and Rouaud, *Pour une littérature-monde*, 126–7. Our translation.
72 Polet, "L'atlas du monde," 125.
73 See Aamir R. Mufti, *Forget English! Orientalism and World Literatures* (Cambridge, MA: Harvard University Press, 2016), 16: "Any critical account of literary relations on a world scale—that is, any account of World Literature as such—must thus actively confront and attend to this functioning of English as vanishing mediator,

rather than treat it passively as neutral or transparent medium, both as world language of literary expression and as the indisposed language of global capitalism."
74 Emily Apter, "Afterword: The 'World' in World Literature," in Hargreaves, Forsdick, and Murphy, *Transnational French Studies: Postcolonialism and Littérature-monde*, 288.
75 Leservot refers to this reaction—nationalist or less so—on the part of French critics who worry about the escalating "Americanization" of Francophone studies. See, on this very subject, her essay "From *Weltliteratur* to World Literature to *Littérature-monde*," 37.
76 Lionnet, "Universalisms and Francophonies," 300.
77 Christian Moraru, "The Global Turn in Critical Theory," *symploke* 9, nos. 1–2 (2001): 80–92.
78 See, for instance, Christian Moraru, "'World,' 'Globe,' 'Planet': Comparative Literature, Planetary Studies, and Cultural Debt after the Global Turn," in *Futures of Comparative Literature: ACLA State of the Discipline Report*, ed. Ursula K. Heise, with Dudley Andrew, Alexander Beecroft, Jessica Berman, David Damrosch, Guillermina De Ferrari, César Domínguez, Barbara Harlow, and Eric Hayot (New York, NY: Routledge, 2017), 124–33.
79 Apter, "Afterword: The 'World' in World Literature," 289.
80 Lionnet, "Universalisms and Francophonies," 308.
81 Pierre Halen has described the Francophone literary system in a series of articles including "Notes pour une topologie institutionelle du système littéraire francophone." The text is available at: https://www.limag.com/Textes/Halen/Riesz.PDF (accessed May 23, 2019).
82 Achille Mbembe, "Pièce d'identité et désirs d'apartheid," in Le Bris and Rouaud, *Je est un autre. Pour une identité-monde*, 116.
83 Lionnet, "Universalisms and Francophonies," 300.
84 See Véronique Porra, "Malaise dans la littérature-monde (en français): de la reprise des discours aux paradoxes de l'énonciation," *Recherches & Travaux* 76 (2010): 126.
85 Michel Le Bris, "Pour une littérature-monde en français," in Le Bris and Rouaud, *Pour une littérature-monde*, 25.
86 Juan Goytisolo, "Défense de la hybridité ou La pureté, mère de tous les vices," in Le Bris and Rouaud, *Je est un autre. Pour une identité-monde*, 213.
87 Le Bris and Rouaud, *Pour une littérature-monde*, back cover presentation. Also see p. 18.
88 See, for instance, Mbembe, "Pièce d'identité et désirs d'apartheid," 116–17. On Derrida, Nancy, and *monde/mondialisation* as a basis for a community in and "other" to "globe" and "globalization," see Moraru, *Cosmodernism: American Narrative, Late Globalization, and the New Cultural Imaginary* (Ann Arbor, MI: University of Michigan Press, 2011), 52–3.
89 Le Bris, "Pour une littérature-monde en français," 24.
90 Gayatri Chakravorty Spivak, "Imperative to Re-imagine the Planet," reprinted as chapter 16 in her book *An Aesthetic Education in the Era of Globalization* (Cambridge, MA: Harvard University Press, 2011), 335–50; *Death of a Discipline* (New York, NY: Columbia University Press, 2003).
91 Masao Miyoshi, "Turn to the Planet: Literature, Diversity, and Totality," *Comparative Literature* 53, no. 4 (Fall 2001): 283–97.

92 Susan Rubin Suleiman and Christie McDonald, "Introduction: The National and the Global," in *French Global: A New Approach to Literary History*, ed. Christie McDonald and Susan Rubin Suleiman (New York, NY: Columbia University Press, 2010), xvii.
93 Suleiman and McDonald, "Introduction," xvii–xviii.
94 Thérèse Migraine-George, *From Francophonie to World Literature in French: Ethics, Poetics, and Politics* (Lincoln, NE: University of Nebraska Press, 2013), x; Nadège Veldwachter, *Littérature francophone et mondialisation* (Paris, France: Karthala, 2012). Achille Mbembe and Felwine Sarr, eds. *Écrire l'Afrique-Monde* (Dakar, Senegal: Philippe Rey/Jimsaan, 2016).
95 Spivak, *Death of a Discipline*, 72–3.
96 Spivak, *Death of a Discipline*, 73.
97 Moraru, *Cosmodernism*, 48–9.
98 Christian Moraru's books on the subject are primarily the monographs *Cosmodernism* and *Reading for the Planet: Toward a Geomethodology* (Ann Arbor, MI: University of Michigan Press, 2015), as well as the essay collection *The Planetary Turn: Relationality and Geoaesthetics in the Twenty-First Century* coedited with Amy J. Elias (Evanston, IL: Northwestern University Press, 2015).
99 On "planetarity" and the "geoaesthetic" structure of the planetary world model, see Moraru, *Reading for the Planet*, 19–76.
100 Le Bris, "Pour une littérature-monde en français," 28.
101 Moraru, *Reading for the Planet*, 36–9.
102 Sarika Chandra, *Dislocalism: The Crisis of Globalization and the Remobilizing of Americanism* (Columbus, OH: Ohio State University Press, 2011), 4.
103 Emily Apter, *Against World Literature: On the Politics of Untranslatability* (London, UK: Verso, 2013), 78.
104 See Amy J. Elias and Christian Moraru's coedited essay collection, *The Planetary Turn*.

Part I

Systems and Institutions of Literary Francophonie: Language, Written Culture, and the Publishing World

1

African Literature, World Literature, and Francophonie

Bertrand Westphal

There once was a tower in Babel. Afterwards, it was a real mess.

—Raharimanana

Each African country is a living Babel.[1]

—Nimrod

If one considers literature on any scale other than that of the text alone, one wonders if we have been paying sufficient attention to the deep and multiple impact of globalization, a phenomenon that, in keeping with a certain tradition of cultural exception, one prefers to call, in French, *mondialisation*. Skeptical about such a possibility, Achille Mbembe observes in "L'Afrique qui vient," an essay published in the impressive 2017 collection edited by Alain Mabanckou *Penser et écrire l'Afrique aujourd'hui*, that "we have, then, shifted away from the human condition to the planetary condition."[2] The suggestion, accordingly, is that literature is now inscribed in the world, if by "world" we mean real, daily life, or, in more theoretical terms, literary discourse's "referent." But literature is also inscribed in the world in another sense, namely, the world perceived in its macroscopic dimension, as a *globe*. The latter evokes a playground for planetary stakeholders in a borderless economy or, conversely, the grievances following lost illusions for the planetary victims of an economy that erects barriers of water, brick, concrete, or barbed wire at every crossroads. The planetary condition evoked by Mbembe defines, however, the Age of Diasporas, and, to use one more time the Cameroonian philosopher's language, this condition has inspired, for example, "Afro-diasporic creations."[3] Likewise, and from a more strictly literary perspective, we could also speak of the diasporic readership that emerged at this planetary moment. Furthermore, Mbembe's statements prompt us to ask what exactly this refocusing of scholarship on the planet and its scale means for African literature in general and Francophone African literature in particular. What are the conditions under which this literature is produced, circulated, and interpreted? Which institutional and market factors shape its reception, and in what ways are these planetary relationships amenable to change? Under which circumstances can African literature be said to break out of lingering colonial dynamics and reposition itself in the international canon? The following pages take stock of how we got where we are and prospect future modalities of achieving more equity on the world literature scene.

1. Out of the "Colonial Library"

We did not have to wait until recent years to take a macroscopic approach to literary studies and their infinite variations.[4] It was just that we had to wait a little more in a country like France than elsewhere. In the 1960s, critics began to realize that literature should no longer be the prerogative of a small number of European and North American theoreticians. It was not acceptable any more to reserve the monopoly on literary analysis to a culture and generation whose education had been framed by the ethnic, gender, and sexual norms in place in nations jealously protective of an often-colonial past imbued with a presumed civilizing mission. Consequently, in the human and social sciences, the situation started evolving. In France, this happened as the ideas of Jean-Paul Sartre and Frantz Fanon, among others, received significant response. Here and elsewhere, the 1970s were decisive, for it was at this juncture that a shift occurred, and, henceforth, the articulation of new approaches to literature and theories thereof would take the cultural, historical, and political particularities of the subject of enunciation into account. At the beginning of those years, it was still conceivable, however, that Michel Foucault and Noam Chomsky could debate the meaning of history and human nature on the set of a Dutch TV program without ever considering the heterogeneity of planetary cultures.[5] At the end of the decade, their discussion was to take a different turn, as demonstrated by their growing militancy on various political fronts. Then, in 1978, Edward Said published *Orientalism*, which was translated two years later into French. Thus definitively launched, postcolonial studies provoked a questioning of epistemological foundations on university campuses, especially in the United States. The novelty of Said's intervention was—to state the obvious—of great importance: it became apparent that, at the heart of the academy, there was not just a single point of view in matters of representation and its politics, but such angles were legion, and, finally, their ongoing multiplication became widely accepted. At the same time, scholars realized that the ultra-dominant perspective that had hitherto characterized Western literary studies was perfectly identifiable. It was the one that was soon to be subsumed under a stock catchphrase: Dead White Males. To have any chance at entering the international literary canon, you had better be white, male, and dead, that is to say, "sanctifiable." In this context, the spring of 1988 could be considered a symbolic date. In this last year of the Reagan era, 500 Stanford University students marched through the campus, accompanied by Reverend Jesse Jackson. Their demand was more pluralism in syllabus development and especially in reading lists. The students' warrior-like slogan spread beyond the walls of Stanford and even past California's borders: "Hey hey, ho ho, Western culture's got to go." The protestors did specify, however, that the issue was in no way about expelling Plato or Aristotle from the Republic of Letters; if that had been the case, it would have been a serious mistake, for these thinkers themselves were the first to demand the ideal society not be reduced to the heritage of Dead White Males. In any event, the bottom line is that, from this point forward, when analyzing, say, William Shakespeare's *The Tempest*, no one hesitated to weigh it in comparison to Aimé Césaire's anti-colonial play, *Une Tempête* (1969).

Postcolonial studies substantially altered the world's Anglophone university landscape, for it was not just the US academy that was affected. France, however, at least between 1980 and 1990, still had a long way to go. I will limit myself here to just one example, namely, cinema. A mere few months after the protest at Stanford, the jury of the Venice *Mostra* awarded its special prize to *Camp de Thiaroye* by Ousmane Sembène. The film commemorates a bloody episode whose responsibility was incumbent on the colonial occupier: the massacre of seventy Senegalese soldiers in December 1944 in the camp referred to in the movie's title. Like *The Battle of Algiers* (1966) by Gillo Pontecorvo, Ousmane Sembène's film, coproduced with movie studios from Tunisia and Algeria, was only shown in French cinema theaters in 1998, after a considerable ten-year delay (while it took, I might add, *The Battle of Algiers*, whose initial projection was censored, only five years to be distributed).[6] In both cases, the subject embarrassed those, still numerous, who were reticent to evoke what former president François Hollande finally acknowledged, on the occasion of an official visit to Dakar in October 2012, as "the shadowy part of our [French] history." He confirmed his position during a commemorative ceremony held in the Thiaroye camp, in November 2014, in the presence of Macky Sall, president of the Senegalese Republic.[7] At the same time, I might note that *La Victoire en chantant* (*Black and White in Color*) by Jean-Jacques Annaud received the Oscar for Best Foreign Film in 1977. The result of a Franco-German-Swiss coproduction with the Ivorian Film Society, the film stages a vehement satire of colonialism. It went practically unnoticed in France, as it did in West Germany. Côte d'Ivoire, where the film was shot, entered it into competition under its own banner, and that is how *La Victoire en chantant* won the Hollywood trophy. This reaction is symptomatic of a context in turn accounting for the belated emergence of postcolonial studies and postcolonial concerns overall in France, at the beginning of the new millennium.[8]

2. "I Don't Know What *littérature-monde* Is. I Don't Know What French Literature or American Literature Is Either"

At the same time the postcolonial model of analysis was permanently settling into the Anglophone university landscape and speculation about the substance of the literary canon was growing, a new reflection on Goethean (and, though we forget it sometimes, Marxian) *Weltliteratur* took off, especially in comparative literature departments in the United States.[9] Of course, the conversations that brought Johann Wolfgang von

Goethe and Johann Peter Eckermann together in Weimar are well known and need not be rehearsed here. I will only remind the reader that one of them, dating from 1827, relates to the opening up of literature to the world and the ensuing necessity to conceive of a *Weltliteratur*. While a segment of the European intelligentsia was coming under the sway of nascent Orientalism, Goethe argued in favor of including non-European works in the international canon. He admired in particular Persian, Chinese, and Indian literature. There were limits to this inclusivity, however. For instance, African literatures, especially those from the sub-Saharan region, went completely unrecognized, a situation that changed with the rise of postcolonialism and, then, with the discipline of World Literature, which, on this and other grounds, has now succeeded *Weltliteratur*. Parallel to that of postcolonial studies, the growth of World Literature involved taking up immediately the question of the place of literatures on the bookshelves of the planetary library at a time critics across the academy were probing the impact on Western culture of traditions considered extrinsic to it. Thus, those we wrongly or rightly call "minorities" finally saw themselves "centered"—at least by comparison with the more marginal positions previously occupied in the literary world-system—under the combined pressures of postcolonial, gender, and queer studies. Reread in this way, world literature has opened up literary scholarship to creolization, cultural hybridization, as well as inter- and trans-culturality.

Importantly, the study of world literature is not confined to abstract reflections concerning the state of literature in the age of globalization and "fluid" societies. World literature also feeds a ripe editorial market, and to the extent that inclusion in the global implies considerations of an economic nature, the study of world literature must attend to these. Moreover, we cannot forget that between Goethe and the 1990s came Karl Marx, as did Pierre Bourdieu. The first really material reflection on the vagaries of what could be thought of as world literature emerged at the very beginning of the twentieth century, at the same time as the Nobel Prize for Literature. The irony of the story is that Alfred Nobel, the man who invented dynamite, also gave his friends the idea of making a canon—a cultural canon with a "humanist" vocation, in keeping with the terminology of the time. This humanism had very local ties, and its universalism was biased; to put it bluntly, it was Eurocentric. Consequently, African literature was, for a long time, confined to the margins of European attention or even ignored altogether. The world had to wait until 1986, when Nigerian Wole Soyinka was awarded the Nobel Prize in Literature, for this marginalization to come to an end. Subsequently, though, only three African laureates garnered the distinction: Egyptian Naguib Mahfouz (1988) and South Africans Nadine Gordimer (1991) and J. M. Coetzee (2003), who has since become an Australian citizen. The works of Ahmadou Kourouma, Assia Djebar, and Chinua Achebe were not recognized by the prize; the work of Ngũgĩ wa Thiong'o might still have a chance.

But there is, beyond the coveted Nobel, another internationally prominent forum of recognition, complete with its own market with a long-established tradition: literary anthologies designed for student use. The third edition of the *Norton Anthology of World Literature* (2001), for example, shows the evolution of this market in a particularly instructive way. Consisting of six volumes arranged from A to F, the Norton establishes a corpus of works among which instructors and students may select, and, like similar anthologies, reflects through its thematic organization the principles intended to guide that selection. An excerpt from a syllabus distributed to students in a World Literature course at Creighton University in Omaha, Nebraska, exemplifies these principles well and highlights the structural role anthologies play as material supports in curriculum development:

> In making selections from the sections below, instructors must strive to create a balanced reading list featuring a range of genres (epic, lyric, drama, short narrative, novel, essay); works from all the major historical periods (Antiquity, the Middle Ages, the Renaissance); works by authors from diverse backgrounds, genders, and racial/ethnic origins; and coverage of as many different cultures and literary traditions as possible.[10]

From the outset, we can sense the impact of these choices. While the traditional genres and the great literary periods are still mustered here, there is at least an effort to decenter the cultural canon and to contain its ethnocentric tendencies. Given that this concern was not even on the horizon in 1956, when the first edition of the anthology appeared, we can see just how significant a shift in thinking about the world's literatures has taken place in the interval since.[11]

A beneficiary of this change, Africa is no longer the great absent of a world literary history "made in the U.S.A." The continent's literature appears in volume C of the *Norton Anthology* of 2001 with an excerpt from a written version of the epic of Sunjata Keita. In turn, volume D features British writer Aphra Behn, who published *Oroonoko, or the Royal Slave* (1688), a novel whose protagonist is the grandson of an African king reduced to slavery and deported to Suriname with his beloved. Volume E makes room for Olaudah Equiano, who comes from an Igbo family, is forced into slavery, emancipated, and then becomes the author of a 1789 autobiography, *The Interesting Narrative of the Life of Olaudah Equiano, or Gustavus Vassa the African, Written by Himself*. The same Norton segment also includes the oral history tradition, which is represented by narratives gravitating around the mythical figure of Anansi and by excerpts of *hain-teny*, a Malagasy poetic form. It is nevertheless up to the last volume, F, to introduce African and Caribbean literature more substantially. Divided into three sections, this volume acknowledges, for the period 1900-45, *Cahier d'un retour au pays natal* (1939) by Aimé Césaire. The years 1945-69 are grouped together under the heading "Postwar and Postcolonial Literature." In terms of periodization, this grouping has the merit of placing the post–Second World War period and decolonization on equal thematic footing. Here, we find Léopold Sédar Senghor, whose work is present through eight translated excerpts. The place given to Senghor is particularly noteworthy in a volume that makes room only for three other Francophone or partially Francophone authors for the period between 1900 and 1968: Marcel Proust, Albert Camus, and Samuel Beckett. Moreover, Senghor is not the only African author in the *Anthology*; Tayeb Sahib, Naguib Mahfouz, and Chinua Achebe take their places alongside him. The African contribution is reinforced in the third section of volume F, which is devoted to "contemporary world literature," said to begin in 1968. Next to three authors of Caribbean origin (Derek Walcott, the British V. S. Naipaul, and Jamaica Kincaid), two Nigerians are recognized (Wole Soyinka and Niyi Osundare) along with a Ghanaian (Ama Aida Atoo), a Kenyan (Ngũgĩ wa Thiong'o), a South African (Bessie Head), and an Egyptian (Nawad El Saadawi). Nevertheless, Africa's Francophone writers or Portuguese-speaking African writers such as Mia Couto, for that matter, are, overall, singularly absent from the panorama of the contemporary era as envisaged by the Norton. For the same period, Europe is represented by the Irish Seamus Heaney, Great Britain's Naipaul and Salman Rushdie, and the Turk Orhan Pamuk, who is, as a result, the only non-Anglophone European writer accepted by the *Norton Anthology* editors in their post-1968 selection. The great emptiness characterizing the literary space between the Channel and the Aegean Sea is surprising. The choice to ignore such a vast expanse of Europe is undoubtedly a first in the construction of Western literary history.[12] Finally, I should point to the four authors from the United States, who are all from "ethnic minorities" in the American sense of the term: Leslie Marmon Silko (Native American Literature), Toni Morrison (African American Literature), Sandra Cisneros (Chicana Literature), and Junot Díaz (Dominican-American Literature).

Tentative and insufficient as they may be, the mutations in the Norton reflect the stakes involved in canon formation, which is always selective, subject to changing norms, and never neutral.[13] What further complicates the problem of a *representative* world canon is the very notion of representativity, which has been traditionally understood in national terms. For what the global era has taught us is that it is no longer possible to establish a strict equivalence between the nation and literature, if this correlation ever had any meaning at all in the first place. This is, in fact, what Haitian writer Gary Victor hints at when he insists in the quotation reproduced in the subheading above that "I don't know what *littérature-monde* is. I don't know what French Literature or American Literature is either." With the passing of time, national perimeters seem more and more confining for the literatures inside them. But, then, even a world literature or a *littérature-monde* defined in an excessively rigid way can come to feel constraining. Literature has, to state the obvious, an undeniable transnational dimension, one that has never been more obvious than in our time, that is, in the era of planetary mobility. Yet this mobility requires us to think the global differently, as an evolving complex of relations within and across nations, not just as contacts between discrete entities bounded by stable and coherent national identities. From this point of view, Africa constitutes a major paradigm of globality, if that globality is reconceived with a focus on relational connections among individuals and cultures. Yet again, let us listen to Achille Mbembe: "About 'Africa' we can only speak of an assembly of spaces constantly produced in the mode of entanglement and circulation. Africa is, first, multiplicity—and therefore relation."[14] From the standpoint of its literary "entanglements"—internal and external—as well as from other perspectives, Africa's place in the world is anything but peripheral.

3. "Language. Here We Are"

The sheer amount of world literature volumes—anthologies, textbooks, and studies of all sorts—that have come out of late indicates that, at least in the United States and in many other Anglophone countries, the university system is now assigning a more reasonable place to Caribbean and African literatures.[15] Another sign of the growing health of the scholarship in the field is the increase, especially in postcolonial studies, in critical attention devoted to the problems inherent to the creation and presentation of world literary corpuses.[16] Such bodies of work—those of anthologies, for example— are certainly varied, but their establishment and management, critics argue, remain the prerogative of a small group of people. Long ago, Goethe spoke about the same problem in different terms:

> National literature [*Nationalliteratur*] means little these days; the epoch of world literature [*Weltliteratur*] is at hand, and everybody must endeavor to hasten its coming. But again, in such estimation of things foreign, we must not cling to a particular work and regard it as ideal. We must not think it is the Chinese, or the Serbs, or Calderon, or the *Nibelungen*. In our need for the exemplary, we rather must always return to the ancient Greeks, for in their works it is at all times man in his beauty that is depicted. Everything else, we must regard merely from an historic point of view, and adopt as much of the good in it as we can.[17]

And herein lies the difficulty. What Goethe thought to be natural and completely spontaneous is hardly self-evident, though. Turning to the world for one's own aesthetic thrills and then just falling back on the old habits of Dead White Males will simply not do. On the other hand, those efforts to promote world literature without harking back on atemporal and ethnocentric ideals still have to overcome material and cultural-linguistic obstacles to an equitable treatment of the daunting variety characterizing the world's literary production. This is not a path-breaking realization, of course, for numerous theoreticians of postcolonial and subaltern studies have already paved the way to it. But, in her excellent 2013 monograph, *Against World Literature: On the Politics of Untranslatability*, Emily Apter articulates such concerns most effectively, as she questions the consequences of large-scale translation practices, notably in the Anglophone sphere.[18] Obviously, translation is neither innocent nor inoffensive, for, as Aamir R. Mufti has underscored, "any critical account of literary relations on a world scale—that is, any account of world literature as such—must thus actively confront and attend to this functioning of English as vanishing mediator, rather than treat it passively as neutral or transparent medium, both as world language of literary expression and as undisputed language of global capitalism."[19]

Granted, translation allows for the dissemination of works that would otherwise be confined to zones that are linguistically inaccessible to most people outside those spaces. Translation also ensures a modicum of cultural democracy through the "horizontal" links it sets up. By the same movement, translation also reinforces the hegemonic status quo because it can never be a *vanishing mediator*. Particularly in the context of a world literature anthology, rendering into another idiom entails making a selection, and this raises some thorny issues since, it goes without saying, not everything can be translated. One wonders, then, how can one justify the choice to translate some works and not others? The question is key because choices made now will have consequences whose significance cannot necessarily be determined in advance. If an English version introduces to wider publics a writer from a linguistic area that is little known on the world stage, his or her promotion will have wide repercussions, *even on the author's culture of origin*. To put it differently, by translating on a worldwide scale, one is contributing to imposing on the source literature a literary canon that is not necessarily its own.

But even before considering the impact of translation once the decision to produce a foreign-language version of a certain work has been made, there is another major problem one must consider: Which criteria will be used in making the decision to include a text or not in a world literature anthology? There are multiple possible answers to this question. The most neutral would basically consist in declaring that one must follow the canon of the source cultures. This solution is, at least in part, plausible for authors belonging to literatures whose historical development rests on the written word and a planetary reputation. Such figures might include, for example, Shakespeare, Miguel de Cervantes, Victor Hugo, and Cao Xueqin— though, apropos of Cao, we might add for practical purposes, as it were, "the author of *Dream of the Red Chamber*" (in the Eurocentric West, a Chinese classic will always be less classic than a European one). The case is quite different for literatures whose history is scarred by external aggressions such as colonization, but which are now booming. In this instance, it would be appropriate to ask whether the canon of African literature—or literatures—established by American anthologies corresponds to African universities and readers' view of things even though, it goes without saying, this is an issue of international, intercultural, and even global critical reception. This matter is just as pertinent in Francophone environments, where the problem of anthologies is further complicated by that of the book market and all of its related stakes. Moreover, the questions of selectivity and inclusion are not limited to works produced in the tongues and sites of the former colonies, which works still have to be recognized at metropolitan centers whose languages are those of the colonizers of yesteryear such as the French. Rumor has it that, to win the Nobel Prize for Literature, the nominee must have been translated into the native language of the distinguished members of the Swedish Academy.[20]

Whether we like it or not, what gets translated, anthologized, taught, and promoted by the book industry is also affected by a whole series of stereotypes engrained in the target country's sometimes ethnocentric vision of itself and others in the world. In this vein, it would not be too farfetched to point out that what is actually taking place in World Literature in terms of both literary practice and management thereof recalls what happened at the time when Orientalism was gaining momentum—

along these lines, let us not forget that Goethe, in championing *Weltliteratur*, was doing so in an Orientalist context where he and others would devise general, world-inclusive schemas whose implementation, however, was sometimes handled without discernment. Several prominent studies have been carried out, for instance, on the modifications affecting the Indian literary patrimony following the British occupation and on the manner in which they were adopted by local intellectuals. Ranajit Guha, one of the founding members of the Subaltern Studies school, and Mufti have made notable contributions on this topic.[21] Mentioning Kālidāsa and his play *Śākuntala* (*Shakuntala*), Mufti observes that Kālidāsa, transformed into an "Indian Shakespeare" by the colonizers and therefore enduringly knighted as such, as it were, became a cog in the wheel of the canonization process propagated in India by the native nationalist intelligentsia itself. As the critic specifies, "The national consciousness finds itself, so to speak, precisely by adopting the colonizer's orientation toward 'Indian literature' and can therefore only be understood, to be more precise, as an Orientalized consciousness."[22]

Involving a translation—or mistranslation, rather—of sorts, this "Orientation," one is tempted to write, suggests once more that translation is not solely a matter of language. Nor is it restricted, in terms of its mechanics and ultimate objective, to producing an "equivalence" between concepts from different languages, an issue that has largely already been addressed.[23] What is more, translation is not even limited to the swing from language to language that Souleymane Bachir Diagne pointedly evokes in the volume of essays edited by Mabanckou. "To think about Africa," says Diagne, "to think in Africa, is to think in translation, in African languages and in the languages of Africa, which today are also Portuguese, French, and English. It is to think in the modality of to-ing and fro-ing [*dans le va-et-vient*], it is to think from one language to another."[24] Certainly, we need to think about the relationship between idioms, which is the one that places the African speaker in a constant process of translation and inscribes his or her writing in a broader environment. The languages of former colonizers have undoubtedly become African, a notion that has the immense merit of "decentering" the Hexagon's place in the Francophonie debate, of liberating the entire discussion from academic and other institutional constraints. But, at the same time, the idiom—in this case, French—becomes the vector of unique linkages to the country from which it comes, that is, France.[25] In view of the worship of French in France—compared, say, to English, which is not even the official language of the UK—the linguistic relationship between former African colonies and their French metropolis is necessarily complex, "a kind of ambiguous matriarchy, [which] fools no one, especially the writers," as Tahar Ben Jelloun has said.[26] As delicate and ample as the language controversy has been, especially as far as French goes, there is today an even broader one, which involves the entire cultural and literary planet. For, most significantly, relationships among writers or idioms are no longer organized primarily into binary oppositions such as former colony-former colonizer; they have been absorbed into a global, largely rhizomatic network.[27]

4. "No One Should Give Us Lessons as Long as They Ignore Economic Domination: It Conditions All the Rest"

This is not to say, though, that this world network is evenly balanced or equitably set up, nor to deny, accordingly, the persistence of hegemonic poles and power discrepancies. Rather, it is to draw attention to the need to attend to the new and specific forms these relations take in our global era. We may note—and frankly, this should come as no surprise either—that the hypotheses applied to translation and its repercussions are of interest to a whole series of linguistic areas subjected to historically determined power relations, even though these relations might vary in nature from place to place.[28] From a global standpoint, writing in an uncommon language can be an obstacle when one has the ambition of being read urbi et orbi. On this ground, the intermediary role played by translation becomes unavoidable. Another stumbling block, perhaps less visible but no less restrictive, has to do, regardless of idiom, with effective access to what I have called the world scene. In other words, a book may well be written in a twenty-first-century *lingua franca*—in English or, to a lesser extent, French—and yet that work's dissemination will still be economically conditioned by the relationships that usually develop between center and periphery, a dynamic no analysis of world literature can afford to ignore. Publication itself and then the conditions for the establishment of a literary canon, and, more generally, the prerequisites for a genuine cultural autonomy, are here at stake. As Mufti has aptly argued, it would be quite wrongheaded—and, indeed, anachronic— for World Literature as a literary and scholarly field expanding during these times of accelerated globalization to build itself up by ignoring the pitfalls of Orientalism and of the cultural-colonization logic conditioning it. For the risk of replicating, over a much wider expanse, in the twenty-first century—a time filled with a lot of uncertainty worldwide—what once occurred in India should not be underestimated. There is no doubt, then, that the main question to explore at present concerns not only the circulation of texts but also its specific circumstances and cultural-political upshots. If, as Lydie Moudileno recalls, the questions asked during the First Congress of Black Writers and Artists organized at the Sorbonne in 1956 through the initiative of the journal *Présence africaine* revolved around the nature of Pan African intellectuals' *engagement*—"What is the mission of the African writer? For whom are we [African authors] writing? On what subjects should we write? In which terms, in which language, even?"—we can reiterate today some of these questions and even add others: Who publishes? Where can one get published? With which press? What is published? Who reads whom? Who reads what?[29] All these are worthy of debate, and if they are not addressed up front, any discussion of world literature—or, after *Le Monde*'s 2007 publication of the famous manifesto, *littérature-monde*—will become pointless.

At the 2015 Salon du Livre de Genève, Cameroonian writer Max Lobe, who lives in Switzerland, raised these very issues in an editorial published in *Le Monde*, where he took a hard look at the distribution mechanisms for African authors and books. In response to the more specific question, "Are African authors obliged to go through Paris?" he said:

Even if their efforts are not enough, African governments *are* promoting the literature of their countries. Cheikh Hamidou Kane, Léonora Miano, Calixthe Beyala, Gaston Paul Effa, or even Alain Mabanckou are largely read in Francophone Africa. They are included in school curricula. This is one of the most important means by which African authors can be read on the continent. However, what strikes me most regarding the handful of contemporary authors mentioned above is that they have all been published in France, and more precisely, in Paris. . . . Should we say that a Francophone African writer will never be read in Africa if he does not go through Paris? Maybe. But this is an old question, and to me, a secondary one. And it is not specific to African authors either. . . . As far as African publishing is concerned, the real question that begs to be asked is that of distribution. On the one hand, how can we remedy the virtual monopoly of the major Western publishing groups over low-cost editions of African-authored books included in African school curricula? On the other hand, how can the literature produced in Africa be better disseminated not only on the continent, but also, especially, in the West in an increasingly globalized cultural context? Once we have answered these two questions, we will probably benefit more not only from publishing African literature generally but also from publishing it in Africa.[30]

Lobe makes here several fundamental points while also taking inventory, from an African perspective, of a few of the canonical writers of the continent. These are not always the same as those of American anthologies, which neglect, to some extent—Lobe seems to imply—authors of French expression. In *Penser et écrire l'Afrique aujourd'hui*, Togoan novelist Sami Tchak has a similar list fleshing out a locally informed perspective on the African canon, books that give "the impression of knowing more about the continent when we read them": Kateb Yacine's *Nedjma*, Chinua Achebe's *Things Fall Apart*, Cheikh Hamidou Kane's *L'Aventure ambiguë*, Ahmadou Kourouma's *Les Soleils des indépendances*, Sony Labou Tansi's *La vie et demie*, Abdourahman Waberi's *Aux Etats-Unis d'Afrique*, Mia Couto's *The Tuner of Silences*, and J. M. Coetzee's *In the Heart of the Country*.[31]

This is another indication that, globally speaking, the situation is asymmetrical if not utterly unequal and unjust. In a 2016 article tellingly titled "When African Publishing Emancipates Itself," Raphaël Thierry analyzed in detail the production and distribution of books in French-speaking Africa.[32] Perhaps taking inspiration from the 2006 novel *Aux Etats-Unis d'Afrique*, where Waberi paints an upside-down version of today's world, in which the African continent has become the great power holding the reins of world economy and sheltering European refugees, Thierry writes:

> Imagine for a moment that a Cameroonian editorial group is gradually absorbing some 90% of French school programs, [and] that Ivorian cultural diplomacy coordinates the overhaul of the French public reading network. Suppose, then, that African non-governmental organizations send millions of books to French libraries, and almost exclusively fill them with books published in Africa, to the detriment of the diversity of local publishing. Finally, picture a situation in which

some great names in French literature—who would have always been published in Africa: Victor Hugo, Albert Camus, Jean-Marie Gustave Le Clézio—are very rarely republished by French publishers, who obtained the rights thanks to the generous intervention of the Cultural Institute of Senegal.[33]

If we translate Thierry's als ob reasoning into the terms of today's historical context, we do get a good grasp of the real state of affairs in publishing in Francophone Africa, where, I might note, things look hardly different from what is happening in the continent's Anglophone zone, which is structured around British and American poles. This is an example, as Gary Victor would rightly say, of "a form of colonization that remains unspoken."[34] But precisely because it is seldom if ever spoken about, this topic deserves to be dealt with extensively, and other critics have done so.[35] Here, I would only add, as Thierry himself has done using figures provided by the *Syndicat national de l'édition*, the Foreign Trade Portal of France, and the French Ministry of Finance, that the ratio between books exported to Francophone Africa and those imported into France from the same region from 2014 to 2015 is 98 to 2! At the same time, African countries are not, as he reminds us, France's main Francophone book customers. Belgium is first on the list; Algeria, which is partially Francophone, is seventh; and Côte d'Ivoire, the largest client in sub-Saharan Africa, is twelfth. In terms of imports into France between 2015 and early 2016, no African country is among the top seventeen publishing exporters. The deficit is also worrying in educational publishing, since more than half of the textbooks of Francophone Africa are French. As emphasized by Thierry, Côte d'Ivoire is an exception, since schoolbooks are manufactured and distributed there locally.

Should we despair? I do not think so. Taking the first steps down the path to a more equitable situation is the prerequisite to an effective presence of African literatures in the world, and Thierry enumerates many reasons we can expect significant improvement ahead. The first has to do with statistics and the ability to gather and analyze information. Granted, this capacity does make a difference whenever markets with developed statistical instruments (institutes, research logistics, etc.) are compared to others that are deprived of adequate measuring instruments. Since data collection tends to be exhaustive for the former and incomplete for the latter, the abovementioned disparities may be artificially accentuated. What is left to do then, as Thierry suggests, is to take into consideration several other factors with firm groundings. One of these is the published volume's *visibility*, for, quite logically in my view, books must be physically visible in order to circulate. Therefore, they have everything to gain by taking center stage at bookfairs in Paris, Geneva, Frankfurt, and elsewhere. Capturing the spotlight this way, he says, is happening and matters, more and more frequently, and the degree of publicity is increasing every day. In addition, digital publishing is expanding at a fast clip, and this development in particular is an obvious source of hope due to reduced costs and the inbuilt superior potential for global interconnectivity and dissemination. At the same time, efforts must be made to avoid privileging the French or European markets; it is indeed imperative to bring both readerships and book industry decision-makers to African countries, and in this regard, too, things appear to be moving in the right direction. As Thierry points out, UNESCO made Conakry the book capital of the world in 2017, while a first *Salon de l'écrit et du livre en langues africaines* (SAELLA) was organized in Bamako in January 2016.[36] In a more traditional way, many African countries are organizing bookfairs such as Côte d'Ivoire's Salon International du Livre d'Abidjan (SILA). The goal here, as Thierry concludes, is to start broadening the African publishing industry spectrum so as to bring it in line with international publishing norms while also taking into account the specifics of Africa's book market. Finally, another effective and actually well-known strategy that might work is increasing collaborations among Francophone publishers, be they African, European, or North American. In fact, since copublishing reduces manufacturing costs and ensures better distribution, some authors themselves have founded presses, with noted figures such as Mali's Moussa Konaté, Senegal's Felwine Sarr, Congo's Caya Makhélé, and Cameroon's Paul Dakeyo leading the way.[37] Not only that but when the opportunity arises, they cooperate with French or Québécois publishers. That is exactly what Boubacar Boris Diop has done, as indicated by Waberi, in creating the publishing label Céytu (Dakar), a joint venture with Laure Leroy of Éditions Zulma (Paris) and Rodney Saint-Eloi of Mémoire d'encrier (Montreal).[38] All of them have helped bring greater international visibility to the African book market and encourage African writers to publish in Africa.

These are some of the essential venues and modalities for diversifying book production, for taking into account multiple viewpoints and actors involved, or who *should be* involved, in the publishing world, and thus for gaining greater control in the fostering of a representative African literary canon.[39] African literatures, particularly the Francophone ones, must be able to better manage their positioning in terms of where they stand within planetary literature and of their study *as* part of it, whether it is labeled World Literature or *littérature-monde*. The stakes are undoubtedly high. After putting together a list of recommended readings by African writers, Tchak added: "These texts constitute elements of a puzzle whose reconstruction would make it possible to attain an 'us.'"[40] This "us" may be African but goes, most likely, beyond that. It includes the world, a gigantic puzzle that we must solve together regardless of the languages in which it is written.

Notes

1 Raharimanana, "Le creuset des possibles," in *Pour une littérature-monde*, ed. Michel Le Bris and Jean Rouaud (Paris, France: Gallimard, 2007), 312; Nimrod, *Tombeau de Léopold Sédar Senghor* (Cognac, France: Le Temps qu'il fait, 2003), 22.
2 Achille Mbembe, "L'Afrique qui vient," in *Penser et écrire l'Afrique aujourd'hui*, ed. Alain Mabanckou (Paris, France: Seuil, 2017), 19.
3 Mbembe, "L'Afrique," 29.
4 The famous expression "colonial library" is from V. Y. Mudimbe's classic *The Invention of Africa: Gnosis, Philosophy, and the Order of Knowledge* (Bloomington, IN, and London, UK: Indiana University Press-James Currey, 1988), 188.

5   The recording of this November 1971 debate may be viewed at: https://www.youtube.com/watch?v=OY93gHVynaY (accessed June 11, 2019). It was transcribed in Michel Foucault, *Dits et écrits, II* (Paris, France: Gallimard, 1994) and in *The Chomsky-Foucault Debate: On Human Nature*, foreword by John Rajchman (New York, NY, and London, UK: The New Press, 2006).
6   We might include *Les Statues meurent aussi* in the list of films subjected to political censorship. At the initiative of *Présence Africaine*, Chris Marker and Alain Resnais produced this documentary in 1953, but its permit for distribution in France was denied for a period of ten years.
7   François Hollande, "France-Afrique: Le texte du discours de Dakar prononcé par François Hollande," *Jeune Afrique*, October 15, 2012, http://www.jeuneafrique.com/173903/politique/france-afrique-le-texte-du-discours-de-dakar-prononc-par-fran-ois-hollande/ (accessed August 3, 2017).
8   See the highly critical Jean-François Bayart, *Les Études postcoloniales: Un carnaval académique* (Paris, France: Karthala, 2010). For a more nuanced overview, see Nicolas Bancel, "Que faire des *postcolonial studies*? Vertus et déraisons de l'accueil critique des *postcolonial studies* en France," *Vingtième Siècle: Revue d'histoire* 115 (2012/2013): 129–47. Bancel notes that Mudimbe's *Invention of Africa* has never been translated into French. In taking a closer look at Mudimbe's bibliography, it becomes apparent that he abandoned French in favor of English in 1982. None of his English works have been translated into French to this day.
9   The quoted sentences opening this section are Gary Victor's. See Gary Victor, "Littérature-monde ou liberté d'être," in Le Bris and Rouaud, *Pour une littérature-monde*, 315.
10 Creighton University, "ENG/CNE 120/122: World Literature I Master Syllabus," https://www.creighton.edu/ccas/english/programs/worldliteratureprogram/courses/worldliteraturei/ (accessed August 13, 2017). In this course, reference is mainly made to the *Bedford Anthology*.
11 The coordination of the collection was entrusted to Martin Puchner (General Editor), a professor of Theater, English Literature, and Comparative Literature at Harvard. Puchner was assisted by a team of academics working in North America: Suzanne Conklin Akbari (Editor, University of Toronto), Wiebke Denecke (Editor, Boston University), Vinay Dharwadker (Editor, University of Wisconsin-Madison), Barbara Fuchs (Editor, University of California-Los Angeles), Caroline Levine (Editor, University of Wisconsin-Madison), Pericles Lewis (Editor, Yale University), and Emily Wilson (Editor, University of Pennsylvania).
12 This data points to a reality totally opposite to what Nobel Prize history suggests. Whereas there have been four prizes for African writers since 1985—and this is, in fact, the number of *all* African authors ever recognized by the Nobel Committee—there have been eighteen Nobels for European writers during the same period, four of which went to French authors alone: Claude Simon, Gao Xingjiang, J. M. G. Le Clézio, and Patrick Modiano. African cinema has not fared any better either. Quite the contrary. Among the winners at three European film festivals (Cannes, Berlin, and Venice), there is only one film whose director is African: *Chronique des années de braise* by the Algerian Mohammed Lakhdar-Hamina, who got the *Palme d'or* in 1975. As for Hollywood, the only Oscar for the Best Film in a Foreign Language awarded to an African director went to the South African Gavin Hood for *Tsotsi*, in 2005.

13 The Norton is, of course, not the only world literature anthology. There are at least two others in English alone, the Longman (Pearson, 2004, for the latest edition) and the Bedford (Bedford/St Martin's, 2003). This is not the place to review in detail either their contents or content variation across editions. It will be sufficient to note that, for the Longman, the cover of the volume dedicated to the eighteenth century features the portrait of Olaudah Equiano, and the list of African and Caribbean authors of the twentieth century faithfully reflects that of the Norton. Here, in capital letters, we find Naguib Mahfouz, Léopold Sédar Senghor, Aimé Césaire, Chinua Achebe, and Wole Soyinka. Featured are also Assia Djebar, V. S. Naipaul, Ama Ata Aidoo, Jamaica Kincaid, and Nadine Gordimer, as well as the Libyan Ibrahim al-Koni. In a compact version of the anthology, we come across Ngũgĩ wa Thiong'o, Derek Walcott, and Georges Ngal. In the *Bedford Anthology*, the excerpts are longer, and therefore the list of authors is shorter. Senghor, Césaire, Achebe, Mahfouz, and Walcott remain the undisputed headliners of African and Caribbean literature, while new entries are reserved for the Egyptian Alifa Rifaat and Claude McKay, who was born in Jamaica and moved to the United States in 1912, before becoming an American citizen and one of the major members of the Harlem Renaissance. Also included is Edwidge Danticat, an Anglophone writer who, at the beginning of her adolescence, moved to Brooklyn with her parents, who were originally from Port-au-Prince.
14 Mbembe, "L'Afrique," 30.
15 The phrase "Language. Here we are" is Raharimanana's. See Raharimanana, "Le creuset des possibles," 305.
16 Sharae Deckard et al., *Combined and Uneven Development: Towards a New Theory of World-Literature* (Liverpool, UK: Liverpool University Press, 2015); Pheng Cheah, *What Is a World? On Postcolonial Literature as World Literature* (Durham, NC: Duke University Press, 2016); Aamir R. Mufti, *Forget English! Orientalisms and World Literatures* (Cambridge, MA: Harvard University Press, 2016); B. Venkat Mani, *Recoding World Literature: Libraries, Print Culture, and Germany's Pact with Books* (New York, NY: Fordham University Press, 2016).
17 J. P. Eckermann, *Conversations with Goethe: Selected, with an Introduction and Annotated Index*, ed. Hans Kohn, trans. Gisela C. O'Brien (New York, NY: Frederick Ungar Publishing, 1964), 94.
18 See also Rebecca L. Walkowitz, *Born Translated: The Contemporary Novel in an Age of World Literature* (New York, NY: Columbia University Press, 2015).
19 Mufti, *Forget English!*, 16.
20 See, for example, Kelly Washbourne, "Translation, *Littérisation*, and the Nobel Prize for Literature," *TranscUlturAl* 8, no. 1 (2016): 57–75, http://dx.doi.org/10.21992/T92H02 (accessed August 9, 2017).
21 See Ranajit Guha, *History at the Limit of World-History* (New York, NY: Columbia University Press, 2002).
22 Mufti, *Forget English!*, 115.
23 In Africa, one of the figureheads of this line of thinking is the Ghanaian philosopher Kwasi Wiredu. See his *Cultural Universals and Particulars: An African Perspective* (Bloomington, IN: Indiana University Press, 1996) and *A Companion to African Philosophy* (Oxford, UK: Blackwell, 2003).
24 Souleymane Bachir Diagne, "Penser de langue à langue," in Mabanckou, *Penser et écrire l'Afrique aujourd'hui*, 79.

25 My comment echoes, if obliquely, what Le Bris declares in his piece "Pour une littérature-monde en français" from his and Rouaud's *Pour une littérature-monde*: "The survival of French on the world scale will depend on our ability to liberate the language from its pact with the nation" (47). In the same volume, Waberi insists, in a similar vein, that "the point here is to make clear that the literature of France is no more than a small island that murmurs, psalmodies, and creates in French within the greater archipelago of the French language" (72).

26 Tahar Ben Jelloun, "La cave de ma mémoire, le toit de ma maison," in Le Bris and Rouaud, *Pour une littérature-monde*, 117.

27 See Thérèse Migraine-George, *From Francophonie to World Literature in French: Ethics, Poetics, & Politics* (Lincoln, NE, and London, UK: University of Nebraska Press, 2013), where the critic underscores "the ever-increasing mobility of literary and cultural producers—for example, a great number of African and Caribbean writers now live and publish in Europe and in North America—and the concomitant intricacy of literary aesthetics that strive to account for *rhizomatic relations between the local and the global, the particular and the universal*" (xi; emphasis added).

28 The statement opening this section is Nimrod's. See Nimrod, *Tombeau de Léopold Sédar Senghor*, 33.

29 Lydie Moudileno, "Penser l'Afrique à partir de sa littérature," in Mabanckou, *Penser et écrire l'Afrique aujourd'hui*, 144.

30 Max Lobe, "Editeurs africains, mondialisez-vous donc!" *Le Monde*, April 24, 2015, http://www.lemonde.fr/afrique/article/2015/04/24/editeurs-africains-mondialisez-vous-donc_ 4622325_ 3212.html (accessed August 7, 2017).

31 Sami Tchak, "Le Moi au miroir fragmenté du Nous," in Mabanckou, *Penser et écrire l'Afrique aujourd'hui*, 203.

32 Raphaël Thierry's study follows in the line of his Comparative Literature thesis defended in 2013 and written under codirection from the University of Lorraine and the University of Yaoundé.

33 Raphaël Thierry, "Quand l'édition africaine s'émancipe," *INA Global* (Institut National de l'Audiovisuel), April 20, 2016, http://www.inaglobal.fr/edition/article/quand-l-edition-africaine-s-emancipe-8944 (accessed August 9, 2017).

34 Victor, "Littérature-monde ou liberté d'être," 319.

35 Bernard Mouralis, *Littérature et développement* (Paris, France: Silex, 1984); Raphaël Thierry, *Le marché du livre africain et ses dynamiques littéraires. Le cas du Cameroun* (Pessac, France: Presses Universitaires de Bordeaux, 2015); Haby Niakate, "Côte d'Ivoire: le livre de comptes de Dramane Boaré, éditeur et fin gestionnaire," *Jeune Afrique*, January 13, 2016, http://www. jeuneafrique.com/mag/289602/culture/cote-divoire-livre-de-comptes-de-dramane-boare-editeur-fin-gestionnaire (accessed August 9, 2017).

36 Here is an excerpt from the Salon's presentation on *Afrolivresque*, an online magazine dedicated to African literature: "SAELLA's stakes are of a capital importance in Francophone Africa, where most children (about 83%) are schooled in French or in Arabic while they neither write nor read in their maternal language. This native multilingualism tends to get lost over the course of their education" ("Mali—Premier Salon de l'écrit et du livre en langues africaines du 03 au 06 décembre 2015," *Afrolivresque*, November 13, 2015, https://www.afrolivresque.com/premier-salon-de-lecrit-et-du-livre-en-langues-africaines-du-03-au-06-decembre-2015/ (accessed August 10, 2017).

37 These presses are Éditions du Figuier (Bamako), Jimsaan Éditions and Silex, later known as Nouvelles du Sud (Dakar), Acoria Éditions (France).
38 Abdourahman Waberi, "'Les enfants de la postcolonie' précédé d'une note liminaire," in Mabanckou, *Penser et écrire l'Afrique aujourd'hui*, 151.
39 See the bibliography provided by Lydie Moudileno in her text "Penser l'Afrique à partir de sa littérature"; Bernard Mouralis, "Qu'est-ce qu'un classique africain?" *Notre Librairie* 160 (December 2005): 34–9; Claire Ducourneau, "Qu'est-ce qu'un 'classique' africain? Les conditions d'accès à la reconnaissance des écrivain(e)s issu(e)s d'Afrique subsaharienne francophone depuis 1960," *Actes de la Recherche en Sciences Sociales* 206–7 (2015): 34–49; János Riesz, "A propos des 'classiques africains': Quels modèles pour un canon des littératures africaines?" *Etudes Littéraires africaines* 32 (2011): 147–56.
40 Tchak, "Le Moi au miroir fragmenté du Nous," 203.

2

Francophone African Publishing and the Misconceptions of World Literature

Raphaël Thierry

In this essay, I wish to address some widespread misconceptions that surround the African book industry and thereby contribute to limiting the circulation of Africa's literature around the world. These commonplaces, I suggest, present African publishing as an endangered and subaltern species that requires protection, as a niche of the international book market rather than an equal-footing partner in this trade and, by extension, in the world literature corpus. Such clichés persist even though literature that has long been categorized as "African" has consistently interrogated hegemonic and classificatory modes of conceptualizing "African literature" and, moreover, despite the salient rise of World Literature and of interest in new paradigms through which one might get a better grip on global cultural realities.[1] Although the Global North has been factoring the African publishing industry into its thinking for the last thirty years, it has been viewing Africa through the narrow lenses of ever-"emerging markets" fraught with difficulties and of "developing countries" caught in a state of constant technological, economic, and self-expressive or "stylistic" flux. One could attribute this outlook to widespread ignorance as well as to a misguided approach to African markets, which are treated as just another piece in the global puzzle rather than as an economy that must be analyzed, assessed, and supported according to its own complex morphology and tradition. The conversation around such issues also fails to take into account the industry's actual output far too often. The critical-historical narrative that follows sets out to correct this situation.

One recent illustration of this state of affairs was supplied by the 2017 Frankfurt Book Fair, when the world's largest gathering of this sort hosted a roundtable on publishing in Africa. During this meeting, three Francophone publishers were asked about illiteracy rates and the challenge of accessing reading material in their countries.[2] Such questions betray the problematic conservatism of the epistemological frameworks still dominant today, which have been perpetuated through six decades of pseudo-analysis providing a picture of the African literary marketplace as still nascent and hampered by obstacles such as poor education of local audiences. The sheer absence of precise, contextual data on the realities of publishing in African countries has allowed this kind of talk to go unchallenged.[3]

To explain the paradoxical persistence of Eurocentric epistemologies and the marginalization of African publishing in a contemporary moment when terms like "World Literature" and "cultural diversity" are on everyone's lips, we must consider the lack of African representation in international publishing platforms and in ostensibly collaborative efforts, as well as the tendency to see African publishers, when they appear in such arenas at all, as venues for "specific" literary themes and individual authors.[4] We must also revisit, however, the conceptual-analytic frameworks built from the 1960s to the 1980s, which repeatedly reproduced a radical division between "African publishing" and "African literature," splitting the one from the other and reinforcing their confinement to separate categories. Furthermore, it is important to question the role of publishers in fostering a canon of postcolonial literature whose African representatives have been published mainly in France—a canon that, I might add, has become since the 1980s one of the most visible branches of the world's literature, and that has been identified of late with the so-called *littérature-monde* movement.[5] Assuming that such visibility of a body of literature is based on a certain number of symbolic positions, it is useful to recall French sociologist Gisèle Sapiro's observation that "the book trade is primarily a matter of geographical distribution areas, national borders defining juridical spaces and public policies, and imaginary territories linking identities to places that shape a horizon of expectation."[6] Even though the field of African literatures is growing more diverse every day, the global face of African literature is still shaped chiefly by "expectations" in turn underpinned by economic developments driven by outside, Western forces. Consequently, when African writers are increasingly dissociated from the category "African" in order to fit into the frameworks of "World Literature," they are most likely to be published by houses based in the West and, as far as Francophone authors go, more specifically in France.

This economic reality becomes particularly visible during bookfairs and similar activities devoted to Francophone literature. To give a recent example, Francophone literature took center stage at the 2017 Frankfurt Fair, which was devoted to the theme "*Frankfurt auf Französisch*." This edition meant to highlight diversity in French literature and publishing, with particular attention paid to presses from Francophone sub-Saharan Africa, eighteen of which were invited by the Bureau International de l'Édition Française (BIEF), with the financial support of the Organisation Internationale de la Francophonie (OIF) and the French Centre National du Livre.[7] But which were the most highly promoted events here? They were essentially those that concerned Francophone authors whose works had come out from French houses.[8] No author published by any African press was invited, and only two events highlighted African presses during the fair, including the roundtable mentioned earlier, which focused on the subject of literacy in Africa as well as on the difficult "job of the African publisher" today.[9] Questionable as it was, this way of handling diversity in the industry foregrounds the issue of the kind of networks in which African publishers most often participate as well as the porous nature of the linguistic boundaries inherited from institutionalized Francophone projects in place since 1970.[10] It is also worth bearing in mind here that behind every institutionalization process through which books appear and make an impact lie methodological and political decisions not always driven by theoretical or transcultural issues. Yet although the politics of African publishing is relevant, we must still return to the questions of the economic leverage and international reputation of publishers in Francophone Africa since the 1960s, which have brought out books that are still not deemed "attractive" enough to be truly global in reach.

1. From Third-World Literature to World Literature— without Africa?

We will therefore start with the ways in which African literature is disseminated and in particular with those agents who have shaped a Francophone literary ecosystem that is exclusive in nature and centered on French presses since the 1950s. This ecosystem is still enormously influential, as can be witnessed at prestigious literary and publishing events. Its origins can be traced back to 1956 and the First Congress of Black Writers and Artists held in Paris at the Sorbonne under the auspices of the journal and publishing house Présence Africaine. Examining the gradual unfolding of activities in this area since this First Congress allows one, I maintain, to better understand how the Francophone African literary economy came to be "vertically" structured, and why, accordingly, the publishing circuit remains ultimately, and definitely, French, even in the geographically rather indefinite landscape of *littérature-monde.*

Let us begin with the role and, in a manner of speaking, the mythology resulting from the 1956 Congress. Taken by critics as a *ground zero* for major developments to come, the Congress impacted both the academic and the journalistic spheres and held a decisive role in the creation of a centralized African literary marketplace in France and, more generally, in Europe.[11] One of the main outcomes of the Congress was the creation of the Society of African Culture (SAC) in order to spread Présence Africaine's work worldwide. One sign of SAC's importance was its success in obtaining consultative status with UNESCO in 1958. Favored by the French publishing context, the Congress functioned as a kind of matrix both for scholarship and for the rise of a French book industry concentrating on African literature.[12] If the categories governing the reception, classification, and analysis of African literature that emerged from this event have regularly been brought into question ever since, the Congress did play a major part in the constitution of an uncontested African literary field-*sur-Seine*, up through the 2009 Présence Africaine conference at the Musée du Quai Branly in Paris, Présence Africaine: A Forum, A Movement, A Network (Présence Africaine. Une tribune, un mouvement, un réseau). Thus, we return to the paradox of France's centrality in the publication of African literature, an idea highlighted by Claire Ducournau in her book *La fabrique des classiques africains* (2017)—this paradox, I should specify in passing, has been present in French literary culture since the 1950s and bears witness to the development of what Ruth Bush calls "a Parisian third worldism."[13] Until the famous 2008 book-manifesto *Pour une littérature-monde*, which, as is well known, came out from Gallimard, it had been indeed unusual for a principally Parisian publishing field to make claims to diversity and, in so doing, to promote Africa's authors, when said field had basically followed French aesthetic and economic standards rather than diversifying its norms and redistributing African literatures across the Francophone world.[14] At any rate, one major element remains unchanged to this very day, namely, the central publishing hub that determines the framing values governing the promotion of African works worldwide to a global readership. Still largely French, that hub, that core space, renders, especially in France, African literature a corpus with varying degrees of success and whose primary sales come from a sort of "second-tier" bestsellers.[15]

Geopolitical elements also shaped, of course, the 1950s and 1960s, when Francophone African authors began to be widely translated and disseminated. Notably, this was a period that saw both postcolonial independence and the beginning of the Cold War. Présence Africaine's Congress, which was organized in the midst of the rise of the Third World—that is, one year after the Bandung Conference—thus contributed directly and indirectly, just like other French publishers of African writings did, to the consolidation of a hierarchically organized African literary market.[16] The latter was politicized, in the sense that Francophone Africa represented at the time an inconsistently strategic and insufficiently effective promotion apparatus rather than a central economic driver on an international scale.[17] One can take as examples the literary journal *Black Orpheus*[18] or the first Asian and African Conference of Writers held in Tashkent, Uzbekistan, in October 1958.[19] Reflecting the influence of Présence Africaine, these contributed to the internationalization of so-called black literature, which would go on to become a favorite topic of certain Western critics, whose promotion of this literary category became a major factor in the centralization of African-literature scholarship in Europe. Consolidating this criticism were earlier interventions such as Lilyan Kesteloot's 1963 *Les écrivains noirs de langue française: naissance d'une littérature*, Janheinz Jahn's 1965 *Die neoafrikanische Literatur: Gesamtbibliographie von den Anfängen bis zur Gegenwart*, and Jacques Chevrier's 1974 *Littérature nègre. Afrique, Antilles, Madagascar*.

In a sense, the impact of Présence Africaine, in addition to the flurry of debates spreading in the English-speaking world around African independence, contributed to the expansion of African literature in French but also to its isolation as an autonomous corpus marked by its own ecosystem, economic legitimacy, and self-references animated by a spirit of *fiat lux*, as it were, that would never go away. From the proceedings of Présence Africaine's 1956 Congress, one could conclude that, in order to exist, a body of work of this sort must put forth its own viable economic model or rationale and create its own history *by articulating its own narrative*. It is therefore remarkable to note that Présence Africaine has built its own legacy by legitimizing itself *from within the French literary space*. Yet while Présence Africaine has had direct commercial results, one cannot give credit for such success to any single press or journal but rather, and more broadly, to this space's ability to redefine itself, from the 1960s onward and more emphatically in the 1980s, as a publishing hotbed for Francophone literatures so as to capitalize more lucratively on the fiction and nonfiction output of African writers.

2. Development without Literature

Following the Présence Africaine-spearheaded fostering of "Black literature," African writers gained new and important positions in the Global North. For these authors, literary opportunities came as often in publishing as in translation. Opening up the field mobilized political agendas, in the US-sponsored Area Studies programs, for example, which, driven by American interests as they were, nonetheless funded newspapers, cultural projects, and conferences, allowing Francophone African writers access to a global audience.[20] It is equally important to point out here the role of emerging African universities[21] and of literary exchange programs implemented in the USSR by the Soviet Afro-Asian Solidarity Committee (SKSSAA).[22] New or newly energized institutions also fueled the emergence of an African Third World whose "developing" countries direly needed to step up their educational efforts in order to respond to increasing demand from also growing populations. It is in this context that UNESCO intervened decisively by convening a crucial 1960 Addis Ababa meeting of ministers and directors of education of Tropical African Countries. This led to the ambitious "Addis Ababa Plan," which covered the 1960–80 period and advocated integrating economic, instructional, and social development. The plan took publishers in the Global North to be the most obvious available resource for African countries,[23] whose local book industries were still in their infancy.[24] In the early 1960s, UNESCO endorsed international cooperation in publishing and book distribution and supported the establishment of a program to promote press development in Africa.[25] In 1965, the director general of UNESCO, René Maheu, participated in the International Congress of Publishers held in Washington, DC. There, he defended UNESCO's technical assistance in the development of textbook-publishing facilities in Francophone African countries, including Cameroon, Central African Republic, Gabon, Chad, and Republic of the Congo, but also a partnership in Ethiopia. Maheu also spoke of UNESCO's role in entrusting Yugoslavia with the production of these textbooks for Africa's educational systems.

Notably, it was part of this campaign that UNESCO funded the publication of sociologist Robert Escarpit's *La révolution du livre* in 1965, which was issued in English in 1966.[26] This was the first large-scale study to evaluate book sales in Africa. It must be noted, however, that Escarpit's focus was book consumption, not production, and even less the process of literary creation. Along these lines, Escarpit's statement is eloquent: "These 90,000 tons [of paper] do not represent much in the world economy, just as African literature does not yet count for much in world culture."[27] Arguably, Escarpit's work sparked a turning point in UNESCO's involvement in African publishing, which, from then on, UNESCO envisioned as a mass-production industry, preferably locally based, and the organization's recommendations on these matters throughout the 1960s invariably emphasized this direction. As I will discuss in more detail later, until 1973, African publishing was not regarded by UNESCO as a literary field but rather as one element in ongoing, wide-scale development phenomena on a continent with a population made up predominantly of young people. Publishing, therefore, came to be considered by UNESCO a tool for implementing mass literacy. In the September 1965 issue of *UNESCO Courier*, titled "The Book Revolution," Clifford M. Fyle penned what was probably the first large-scope article devoted to publishing in Africa, "A continent in quest of a publishing industry."[28] In his piece, Fyle considered the African book market solely in its utilitarian and educational dimensions. He contended that "Africa's greatest demand is for children's books, books on all the basic and applied sciences and on history and geography. . . . Top priority is given to books that contribute to economic development."[29] Just as Escarpit disregarded the influence of Présence Africaine's 1956 Congress as well as UNESCO's support for the SAC and the 1962 Makerere Conference when he claimed that "African literature does not yet count for much in world culture,"[30] Fyle only refers here to the work of Ibadan Mbari Club's books for youth although, by 1961, the Mbari Artist and Writer's Club, cocreated by German publisher Ulli Beier, had already become affiliated with Nigerian writers Wole Soyinka, Christopher Okigbo, and John Pepper Clark, as well as with the South African writer Ezekiel Mphahlele. Indeed, by 1965, Mbari had published Soyinka, Achebe, and Senghor and would, moreover, go on to become a major source of titles for the "African Writers Series" set up by the British agency Heinemann, bringing the continent's authors onto the world stage.

African writers witnessed the expansion of their publication prospects at the same time as an international market for the translation of African texts was beginning to develop. However, African presses, such as the Cameroonian based Clé, were not part of this general movement. It was not until the 1968 conference organized by UNESCO in Ghana, Book Development in Africa: Problems and Perspectives, that the organization, under the leadership of Julian Behrstock, director of UNESCO's Office of Free Flow of Information and International Exchanges from 1967 to 1976, clearly addressed the issue of developing publishing broadly.[31] At the same time, and also due largely to UNESCO's continuous efforts to support educational development in Africa—endeavors that also benefited Europe's educational publishers—it is not surprising that other European presses seized the economic opportunities this afforded and established African-literature collections aimed at African curricula. Major initiatives of this sort include the creation of Heinemann's African Writers Series in 1962 and Nathan's Classiques du Monde series in 1964, which, together, helped several authors, initially published by Présence Africaine, rise to prominence throughout Africa as "classics of African literature."

However, Escarpit and Ronald E. Barker lamented that in 1964, "75 per cent of books sold in Africa were imported from other continents . . . represent[ing] 24 million copies . . . against [a] local printing of 7.3 million copies."[32] Their views were echoed in a 1969 pioneering article published in the UK by John Nottingham, who was associated with Tanzania's East African Publishing. The title of Nottingham's text was "Establishing an African Publishing Industry: A Study in Decolonization." In his work, the author concluded that "there is no technological reason why all the basic educational course books, and indeed most of the supplementary ones, at both primary and secondary level, should not be written, designed, printed and published in Africa rather than in

London, Malta, or Hong Kong."[33] Nottingham asked UNESCO and the World Bank to support local publishers. He highlighted the challenges facing an African industry nonetheless better and better prepared to satisfy the needs of a national and, in the case of the Swahili market, regional readership.[34] Nottingham's call for action would eventually be answered by the 1970s workshops and conferences that gradually incorporated the matter of African-based literary publishing into their agendas instead of attending to educational issues broadly. This shift would lead UNESCO to support the founding of the Regional Centre for Book Promotion in Africa (CREPLA) in Cameroon in 1977.[35] At the same time, UNESCO helped open up new avenues for African publishing by proclaiming 1972 the "International Year of the Book" under the motto "Books for All" and pursuing four major themes: "Encouragement of authorship and translation with due regard to copyright; production and distribution of books, including the development of libraries; promotion of the reading habit; and books in the service of education, international understanding and peaceful co-operation."[36]

Unsurprisingly, an International Conference on Publishing and Book Development in Africa was held the following year at the University of Ife, Nigeria. Indeed, Nigeria became one of the centers for African literature in English, with a vibrant literary, academic, and publishing environment that had been expanding steadily since the late 1950s. This reunion was funded by the University of Ife Press and UNESCO— once again with Julian Behrstock's involvement—and with additional support from the British Council, the Nigerian Publishers' Association, and the Börsenverein des Deutschen Buchhandels. If the previous 1968 UNESCO Conference had fully engaged with the institutions of African publishing, bringing together consultants, technical assistants, managers of institutional programs, and librarians, with a few Francophone speakers among them, the second meeting diversified the dialogue by inviting journalists, writers, publishers, academics, and bookfair officials. In fact, the whole Anglophone literary world appeared to be present in Ife. It is in this context that Nigerian writer Chinua Achebe took up the challenge of indigenous publishing and called upon established writers to give it a chance.[37]

Undoubtedly connected to the concurrent birth of the Paris-based Agence de Coopération Culturelle et Technique (ACCT), whose main task was to strengthen the ties between different facets of the Francophone world community, the absence of Francophone representatives did not diminish the success of the Ife Conference, which went a long way to advance the internationalization of African publishing during the 1970s. For its part, the Frankfurt Book Fair's early role was further bolstered in 1980 through the Frankfurter Buchmesse's "African" program. Accordingly, it bears noticing the presence of FBM's director, Sigfred Taubert, among the participants in Ife. Taubert's attendance recalls how FBM had begun to invite publishers from Ghana, Kenya, and Uganda in 1968 and went on to support several workshops on "Economic Publishing" in Nigeria, Kenya, and Zambia over the following years.[38] Tanzanian translator and publisher at the East African Publishing House, Said Mzee was at this time the main "Africa" consultant for FBM. His work was behind the ambitious program "Africa: A Continent Asserts Its Identity" in 1980.[39] Furthermore, the Ife Conference coincided with the impending nomination of Peter Weidhaas as the head of FBM in 1975, which constituted a political turn for the fair, which change was evident in the choice of central themes from 1976 onward.[40] This nomination also led to the aforementioned landmark 1980 fair and its focus, "The Literature of Black Africa," which had been anticipated by a five-week tour undertaken by FBM representatives around Cameroon, Ghana, Côte d'Ivoire, Senegal, Kenya, Tanzania, and Zambia.[41] The 1980 Frankfurt Fair showcased actually some 2,000 books put out by 180 publishing houses from twenty-nine African countries, while also featuring as guests a large number of leading African writers published both in Europe and Africa.[42] Organized with the financial support of the German Foreign Office, the 1980 event was, and remains, the largest ever Africa-focused book event in Europe to gather together publishing representatives from across Africa.

The fostering of such links between European institutions and the African literary scene influenced, in turn, research, what with scholarship such as Phillip Altbach's 1975 article "Literary Colonialism: Books in the Third World" and Hans Zell's *African Book Publishing Record*, which Zell started editing the same year.[43] Moreover, it is interesting to observe the crossovers between African publishing and African literature during the 1960s and 1970s. Notable literary gatherings such as the 1956 Paris Congress, the 1958 Tashkent Summit, and the 1962 Makerere Conference attracted writers of all linguistic backgrounds including African Francophones, whose commonality, apart from their language and African birthplace, had to do mainly with the Western location of their publishers. Events highlighting Africa's book industry were organized later than other similar meetings and exhibits; it was not until 1973 and the Ife Conference that writers and publishers became jointly involved in them, the glaring absence of Francophones notwithstanding. And, with the creation of CREPLA in Yaoundé at the end of the 1970s, twenty years after Présence Africaine's Congress in Paris, the Anglophone/Francophone linguistic division began to count less and less also.

3. Francophone Insularity

With regard to Francophone publishers especially, it was not until the opening of the private sector and the 1980 Frankfurt Book Fair that these presses took up the "African theme" fast emerging in the international literary marketplace. In essence, their case was unique even though it was also indelibly connected to Western cultural and financial institutions, as well as to the mechanics of the international literary market. The first observation I would like to make apropos of such developments of the 1980s and 1990s is that for quite a long time, discussions of literature in Francophone Africa were not disseminated by African-based publishers such as John Nottingham, Said Mzee, Walter Bgoya, and Henry Chakava, but rather only by academics and consultants from the Global North like Escarpit and Robert Estivals. While major authors from Africa's Anglophone sphere remained prominent in the international African literary landscape, there were fewer well-known figures from the Francophonie zone before the 1980s, and no Francophone publisher took part in the workshops on "Economic Publishing" organized by the Frankfurt Book Fair in Africa in the 1970s.[44] Consequently, no project similar to the "Hans Zell Publishers imprint," launched in 1975 after the Ife Conference, actually saw the light on the Francophone side. On the other hand, from the 1960s to the beginning of the 1970s, the only Francophone African publishing house with an international or continental reach was Cameroon's Éditions Clé (Centre de Littérature Evangélique), which was founded in 1962 by the evangelical churches of Central Africa and the Netherlands.[45] While Clé brought out important African writers—it was, for instance, Soyinka's first Francophone publisher—the semi-religious bent of its catalog likely accounted for the press's weak visibility abroad.[46] Buttressing the visibility and legitimization of Clé, and of Francophone African publishing more broadly, was the French Association Des Écrivains de Langue Française (ADELF) and the affiliated Grand Prix Littéraire d'Afrique Noire, which distinction recognized, on four occasions between 1968 and 1975,[47] writers published by Clé, out of a continent-wide pool of authors whose works came out mainly from French publishing houses.[48]

My second observation concerns the institutional infrastructure of the Francophone African landscape. After the 1970 creation of ACCT, OIF's precursor, the Francophone African book business evolved its own dynamics in response to developmental models keyed to growth in literacy and education, and this process resulted in a publishing economy that, as mentioned earlier, was "vertically" organized and in which, accordingly, France's presses lay at the top. In parallel, from the 1970s to the 1990s, Francophone Africa built, as Escarpit observed, a partly autonomous system closely and sometimes exclusively linked, outside the continent, to French houses and cultural cooperation. Consequently, Francophone African publishing remained largely isolated from the greater international market, with the exception of publishers involved in CREPLA between 1977 and 1983.

Coauthored by Escarpit and Barker for UNESCO, *The Book Hunger* (1973) helps grasp the 1970s changes, continuing the work that began with UNESCO's designation of 1972 as "The International Year of the Book."[49] In their study, the two critics observed that "African publishing is not at present able to meet its total needs on its own. A large number of the books produced in Africa are at present still produced by foreign publishers."[50] The authors updated and expanded the data presented in *Books for All* and in *The Book Revolution*, while at the same time maintaining the angle of "educational priority," which left aside the question of literature and implied significant involvement from foreign presses. "All the regional meetings on book development organized by UNESCO," they wrote, "have agreed that priority must be given to educational books, particularly those used in first-level education."[51] Overall, Escarpit and Barker suggested that the local book industry should be shored up in order to satisfy these educational needs. The authority of *The Book Hunger* was notably invoked in support of the interventionist policy of French cultural cooperation in Francophone Africa during the 1970s, which stressed the development of documentation centers and whose masthead was the journal *Notre Librairie* founded by the French Ministère de la Coopération in 1969 with the aim of assisting the libraries belonging to the French cultural network in Africa.[52] The name of the organization running *Notre Librairie* is unequivocal: "Association for the Dissemination of French Thought" (ADPF). Until the 1990s, and as part and parcel of France-Africa bilateral collaboration, *Notre Librairie* would be heavily involved in spreading the French cultural network across Francophone Africa, aggressively promoting African literature published *in France*.[53]

ACCT came about in this context. It was also in the spirit of continuing, French-backed institutional solidifying of African Francophonie that Senegalese president Léopold Sédar Senghor supported the creation of the Nouvelles Editions Africaines (NEA), which was jointly managed by Togo, Senegal, and Côte d'Ivoire. Significantly, participating in this publishing venture were French publishers such as Armand Colin, Nathan, Présence Africaine, Seuil, and Edicef, a subsidiary of the Hachette group and an educational publisher whose presence in Francophone Africa goes all the way back to the colonial period. NEA went on to supplant Clé in the Grand Prix Littéraire d'Afrique Noire.[54] Its authors got either the main prize or a special mention in 1978, 1979, 1980, 1983, and 1985.[55] Senegalese writer Aminata Sow Fall, a 1979 winner, was also short-listed that year for France's main literary award, the Goncourt, with her novel *La grève des bàttu*. This is the only time a book published *in* Africa became a finalist for a major French literary prize. In fact, the end of the 1970s and the beginning of the 1980s were a period of recognition for the NEA itself rather than for Francophone African publishing in general, and Hans Zell did suggest in 1996 that "it can be argued that [NEA's] dominance and quasi monopoly probably stifled the growth of small independent publishers."[56] It is therefore not surprising to see NEA once again under the spotlight at the 1980 Frankfurt Book Fair, during which the Senegalese writer Mariama Bâ received the first Noma Award for African publishing for her novel *Une si longue lettre*,[57] which was then translated into no fewer than fourteen languages.[58] Advised by Julian Behrstock, who served at that time as a consultant for Kodansha Publishers in Tokyo, Noma had been funded by the Japanese Foundation Shoïchi Noma, which also sponsored CREPLA, of which the NEA was an active member. Taubert himself was a member of the Noma jury, like the director of CREPLA William Moutchia, and CREPLA hosted the third edition of the award ceremony in Yaoundé in 1983.[59]

We reach here a turning point in the recent history of international literature as a field: on the one hand, we are witnessing the dawn and then the peak, in the 1980s, of the postcolonial movement—whose roots are also firmly planted in the work of Présence Africaine—followed by a resurgence of interest in the concept of World Literature. On the other hand, African writers became, for the first time, recipients of the world's most prestigious literary awards—Wole Soyinka with the Nobel Prize in 1986 and Ben Okri with the Booker Prize in 1992. "World Literature" would then go on to absorb within its canon a more extensive body of African works, an expansion that would produce trickle-down benefits for Francophone African writers published by French presses from 1980 to 2000. Karthala, L'Harmattan, Le Serpent à Plumes, and the "Afriques" and "Continents Noirs" collections at Actes Sud and Gallimard, respectively, are the most notable examples. Several writers published by a wide range of houses were promptly picked up and promoted by *Notre Librairie* at this time, among them Alain Mabanckou, Abdourahman Waberi, Sami Tchak, and Kossi Efoui, who would later participate in the Étonnants Voyageurs festival and afterward contribute, as is well known, to the *littérature-monde* movement. This group would then serve as a base for the partnership between Étonnants Voyageurs and the World Alliance, the world's largest platform for the promotion of World Literature.[60]

It was during the same tumultuous period of the 1980s that Francophone initiatives increased emphasis on publishing *on* literature rather than solely *of* literature, as before.[61] Thus, under the impetus of ACCT and French Cultural Cooperation conferences, programs for Francophone regions turned to the editing and production of thesauruses and encyclopedias of Francophone African literatures, whether such reference instruments would come out in Africa or not.[62] The general absence of research on the Francophone African publishing industry, to which such projects responded, correlated with the crisis faced by the industry itself in the 1980s and the 1990s, as well as with the simultaneous rise of French publishers of African literature and the further consolidation of the institutions involved in the management of the Francophone literary environment. This period gave birth to a concentric movement that gathered together French publishers, African writers of the diaspora, journals edited in France, and literary events based in the Global North, as well as to literary prizes and to academic departments studying Francophone African literatures. Outside this movement, however, the presses from Francophone Africa remained marginal, with some ultimately fading away altogether. The economic crisis that broke out in Africa brought to a grinding halt publishing programs of many players in the business, beginning with the NEA, which would eventually be dismantled in 1988.[63] Some of NEA's award-winning authors were subsequently republished in France, notably by Éditions du Serpent à Plumes.[64] Furthermore, UNESCO, which was preparing for the 1988–97 "World Decade for Cultural Development,"[65] had to discontinue a number of investments, including CREPLA, in order to focus on other priorities. This caused the steady decline of CREPLA's activities, and its continental involvement abated after the cessation of UNESCO's and African states' support in 1983.[66] Apart from CREPLA, literary prizes recognized fewer and fewer works published in Africa from the late 1980s onward. Thus, the Grand Prix Littéraire d'Afrique Noire failed to honor any writer whose books came out in Africa between 1992 and 2012, and the Noma Award went only occasionally to works that appeared in Francophone Africa, not to mention that, in general, few books were actually accessible to prospective judges as a consequence of the economic crisis.[67] Among the thirty-five authors who were awarded prizes by Noma, three of the seven Francophones (Mariama Bâ, Bernard Nanga, and Pierre Kipré) were published by NEA, two (Kitia Touré and Werewere-Liking) by Nouvelles Éditions Ivoiriennes (NEI), and one (Djibril Samb) by Nouvelles Éditions Africaines du Sénégal (NEAS); both NEI and NEAS stem from the dismantling of NEA. In fact, the Algerian writer Souad Khodja, brought out by Entreprise Nationale Algérienne du Livre (ENAL), was the only one of the Francophone laureates who was not linked to NEA. Moreover, *all* Francophone publishers awarded by Noma—NEA, NEI and NEAS directly, and ENAL (due to the nationalization of Hachette Algeria)—were connected financially to French publishing.[68]

Two final examples help us understand the Francophone African publishing field's loss of visibility in this period. Introduced in 1980, the "Monde-Noir Poche" series of the French Éditions Hatier is the first. Run by researcher and ADELF president Jacques Chevrier, it further oriented French publishing to African educational programs across the Francophone regions. The second example is the advancement of collaboration between France and Francophone Africa in the 1990s. Yet again, this cooperation linked development to literacy and by the same token impacted publishing in several ways. Following French president Mitterrand's "Discours de La Baule,"[69] which tied aid to democratic reforms, France contributed greatly to the setting up of a public library network to improve literacy, while ACCT launched the program for Centres de Lecture et d'Animation Culturelle in Africa, which effectively discounted the continental publishing scene.[70] As a result of the priority given to eradicating illiteracy, the majority of works coming out during the economic crisis in Francophone Africa were children's literature. The Francophone African publishers Le Figuier (Mali), Ganndal (Guinea), Ruisseaux d'Afrique (Benin), and Tropiques (Cameroon) did gain some limited visibility at this time, but this must be seen as an upshot of the activity of the French journal *Takam Tikou*, which was responsible for curating the *Amabhuku* exhibition dedicated to children's book publishing in Africa at the 1999 Bologna Children's Book Fair.[71] Stepped up during the food crisis of the mid-1980s, book donations by Western NGOs boosted library holdings in various African countries but did so largely to the detriment of a local publishing industry that, already feeling the pressure of the economic downturn, had to cope with further shrinking of demand on local markets. Oddly enough, this donation phenomenon caused, at least in part, the misconception of a "book famine in Africa," now viewed by some as a "continent without publishers."[72] Compounding this misperception were, albeit indirectly, the rapid—some might say, disproportionate—increase in the number of children's book presses in Francophone Africa, as well as the uptick in donations of used literature books published largely in France. Arguably, both trends widened the gap between the World Literature system, which would continue to incorporate Francophone African authors during the first decade of the third millennium, and the Francophone African publishing field itself, which was still in the process of recovering from the crisis.

These tendencies and their effects are by no means isolated. The awards received in France by African writers with French publishers over the last twenty years, literature festivals such as the Étonnants Voyageurs festival, which was bolstered by the *littérature-monde* movement, and OIF's creation of the Prix des 5 Continents in 2000, which, until 2014, recognized only works published in the Global North, have all contributed to the growing isolation of Francophone literature from world networks.[73] These events and initiatives have largely reinforced France's central position in Francophone African literary production since the 1950s as well as African continental publishing's relegation to the peripheries of global literary circulation. These realities give the lie to globalization paradigms that mistake the visibility of individual Francophone African authors for broader and substantial material shifts in the book economy. If publishers and critics of World Literature mean to engage globalization more accurately and effectively, then they would do well to revisit celebrations of diversity, expansion, and access that pay little attention to publishing infrastructures and the financial, logistic, and epistemological factors instrumental to their reinforcement.[74]

Notes

1. Sarah Burnautzki, "Penser le pouvoir de racialisation des catégories d'études littéraires," in *Penser les catégories de pensée. Arts, cultures et médiations*, ed. Chloé Delaporte, Léonor Graser, and Julien Péquignot (Paris, France: L'Harmattan, 2016), 67–86.
2. Interkontinental, "Frankfurt Book Fair 2017," Interkontinental.org, October 19, 2017, https://www.interkontinental.org/en/2017/10/19/frankfurt-book-fair-2017 (accessed December 9, 2018).
3. Hans Zell, "African Book Industry Data & the State of African National Bibliographies," *The African Book Publishing Record* 44, no. 4 (2018): 367.
4. See especially UNESCO's 2005 "Convention on the Protection and Promotion of the Diversity of Cultural Expressions."
5. Caroline Davis, "The Politics of Postcolonial Publishing: Oxford University Press's Three Crowns Series 1962-1976," *Book History* 8 (2005): 227–44.
6. My translation of Gisèle Sapiro, *Les contradictions de la globalisation éditoriale* (Paris, France: Éditions Nouveau Monde, 2009), 7.
7. See Bureau international de l'édition française, "Portraits," Promotional poster, 2017, https://www.bief.org/fichiers/operation/4010/media/9621/PortraitsEditeursFrancophones_Francfort2017Envoi.pdf (accessed December 9, 2018).
8. Catherine Fruchon-Toussaint, "La France, invitée d'honneur à la Foire du Livre de Francfort," Radio France International, June 22, 2017, http://www.rfi.fr/culture/20170622-france-invitee-honneur-foire-livre-francfort-langue-francaise (accessed December 9, 2018).
9. "Quelles évolutions pour le marché de l'édition francophone?" (Frankfurt Book Fair, Frankfurt, Germany, October 12, 2017) and "Publishing in Africa" (Frankfurt Book Fair, Frankfurt, Germany, October 13, 2017).
10. Albert Gérard, "Littérature africaine et identité(s) maghrébine(s)," in *The Growth of African Literature: Twenty-Five Years After Dakar and Fourah Bay*, ed. Edris Makward, Thelma Ravell-Pinto, and Aliko Songolo (Trenton, NJ: Africa World Press, 1998), 80–1.
11. Julien Hage, "Les littératures francophones d'Afrique noire à la conquête de l'édition française (1914-1974)," *Gradhiva* 2, no. 10 (2009): 80–105.
12. Ruth Bush, *Publishing Africa in French* (Liverpool, UK: Liverpool University Press, 2016), 56; Servanne Woodward, "French-Language Fiction," in *A History of Twentieth-Century African Literatures*, ed. Oyekan Owomoyela (Lincoln, NE: University of Nebraska Press, 1993), 177.
13. Bush, *Publishing Africa in French*, 64.

14 Claire Ducournau, *La fabrique des classiques africains* (Paris, France: CNRS éditions, 2017), 80.
15 Raphaël Thierry, *Le marché du livre africain et ses dynamiques littéraires* (Pessac, France: Presses Universitaires de Bordeaux, 2015), 52–5.
16 Nathan, Hachette, Seuil, Grasset, Gallimard, Maspero, Julliard, Robert Laffont, and others.
17 At the occasion of events such as the "World Festival of Black Arts" organized by Présence Africaine and the Society of African Culture in 1966 in Dakar (Senegal), under UNESCO's patronage.
18 *Black Orpheus* was founded in 1957 in Ibadan (Nigeria) by the Germans Ulli Beier and Janheinz Jahn. It served as a venue for the Mbari Club and ultimately as a springboard for many Nigerian and African writers, as well as for the translation into German of texts by Senghor and Césaire by Jahn (Peter Benson, *Black Orpheus, Transition, and Modern Cultural Awakening in Africa* [Berkeley, CA, Los Angeles, CA, and London, UK: University of California Press, 1986], 92–9).
19 Constantin Katsakioris, "L'Union Soviétique et les intellectuels africains," *Cahiers du Monde Russe* 47, no. 1–2 (2006): 19–23.
20 John Krige and Helke Rausch, *American Foundations and the Coproduction of World Order in the Twentieth Century* (Göttingen, Germany: Vandenhoeck & Ruprecht, 2012), 244.
21 Ibadan, Dakar, Yaounde, Kampala, and others.
22 Katsakioris, "L'Union Soviétique et les intellectuels africains," 18–19.
23 In December 1961, a report by Jean-Claude Pauvert for Orstom already pointed out that the Addis Ababa Conference was "too strictly economic" (my translation of Jean-Claude Pauvert, "Les trois aspects positifs de la conférence d'Addis Abeba," *Bulletin de Liaison de l'Orstom*, December 1961, 13, https://core.ac.uk/download/pdf/39893244.pdf [accessed December 9, 2018]).
24 Robert Estivals, "Le livre en Afrique noire francophone," *Communication et Languages* 46 (1980): 65.
25 Robert Escarpit, *La révolution du livre* (Paris, France: UNESCO, 1969), 7, https://unesdoc.UNESCO.org/ark:/48223/pf0000161128 (accessed December 9, 2018).
26 The book followed Ronald E. Barker's previous study *Books for All: A Study of International Book Trade* (Paris, France: UNESCO) in 1956.
27 Robert Escarpit, *The Book Revolution* (London, UK, and Paris, France: Harrap, UNESCO, 1966), 68–9, https://unesdoc.UNESCO.org/ark:/48223/pf0000003119 (accessed December 9, 2018).
28 The French version was titled "*Un continent en quête d'éditeurs*" ("A continent in quest of publishers"), and it is interesting to note the shift in it away from the book industry to the global function of publisher.
29 Clifford M. Fyle, "A Continent in Quest of a Publishing Industry," *UNESCO Courier* (September 1965): 28–9, https://unesdoc.UNESCO.org/ark:/48223/pf0000060619 (accessed December 9, 2018).
30 Sentence reproduced in the 1965 issue of UNESCO's *Courier* and in the 1969 second edition.
31 S. I. A. Kotei, *The Book Today in Africa* (Paris, France: Les Presses de l'UNESCO, 1982), 5.

32 Ronald E. Barker and Robert Escarpit, *The Book Hunger* (London, UK, and Paris, France: Harrap, UNESCO, 1973), 25, https://unesdoc.UNESCO.org/ark:/48223/pf 0000005699 (accessed December 9, 2018).
33 John Nottingham, "Establishing an African Publishing Industry: A Study in Decolonization," *African Affairs* 68, no. 271 (1969): 139.
34 He gives the example of a best-selling Swahili poetry collection, *Song of Lawino*, published by Ugandan Okot p'Bitek with East African Publishing House (Nottingham, "Establishing an African Publishing Industry," 139).
35 Thierry, *Le marché du livre africain*, 224–9.
36 Barker and Escarpit, *The Book Hunger*, 5.
37 Edwina Oluwasanmi, Eva Mclean, and Hans Zell, *Publishing in Africa in the Seventies* (Ile-Ife, Nigeria: University of Ife Press, 1975), 45–6.
38 Peter Weidhaas, *A History of the Frankfurt Book Fair* (Toronto, Canada: Dundurn, 2003), 186.
39 Barbara Harrell-Bond, "Africa Asserts Its Identity. Part 1: The Frankfurt Book Fair," *American Universities Field Staff Reports* 9 (1981): 1–15; Peter Weidhaas, *See You in Frankfurt! Life at the Helm of the Largest Book Fair in the World* (New York, NY: Locus Publishing, 2010), 147.
40 Weidhaas, *See You in Frankfurt*, 193.
41 Weidhaas, *See You in Frankfurt*, 211.
42 Harrell-Bond, "Africa Asserts Its Identity. Part 1," 2–3. Here, I also refer the reader to Weidhass, *See You in Frankfurt*, 149–50.
43 Philip G. Altbach, "Literary Colonialism: Books in the Third World," *Harvard Educational Review* 15, no. 2 (1975): 226–36.
44 Weidhaas, *A History of the Frankfurt Book Fair*, 171.
45 Thierry, *Le marché du livre africain*, 219–23.
46 Authors published by Clé include Guillaume Oyono Mbia (Cameroon), Julius Nyerere (Tanzania), John Mbiti (Kenya), Bernard Dadié (Côte d'Ivoire), and Henri Lopes (Republic of the Congo), among others.
47 These are Francis Bebey with *Le Fils d'Agatha Moudio* (1969), Guy Menga with *La Palabre stérile* (1970), Henri Lopes with *Tribaliques* (1972), and Etienne Yanou with *L'Homme Dieu de Bisso* (1975).
48 Ruth Bush and Claire Ducournau, "La littérature africaine de langue française, à quel(s) prix? Histoire d'une instance de légitimation littéraire méconnue (1924–2012)," *Cahiers d'Etudes Africaines* 3, no. 219 (2015): 555.
49 Attending the Accra 1968 Conference, Escarpit did not take part in the Ife Conference of 1973.
50 Barker and Escarpit, *The Book Hunger*, 26.
51 Barker and Escarpit, *The Book Hunger*, 132.
52 These issues are available through the Bibliothèque nationale de France's digital platform, Gallica. See https://gallica.bnf.fr/ark:/12148/cb34387430t/date.r=%22Notre+Librairie%22.langFR (accessed December 9, 2018).
53 I will mention here Virginie Coulon's *Bibliographie francophone de littérature africaine*, which grew from an issue of *Notre Librairie*, "2500 titres de littérature africaines: Afrique subsaharienne," coedited by Coulon and Monique Hugon (*Notre Librairie* 94 [July–October 1988]; Virginie Coulon, *Bibliographie francophone de littérature africaine* [Vanves, France: Edicef, 1994], 4).

54 Ramatoulaye Fofana, *L'Édition au Sénégal: bilan et perspectives de développement*. Mémoire pour l'obtention du diplôme de conservateur des bibliothèques (Lyon, France: ENSSIB, 2003), 15.
55 Idé Oumarou, *Gros plan* (1978), Lamine Diakhate, *Chalys d'Harlem* (1979), Aminata Sow Fall, *La grève des bàttu* (1980), Mariama Bâ, *Un Chant écarlate* (hors-concours: 1983), Jean-Pierre Makouta-Mboukou, *Introduction à l'étude du roman négro-africain de langue française* (1985).
56 Hans Zell, "A Sixteen-Year Japanese Contribution to African Publishing," *Logos* 7, no. 2 (1996): 165.
57 Barbara Harrell-Bond, "Africa Asserts Its Identity. Part 2: Transcending Cultural Boundaries through Fiction," *American Universities Field Staff Reports* 10 (1981): 2–12.
58 Weidhass, *See You in Frankfurt*, 149.
59 William Moutchia, *Le CRÉPLA depuis 1975* (Yaounde, Cameroon: Clé, 2000), 17.
60 Thierry, *Le marché du livre africain*, 194.
61 Hans Zell, *The African Book World & Press: A Directory* (Munich, Germany: K.G. Saur, 1980); S. I. A. Kotei, *The Book Today in Africa* (Paris, France: UNESCO, 1981), translated into French in 1982; Philip G. Altbach, Amadio A. Arboleda, and S. Gopinathan, eds., *Publishing in the Third World: Knowledge and Development* (Portsmouth, NH: Heinemann, 1985). Works such as Bernard Mouralis's *Littérature et développement* (Paris, France: Silex, 1984), which took socioeconomic conditions into account, contributed to the expansion of Francophone African literary scholarship during this time.
62 For instance, the Congrès Mondial des Littératures de Langue Française held in Padua, Italy in 1984; the *Guide de littérature africaine* by Patrick Mérand and Séwanou Dabla (Paris, France: L'Harmattan/ACCT, 1979) and *Dictionnaire des œuvres littéraires négro-africaines de langue française* directed by Ambroise Kom (Paris, France, and Sherbrooke, Canada: Éditions ACCT/Naaman, 1983), which were both funded by ACCT. Fewer such works appeared in the 1990s. Coulon's 1994 *Bibliographie francophone de littérature africaine* can be considered an exception. This bibliography represents the core of the Litaf database (Littérature Africaine Francophone), which was still running in 2018: http://www.litaf.org (accessed December 9, 2018). During the 1980s, English-language scholarship increased its focus on publishing in Anglophone Africa and the Third World.
63 Fofana, *L'Édition au Sénégal*, 15.
64 Aminata Sow Fall's and Mariama Bâ's novels are notably republished by the French Editions du Serpent à Plumes in the 2000s.
65 Raymond Weber, "Culture et développement: vers un nouveau paradigme?" in *Cooperación cultural entre Europa y África. Actas del 1er Campus Euroafricano de Cooperación* (Madrid, Spain: Agencia Española de Cooperación Internacional para el Desarrollo, 2010), 100.
66 Thierry, *Le marché du livre africain*, 230.
67 See Association des Écrivains de Langue Française, "Grand prix littéraire de l'Afrique noire," http://www.adelf.info/data/documents/HISTORIQUE-GRAND-PRIX-L ITTERAIRE-dAFRIQUE-NOIRE-.pdf (accessed December 9, 2018).
68 Nadège Veldwachter, *Littérature francophone et mondialisation* (Paris, France: Karthala, 2012), 60.

69 Alan Riding, "France Ties Africa Aid to Democracy," *The New York Times*, June 22, 1990, https://www.nytimes.com/1990/06/22/world/france-ties-africa-aid-to-democracy.html (accessed December 9, 2018).
70 Hans Zell and Raphaël Thierry, "Le don de livre, mais à quel prix, et en échange de quoi? Un regard sur le don de livre en Afrique francophone," *African Research & Documentation. Journal of SCOLMA (the UK Libraries and Archives Group on Africa)* 127 (2015): 161–5.
71 Viviana Quiñones, "La littérature de jeunesse, un art africain: Panorama 2000-2015," in *Takam Tikou, Dossier annuel: La belle histoire de la littérature africaine pour la jeunesse: 2000-2015 (online)*, 2016, http://takamtikou.bnf.fr/dossiers/la-litt-rature-de-jeunesse-un-art-africain-0 (accessed December 9, 2018).
72 Zell and Thierry, "Le don de livre," 155–60.
73 A few examples include Alain Mabanckou, Leonora Miano, Tierno Monenembo, Scholastique Mukasonka, and David Diop.
74 I am indebted to Hans Zell, Mary Jay, Stephanie Kitchen, and Emma Crowley for their help with this essay.

3

Malinke, French, Francophonie: African Languages in World Literature

Bi Kacou Parfait Diandué

In an important sense, African literature written in Africa's local languages reclaims a space of expression for idioms historically marginalized or even suppressed by French colonization. In West Africa, for example, French was imposed for a century as the lingua franca of research and knowledge transmission, as well as the exclusive idiom of colonial administration and education. Children who spoke their mother tongue at school were flogged or otherwise punished and forced to wear a distinctive "symbol"—a "reprobation" collar—all day long.[1] In areas under strict imperial control, it was similarly forbidden to speak one's native tongue, a practice which forced the indigenous inhabitants to distance themselves from their first language. French was thus resorted to out of obligation—not by choice but rather by coercion. We can see why local idioms were banned by colonial power when we look at history, which tells us, for instance, that for the Abbeys, a population from southern Côte d'Ivoire, their language was instrumental to their revolt.[2] They planned their uprising against colonial brutality in messages sent to their comrades in their mother tongue, which the colonizers neither spoke nor understood. Domestic servants, abusively employed in the colonizers' houses, organized themselves in the Abbey language and coordinated an attack against the railroad as well as the sabotage of numerous facilities. The French, in turn, saw well the threat posed by local idioms and therefore targeted them for destruction, thereby preventing transmission of the values, philosophy, and culture of preexisting, ancient African tongues.

The repressive policies of colonial administrators can also be attributed to the fact that colonization assimilated the conquered space to French space. This desire to expand France's territory accounts for the search for new markets to which to deliver a surplus of products manufactured by the metropolis. Let us recall that it was the European industrial revolution that generated capitalists' thirst for new outlets for trade and lands to dominate. Colonization was initially undertaken for commercial rather than cultural purposes, though the two have been intertwined. The spirit of mercantilism is, of course, bound up with acquisition, possession, and ownership. Furthermore, commerce justified colonial settlement and all kinds of violence. Even before the great colonization movements of the nineteenth century began, the quest for slave labor had similarly passed through the empire's outposts and forts, those military and mercantile symbols of what should be called commercial territoriality. European expansionism's objective was, for centuries, to create properties outside Europe for the West's use. Spatial extension represents and ensures property ownership of territory, minerals, and humans and lies at the heart of colonial conquest. Yet land cannot be separated from the people and cultures that inhabit it, and it is the interconnection of land, social structures, political power, and idiom that explains the pressure on local tongues and dialects and the bans they endured during the century of active colonization. For the French, destroying the plurality of languages was a correlate to imperial expansion. As indicated earlier, then, any discussion of literature in African idioms necessarily entails addressing the problem of territorial reconquest, for the target of colonization was not only land but also, symbolically and materially, the Babel Tower—the continent's wealth of languages.[3]

The subject of Franco*phonie*—which evokes at once the locutory-acoustic dimension of *spoken* and *heard* language, the collective, political organization of communication, and the space of an idiom's extension—casts the debate over idioms and their sphere of influence in sensory terms to which I would like to attend here. Naturally, considering a language's space of conquest inevitably prompts geopolitical and geocultural questions. No doubt, the reign of one tongue over territories lying beyond its initial site of emergence is an expression of a hegemony that needs to be understood politically, culturally, and otherwise. Though I will focus below on French as a vehicle of communication rather than on its role in this exercise of colonial and cultural power, I would nevertheless like to look more closely at the "French-speaking" *space* that is bound up with these political concerns. Taking up a three-pronged, geocriticism-informed approach to this complex problematics and its reverberations in one of Africa's major Francophone authors, Ahmadou Kourouma, I will discuss why and how French must be grasped as a "topolect"; in what sense the latter's expansion into Africa has affected indigenous communities and languages such as Malinke to the point that today's Francophonie might be seen as a "collective destiny" on the continent and in the world at large; and how Francophonie and, more specifically, "hearing French" have also impacted Africans at the individual level.

1. French as Topolect: The Discourse of Space and the Space of Discourse

Two ways of characterizing spatial discourses can help us get a grip on the topolect notion: "speaking space" and "spoken space." I define topolects both as the discourse of space—speaking space or the construction of space through discourse—and as the space *of* discourse or spoken space that gives rise to particular modes of speaking and hearing.[4] This understanding of language, the world, and the fiction bringing them together is built around geocriticism as a methodology for analyzing literature in its relation to anthropological reality.⁵ To rehearse quickly the basic principles and modus operandi of geocritical studies, let me note that they articulate the relationships between the existing world and the literary imagination around three axes: spatiotemporality, or the space-time continuum, transgressivity, and referentiality. The relationship between time and space constitutes the framework for all artistic creation and is also what allows reality and fiction to bear on one another. The second principle, transgressivity, holds that exogenous contributions actualize the self through time and space. In other words, connecting with the other, stepping across borders and barriers, opening up breaches help, in short, decompartmentalize thought and stimulate creation. Dynamic and static movement, material, virtual, and symbolic crossings, all reveal the spatial dimension of human invention, the "cross-territorial" quality of cultural and, indeed, multicultural identity. More than ever before, today's multicultural person is a traveler. His or her artistic creation systematically bears the marks of the other. His or her senses are open to all sounds and tastes. Everything he or she smells gives off the scent of otherness. All of these links between the self and the other, all of these avenues of exchange are as much a presence of the other in the self as they are also imprints of the other in the creation of the self. As for the third principle, referentiality, it is intimately linked to the first two. Fiction and the "referent" of reality cannot be walled off from one another; rather, they are produced in dynamic, transgressive relation to each other through discourses of space and within spaces of discourse.⁶

As discourses of space, topolects give meaning, but meaning-making also draws from the semantic "range" or spatial gambit of a work of fiction. That is to say, because writing is a complex, referential, and symbolic act of spatialization, territory itself and its play in texts, films, and paintings are also key for these works' reading. The topolectal construction of space in literature can be divided into three categories: *topomorphemes*, *topolexemes*, and *toposemes*. Helping explain how fictional or textual space both creates autonomy vis-à-vis the extratextual space, this terminology also elevates the latter, emphasizing its dependence on "referential" spatiality. *Toposemy*, I might add, allows us to study the relationship of interdependence that obtains between time and space in any act of fictional creation. It is this nexus that makes reality and fiction interconvertible in fictional texts, for the latter configure and reconfigure the parameters of the interchange between space and time. Literary poiesis thus reorganizes the metaphorical distance between reality and fiction. If we understand *toposemy* as the operation and interconvertibility ratio of different types of spaces—one that puts the pastiche and parody of space side by side, for example—*chronosemy* can therefore be read as the operation of time in fiction within a relation of self-reference or chrono-reflected figurative mimesis of the extratextual, the *hors-texte*. From this fruitful contradiction between real and fictional spaces, *chronomorphemes*, *chronosemes*, and *chronolexemes* arise.

The topomorpheme is a compound lexical creation. It joins together the concepts of *topos*—place—and *morpheme*—a morphological unit of a linguistic sign. A topomorpheme thus designates the first categorical unit of spatiality. That is, it constitutes a concept that foregrounds the primal character of spatiality in a given text. It is a syntactical feature that differs from the toponym in that the latter is only a name for the fictional space, while the topomorpheme encompasses both the name and the spatiality characteristic of all space. In proportion to its semic density—relative, that is, to the concentration of topolectal *semes* or space-related semantics within it—a topomorpheme becomes either a topolexeme or a toposeme. Every space is first a topomorpheme. For in any given fiction, a space can exist without a name, but not without characteristics. If we take, for example, a fiction in which the space is unidentified toponymically but exists just the same, if only as the generative matrix in which the characters are placed, it follows that space exists in this fiction through its very nature, so to speak, and not primarily through what it is called. From there, it becomes apparent that in its functionality, space is more closely linked to its character *qua* space—space as such, as physical expanse—even if the toponym can sometimes be a determining factor too. The topomorpheme is therefore the first stage in the operation of fictional spaces. Following after this, the toposeme is a construction integrating *topos* and *seme*. The addition of the lexical particle -seme to *topos* implies that the latter is open to variation and change. The toposeme thus fluctuates, and so it can appear in several guises. Above all, it is characterized by its semic instability, which leads to its semantic instability. Consequently, it is a semantically volatile fictional space capable of developing all sorts of relationships with the extratextual, ranging from the paradigmatic to the homologous, antithetical, and hyperbolic.

Now, when one considers topolects as the space of discourse or spoken space, one implies, most notably, that space is *read and perceived through language*. Words and expressions carry the spaces in turn secreting them. In taking up this perspective, one situates oneself halfway between sociolinguistics and geocriticism so as to analyze the interactions between human ("referential") and figurative space. Spoken space is presented in intonations, accents, and speech particularisms. Intonation can be compared to an "envelope" for utterance, creating as it does acoustic poetry in and through the spectrum of auditory perceptions. Hearing, I must also stress, is *cultural*, and so the perception and production of sound unfold within a precise cultural situation. Here, I point to rhythm, for example, which, to a certain extent, actualizes intonation in song or poetry. Accent sets the bounds of curvatures, marks the stops, and specifies the inclinations of the oratory flow. Pitch and tone belong to oral discourse and characterize the space of expression in discourse as it is received by its audience. Accent and intonation thus become the cultural content of oral discourse. Hearing and culture, which are forms of knowledge, help us comprehend the space of expression contained in the discourse of the speaker.

When one looks at speaking space from this angle, one begins to notice this domain's social and extratextual dimensions. One form of speaking space that bridges fictional texts and extratextual social life is linguistic particularism. Particularisms are discursive specificities typical of certain individuals, communities, and spaces. At the same time as particularisms identify their speakers, they specify the space of expression that is readable or perceptible when they are used. They are phrases, words, or expressions that, over time, give birth to a slang proper to a certain society or city (the example of "nouchi" in Côte d'Ivoire is illustrative). Slang, in its communicative use, can represent a dialectal variety within a set of languages sharing a common root. Ivorian novelist Ahmadou Kourouma would be a good example here, for his writing pursues the creative avenue afforded by linguistic particularisms in his portrayal of characters whose ways of speaking conjure up a space that is both social and cultural. In his 1993 novel *Monnew*, Djigui Keita, king of Soba, speaks like the Soba people. Indeed, the author evokes the characters' circumstances of enunciation in order to achieve realism in his fiction. His numerous borrowings from spoken idiom ensure the relevance of the text to an audience familiar with this idiom. To capture, for example, the level of French fluency of the king of Soba and his followers, the narrator reports a scene at an adult literacy class for Soba people. Asked to repeat the phrase "the cat sees well even at night" ("*le chat voit bien même la nuit*"), the Malinke courtiers and their ruler repeat together "*zan ba biè na nogo*," which literally means "the vagina of the mother of John gooey sauce."[7] A similar "translation" occurs in conjunction with the concept of freedom ("*liberté*"), which becomes first "*Gnibaité*," which means "having lost all teeth," then "*Nabata*," or "come take or mama takes." This rehearsal exercise is also applied to the translation of the phrase "Mamadou brings her sister" ("Mamadou *amène sa sœur*"), which becomes "Mamadou *amina ka siri*" ("Mamadou seizes and ties up"). Portraying these alterations of auditory perception merged into illocutionary distortions shows the author's desire to reproduce the learners' search for corresponding sounds in their own language. While the students translate the chunks of French phonologically, the author, through his narrators, "translates," as it were, the illiteracy of the "Sobaka." This fictional treatment of a specific linguistic situation deploys what one might dub "representational mimesis." Enacting such a mimesis, Djigui as a Malinke of Soba "hears" a homophony or, more precisely, a semblance or impression of homophony between different expressions. Upon auditory reception, this homophony yields a semantic distortion. The illusory perception of Malinke words and formulas in French phrases leads to a shift in phonetic perception in Kourouma's text, so much so that linguistically competent readers can easily infer that it is the familiar Horodougou space that actually speaks to Djigui's ear.

Kourouma's portrayal of Birahima, the child soldier who narrates the 2000 *Allah n'est pas obligé* (*Allah Is Not Obliged*) and the 2004 *Quand on refuse on dit non* in a playful, inventive language, is also relevant to this discussion.[8] Here, the distinct topolect in the book's spoken space opens the structuring dialectic of topos. The latter shapes language curvatures and overall structures speech as a flexible medium. It should be noted that topolectal discourse does not express who the speaker actually is; it may shed light on his cultural identity, and it may certainly illuminate his spatial identity, where he is located or comes from. Spoken space "voices" more precisely the identity of the space featured in the novel, and it creates above all a relation of "complicity," as it were, between the speaker and spoken space in the sense that they identify each other. The topolect is from this point of view a designator and a marker, a kind of beacon that punctuates speech and locates the speaker in his cultural space of origin. One should understand "origin" here as the source space from which the speech flows. Here too we can specify that cases of homophony (in oral communication) or homonymy (in writing) can create links with multiple source spaces. Instead—and in contrast to this potential ambiguity—the topolect is fundamentally marked by recurrence, by stable references to a certain spatial domain from outside the book.

2. Francophonie as Collective Destiny

What is Francophonie? Above all, it is a question of contact and, by the same token, of linguistic territoriality. Before even gesturing to a future community for countries and speakers who have French in common, "Francophonie" evokes the nagging specters of conquest, colonization, and cultural domination. But the term's heritage is twofold, for Francophonie is both a historical memento and a cultural site of memory for the formerly colonized. The idea recalls the establishment of French ownership over property—land, resources, people, language—outside of France. The word brings us face to face with the colonial policy of a geopolitics of extraversion of sorts, which is underpinned by an imperial expansion guided by territorial contiguity—the principle of the continuous presence of the colonizers with the empire, hence the disappearance of borders inside the latter. Settler migration to Africa reflects the true manifestation of contiguous territoriality, whose spatial extension under colonization was, again, motivated by the desire for ownership. The consolidation of territorial continuity thus understood was required to ensure property rights over lands and their riches.

This explains why the conquerors reorganized spatially the ethnoculturally and linguistically distinct territories they acquired, which resulted, as one might expect, in linguistic and other sorts of tensions and clashes. The relationship between French and local African tongues became, however, one of multifaceted cohabitation, where native idioms continued to thrive in everyday confrontation with the empire's "supralanguage." The domination of French over these local languages has been institutional: in countries formerly colonized by France, institutions continue to develop and carry out policy in French to this very day. In these areas, French officially has become the main language, which was not and is still not the case in concrete linguistic practice. This surprising phenomenon, which might be described as an "inversion" of linguistic polarities in territory, is noticeable in two prevailing scenarios in plurilinguistic contexts. Thus, the dominant communicational matrix in some linguistic zones is a "Creole" language mixing French and indigenous idioms. In other cases, however, these languages remain distinct, but the grammatical structures of French influence native languages, and, vice versa, the morphosyntactic patterns of African tongues leave their imprint on French. That is to say, even if it is adopted as the literary and institutional vehicle of communication, French is altered by the integration into it of structures typical of local thought, sentence construction, and other forms of linguistic expression, all of which are constantly renewing the former colonizer's language and giving rise to a "new French." In all situations, we witness the birth of a hybrid linguistic code in formerly colonized spaces. On the one hand, there occurs a fusion of languages that culminates in a creolization of French, where borrowings and neologisms remain visible as such. On the other hand, French words are fertilized by the structures of African ways of seeing and thinking about the world. The envelope and the content of "new French" are, in this case, asymmetrical, belonging as they do to different geocultural spaces, but they are conjoined so as to create and renew that same language. Cohabitation, linguistic and otherwise, makes language evolve.

Kourouma experimented with such linguistic encounters in his best-selling book *The Suns of Independence*.[9] Here, his style can be considered as emerging from a hybrid space that has instilled a bicultural creativity in the author, superimposing as it did his original Malinke culture on his adopted French one. This creative "schizophrenia" is symptomatic of the double formative influence marking the novelist, a situation shared, as is well known, by colonized people broadly. The schizolinguistic state at issue here is, indeed, a collective condition in a postcolonial context, and so is the Francophonie the formerly colonized inherit. The linguistic creations and lexical innovations found in postcolonial writing, which have baffled the censorious purists from the so-called "center" of French language, seem sometimes to stem simply from the expression of an author's feelings. That is, the illocutionary effect of these inventions on a text's receivers sometimes occurs without any authorial intention of originality or desire to surprise readers. Kourouma's writing is an appropriation of French, an adaptation of French to his mental reality. As he has declared, "I think in Malinke, and I write in French."[10]

Schizolinguistic communities have expressive needs that require approaching French as an integrated but composite medium. French incorporates the features of endogenous thought at the same time as this way of thinking defines the grooves of French expression. This is certainly the reason working in and, inevitably, *on* a language in a schizolinguistic territory brings about original texts whose solecisms and "barbarisms" strike audiences as interesting and intriguingly crafted through writing. In Kourouma's works, Malinke thought fertilizes French speech through the words of the griot, through the "donomana" mysteries of the initiate "Sora," through the gossip of the king of Soba, and through the obscene elucubrations of Birahima, the child soldier. Kourouma's art leans on social mimesis in that it not only translates the language of the community but also conveys the creative, schizolinguistic needs that drive the communicative strategies of the community.

3. Kourouma and Francophonie as Individual Identity

It bears reiterating that, etymologically and institutionally, Francophonie emphasizes the actual use of French. As such, it essentially favors language in a communicative context in which the speaking subject's "hearing and understanding of French" prove paramount. Thoroughly implicating the individual, this Francophonie concept rests on a Ricœurian dialectic of sameness and selfhood where the collective and communal dimension of Francophonie emphasizes sameness while its individual dimension privileges selfhood. Language cannot be reduced to spoken or written speech either, to utterance as something one produces by speaking, putting things in writing, and otherwise just sending a message; language is also reception of that message, which is why there is a sensory dimension to linguistic acts. Because of the sensorial character of such acts, the auditory and mental perceptions that characterize communication place the individual at the core of linguistic encoding and decoding, at the heart of the very purpose of language itself. Just as it does in society, the "self," by itself, determines its own linguistic identity by "speaking" and "understanding" a given language.

All this may be well known but is worth repeating here because in literature—and African literatures are no exceptions—an "individual" style is built *in* the language of writing, and literary identity, an "effect" of this style as it may be, is equally a daughter of cultural identity. Thus, Kourouma's writing appears as the actualization or "updating" of his culture linguistically and, on another level, novelistically. Accordingly, the structure of the 1998 *En attendant le vote des bêtes sauvages* (*Waiting for the Wild Beasts to Vote*) and of *Allah Is Not Obliged* is based on both "donsomana" and Malinke myths.[11] The author asserts himself here through metaphors and allegories. In the 1992 *Les Soleils Des Independances* (*The Suns of Independence*), he tells the story of Fama Doumbouya, a Malinke prince deposed by anti-colonial independence, and affirms his identity through the unabashed expression of a mixed culture that "particularizes" French, converting it to a local variety—to a "regional" phenomenon—within the mind-bogglingly diverse postcolonial world. The expression of identity through artistic practice is, here too, an extension of the quest for identity, which, moreover, forefronts the consubstantial problem of the ability to define oneself in a cultural context increasingly marked by complexity, change, conflict, and "impurity" and where the interconnections between literature and identity are bound to come across through the individual language of an author like Kourouma. The creative adventure the author embarks on consists in an attempt to crystalize the experience of what exists and what is lived. Encountering the unknown, challenging the foreseeable, and testing the possible—this is what his characters explore in order to open themselves up to the world and to the vast imaginary helping them picture it.

Failing to write in Malinke, Kourouma wrote in a French that he molded into the structures of the Malinke language. This was his "dual" linguistic approach to novelistic writing, a notion and, again, a practice that in turn speak to a twofold dialectic of content and form, on the one hand, and mind and body, on the other. The body or form of Kouroumian texts is French, but its spirit or content is Malinke, and it is between the "Malinkization" of French and "Frenchifying" of Malinke that Kourouma weaves his novel's linguistic web. In his fiction, the writer shows the cultural cohabitation of the local tongue and the borrowed idiom, of the colonized and colonial language, Malinke and French. Dizzying in its convolutions and dynamic hodgepodge of oral and written forms, Kourouma's writing—much like other African authors'—might appear, from the standpoint of cultural and linguistic orthodoxy, mixed, bastard, and illegitimate, which, incidentally, is why, in 1967, Seuil refused to publish the first version of *Les Soleils des indépendances*. And, to be sure, the author's twin linguistic heritage bestows on his work a disturbed, and perhaps disturbing, identity. But one should keep in mind that this identity, real as it is, is also a product of the history of Africa itself and in that a microcosm of Africa's identity. No wonder, then, that in his texts French becomes the "civilizing" varnish that functions like a cover for the author's deep, Malinke way of thinking and imagining the world. Reading Kourouma's work is like stumbling on a treasure trove of Malinke myths, rites, cults, emblems, symbols, and knowledge, all of them rooted in a culture for whose expression his Francophone fiction has pressed into service a French that no longer looks and sounds like what its past and present purist guardians thought and think it should.

Notes

1. On efforts to rectify this practice and its legacy, see Birgit Brock-Utne and Malcom Mercer, "Using African Languages for Democracy and Lifelong Learning in Africa: A Post-2015 Challenge and the Work of CASAS," *International Review of Education* 60, no. 6 (2014): 777–92, and Bruno Maurer, *Les langues de scolarisation en Afrique francophone: enjeux et repères pour l'action* (Paris, France: AUF, 2010), http://www.bibliotheque.auf.org/doc_num.php?explnum_id=825 (accessed October 26, 2018).
2. As Wikipedia informs us, Abbey or Abé populations are composed of various subgroups (Abé properly speaking, Abè-N'Damé, Abé-évé, Abé-Krobou, Abbey-agni, Abéanou, which has resulted from a fusion of the Agba and the Abé, then the Abé-Dida, the Abidjis, and the Mbattos, ethnic groups stemming from the Abbey, and Abbey-M'bochi). The Abés were the warriors in Queen Abla Pokou's army. They belonged to the Akan group, which also included the Ashanti, also natives of Ghana, who migrated to Côte d'Ivoire between the seventeenth and eighteenth centuries. Wikipedia, "Abés," https://fr.wikipedia.org/wiki/Ab%C3%A9s (accessed October 20, 2018).
3. This economic imperative persists in different forms today but remains intimately tied to language and to the use of language as an instrument of economic enhancement. On this aspect, see, for example, a 2014 report prepared for French president François Hollande and laying out measures France can take in order to tap what the author identifies as the "underexploited" economic potential of Francophonie. See Jacques Attali, *La francophonie et la francophilie, moteurs de croissance durable*, La Documentation française, August 2014, https://www.ladocumentationfrancaise.fr/rapports-publics/144000511/index.shtml (accessed October 20, 2018).
4. For an extended treatment of this topic, see Bi Kacou Parfait Diandué, *Topolectes 1* (Paris: Publibook, 2005) and *Topolectes 2* (Abidjan, Côte d'Ivoire: Baobab, 2009).
5. See, for example, Bertrand Westphal, *Geocriticism: Real and Fictional Spaces*, trans. Robert Tally (New York, NY: Palgrave Macmillan, 2011).
6. On "referentiality" in fiction after structuralism, see also Thomas Pavel, *Fictional Worlds* (Cambridge, MA: Harvard University Press, 1986).
7. Ahmadou Kourouma, *Monnew: A Novel*, trans. Nidra Poller (San Francisco, CA: Mercury House, 1993), 232.
8. Ahmadou Kourouma, *Allah Is Not Obliged*, trans. Frank Wynne (Portsmouth, NH: Heinemann, 2006) and *Quand on refuse on dit non* (Paris, France: Seuil, 2004).

9 *The Suns of Independence*, 1981, trans. Adrian Adams (Teaneck, NJ: Holmes & Meier Publishers, 1997). The original edition of *Les Soleils des indépendances* came out in 1968 from Presses de l'Université de Montréal. On Kourouma's language in this work, see also Logbo Blédé, *Les interférences linguistiques dans Les Soleils des indépendances d'Ahmadou Kourouma* (Paris, France: Publibook, 2006) and Makhily Gassama, *La langue d'Ahmadou Kourouma, ou, Le français sous le soleil d'Afrique* (Paris, France: Karthala, 1995).

10 When asked about the originality of his writing, during an interview in Abidjan in 1998, Kourouma attributed this quality to such an encounter among languages. He declared on that occasion that "I think in Malinke and I write in French." Responding in another interview to a question about the ways in which his writing has evolved, Kourouma answered: "I spent ten years in Lomé where I wrote *Monnew*. My writing style changed slightly there because while I am still Malinke, I was no longer thinking in Malinke." See the December 10, 1998, and August 9, 2000, interviews included in the appendices to Diandué, "Histoire et Fiction dans la production romanesque d'Ahmadou Kourouma" (doctoral dissertation, Université de Limoges, France, June 10, 2003).

11 Ahmadou Kourouma, *Waiting for the Wild Beasts to Vote*, trans. Frank Wynne (Portsmouth, NH: Heinemann, 2003).

4

Globalizing the Spiritual and the Mythological: Indian Writing in French from Pondicherry

Vijaya Rao

> World literature has often been seen in one or more of three ways: as an established body of *classics*, as an evolving canon of *masterpieces*, or as multiple *windows on the world*.
>
> —David Damrosch, *What Is World Literature?*

Satya Mohanty makes an important point when urging scholars to consider that "Indian modernity does not begin with colonial rule." He further asks if "[an] interdisciplinary focus on alternative modernities [can] contribute to our understanding of what world literature is."[1] To answer this question, Mohanty takes up a more inclusive corpus: oral literatures, folk art forms, proverbs, wedding songs, and so on, in different Indian languages and dialects that have existed since "premodern" times. Mohanty is not alone in contesting the limits of the European vision of World Literature, as critics today are looking beyond the European continent to find networks within other continents and countries. For instance, David Damrosch quotes Amiya Dev who points out that "India's twenty-two principal literary languages themselves form a plenum comparable to that of European literature."[2] If we consider countries surrounding India, which share similar cultural contexts and overlapping languages, there is a vast terrain—full of potential but only partially explored—for the circulation of texts and ideas. Indeed, it is a world within the world. It is in this vein that Damrosch adds that, in India, "world literature takes on a very particular valence in the dual contexts of the multiplicity of India's disparate languages and the ongoing presence of English in post-Raj India."[3] Though contained in small enclaves of former colonies and used by even smaller groups, French and Portuguese could be added to the multiplicity of India's idioms. This leads me to my main questions in what follows: What is the status of Indian writing in French? Who wrote in French and continues to write in the language? Is there any readership at all for French-language texts in India save the academic networks?

It would not be fallacious to state that Indian writing in French happened in spite of the French administration. There were certainly no policies of promoting writing in the language of Molière or of setting up publishing houses in Pondicherry, owing perhaps to the idea that writing from outside the confines of the Hexagon was of no literary value. A quick glance at the catalogs in libraries and archives in Goa, a former Portuguese enclave in India, reveals, however, a wealth of fiction and essays in Portuguese, along with a slim corpus in French.[4] The existence of measures to encourage reading,[5] publishing, and circulation of texts beyond the colony seems obvious, evidenced as it is by three volumes of annotated Goan literature reference works.[6]

The first book to be written in French by an Indian was *Le journal de Mlle D'Arvers* by Toru Dutt. Didier published it posthumously in 1879 in Paris. Its example was never replicated. Indian writings in French have been few and far between, or so it would appear from what has been gathered from libraries, archives, and personal collections. The very purpose of the anthology *Ecriture indienne d'expression française*[7] was to pursue traces of French writing from India by bringing together a small body of disparate works, although they were mainly from Pondicherry, with a few from Goa. This corpus ranges widely in topics: fiery nationalist writing, depictions of simple rural lives that serve as an identity marker to distinguish from the urban milieu touched by European modernity, the ponderings of a spiritual poet, and retellings of mythological stories through prose or drama. At the heart of these themes, however, is India, or the quest for Indianness. Both the spiritual and the mythological—symbols par excellence of Indian identity—can be read as a mode of self-definition or a response to colonialism. My claim is that Indian writing in French from Pondicherry has piggybacked on these modes to gain attention, restricted though it may be to a particularly niche audience. In that sense, this writing can at best represent "a mode of circulation and of reading" in specific circles but definitely not a canon of works.[8] This chapter will examine the context of Pondicherry writings on the spiritual and mythological against the backdrop of the place's colonial past, with particular focus on the formation of networks of dissemination of this literature in world zones one might not expect these works to be read. The Sri Aurobindo Ashram in Pondicherry, for instance, has its followers both in India and in the West, where the message of spirituality is further spread across the globe, albeit its impact is a far cry from the worldwide circulation enjoyed by Salman Rushdie, Amitav Ghosh, Arundhati Roy, or Rohinton Mistry, whose works have been extensively translated.

1. Aurobindo's Humanism and *Viswa Sahitya*

The editors of *La modernité littéraire indienne: Perspectives postcoloniales* give valence to Indian literatures written in regional languages that very often suffer from a lack of representation as compared to Indian writing in English, which has not only dominated the literary scene in India but gained currency in the international arena.⁹ While the debates around these bodies of work have been occupying center stage for decades now, most Indians are understandably oblivious to Indian writing in French, as it is practiced by only a handful of writers. These writers invariably come from the erstwhile French colonies of Pondicherry, Chandernagore, Karaikal, Mahe, and Yanon. "We have a base for the French language in Pondicherry which has been existing for a long time. We want to take advantage of that and to keep Pondicherry as a window to French culture," said Jawaharlal Nehru in regard to preserving French in the former colony.[10] Contrary to his vision, the sweep of English and Tamil has left few traces of the language of Molière. Yet despite the lack of efforts by succeeding governments, a small "window" still exists, primarily within the precincts of the Aurobindo Ashram and the Lycée français in Pondicherry. The ashram was established in 1910 after Aurobindo came to Pondicherry to flee the British police during the independence movement in India,[11] when he was actively involved in writing fervently against British rule.

Having spent close to thirteen years in England pursuing his studies, he mastered English, French, German, Italian, Greek, and Latin. He was also well versed in Sanskrit and Bengali. But it was after his return from England, in the princely state of Baroda—where he taught English and French—that he relentlessly worked on classical as well as modern texts from both Western and Indian traditions. It was from 1910 onwards, in Pondicherry, that Aurobindo turned to spiritual experience and initiated a number of disciples who continued his work thereon. It was also in Pondicherry that he met Maria Alfassa Richard (known as The Mother), a French national, who became his spiritual companion, gave structure and rigor to the ashram, and maintained the French language there.[12]

Although Aurobindo read extensively in French and could write in several languages, he chose to do so in English. His reasons were both spiritual and political, as testified by his correspondence with his disciple Nirodbaran:

(1) The expression of spirituality in the English tongue is needed[13] and no one can give the real stuff like Easterners and especially Indians. (2) We are entering an age when the stiff barriers of insular and national mentality are breaking down (Hitler notwithstanding), the nations are being drawn into a common universality with whatever differences, and in the new age there is no reason why the English should not admit the expression of other minds than the English in their tongue. (3) For ordinary minds it may be difficult to get over the barrier of a foreign tongue, but extraordinary minds (Conrad etc.) can do it. (4) In this case the experiment is to see whether what extraordinary minds can do, cannot be done by Yoga.[14]

From the above, at least three points are clear: that spirituality needs to be "globalized," and conceivably one of the ways to disseminate spiritual expression is through the English language; that nations, as the author observes, are entering universality; and that yoga has the power to achieve what only extraordinary minds are able to do.

Aurobindo's very purpose in founding the ashram in Pondicherry was to spread his universal spiritual message to humanity at large. This message, propagated in turn by his disciples in their respective poetic works, is to reveal or manifest the hidden spirit or soul in the material.[15] A close look at Aurobindo's only poem written in French reveals the eternal opposition of the spirit and the material.[16] Composed in the alexandrine, an experiment with which Aurobindo engaged more broadly, this fragment shows the poet's quest to find a form that can best express the spiritual message. Aurobindo's reflections on poetry as an aesthetic experience are found in *The Future Poetry*. Here the poet defends the choice to adopt the alexandrine: "The Alexandrine is an admirable instrument in French verse because of the more plastic character of the movement, not bound to its stresses but only to an equality of metric syllables capable of a sufficient variety in the rhythm."[17] This poem in French was possibly never completed, or perhaps it was, but it was ultimately destroyed by the British police when his works and entire library were confiscated during the struggle for independence. While all his works written in Pondicherry have been carefully preserved in the Aurobindo Archives there—most of it now digitized—it is impossible to know the extent of the loss of the texts written in Baroda.

Aurobindo's disciples arguably pursued his message in their poetic works, which were written, though not exclusively, in French. Nolini Kanta Gupta, Prithwindra Mukherjee, and Ranajit Sarkar were initiated into the world of spirituality and introduced to French literature at the ashram. All three wrote in English, Bengali, and French. While the content of their writings invariably followed the tradition of Aurobindo's aesthetics and spirituality, they carved out their own distinct style. Nolini Kanta Gupta's work in French was marginal—roughly twenty-five pages—as compared to his eight volumes of writings and poetry in English.[18] The French section, which appears in volume five, is divided into two parts, namely *Mater Dolorosa* and *Mater Gloriosa*. In the first, the poet professes to renounce worldly and mundane pleasures in order to enter the world of the spiritual. His poetry is as much informed by the French Symbolists as it is by the bhakti movement. Similarly, the myriad influences of European as well as Indian traditions have marked the poetry of Prithwindra Mukherjee. In the preface to *Le serpent de flammes*,[19] Gérard Mourgue remarks that Mukherjee's poems have been nurtured by Vishnouite, Sufi, Biblical, tantric, and Symbolist poetry, which all search for an aesthetic form to express spirituality.[20]

While the common thread that binds all the poets of the ashram is spiritual growth, Ranajit Sarkar comes to this growth in a unique manner—by ingeniously employing simple or ordinary themes from his immediate environment. In "Le métro parisien,"[21] Sarkar deftly uses the metaphor of the underground where the modern human descends blindly, struggling to fulfill each of his or her desires. The poet reminds the soul that it can surge upward to reach its destination provided he or she chooses the right direction. That the universal human should be at the center of ruminations in the ashram is no surprising revelation, for it *is* an ashram's *raison d'être*. Aurobindo, like many gurus, aspired to reach out to the world with the message of spiritual awakening. Ashish Nandy's incisive study of the uncolonized mind partly draws on the life and beliefs of Aurobindo. He notes that "Aurobindo's response to colonialism included a cultural self-affirmation which had a greater respect for the selfhood of the 'other' and a search for a more universal model of emancipation. . . . Aurobindo's spiritualism can be seen as a way of handling a situation of cultural aggression . . . seeking to make sense out of the West in Indian terms."[22] Nandy adds that Western culture was a vehicle of Aurobindo's self-expression and that he always had human evolution in mind. In this vein, Aurobindo's thoughts resonate with those of Rabindranath Tagore, who spoke as early as 1907 on *Viswa Sahitya*, or World Literature. "To see literature through the mirror of nation, time and people," Tagore said, "is to diminish it, not see it fully. If we understand that in literature the universal man (*vishva-manav*) expresses himself, then we can perceive what is truly worthy of observing in literature."[23]

If Tagore defined World Literature through the evocation of the *vishva-manav* and the latter's search for kindred spirits, we can surmise that this humanist view puts the creator at the center, for it is his or her ability, through his or her expression, to reach out to the world. "How man expresses his joy in literature, how and in what form the human soul chooses to manifest its diverse, variegated, multiple images of self-expression," Tagore insisted, "that is the only thing worth considering in world literature. Literature must actually enter the world—whether it pleases to express itself in the form of the diseased, the accomplished, or the ascetic person—to know how far man can find his kinship in the world, and to what extent he can realize truth."[24] Goethe's *Weltliteratur* idea was to move beyond the limits of national boundaries. He believed that literatures need to be suffused with vitality and freshness, which would only happen in contact of one literature with another. "It is to be hoped," he wrote, "that people will soon be convinced that there is no such thing as patriotic art or patriotic science. Both belong, like all good things, to the whole world, and can be fostered only by untrammelled interaction among all contemporaries, continually bearing in mind what we have inherited from the past."[25] While Tagore envisions the universal man, his search for kinship, and the realization of truth as prerequisites for World Literature, Aurobindo does not set out to define World Literature but rather attempts to "preserve the ideas of the oneness of man, and of man as a part of an organic universe."[26]

2. Epic Circulation: K. Madavane's *The Mahabharata of Women*

Peter Brook's *Mahabharata* was recognized as a world event in the 1980s. First performed at the Avignon Festival near a quarry, the eleven-hour play, scripted by Jean-Claude Carrière, toured the world for four years. Subsequently, it was made into a film in 1989. Brook's *Mahabharata* has come to be associated with the epic itself. Although the epic was introduced to Europe by way of translations and traveler's accounts as early as the seventeenth century, it was really not until Brook's production that it gained such unprecedented circulation outside India. For many non-Indians, Brook's version is their very first introduction to this monumental epic, circulated in a format that is accessible to the uninitiated. "Accessibility," complains eminent scholar Rustom Bharucha, "is the determining principle of his adaptation. In this respect, Brook is greatly facilitated by Carrière, who ... has reduced the epic to a chronological sequence of episodes."[27] Along similar lines, for postcolonial scholars like Gautam Dasgupta, "Brook's *Mahabharata* falls short of the essential Indianness of the epic by staging predominantly its major incidents and failing to adequately emphasize its coterminous philosophical precepts."[28] Bharucha too wonders: "What is the Mahabharata without Hindu philosophy?"[29] Later in the same article, he asks if "a story [can] be separated from the ways in which it is told to its own people?" and goes on to point out that the audience at the New York production laughed on hearing Krishna's advice to Arjuna: "Act, but don't reflect on the fruits of the action."[30] Krishna's advice forms the basis of the *Bhagavad Gita*. Without sufficient background, the audience cannot be expected to comprehend the basic tenets of Hindu philosophy. In fact, no Indian has ventured to present the *Mahabharata* in its totality; even during the all-night Paratam festivals in Tamil Nadu, only a small section of the epic is played out every evening. But the question—one that Damrosch himself poses in his essay on World Literature—really is: What is circulation if the basic meaning of the text is lost to a foreign audience?

In India, for the past two decades, the publishing industry has been replete with retellings, rewritings, translations, dramatizations, and annotations of the country's two major epics, the *Mahabharata* and the *Ramayana*, not only in English but also in several regional languages. "It is said in India," notes scholar Pupul Jayakar, "that there is nothing in human existence which does not have a place in the *Mahabharata*. ... [The work] contains all the contradictions of life, and its legends and stories have been told and retold in every generation."[31] There are at least 500 versions of these epics, both in oral and written traditions. Often, retellings explore the oral versions that abound in folktales, songs, and performing arts. As Aditya Iyengar, author of *The Thirteenth Day* (a 2015 retelling of the *Mahabharata* that focuses on the little discussed character, Yudishtira), insists, "The question of what is mythology and mythological fiction is quite moot. Let's face it; no one today is going to read the original *Mahabharata* in Sanskrit. Most of us have heard it orally first and then read various interpretations of the text, so as a writer who is reimagining the epic today, I am only trying to humanize it for my readers."[32] Here, Iyengar puts forth two ideas: that the paucity of readership for the epic in the original Sanskrit calls for more translations and retellings and that the epic can be reimagined and humanized for the reader. Perhaps the way to keep epics alive is by assuring several modes of dissemination concomitantly so as to reach different sections of society.

La malédiction des étoiles ou le Mahabharata des femmes (The Curse of the Stars or the Mahabharata of Women) by K. Madavane was commissioned in 1994 by a Francophone university in Montreal to prepare drama students for a stage production.[33] Madavane's assignment responded to the lack of Indian plays with major female roles. Little did the playwright know that his work would circulate in unimaginable ways.

It has been, indeed, subsequently staged in many languages in different productions, in professional and community theater venues, in German translation for the Baden-Württemberg Festival at Karlsruhe, in the original French in Paris and on Réunion Island, and in English translation at Melbourne. In India, it has been performed in many cities in English, Hindi, Tamil, and Kannada. Besides these productions, a theater company in Prague has conducted a reading in Czech. Incidentally, the theater companies that have produced these plays and invited Madavane to direct were relatively small but open to texts and performances from abroad.

In the *Mahabharata des femmes*, Madavane introduces three contemporary characters: Mother, Son, and Sister. By doing so, he offers different temporal perspectives to the epic. Mother tells the story of the *Mahabharata* to her son and daughter and also evokes the story of the Young Woman, a local legend from the environs of Pondicherry. At least three temporal frames are here intertwined: the present, which is also a flashback and therefore involves more than two moments; the time of the epic; and the past of the Young Woman, whose time frame remains undetermined due to Mother's senility. Within this continuous emboîtement of time, we witness complete identification of the contemporary characters with those of the epic. "Mythology," explains Madavane, "has been known to establish solid and valuable links between two epochs. The sheer confrontation of two different myths raises a number of questions. As far as I am concerned, *The Mahabharata of Women* was a pretext to talk about a local legend that has nourished my imagination ever since my childhood."[34] "The Young Woman" episode essentially recalls the power of collective memory and imagination. Often our perception of the larger world is shaped by what is closer to home, by the smaller or the more immediate. The concept of framing the epic through a regional legend illuminates human strategies of comprehension. Scholar and critic Carpanin Marimoutou compares Madavane's play to a *"texte banyan,"* an analogy that points to the constant crisscrossing of words, stories, and time frames. Receiving a text through another, which is what the reader experiences here, can be seen as another mode of translation and therefore circulation.[35]

Le Mahabharata des femmes was first published in French in 1998 by a Chennai-based press, but soon it was translated and published in Tamil. This is perhaps the biggest irony, namely, that an Indian epic originally dramatized in French was later translated into the author's mother tongue! Such anomalies are usually found in colonial contexts. Having studied at the Lycée français, Madavane always wrote in French even though he could read and speak Tamil. "As someone belonging to Pondicherry," he confessed, "I inherited two languages—Tamil and French. My entire education was in French. But I stayed on in India unlike my classmates whose families chose to migrate to France. My roots are profoundly Indian and my readings international."[36] Madavane's French, at least in his prose, reflects this background and, what is more, is somewhat "domesticated" by an array of basically untranslatable Tamil words.

While the translation of the play into English and its subsequent publication in *Theatre India*, a journal run by the National School of Drama, assured visibility in theater circles, his 2004 collection of short stories, *Mourir à Bénarès*, had to wait fourteen years before it was translated into English as *To die in Banaras* and published by Picador/PanMacmilan in 2018. The problem of distribution in French, however, remains for several authors, including Madavane. With the option of being translated into English and published in India, how many authors, one wonders, will stand patiently in the long queue of Francophone writers waiting to be noticed? As Blake Smith puts it, "[Madavane's] fiction, such as the haunting collection of short stories, *Mourir à Bénarès*, is . . . difficult to find even in the French-speaking world. This is a pity, because his stories, in which a lucid prose style passes from bittersweet reverie to grim humour or a devastating twist of fate, offer an unrivalled perspective on a forgotten corner of Indian history."[37]

3. Conclusion

For Damrosch, World Literature "encompass(es) all literary works that circulate beyond their culture of origin, either in translation or in their original language."[38] Departing from this broad and generous definition of World Literature, I wish to quote Mohanty once more and invoke his stance so as to understand the phenomenon of cross-cultural exchange in a pluralized cultural space:

> The term "world lit," as I use it, is a goal of critical practice, of cross-cultural conversations. It does not refer to a canon of literary works. Even Goethe, when he initially came up with the term *Weltliteratur* in the early nineteenth century, thought of it less as a body of literary works—fixed or growing—and more as the process by which critics and general readers learn how to live consciously and intelligently in a pluralised cultural space, a space shaped by increased travel and cross-cultural contact through translations and criticism.[39]

The case that best exemplifies Mohanty's point is that of M. Mukundan. A writer hailing from Mahe, a former French enclave on the western coast of India, Mukundan can speak and write in French with relative ease but chose to write in Malayalam, his mother tongue, which is used in the state of Kerala.[40] An acclaimed writer, he has won several prestigious awards[41] in the country and has been even recognized by an official French distinction.[42] Critics credit him with infusing modernity into Malayali literature. Influenced greatly by writers such as Jean-Paul Sartre and Albert Camus, Mukundan's novels and short stories form an incisive study of identity, its loss, and the individual's efforts in grappling with constant challenges. The novel that probably propelled Mukundan out of the more limited Malayali circuit, *On the Banks of the Mayyazhi*,[43] became available to a wider readership after being translated into English. It was later rendered into French as *Sur les rives du fleuve Mahé* and brought out by Actes Sud in France.[44] Through a multitude of characters that represent not only the whites and the browns but also the *métis*, the novel deals with the retreat of the French from the colony. More importantly, the book shows the divided reactions to the departure of the French. While a handful of youth, led by their Communist master, strive to fight for the liberation of Mahe, others, having internalized colonialism so well, wonder why the French even needed to leave, as the circumstances at that time seemed natural to them. The sequel to this novel, which looks at the aftermath of colonization, was also translated into English under the title *God's Mischief*. What makes the two novels noteworthy—apart from the treatment of the subject—is the mere portrayal of the French colony. Nowhere in Indian fiction has this space been spoken about or represented. Surprising as it may sound, the average Indian reader is rather ignorant of the history of French presence on his or her soil, making Frenchness in the texts all the more exotic to the reader both in India and in the Indian diaspora.

The reception of such works in Indian diasporic sites around the world is worthy of analysis as these communities often have parallel networks in the countries where they live, broadening circulation in diversified circuits of interaction. These circuits make translations possible and also create platforms for critical reading. For instance, one can imagine an Indian teaching Tamil in a French university and translating an exiled Sri Lankan poet's work written in French into Tamil, which has its readership not only among Indian Tamils but also among Sri Lankan Tamils. Similarly, a Pakistani living in France may translate an Indian writer's prose from Urdu into French, or an Indian Bengali may read and/or translate a Bangladeshi's poetry from French into Bengali or vice versa. The Indian subcontinent provides multiple permutations and combinations within and outside its confines, which already creates cultural spaces of readership distinct from the latter's geographical origins.

As mentioned earlier, writings from Pondicherry occupy a special place among populations of Indian descent residing in the French islands of the Caribbean or of the Indian Ocean. Since Indians left their shores to work as indentured labor for the thriving sugarcane plantations in British and French colonies on these islands, the affinity with India is understandably strong. Theirs is a community that devours literary production from India accessible through original writing in French or through translation. Further, they constitute an audience that can partake of a "shared experience" through a collective memory kept alive by almost five generations. To date, the *Mahabharata* and the *Ramayana* continue to appeal to them a great deal, be it in Mauritius, Réunion Island, or the French Caribbean. But, at least in these Francophone zones, Indian writing in French, too, has not lost its relevance.[45] As Smith notes, "On the border between the Francophone world and the Indian Subcontinent, rich with unique perspectives, [Indian writing in French] could be poised for a global renaissance—if scholars, translators and critics can bring it to a new generation of readers."[46] Smith could not be more right in his assessment of the kind of circulation that Indian writing in French could enjoy. To that effect, a proactive policy of translation in India not only into English but also into regional languages would help, as would mapping Indian literature in French, through publication and critical study, before the last generation of writers from the erstwhile colony fades into oblivion.

Notes

1. Satya P. Mohanty, "Literature to Combat Cultural Chauvinism. From Indian Literature to World Literature: In Conversation with Satya P. Mohanty," by Rashmi Dube Bhatnagar and Rajender Kaur, *Frontline: India's National Magazine*, April 6, 2012, 91.
2. David Damrosch, *What Is World Literature?* (Princeton, NJ, and Oxford, UK: Princeton University Press, 2003), 27.
3. Damrosch, *What Is World Literature?*, 26.
4. French was the second language in the Portuguese colony of Goa but also the language of the elite.
5. Modes of literary circulation in the nineteenth century were fascinating. Francisco Luis Gomes, a Goan, wrote to the French poet Lamartine, lamenting about India's situation: "Je demande pour l'Inde la liberté et la lumière!" In a letter dated January 5, 1861, he praises Lamartine's *Confidences* and *Graziella* and mentions that he will send Lamartine books through a friend as an act of gratitude. See Felizardo Gonçalves Pereira, *Apontamentos para a biographia de Franciso Luis Gomes* (Bombaim, India: Tipografia Anglo-Luisitano, 1892), 256–7.
6. Aleixo Manuel da Costa, *Dicionário de literatura goesa* (Panjim, India: Fundação Oriente, 1997).
7. Vijaya Rao, *Écriture indienne d'expression française* (New Delhi, India/Réunion: Yoda Press/Le GERM, 2008).
8. Damrosch, *What Is World Literature?*, 5
9. Anne Castaing, Lise Guilhamon, and Laetitia Zecchini, eds., *La modernité littéraire indienne: Perspectives postcoloniales* (Rennes, France: Presses Universitaires de Rennes, 2009).
10. Jawaharlal Nehru, *Selected Speeches*, vol. 5, *1963-64* (New Delhi, India: Publications Division, 1983), 35.
11. Aurobindo was one of the leaders of groups that were fighting against British rule. Charged with sedition, he was imprisoned for a year, during which he practiced yoga and engaged with spirituality.
12. Ashish Nandy, *The Intimate Enemy: Loss and Recovery of Self under Colonialism* (New Delhi, India: Oxford University Press, 1983).
13. Aurobindo's spiritual quest did not stop him from being drawn into the nationalist movement. Interestingly, Aurobindo makes a statement contrary to his point of using English ("When a Maratha or Gujarati has anything important to say, he says it in English; when a Bengali, he says it in Bengali. . . . English is being steadily driven out of the field. Soon it will remain to weed it out of our conversation") in *Indu Prakash*, July 23, 1894. Quoted in Nandy, *The Intimate Enemy*, 92.
14. Nirodbaran, "Correspondence with Sri Aurobindo," February 28, 1936, 508, https://www.aurobindo.ru/workings/nirodbaran/corresp_1/0004_e.htm (accessed October 5, 2018).
15. See Dhir Sarangi, "L'inspiration spirituelle dans la poésie de Sri Aurobindo, de Nolini Kanta Gupta et de Prithwindra Mukherjee," in *Écriture indienne d'expression française*, ed. Vijaya Rao and Shantha Ramakrishna, special issue, *Rencontre avec l'Inde* 29, no. 3 (2000): 22.
16. Sri Aurobindo, "Fragment d'un poème," in Rao, *Écriture indienne d'expression française*, 3.

17 Sri Aurobindo, "The Alexandrine," *The Future Poetry*, https://www.sriaurobindoashram.org/sriaurobindo/downloadpdf.php?id=39 (accessed January 16, 2019).
18 *Collected Works of Nolini Kanta Gupta* (Pondicherry, India: Sri Aurobindo Centre of Education, 1974).
19 Prithwindra Mukherjee, *Le serpent de flammes* (Paris, France: Editions Estienne, 1979).
20 See Sarangi, "L'inspiration spirituelle dans la poésie de Sri Aurobindo," 28.
21 Ranajit Sarkar, *Langue étrangère et autres poèmes*, ed. Vijaya Rao (New Delhi, India: Daastaan, 2012), 47.
22 Nandy, *The Intimate Enemy*, 85–6.
23 Rabrindranath Tagore, *Viswa Sahitya*, trans. Rijula Das and Makarand R. Paranjape, in *Rabindranath Tagore in the 21st Century*, Sophia Studies in Cross-cultural Philosophy of Traditions and Cultures 7, ed. D. Banerji (New Delhi, India: Springer India, 2015), 286.
24 Tagore, *Viswa Sahitya*, 287.
25 Quoted in Fritz Strich, *Goethe and World Literature*, trans. C. A. M. Sym (London, UK: Routledge, 1949), 35.
26 Nandy, *The Intimate Enemy*, 97.
27 Rustom Bharucha, "Peter Brook's 'Mahabharata': A View from India," *Economic and Political Weekly* 23, no. 32 (August 6, 1988): 1644.
28 Gautam Dasgupta, "'The Mahabharata': Peter Brook's 'Orientalism,'" *Performing Arts Journal* 10, no. 3 (1987): 9–16.
29 Bharucha, "Peter Brook's 'Mahabharata,'" 1643.
30 Bharucha, "Peter Brook's 'Mahabharata,'" 1644, 1643.
31 Quoted in Steven R. Weisman, "Many Faces of the Mahabharata," *The New York Times*, October 27, 1987, C17, National edition. As Weisman notes, Pupul Jayakar was at the time "cultural adviser to the Indian Government and impresario of festivals of India in the United States and other countries."
32 Mahalakshmi P, "Ramayana and the Mahabharata continue to Inspire Writers," *The Times of India*, March 4, 2017, https://timesofindia.indiatimes.com/city/bengaluru/ramayana-and-the-mahabharata-continue-to-inspire-writers/articleshow/57459220.cms (accessed February 2, 2019).
33 A native of Pondicherry, Madavane studied at the Lycée français de Pondichéry and later pursued his doctorate at Jawaharlal Nehru University, where he taught and from which he retired as professor. After training with theater luminaries like Antoine Vitez and Guy Retoré in Paris (1975–78), Madavane returned to New Delhi to form the drama group *Chingari*. He has since directed over sixty plays in many languages. His acclaimed innovative creations include *Tughlaq* (Girish Karnad), *Tartuffe* (Molière), *The Mahabharata of Women* (Madavane), and William Shakespeare's *Hamlet*. From 2014 to 2016, Madavane was the creative director at the Shri Ram Centre for Performing Arts, New Delhi.
34 K. Madavane, "Penser dans la langue de la mère, écrire dans la langue du père, vivre le mythe comme un agent interculturel," in *Écrire en langue étrangère: intérferences de langues et de cultures dans le monde francophone*, ed. Robert Dion, Hans-Jürgen Lüsebrink, and János Riesz (Sainte-Foy, France, and Frankfurt, Germany: Nota bene and Iko-Verlag, 2002), 522.

35 Carpanin Marimoutou, "Draupadi aux frontières: une lecture de *la Malédiction des étoiles ou le Mahabharata des femmes* de K. Madavane," in *Draupadi: textures et tissages*, ed. Valérie Magdelaine Andrianjafitrimo (La Réunion: Editions K'A, 2008), 347.
36 My translation. K. Madavane, "'Le geste de l'acteur sur scène est une écriture sur l'eau': Entretien avec K. Madavane," interview by Jean-Luc Raharimanana, in "Identités, langues et imaginaires dans l'Océan Indien," ed. Jean-Luc Raharimanana, special issue, *Interculturel Francophonies* 4 (2003): 261.
37 Blake Smith, "This Indian Author Wrote His Stories in French. Is that Why We Don't Remember Him?" *Scroll.in*, April 1, 2017, https://scroll.in/article/833389/this-indian-author-wrote-his-stories-in-french-is-that-why-we-dont-remember-him (accessed May 19, 2019). Madavane's other plays include *The Veritree or The Falsity of the Gods* (2008), *To be or not to be . . . Macbeth* (2015), *A monologue for a woman on stage* (2011), and *1947—The Man from Lahore*, a play which was short-listed for *The Hindu* Playwright Award in 2017.
38 Damrosch, *What Is World Literature?*, 4.
39 Mohanty, "Literature to Combat Cultural Chauvinism," 90.
40 Four French enclaves spread across India—Karaikal, Chandernagore, Yanam, and Mahe—came under the administration of Pondicherry.
41 The Sahitya Akademi Award in 1992.
42 *Chevalier des Arts et des Lettres* of the Government of France in 1998.
43 M. Mukundan, *On the Banks of the Mayyazhi*, trans. Gita Krishnankutty (Chennai, India: Manas, 1999). Mahe was originally called Mayyazhi, but the French Commodore de Pardaillan changed it to Mahe to acknowledge the role played by the French naval captain, Mahé de Labourdonnais, in capturing Mayyazhi.
44 M. Mukundan, *Sur les rives du fleuve Mahé*, trans. Sophie Bastide-Folz (Arles, France: Actes Sud, 2002).
45 As an interesting parallel, it may be noted that the Francophone Literature of the Indian Ocean is part of the curricula in some Departments of French at Indian universities.
46 Blake Smith, "Indian Literature Speaks French," *The Wire*, April 29, 2018.

Part II

Francophone Spatialities: Cities, Landscapes, Environments

5

Mapping World Literature from Below: Tierno Monénembo and City Writing

Eric Prieto

1. The View from Below

This chapter approaches the question of Francophone literature as world literature from the bottom-up, by which I mean three distinct things. The first results from my approach to the broad domains under investigation. Rather than beginning at the top, with the general categories of World Literature and Francophonie in their institutional dimension—the bird's-eye view—I work my way up toward this perspective, beginning with a single French-speaking author (Tierno Monénembo) and a set of specific thematic preoccupations (the city). The larger project on city writing from which this essay is drawn did not start out with any particular concern for the field of world literature per se, yet the nature of the topic led me, gradually and somewhat grudgingly, to the realization that any meaningful contribution to a study of city writing in the Global South would require understanding how Monénembo's novels are enmeshed in larger—Francophone, African, and transnational—networks of city writing on a planetary scale. What follows then is not a set of prescriptive recommendations on Francophone literature as world literature, but an attempt to take the threads that radiate out from my Guinean starting point and follow them where they lead, which is to say, across the African continent and the world.

The second sense in which this chapter takes a bottom-up approach to world literature involves a model of theoretical insight that, following Henri Lefebvre, I have called "transduction," which is premised on the dialectical interplay between the bottom-up perspective of direct experience and empirical knowledge, on the one hand, and the top-down perspective of theoretical discourse, on the other. "Transduction," according to Lefebvre, "assumes an incessant feed-back between the conceptual framework in operation and empirical observations. The theory or methodology, rather, of transduction gives form to the spontaneous mental operations of the urbanist, the architect, the sociologist, the politician, the philosopher."[1] In this, the concept of transduction prefigures what Lefebvre would later theorize in *La production de l'espace* as the dialectical trio of perceived space (which is bottom-up), conceived space (which is top-down), and lived space (which involves the transductive exchange between the two). And, significantly, Lefebvre cites literature as one of the noteworthy purveyors of the transductive logic of lived space. If Lefebvre is right, then the imaginative representations of the kind carried out by literary writers have an important role to play in the resolution of the world's most pressing social problems, right alongside those of policy makers and theorists of various kinds. In this sense, the notion of transduction provides a more sophisticated way to understand the social efficacy of literature (changing the world by "modifying people's mentalities, however incrementally," as Édouard Glissant has put it) than attempts that rely on appeals to propagandist models like the *roman à thèse* or manifesto, or on idealistic appeals to the utopian function of literature.[2]

The third sense in which this essay takes a bottom-up approach is more properly sociological: it focuses primarily on works that emphasize the perspective of those at the bottom of the socioeconomic pyramid. This is a necessary consequence of the thematic focus on cities in the current historical conjuncture. In the 1990s, amid triumphalist claims about the new (neoliberal) world order and the benefits of economic globalization, much of the talk about cities concerned the importance of what Saskia Sassen has termed "global cities," those sparkling capitals of world finance and trade like New York, London, and Tokyo that form the backbone of the global economic system.[3] What was left out of that vision was the new urban agglomerations that did not benefit from the neoliberal economic orthodoxies but were in fact often left to collapse into deeper poverty and disorder as a direct result of these policies' implementation.[4] It was arguably not until the United Nations 2003 report on cities, *The Challenge of Slums*, that the full scale of this devastation began to enter the broader public consciousness, and works written under the influence of this report, such as Mike Davis's *Planet of Slums* (2005), combined with the media sensations caused by such blockbuster films as *City of God* (2002) and *Slumdog Millionaire* (2008), have made it all but impossible to talk about the command and control centers of the global economic system without also talking about urban poverty.[5] Indeed, many of the thinkers associated with the rise of "global city" and "creative class" rhetoric in the 1990s and early 2000s—including Sassen, Richard Florida, Benjamin Barber, and Edward Glaeser—have turned increasingly to questions of urbanization in the Global South.[6]

It is important to understand the magnitude of the demographic upheaval that is currently transforming cities in the developing world. According to UN figures, 90 percent of future urban growth will happen in the Global South, a fact that has led commentators like Stewart Brand to note that, demographically at least, "the rise of the West is over."[7] This demographic sea change becomes spectacularly apparent in recent lists of the world's most populous cities, which are now entirely dominated by Asian and African agglomerations, many of which have populations in the tens of millions.[8] Of perhaps even greater importance is the fact that over half of urban dwellers in the "cities of the South" (Jeremy Seabrook) live in conditions of extreme poverty and precarity, typically inhabiting self-built or substandard housing in informal settlements. Given the scale and pervasiveness of urban poverty in these cities, it has become impossible, or at least unethical, to talk about contemporary urbanization without taking into account the perspective of those at the bottom.

These developments have begun to have a significant effect on literary studies, generating a great deal of new interest in current and past texts on the subject. (The topic has been an important one in the social sciences for decades.) As the Cameroonian writer Patrice Nganang argues, the first generation of postcolonial writers tended to remain enthralled with the village and the countryside, typically understood as the locus of tradition and authenticity and engaged in a complex and often violent dance with an externally imposed modernity associated with the city.[9] Since the 1980s, however, the city has increasingly come to be seen as a kind of second nature, a now familiar environment, often featured alongside pointed critiques of traditional social patterns and village life. There is a new sense that the city has become a paradigmatic locus of postcolonial African life, one that is able to stand on its own and signify in its own right. This has given rise notably to what Nganang terms *le roman de bidonville*, the shantytown novel, which emphasizes the central role of what Monénembo calls the "bas-fonds."

2. Urban Apotheosis as Representational Crisis

Monénembo's use of the term "bas-fonds" seems meant to invoke the long tradition of lower-depths writing in French literature, reminding us that urban poverty, social conflict, and underworld networks are not a Third-World invention. In France, this tradition could be traced from the Middle Ages through to the present day and includes such figures as François Villon, François Rabelais, and Restif de la Bretonne, as well as the great nineteenth- and twentieth-century social novel tradition, with its fascination for what Pierre MacOrlan called "le fantastique social," exemplified by such figures as Eugène Sue, Victor Hugo, Eugène Dabit, Louis-Ferdinand Céline, Raymond Queneau, Romain Gary, and so on, without forgetting genre fiction like the detective novel, action film, and the post-migration novel, which all thrive on lower-depths imagery.

The group of African writers associated with this kind of literature can be said, in a sense, to belong to this "underground" tradition of city writing, which also extends across the globe.[10] But it might be more accurate to say that these writers represent more of an apotheosis of that tradition, not only because the cultural and social specificities of the places in question differ from their European counterparts but also because of the sheer scale of the African megalopoli and the magnitude of the problems they must address. As cities have scaled up, the structural and resource constraints and potentialities have changed in nature, giving rise to new kinds of urban dynamics that are not necessarily well captured by existing concepts and representational practices. This has in turn created a representational crisis that is felt not only in literature but also in fields like urban planning and architecture. Thus, the Dutch architect and urban theorist Rem Koolhaas, noting the "maelstrom of modernization" that this demographic upheaval represents, suggests that it is "creating a completely new urban substance" that has left the discipline of urban planning struggling to catch up: "The absence, on the one hand, of plausible universal doctrines and the presence, on the other, of an unprecedented intensity of production have created a unique, wrenching condition: the urban seems to be least understood at the very moment of its apotheosis." This leads him to conclude that "the result is a theoretical, critical, and operational impasse [that has led to a state where] the entire discipline possesses no adequate terminology to discuss the most pertinent, most crucial phenomena within its domain nor any conceptual framework to describe, interpret, and understand exactly those forces that could redefine and revitalize it."[11] A long list of urban planners, theorists, and architects—including Tom Avermaete, AbdouMaliq Simone, Ananya Roy, Filip de Boeck, David Aradeon, and Pep Subirós— have made related remarks emphasizing (1) the need for new modes of representation able to make sense of these changes and (2) the need to look for the necessary models in the Global South, to "learn from Third World Cities" rather than seeking to apply external models derived from Western practices.[12] Although all of these thinkers have certain shared notions of what such a language would have to account for, beginning with the housing crisis and the prevalence of urban informality, they have not arrived at any kind of consensus on what the central elements of that language would be. They tend rather to emphasize the gap that needs to be bridged between established urban theory and the new realities of the twenty-first-century city.

This is precisely what Monénembo seeks to do: to help bridge this gap between reality and representation, that is to say, between the facts on the ground and the theoretical concepts used to comprehend and address them, by using a transductive poetics to renovate the language of urban representation in ways that can better depict, understand, and respond to the realities of life in the megalopoli of the Global South.

3. Monénembo as a World Author

Perhaps no one is better attuned to the theme of global interconnectedness so central to the world literature approach than the exile. This has certainly been true of Monénembo, whose professional path as a writer is intimately bound up with his personal and political trajectory. Born in 1947 in Porédaka, Guinea, and forced into exile in 1969 for his criticism of the Sékou Touré régime, he then lived in Senegal and Côte d'Ivoire before going to France in 1973. His subsequent life has taken him around the world, including a number of countries in the new world, notably Brazil and Cuba, which he has also written about in *Pelourinho* and *Les coqs cubains chantent à minuit*, respectively. Although he identifies strongly as a *Peul* and a Guinean, he eschews the kind of ethnic or nationalist chauvinism that can lead to interethnic violence. He has, rather, a cosmopolitan outlook combined with an ongoing attachment to his homeland and its people, and a vision of the extent to which global forces penetrate into the daily lives of individuals that recalls Glissant's notions of *relation* and *Tout-monde*.

Of particular importance, at least from the perspective of this essay, is his focus on the city and his commitment to exploring transnational experience from the bottom-up perspective of migrants and the urban poor. Thus, after a fairly conventional first novel, *Les crapauds brousse* (1973), which offered a straightforward critique of corruption under the Sékou Touré régime in the Afro-pessimist vein, he published a series of four highly innovative urban novels: *Les écailles du ciel* (1986), *Un rêve utile* (1991), *Un attiéké pour Elgass* (1993), and *Pelourinho* (1995). Each of these works is set in a highly distinctive urban locale and contributes to the development of an elaborate narrative style designed to bring to light under-recognized aspects of urban experience. These novels stand out, then, not only for their thematic focus on the city and the bottom of the social hierarchy but also for their innovative representational strategies.

It is, I want to argue, this commitment to representational innovation—motivated by the desire to create a more adequate conceptual framework for the complexities of the modern postcolonial metropolis—that makes Monénembo such an important figure for world literature. Monénembo shows in these novels a deep commitment to creating his own representational idiom, giving his city writing an avant-gardist, experimental dimension. Perhaps because they are so difficult, though, none of these four works has been translated into English, and they have garnered relatively little attention outside of a small but prestigious sphere of Francophone African diasporic writers, which includes Abdourahman Waberi, Sami Tchak, and Patrice Nganang, all of whom cite these novels as significant influences.[13] But with the critical and popular success of his more recent books, the city novels may yet find their way to a global audience, an outcome this study seeks to promote. In what follows, I will be focusing on two novels, *Les écailles du ciel* and *Un attiéké pour Elgass*, whose plots unfold predominantly in African cities. (*Un rêve utile* and Pelourinho are set, respectively, in Lyon and Salvador de Bahia.)

4. *Les écailles du ciel*: (De)Constructing Literary History and the Postcolonial City

One way to think of *Les écailles du ciel* is as a kind of literary history: a tour de force of literary pastiche that runs through a number of prominent modes of African and Africana literature in its search for a style that is more adequate to the challenges of the modern African city. Each of the five sections of the novel (a prologue and four numbered chapters) turns to a different style and engages in an implicit dialogue with the literary figures associated with that style. Thus, the novel's prologue, set in a bar in the fictional *bidonville* of Leydi-Bondi, adopts a semi-comical bantering style of a kind that will be picked up by writers like Alain Mabanckou and Nganang, and that harkens back to the long tradition of drunken tall tales exemplified by works like Amos Tutuola's *The Palm Wine Drinkard*. This discursive style may also be meant to recall the tradition of the *palaver*, where collective decisions are made with the help of drink as a social lubricant. (Emanuel Dongala makes much of this tradition in his short story "Jazz and Palm Wine.") It also prefigures, as we shall see, the discursive strategies of Monénembo's later city novels, albeit in still nascent form.

After the prologue, however, chapter one makes a significant shift in tone and voice as it takes us back through history, first to the precolonial period and then to the incursion and progressive dominance of the French colonizers. This chapter could plausibly be read as a pastiche of the kind of tradition-versus-modernity novel associated with writers like Chinua Achebe or Camara Laye. Indeed, upon closer examination, this chapter begins to evoke Cheikh Hamidou Kane's classic *Une aventure ambiguë* (1961). Like Kane's protagonist, Monénembo's is named Samba. Both go to French schools, and both are sent out in the world by their families to learn the secrets of the French colonists in order to better combat their dominance. But whereas Kane's Samba is a brilliant student and intellect, who learns to despise the soullessness of French materialism even as it shakes his faith, Monénembo's Samba does not have that kind of intellectual capacity. He is at best a blank slate (a shadow, as he is called in the prologue) and at worst a lazy lout. To the extent, then, that Monénembo interacts with Kane's novel, it is in the mode of parody.

With chapter two, the theme of city life comes to the fore. And here again, we have a fairly radical shift in style. If chapter one reads like a critical response to Kane's *Aventure ambiguë*, then chapter two can be read as a reconsideration of Frantz Fanon's urban hypothesis in *Les damnés de la terre* (published, like Kane's novel, in 1961), according to which the city, and in particular the *lumpenproletariat* of the shantytowns, excluded from the city center by the colonizers, will form the backbone of anti-colonial insurrection and guarantee its success.[14] At first, Monénembo seems to follow the Fanonian template. Taking up residence in a *bidonville* called Leydi-Bondi, Samba gets caught up in the revolutionary fervor of the moment and contributes (unwittingly) to the success of the independence movement. But in the aftermath of independence, the Fanonian model begins to break down. The colonial oppressor has been replaced by a homegrown tyrant who is just as allergic to dissent as his predecessors and at least as willing to use violence and oppressive tactics to impose his will. Monénembo, accordingly, leaves behind the Fanonian model of revolutionary fervor and collective action and shifts into the kind of Afro-pessimistic satire of corruption, mismanagement, and tyranny associated with African writers of the 1980s like Henri Lopès.

Having registered his disgust with the failure of the postcolonial regime, Monénembo changes narrative gears yet again. In chapter three, the novel shifts into the mode of social apocalypse, which is recounted in an absurdist, quasi-surrealist style that recalls Sony Labou Tansi. Djimméyabé, the capital of the newly minted nation (clearly modeled on Guinea's Conakry), "had completed its cycle of deterioration and *laisser-aller* and had now engaged in a veritable phase of decomposition."[15] This chapter features, notably, the arrival of the allegorically named Johnny-Limited, come to extract the mineral wealth of the country, and the onset of sectarian violence, a civil war that is described as more of a "collective suicide" than a war (176). The chapter culminates in a kind of quasi-surrealist conflagration in which the entire capital is consumed.

And then, in what is by far the shortest, but also perhaps most original part of the novel, chapter four, Monénembo shifts gears once more and closes with a passage that seems meant to symbolize the death of traditional African ways of life. Indeed, Samba, who seeks to return to his hometown Kolisoko after the destruction of Djimméyabé, finally makes it there only to discover that it has become a place of death in the most extreme sense imaginable. Monénembo makes this point in a kind of semi-lugubrious, semi-comic incantation:

> The men were dead, the men had left Kolisoko. The lambs were dead, the lambs had gone away from Kolisoko. The orange trees were dead. The birds were dead . . . the Yalamawol river cursed with all its waters the village of Kolisoko. . . . There was nothing left but the cola tree. . . . When Samba kneeled at the foot of the cola tree to say a prayer, it struck him with a mighty blow and swallowed him in one gulp. (192; emphasis added)

Literally swallowed whole by his own village's protective spirit (the colatier was the village's totem), Samba looks as though he is being punished by tradition itself. This leaves the griot Koulloun, who has narrated the entire story, alone, "sulking over the roots of the past, fearing the fruits of the future" (192). This chapter, tellingly, is titled "Le commencement des choses," as if to say: this is postcolonial Guinea's new reality.

So what does all of this mean? Geographically speaking, there is an opposition between a city, devastated by mismanagement, civil war, and extractive neocolonialism, and an equally devastated, but also depopulated and actively hostile, traditional village. Symbolically, the novel seems to be using this geographical construct to say that a return to those traditional value systems and ways of life is no longer an option. Although the city has become intolerable, laid to waste by a kleptocratic regime, there can be no return to an idyllic world of precolonial social harmony and cultural plenitude. Thus, after contesting the revolutionary socialist model of Fanon and the cultural identity model of Kane, Monénembo seems to have left us with no options. Indeed, it would be difficult to overstate the unrelenting pessimism of this ending, which takes the themes of Afro-pessimism and pushes them in the direst possible direction.

But it is precisely this hole that Monénembo will try to dig himself out of in the three novels to follow. Although *Écailles* seems to leave readers with no satisfactory options, Monénembo's subsequent novels, which take place entirely in urban contexts, seem to suggest that the city, however compromised, may offer a way forward for Africa. In this sense, the city has become a proxy for modernity itself. This new effort results in a major shift in the representational strategies of his novels, one that, so to speak, attempts to triangulate between the sociopolitical project of Fanon and the culturalist project of Kane. This happens first in *Un rêve utile* (1991), which is set in Lyon and so will not be considered here, and most convincingly in *Un attiéké pour Elgass*, to which I now turn.

5. *Un attiéké pour Elgass*: The Return of the (African) Repressed

This is a miserly city, but that gives everyone a fighting chance.[16]

Un attiéké pour Elgass can be understood as a kind of detective story akin to Agatha Christie's *Who Killed Roger Akroyd* in the sense that the narrator himself turns out to be the guilty party—or rather one of the guilty parties, since there are several crimes under consideration and everyone seems to share part of the blame. The informal inquest that will result in the ultimate revelations of the novel takes place in the latter's long fourth chapter, which occupies over a third of this 170-page, 5-chapter text. There is much to say about the depiction of the city in the book's first three chapters—which give a lighthearted account of the protagonist/narrator's well-lubricated bus trip across Abidjan—but I will focus here on chapter four. This chapter has a complex discursive structure of the kind that was prefigured in the prologue of *Écailles* and developed more extensively in Monénembo's previous novel, *Un rêve utile*.

The scene is set in a Treichville bar, where a close-knit group of Guinean exiles is gathered to celebrate the imminent departure of their friend Idjatou (Elgass's sister) for Belgium, ostensibly to take advantage of a university scholarship (although we learn differently later on). There are several simultaneous discussions going on, which all revolve around a number of crimes involving Elgass, their recently deceased friend and leader, who died in dubious circumstances. Debates, arguments, and accusations about these mysteries, as well as other more or less minor betrayals of various kinds, fly back and forth, intertwining polyphonically with each other in a way that creates a densely complex discursive texture. Further complicating all of this is a thread composed of the exclamations of Tantie Akissi, the owner of the bar, who has fallen asleep and is dreaming out loud about the misdeeds of a mysterious female presence referred to only as *Elle*.

All of the various conversations intermingle in such a way that the reader must make a constant effort to determine who is talking, to whom, and about what. Understanding this apparently chaotic polyphonic texture, where several seemingly unrelated conversations are going on that all end up converging around the same topic, is, as we shall see, crucial to understanding the message of the novel and its urbanistic implications. As the night wears on, the drinking intensifies, lowering inhibitions, and the stakes of these conversations rise until we arrive at the ultimate revelation of the novel: Badio, our narrator-protagonist, suddenly has a realization so traumatic that it can only be understood as a Freudian return of the repressed—he is the one who has most profoundly betrayed Elgass, namely by sleeping with his underage sister (a form of pseudo-incest), forcing her to have an abortion (infanticide?), and eventually pushing her into prostitution to cover the traces of his crime. The magnitude of the betrayal is clear and has immediately tragic consequences: when this revelation is made public, Idjatou takes her own life. As to the question of who is responsible for Elgass's death, it remains unresolved. Although the worst of Badio's revelations seems now to have come to light, it cannot be ruled out that he is harboring one last dark secret, namely, that he is himself responsible for Elgass's death. There are reasons to believe, however, that Monénembo's larger point is that it is the group as a whole that has done away with their leader, following a ritual logic akin to that which Freud postulates in *Moses and Monotheism*.

But what does all of this personal drama have to do with the African city? And how does the polyphonic complexity of this chapter contribute to Monénembo's efforts to renew the representation of the city? In order to answer these questions, we will need to return to Tantie Akissi's prophetic dream about this mysterious *Elle*, whom she imagines to be wreaking havoc on the city of Abidjan. Although many of the other strands might have appeared to be more central to the novel's primary plot, it is Tantie Akissi's dream that is most central to Monénembo's larger intention. Her ravings, although apparently unrelated to the other conversations, suggest that the real problem underlying all of the others, including the various crimes of her fellow Guinean expats, has its origin in this *Elle*.

Of particular importance for Monénembo's urbanistic purposes is the fact that *Elle* seems to be engaged in an elemental conflict with the city itself. Thus, Tantie Akissi exclaims to everyone and no one in particular:

> This woman is too cruel, and the city should not have grown up in this place. If the she-devil moves the wrong way, everything will come tumbling down: the bridges, the buildings, the vanity projects. People don't belong here: this is her home. Everything bears her mark, and everything belongs to her. She worked for thousands of years to give shape to the place. In the beginning, there was only her, the plankton, the mangrove trees. . . . Later, the city grew, the city overreached. (115–16)

Elle appears in passages like these (and there are several) as a kind of force of nature. ("She worked for thousands of years to give shape to the place.") But she also seems to be a kind of trickster, surreptitiously manipulating the lives of the city dwellers, who "are just working and pissing in her pack of lies" (115). We repeatedly get confirmation of this double role. Thanks to her, the city has become a kind of simulacrum or "trompe-l'oeil" and a "lieu dévoyé," a wicked place (145).

Who then is this mysterious feminine presence? The crucial clue turns out to be her privileged relationship to the water. In a key but easily overlooked passage, we are told that she is "la reine de l'eau," the queen of the water:

> I know this woman. A hundred times I've seen her, and a hundred times she was different. She lives far from the people, under the water. She has feathers on her stomach, snakes for a collar. Her heart is the size of a pinhead. She is the queen of the water and everything here belongs to her: the waves, the monsoons, solid land, and even the *fatum* of men. (143)

This watery nature, in conjunction with the iconographic attributes of feathers and snakes, as well as "la reine"'s ability to control men's destinies, makes it clear that Tantie

Akissi is invoking Mami Wata, the West African water deity, or at least a very similar kind of water spirit. She serves here as a kind of *génie du lieu* for the city of Abidjan, which is, of course, a coastal city known for its lagoon and its close relationship with water.

In the West African tradition invoked here, Mami Wata's traditional attributes include, apart from her association with water and her feminine identity, her role as a kind of siren or temptress, but also as a protector of women (who enforces conjugal fidelity and punishes the betrayers) and as a symbol of healing and fertility.[17] She is known as an implacable foe to those who betray her but also as a steadfast ally to those who honor her. These attributes go a long way toward explaining the ambivalent nature of the town, which is simultaneously brutal and magnetic: "Life in 'Bidjan, constantly surprising, Russian roulette and bird whistling. This is a miserly city, but that gives everyone a fighting chance" (51). Tantie Akissi, as we have seen, is especially attuned to the risks associated with Mami Wata and to the havoc she wreaks on the lives of those who cross her. She sees this *Elle* above all as a threat. But to the extent that Mami Wata is associated with the life-giving aspects of the natural environment, as well as, again, with healing, fertility, and the defense of women, she can also be a source of support and sustenance. It would be more accurate, then, to say that she is linked with the *precarious* nature of life in an energetic city that seems to exist always under the dual threat of natural disaster and human folly. The problem with the city revealed in Tantie Akissi's dream is that it has forgotten its interdependent relationship with Mami Wata. And the constant mishaps that Tantie Akissi describes suggest that the city may be on the verge of suffering from a return of the repressed of its own, giving powerful allegorical resonance to the personal catastrophe of Badio and Idjatou.

It is important to note that in Monénembo's hands the Mami Wata figure is not just a personification of nature borrowed from West African folk traditions; she also serves as a second-order symbol of that cultural tradition itself. In this sense, the *problem* with Abidjan is as much cultural as environmental: it has forgotten its roots, culturally and environmentally speaking. Unsurprisingly, this dual lack of attunement to the local cultural and natural environment can be traced back to the colonial era and the incursion of whites:

> Just ask the White man who chased her from Bingerville and Bassam in a flurry of deluges and yellow fever. That restless rabble-rouser had no choice but to make a deal with her so he could put up his bridges and walls in this rascal's den. (145)

But the postindependence era has been just as imbalanced. Blacks too have learned to disdain this connection, or, rather, have forgotten to maintain it:

> After him, the Black man came, victorious like a buffalo and without even making the effort to ask the tribe's opinion. Look at how he is tormenting himself today. The city doesn't suit her, she contests it, she oppresses it. She's like a tortoise in an egg shell. . . . Ah! people of 'Bidjan! Lots of heart but no sense of harmony. Take a look at the shambles it's become. . . . This woman made quite a mess of it. (145–6)

A superficial reading of passages like this might lead an overly hasty reader to conclude that Tantie Akissi's dream implies an anti-modern reading of the novel, as if Monénembo's point was that Africans need to turn their backs on the metropolis in order to find a way to return to a lifestyle more in tune with the natural world and precolonial African traditions. But this would be to forget other important elements of the discursive gumbo that make up the book, not to mention the final lesson of *Écailles*, which, as we saw, was about the impossibility of going back to an unspoiled precolonial past. Indeed, the novel is full of appreciation for Abidjan, with characters repeatedly praising it as a difficult but hopeful and invigorating place to live:

> Tantie Akissi is right: "This town *is* a scandal," as appalling as it is necessary, a scandal born, as they say, of the legendary dis-union of the sea and the forest. City of sadness, city of love, city of cocoa built on illusion and bitterness. Bidjan-là-même is the kind of inconvenience you can't live without once you've tasted the harsh virtues of its ex-centricity. (39–40)

This kind of full engagement with the city's multifaceted complexity is precisely why the polyphonic structure of the chapter is so important. No single character is the bearer of the truth of the novel, or of the city. Rather, that truth results from the interplay of multiple voices. What is clear, especially in contrast with the urban catastrophe of *Écailles*, is that Abidjan is a city that, however stressful, however difficult to survive in, is a vibrant place that has great potential for the future, if only that potential can be successfully leveraged. But what might the keys to that success be?

6. Conclusion: Transductively Reconceptualizing the African City

In its broadest sense, Tantie Akissi's dream is about finding the best ways of promoting the modernization of African cities for the next generation and thereby fostering development in both the economic and human senses of that term. *Attiéké* is a succession story after all (the leader is dead and must be replaced), and Monénembo seems interested in using this story as a way to reflect on the next phase of urban development in Africa, emphasizing the need for solutions that are better attuned to the localized problems these cities face, both material and cultural, without neglecting their place in the larger global order.

In order to develop the implications of this observation, we must keep in mind the sociopolitical resonances of the novel's polyphonic structure. By creating a decentralized mode of discourse, where everyone speaks at the same time, where it is not always immediately clear who is speaking and to whom, where knowledge, success, failure, and guilt are all spread across the group in inextricably complex ways, Monénembo presents us with a certain vision of the social dynamic of large cities as seen from below. This discursive model communicates a sense of the interactions between numerous fragmented groups that are vying for advantages in a multidimensional marketplace, simultaneously in cooperation and competition.

This model of power is diffuse, democratic, competitive, and formulated from the bottom-up perspective of the urban poor rather than the top-down perspective of government agencies, which, in the African context, often do not have the resources to organize urban life (hence the importance of the informal economy and housing settlements) and may in fact be actively oppressive (as is clear in the case of Guinea and its dictatorial regime). Xavier Garnier explains the utility of this model of power in terms of an opposition between "la rumeur" (rumor), which is that of the novel's Guinean expat community, and "le mot d'ordre" (slogan or watchword, and by extension official policy), which is that of centralized governmental power. For Garnier, the *mot d'ordre* loses power as it spreads from the center, whereas *la rumeur* gains power as it circulates. One is vertical, arborescent, the other horizontal, rhizomatic.[18] Thus, although diffuse and apparently weak, the kind of agency associated with *la rumeur* is disseminated throughout the population in a way that makes it better suited to the needs of those on the margins of the economic and political life of the city. In this way, the kind of urban discourse we see in Monénembo's novel gives the book a perhaps unexpected contestatory power. This conception of power resonates strongly with, for example, the Certeauian themes of tactics, underground resistance, and occupation of the interstices of state power. It also resonates with the Situationist themes of *détournement, appropriation,* and *bricolage,* which have obvious relevance in the context of the informal economy and self-built housing. This kind of discourse has been embraced by many urban theorists working on the informal city, including specialists of African urbanism like AbdouMaliq Simone, South Asian sociologists like Ananya Roy, and the Latin American urbanists associated with Alfredo Brillembourg and Hubert Klumpner.[19] For these thinkers, the central strategy for the urban poor, as well as for all those who find themselves marginalized from formal power structures, involves first recognizing such discourse as legitimate and then learning how to leverage it.

To some, such an approach evokes a distasteful sense of "the neoliberal city," where poor communities are atomized and forced to practice a kind of entrepreneurial survivalism rather than organizing for direct, collective political action. I do think it is correct to say that Monénembo's model involves a certain, perhaps not neoliberal but liberal, sense of social process as working through the interactions of autonomous actors who engage with others in that zone where their selfish interests intersect with those of the larger community, as in a marketplace.[20] But like Ananya Roy, I would argue that it is better to promote policies that allow for an incremental process of improvement in the near term than to ask the poor to wait for a radical restructuring of society that may never come.[21]

It is this more diffuse kind of power—the semi-coordinated activity of small communities, carefully attuned to the local landscape of constraints and opportunities that govern daily life in Mami Wata fashion—that, Monénembo's discursive strategies suggest, will provide the best way forward for those in the *bas-fonds*. In a sense, we could say that if *Les écailles du ciel* marked the limits of the Fanonian model of revolutionary struggle and class-based collectivities, *Un attiéké pour Elgass*, like *Un rêve utile* before it, signals a turn to a more of a Glissantian way of viewing social and cultural interactions through metaphors of creolization and relation. These models often entail conflict and injustice, to be sure, but in ways that can be managed by seeking out zones of possible cooperation even between adversaries.

It is, I believe, Monénembo's attempts to bring to life this kind of power structure in his novels that make them such a valuable contribution to that subset of world literature devoted to the *bas-fonds*. By providing another view of globalization—one from below, an alternative to the official top-down vision of city life—his works show some of the ways in which urban theorists might look to the Global South for solutions to the challenges facing cities in the era of globalization.

Notes

1 Henri Lefebvre, "Le droit à la ville," *L'Homme et la société*, no. 6 (1967): 29–35; my translation.
2 See Glissant, *Poetics of Relation* (Ann Arbor, MI: University of Michigan Press, 1997), 197. The definition of poetics that Glissant gives in this passage resonates very strongly with Lefebvre's notion of transduction.
3 See Saskia Sassen, *The Global City: New York, London, Tokyo* (Princeton, NJ: Princeton University Press, 2013).
4 I am thinking here of the harsh austerity measures and Structural Adjustment Programs that were imposed on many developing nations by the IMF in exchange for continued credit in the wake of the 1979 global debt crisis.
5 See UN Human Settlements Programme, *The Challenge of Slums: Global Report on Human Settlements* (London, UK: Earthscan Publications, 2003). Mike Davis, *Planet of Slums* (London, UK: Verso, 2006).
6 See, for example, Benjamin Barber, *If Mayors Ruled the World: Dysfunctional Nations, Rising Cities* (New Haven, CT: Yale University Press, 2013); United Nations Human Settlements Program, *The Quito Papers and the New Urban Agenda* (New York, NY: Routledge, 2018); Edward Glaeser, "A World of Cities: The Causes and Consequences of Urbanization in Poorer Countries" (NBER Working Paper No. 19745, National Bureau of Economic Research, 2013); Richard Florida and Benjamin Schneider, "The Global Housing Crisis" (City Lab, April 11, 2018, https://www.citylab.com/equity/2018/04/the-global-housing-crisis/557639/ [accessed June 24, 2019]), and Florida's "Why So Many Emerging Megacities Remain So Poor" (City Lab, January 16, 2014, https://www.citylab.com/life/2014/01/why-so-many-mega-cities-remain-so-poor/8083/ [accessed June 24, 2019]).
7 Stewart Brand, *Whole Earth Discipline: An Ecopragmatist Manifesto* (New York, NY: Viking, 2009): 29.
8 In 2018, according to the World Atlas, the world's largest city, Shanghai, had a population of 24,256,800 and was followed by Beijing, Delhi, Lagos (16 million), Tianjin, Karachi, Istanbul, Tokyo, Guangzhou, and Mumbai (at number 10, with

12.4 million). New York City clocked in at number 24, with a mere 8.5 million inhabitants (World Atlas, "The 10 Largest Cities in the World," last updated November 2, 2018, https://www.worldatlas.com/articles/the-10-largest-cities-in-the-world.html [accessed June 24, 2019]). Of course, these numbers are highly volatile: the rankings change considerably depending on how the urban area is defined, and African and Asian cities are growing at rates that tend to push them higher and higher on the list from one year to the next.

9   See Patrice Nganang, "Le roman des détritus," *Matatu* 33: 242. One need only think of works like Wole Soyinka's *The Lion and the Jewel* (1951), Chinua Achebe's *No Longer at Ease* (1960), or Eza Boto's (a.k.a. Mongo Beti) *Ville cruelle* (1971) for confirmation. (This list could be extended at will.) Ian Munro makes a related point in "Mapping the Postcolonial Metropolis," in *Representing Minorities: Studies in Literature and Criticism*, ed. Larbi Touaf and Soumia Boutkhil (Newcastle, UK: Cambridge Scholars Press, 2006).

10 A short list of comparable *bas-fonds* works from Africa could start with fiction by Ousmane Sembène and Djibril Diop Mambéty (Sénégal), Mabanckou (Congo), Ben Okri, Chris Abani, and Helon Habila (Nigeria), Naïma Lahbil Tagemouati and Mahi Binebine (Morocco), Waberi (Djibouti), David Gitonga's film *Nairobi Half Life* (Kenya), and Athol Fugard's township plays (South Africa). From there it would have to spread out to take into account the truly global scope of the urbanization problematic and the literature that goes along with it. Again, a brief list would have to include works from India (from Satyajit Ray to Vikas Swarup), Turkey (Orhan Pamuk, Latife Tekin), Latin America, and the Caribbean (Carolina Maria de Jesus, Paulo Lins, Patrick Chamoiseau, Orlando Patterson, Earl Lovelace, C. L. R. James, and Pedro Juan Guttierez), to name but a few.

11 Rem Koolhaas, "Pearl River Delta," in *Great Leap Forward*, ed. Chuihua J. Chung and Bernard Chang (Cologne, Germany: Taschen, 2001), 27.

12 Ananya Roy, "Urban Informality: Toward an Epistemology of Planning," *Journal of the American Planning Association* 71, no. 2 (2005): 147. This is also a central thesis of A. E. Pieterse and AbdouMaliq Simone's edited volume, *Rogue Urbanism: Emergent African Cities* (Auckland Park, South Africa: Jacana Media, 2013).

13 For more on the relative lack of reach of these novels, in particular *Attiéké*, see Ute Fendler, "*Un attiéké pour Elgass* de Tierno Monénembo: Une écriture en fugue ou la tresse narrative," in *Litteratures et societes africaines: Regards comparatistes et perspectives interculturelles: mélanges offerts à János Riesz à l'occasion de son soixantième anniversaire*, ed. Papa Samba Diop, Hans-Jürgen Lüsebrink, Ute Fendler, and Christoph Vatter (Tübingen, Germany: Gunter Narr Verlag, 2001), 493.

14 See Frantz Fanon, *The Wretched of the Earth* (New York, NY: Grove Press, 2004), especially 81, where he describes the *lumpenproletariat* of the shanty towns as the "spearhead" of the inevitable anti-colonial rebellion.

15 Tierno Monénembo, *Les écailles du ciel* (Paris, France: Éditions du Seuil, 1986), 157. This and all following translations from *Les écailles du ciel* are my own.

16 Tierno Monénembo, *Un attiéké pour Elgass* (Paris, France: Éditions du Seuil, 1993), 51. All translations from this novel are my own.

17 See, on this subject, Henry John Drewal's writings on Mami Wata, for example: *Mami Wata: Arts for Water Spirits in Africa and Its Diasporas*, with Marilyn Houlberg (Los Angeles, CA: Fowler Museum at UCLA, 2008).

18 Xavier Garnier, "Poétique de la rumeur: L'exemple de Tierno Monénembo," in *Cahiers d'études africaines* 35, no. 140 (1995): 892, passim. The Deleuzian and Glissantian resonances of this vocabulary are clear.
19 See, for example, Alfredo Brillembourg Tamayo, Kristin Feireiss, and Hubert Klumpner, *Informal City: Caracas Case* (Munich, Germany: Prestel, 2005).
20 It is in this sense, I think, that the Nigerian writer Maïk Nwosu, another novelist of the *bas-fonds*, writes of "markets of memories." See his *Markets of Memories: Between the Postcolonial and the Transnational* (Trenton, NJ: Africa World Press, 2011). See also his novel *Invisible Chapters* (Lagos, Nigeria: House of Malaika & Hybun, 2001), which uses a discursive strategy related to Monénembo's to get across a sense of the power dynamics in the *bas-fonds*.
21 Roy's instinct is always to make social justice the primary goal, but she nonetheless concludes that it would be a mistake to let the perfect be the enemy of the good. Thus, all four of Roy's recommendations for an epistemology of urban informality have an incremental feel to them: (1) mastering "the politics of shit" (i.e., getting authorities to focus on addressing basic needs); (2) ensuring the right to participate in the market; (3) strategically using the state of exception; and (4) scale jumping (i.e., scaling up successful local strategies).

6

Questions of Diversity in the Global Literary Ecology and *banlieue* Literature

Laura Reeck

For the last ten years, it has been a nettlesome proposition to define or move freely between cultural production in French and the world scale. The 2007 "Pour une littérature-monde en français" manifesto suggested that the time had come to end the division between the "French" and "Francophone" categories and sign the death certificate of Francophone literature, making way for a world-literature in French. Meanwhile, in "Cinéma-monde: Towards a concept of Francophone cinema" (2012), film scholar Bill Marshall held the Francophone category in place as useful and meaningful—in fact, his theorization turned on considering the whole of French-language cinema as "Francophone cinema."[1] The manifesto and the article obviously travel in opposite directions, but both grapple with the "Francophone" label and the opportunity or obstacle it provides in globalizing French-language cultural production. Having such a category that notionally locates cultural production beyond metropolitan France has created a divide between "French" and "Francophone" and has at the same time complicated expression for French-language cultural production on the world scale. Somewhat ironically, some of the very same signatories of "Pour une littérature-monde en français" (e.g., Tahar Ben Jelloun, Maryse Condé, Henri Lopès, and Alain Mabanckou) have already been discussed through the lens of world literature, in large part because they have circulated in translation in English.

The "Pour une littérature-monde en français" manifesto spearheaded by Michel Le Bris and Jean Rouaud asserted that based on the 2006 literary prize season, in which numerous non-native French writers received France's top literary awards, the periphery had become the center of French-language letters. Here periphery means the Francophone periphery, especially those ex-colonies in which French remains a spoken and literary language. One of the main tenets of the manifesto was to pull apart the relationship between the French language and nation: from a world-systems perspective, now it was time to speak of a world literature in French with no core and no periphery. The manifesto contains a number of blind spots, one of them consisting in not making any reference to an internal literary periphery in France and its *banlieue* literature despite the fact that the manifesto came on the heels of the 2005 urban riots in the *banlieues*, and a wave of literature issued from them in the wake.[2] Only months after the "Pour une littérature-monde en français" manifesto, a group of multiethnic writers from the *banlieues*, the collective Qui fait la France?, also released a literary manifesto, but they were asking into the world of French letters, not to dismantle or reorganize it.[3]

In what follows, I engage with the argument Alexander Beecroft makes in *An Ecology of World Literature: From Antiquity to the Present Day* (2015), specifically in his final chapter entitled "Global Literature." In a survey of the literary environment of the world in the contemporary era, Beecroft moves away from a world-systems line of analysis, indeed away from both the object and the system of world literature, and instead attends to the highly variegated and more fluid conceptualizations of global literature and the global literary ecology. What comes under consideration in the latter is how all of French-language literature relates to the total literary production of the world; the global literary ecology serves therefore as a means and scale for examining the complex relationships and networks that languages and/or literatures enter into. Interesting in regard to the abovementioned blind spot of "Pour une littérature-monde en français" is that *banlieue* literature is always already included in this ecology, as are all extant literatures. A related consequence in using the global literary ecology as the basis for discussion is that it minimizes the long-standing divide between the French and Francophone literary categories as well as partitions within the Francophone literary category itself. Outlining two different pathways forward, one toward more pluralism and the other toward greater monoculture, Beecroft weighs and balances languages and literatures against the forces acting on them by considering variables such as the number of language speakers, the number of works published, the number of works translated, original and translated languages, the number of cultural and publishing centers, genres published and circulated, and so on. All of this leads to conjectures on possible literary futures.

In relation to the present essay, we must ask why the ecological analogy holds analytical power. A short answer is that ecology concerns itself with the organization of constituent and interrelated parts, all dependent upon each other, and is further interested in the impact of the external environment on a given ecosystem. And so, as an organizational analogy, it is at once spatial (internal and external environments with a conceptual border) and has a temporal dimension when considering the best conditions for the continuance and flourishing of a given ecosystem—what will hold the ecosystem in balance over time and allow it to remain productive. But the foremost reason the ecological analogy resonates in my chapter is that it includes at its crux some related and germane concepts such as diversity, productivity, and stability. In an ecological system, biodiversity is the basis of productivity and stability, and so the stability, or, we could say, sustainability, and productivity of this system depend upon its diversity.[4] Moving over to the global literary ecology, Beecroft finds a parallel: "Beyond sheer size (demographics) and ecological factors, such as the strength of literary institutions or the wealth and literacy of native speakers, I would suggest that there are factors of diversity that are likely to matter."[5] Some of those correlated factors of diversity that matter the most in his analysis range from readership to the array of literary forms—as a rule, the more readers, the more writers, the more hubs, the more nodes for publishing, the more literary varieties, the more experiences captured in those literary varieties, the better for any given literary ecosystem and by extension for the global literary ecology.

Of interest here, then, are the admittedly different scales of the global literary ecology, the French national ecosystem, and the specific case of *banlieue* literature. While other theorizations of world or global literature might look to dispense with the national altogether, I would argue that it is not yet time to do so in the relatively solipsistic French context, which Beecroft also points to as being "a much more highly monocentric, and thus monocultural, literary tradition than English" (266). We do not need to debate whether or not the French national ecosystem and *banlieue* literature take part in the same global literary ecology—they do. Rather, we need to better understand what each of these scales tells us about the others in their points of contact and overlap, and how they coexist in mutually influencing ways. Thus, I look first at the linguistic environment in France and the evolution of *banlieue* literature, signaling obstacles and unevenness as they relate to the containment or exclusion of "langue de banlieues" and *banlieue* literature. Despite these constraints or limitations, I show that *banlieue* literature has grown organically and exponentially over the last twenty years. Then, I ask how the geo-located, sometimes hyperlocal, place narratives of *banlieue* literature fit into the global literary ecology.

1. Measuring Linguistic Diversity in France with "Langue de banlieues"

In the global literary ecology, there are several key factors at play with each other, namely *the linguistic, literary language*, and *literary* phenomena, all of which naturally influence each other: a linguistic environment influences literary language, which, in turn, influences literature. The French case retains particular interest if we consider English and French as the two "*sui generis* languages in the global ecology" (259).[6] In his analysis, Beecroft attributes to French an equal status as English because of the former's comparable (though not equal) global reach, defined as "political and economic power, geographic and demographic weight."[7] It follows that the greater the size and diversity of a language, the greater the chances for viability and survival in a competitive linguistic environment. Correspondingly, however, "there are arguable dangers for a literary language in being small and concentrated (or even large and concentrated)."[8] What is under consideration here is the parenthetical case, and thus the less common of the two—French as a "super-central" language that remains highly concentrated on some measures and may lack diversity on others.[9] While there is admittedly a huge range of expression across the Francophone world, here emphasis falls on the French language in metropolitan France. Specifically, knowing that "langue de banlieues" became essential to the literary language of *banlieue* writing is important here because it brings into focus considerations on linguistic invention, diversity, and the provincialization of difference.

The promotion and the protection of standardized French, which originated from the Francilien dialect spoken around Paris in the Middle Ages, is most notoriously upheld by the Académie Française founded in 1634 by Cardinal Richelieu. In addition to setting the rules for what is acceptable and unacceptable as regards the French language and *bon usage*, the Académie Française is also one of the driving forces to limit the constitutional status of regional and minoritarian languages in France.[10] It is significant that, to this day, France has not ratified the European Charter for Regional or Minority Languages, with successive governments refusing to make the constitutional amendment that would nuance the second article (dating from 1992) to the Préambule of the Constitution, "La langue de la République est le français."[11] The driving argument against it is that doing so would undermine French as the national language and create linguistic communities, which might then politicize regional and minoritarian groups or lead to the *communautarisme* that the French political spectrum opposes in a right-left consensus. All this is to say that centripetal forces have been acting on the French language for centuries and have accordingly informed French language policy and instruction in the national educational system.[12]

As regards literary language, some irreverence toward language is necessary, however, for inventiveness and even style. Meanwhile, one factor in the provincialization of *banlieue* writing has been its variation, which ties directly to the "parler des banlieues," "langue des cités," "langue des banlieues," or "langage de la banlieue," as it has variably been referenced across popular and specialized journalistic writing as well as in scholarship.[13] Though views on this new linguistic form have varied, sociologists and linguists have agreed that it originated as an in-group language among youth responding to their experience of disadvantage in the lived and social environment of the *banlieues défavorisées*, now oftentimes referenced as *quartiers populaires*. Critics also agree on its combination of borrowed words, most especially from dialectal Arabic and "la langue des Gitans," the slang of *verlan*, and forms common to working-class slang from the 1960s.[14] In a study on *verlan*, linguist Albert Valdman links the latter two through comparison extending back further in time: "A form of hip slang, *verlan* is quickly becoming the marker *par excellence* for young people living in the projects in what was formerly the radical-left *banlieue*. Since the end of the nineteenth century, working-class poor from the capital who have grown increasingly excluded from France's post-industrial economy have been declassed here."[15] What is of particular interest in this comment is the comparison of *banlieue* youth with the ex-centered working class of the nineteenth century who inhabited the *banlieue rouge*.

In an early 1997 article, "Trafic de mots en banlieue: du 'nique ta mère' au 'plaît-il?,'" sociologist and writer Azouz Begag pointed to hazards in this new linguistic form, and, among them, he cites amalgamation, over-generalization, and *positivization*. To counter these, he affirms, there is not one "langue de banlieues," but rather location-specific variants. The form in question, he also notes, does not originate with itself but rather combines linguistic precedents and elements as described earlier. And he points out, too, that seeing this new linguistic form in terms of creativity and vitality masks the fact that its speakers struggle to adapt to social communication norms outside of it. Begag suggests that the "langue des banlieues" holds no potential for evolution and will only serve to contain and isolate an already-vulnerable population.[16] A more positive view comes from Nadia Duchêne, who also locates the in-group element (through her use of a "language community") as well as the historic precedents in slang from the faubourgs in the nineteenth and early twentieth centuries. Duchêne insists on the creation and possibilities inherent to the "langue de la banlieue." Returning to the dictionary *Tchatche de banlieue* (1998), Duchêne classifies its 729 lexical items into word origin groups; in terms of the largest percentages found, 18 percent of the lexical items come from *verlan*, and an astonishing 69 percent are neologisms. Duchêne references a further degree of flexibility and invention in the fact that because the "langue de la banlieue" functions as a coded language, when a given lexical item has been appropriated by mainstream speakers, it often undergoes a further mutation to prevent its recuperation. Observing that research intensified at the turn of the twenty-first century, Duchêne notes "a fascination for the language of the *banlieue* comparable to the fascination that existed at the end of the nineteenth and beginning of the twentieth centuries for slang."[17] Finally, and very interestingly, as Maria Candea has shown in her extensive work including "La notion d'accent de banlieue à l'épreuve du terrain" (2017), this new language goes beyond lexical items to include differences in pronunciation, vocabulary, and prosody—she sees it in stylistic and fluid terms, and, as to the first aspect, she relates variation in standard pronunciation back to the French spoken in the working-class *banlieues* in the 1960s.

While early research on the "langue de banlieues" most often characterized it as a linguistic form born of exclusion that could only lead to further exclusion, the form has generalized and has come to take part in youth culture in France. Regarding this point, writer Rachid Santaki has offered in an interview an intriguing and compelling view on the evolution of the idiom: he notes that whereas early in his writing career he got comments back from editors or publishers who wanted him to alter and standardize his literary language, he has had few remarks of this sort in recent years, which he attributes to general interest in the "langue de banlieues" and specific interest by editors "interested in this material that reads as authentic."[18] He goes on to note, on the same occasion, that this new French language ("cette langue française") has found its way not only to spoken conversation among youth but also to youth-targeted film (including Pixar voice-overs), rap, and social media. As to its status, Santaki affirmed, "I consider it a language unto itself, it's another language. . . . It's more vibrant than regional languages in France, especially because it's constantly being fed by music, the Internet, and social media." Interestingly, he compares it to Breton and to other minoritarian languages, suggesting that it might be the most relevant "regional" language in France because of its strong connection to other contemporary cultural forms.

This short overview points to forces acting on the linguistic environment in France that contain linguistic diversity and hold standardized French in place while rendering everything else a derivation or deviation from it. Regional and minoritarian languages as well as "langue de banlieues" speak directly to the diversity of people living in France, but with that they bring the potential of disrupting "abstract individualism," which has historically typified the idealized French citizen.[19] Further, the historical analogy provides important insight: like the proletarian "accent" from the 1960s, "langue de banlieues" has often been characterized as impoverished and provincial, an assessment nonetheless contradicted by research on it as well as by its power to generalize and expand within French society. Finally, while it can be seen as a vernacular language in that it differs from official and standard language, "langue de banlieues" has found its way into literary language in the case of *banlieue* literature, perhaps with a certain cost as *banlieue* literature has itself in turn been provincialized.

2. Locating *BanLit*, Watching It De-center

The evolution of *banlieue* literature has been rapid over the last twenty years; though for writers securing a publisher and full reception have been obstacles, *banlieue* literature has expanded considerably. In this respect, it is remarkable that a literary form with few environmental advantages has grown in the way that it has. To begin a look at the evolution of *banlieue* literature, it will be useful to review the origins of *banlieue* literature as place-based narratives and also as narratives intimately concerned with safeguarding diversity of literary language and expression. While Beur literature gets traced back to Mehdi Charef's *Le Thé au Harem d'Archi Ahmed* (1983), the novel could similarly be seen as the point of origin of *banlieue* literature in that a large part of the novel's specificity derives from its setting in the *cités* and the inclusion of *verlan* and oral texture more generally. From here, we could be led to probe the dominant traits and characteristics of *banlieue* literature. Thus, first and foremost, place matters in *banlieue* literature, which, correspondingly, has come to be viewed as a geo-located literature. Also, as we have already seen, its nonnormative literary language introduced a specificity that hinged on "langue de banlieues," and this literary production spoke to a young-adult audience in part because of this new linguistic form. Finally, *banlieue* literature could be said to turn on human-environment interaction. As Eric Prieto explains, *banlieue* literature "show[s] how the banlieue setting—which provides the environmental constraints within which these characters must operate—plays an active role in shaping their evolution. It is in this sense that they can be considered place narratives."[20]

Broadly, *banlieue* literature most often gets characterized as beginning in the middle of the 1990s and as tied into the film event of *La Haine* (1995). In addition to *La Haine*, a threshold essay appeared the same year, *Territoire d'outre ville*, in which writer-singer Mohand Mounsi provided a forward-looking treatise of sorts on how *banlieue* literature might develop as well as on the importance of developing literary forms and expression in the context of the *banlieues*. In terms of being a place narrative, Mounsi's essay conjures up a center-periphery spatial divide that has remained intact in *banlieue* writing: "I grew up in Nanterre. All you had to do was to cross the ring road to leave the world of research and knowledge and cross into the projects. . . . We lived there, a bunch of brown and black adolescents living in the Tropics."[21] Mounsi does not choose the context of the Tropics lightly, as he goes on to explain how Communist recruiters coming into the *cités* as ethnologists would have entered the Tropics at the time of the "Old" and "New" Worlds. But the Communists found "le zonard joyeux dans sa jungle" (happy rejects in their jungle) (47). This jungle may have been "exotic," because it was unfamiliar, but it was made of concrete towers that spanned the distance between sky and earth, an imagery that would become a hallmark of *banlieue* literature: "In the beginning, there were the towers. The massive towers rose up from ground to sky. They had thirty stories with bars fifteen-stories up. The whole area was encircled by intersecting highways" (47).

In this particular built environment, Mounsi recounts, he first encountered urban writing in the form of the "tags" that blanketed the walls. For him, a natural progression exists between "tags," *verlan*, and a new literary language. Speaking for young people living in the *cités* in the 1990s, Mounsi affirms: "I hope they'll come to a new written language that is rhythmic, very fast-paced, and yet extremely expressive, like tags" (79–80). Nothing in Mounsi's view of the nascent literary language suggests that it would be deviant or minorized; instead, he believes that using it to arrive at literary expression would counteract the view of *banlieue* youth as being un- or ill-cultured. In other words, acceding to the realm of literary expression was to be tantamount to a form of mobility, a means of gaining further cultural capital and becoming literary citizens. Broadly, however, the literary language of early *banlieue* literature did not establish its legitimacy, but rather located its difference from the poetico-aesthetic fiction of the French literary establishment and its literary prize system.

In its beginnings, *banlieue* literature was male-centered, fast-paced, and street-level with first-person narrators who provided original and unmediated perspectives. Its epicenter was the *cités*. No novel epitomizes this better than Rachid Djaïdani's *Boumkoeur*, in which the author-character Yaz intends to write the memoirs of his *cité*. He determines to write a first-person place narrative as a corrective to having the *banlieues* written about from the outside-in by journalists; his account will be written from the inside-out. But in a surprising volte-face, Yaz sets his manuscript on life in the *cités* on fire at the end of *Boumkoeur* and asks the reader to visit in person; with this gesture, the author issues a challenge of proximity to the reader and also hints at the difficult task facing writers seeking to represent the *banlieues*. A phenomenon against which Djaïdani can be seen to work in *Boumkoeur* and his subsequent novels and films is "naturalization," namely how difference gets produced and then normalized and stereotyped. Ultimately, by opting out of interpreting, explaining, or rationalizing difference in his context, his author-character refuses to take part in normalizing.

As sociologist and writer Kaoutar Harchi suggests, that normalization involves a power differential and dynamic. When culture is normalized, assertions such as "banlieue youth naturally like rap music" formalize and harden, but what gets abstracted are the structural and contextual elements that contribute to the normalization.[22] What results in some cases is what Djaïdani has called "intellectual discrimination," which he first encountered when editors from Seuil accused him of having used a ghostwriter to write *Boumkoeur* on the assumption that he alone could not have written it and then experienced again as he began working on his second novel: "But the worst was with *Mon Nerf* . . . because they gave me the impression that an Arab had to write about the *banlieue* and nothing else. That's an example of intellectual discrimination."[23] As regards the status of writer, Harchi turns to Pierre Bourdieu to ask, "who creates creators?" and what forms of domination exist within the highly regarded literary domain in France. One particularity of this domain in the French context is the long-standing romantic ideology of the artistic creator who has not been created and thus escapes all forms of social determinism, which translates to culture and especially to the arts occupying a register independent and separate from social reality and social norms and obeying therefore their own logic.[24] *Banlieue* literature challenged this tradition through its literary language anchored in a particular social reality and by scrutinizing how social norms work to contain people and ideas.

Not knowing that another manifesto was afoot, the signatories of the Qui Fait la France? manifesto issued a challenge from the "ban," asking for full rights of participation "because," as they declared, "classed as *banlieue* writers, etymologically from the zone under seigneurial jurisdiction, we want to invest in the cultural field and transcend borders, and in so doing stake claims to the space that is rightfully ours—all in an aspiration to universalism."[25] As aforementioned, the irony here is that with the "Pour une littérature-monde en français" manifesto published just a few months earlier, the very same metropolitan French periphery had been skipped over and at the same time held in place—the *banlieues*, which speaks, again, to the different and unequal spheres or worlds in the proposition of a "world-literature in French." In fact, *banlieue* literature should be seen as part of "world-literature in French" as it directly engages with the world along the lines of "Pour une littérature-monde en français."

In addition to its release to *Les Inrockuptibles* and *Le Nouvel Observateur*, whose Fabrice Pliskin disparaged it—"Oh diversity," Pliskin wrote, "you are always the same. How you lack diversity"[26]—the manifesto fronted a collection of short stories, *Chroniques d'une société annoncée* (2007), and was followed by a preface featuring the commitments of the writers contributing to the collection: "In espousing reality, the literature that the collective's authors defend and produce is decidedly political and profoundly democratic. Some will no doubt deem it banal."[27] Perhaps in recognition that collectives and literary manifestos are most often bound to the avant-garde, these writers aspired to the "avant-garde du réel." In the preface, they characterize their efforts in terms of representing "invisible" France, demanding at the same time that their writing become visible and brought out of its moratorium.

Though it would be impossible to establish a causal relationship between the release of the manifesto and what occurred in its immediate aftermath, it is fair to say that what ensued was the diversification of *banlieue* literature. If the latter has ever had a pure form, it may well be in evidence in *Chroniques d'une société annoncée*, as well as in the individual novels written by the collective members in the same time frame, many of them published by Stock, who also published the short story collection. From there, the floodgates opened.[28] One notable trend was that more women writers came to the fore, in part through the collective with Guène and Habiba Mahany but also with such writers as Houda Rouane and Dali Misha Touré. In their cases, the external environment of the *banlieues* continues to impact story lines; however, inner worlds matter as much and also contribute to an understanding of the external environment: Rouane (*Pieds-blancs* 2006) explores a love relationship; Mahany (*Kiffer sa race* 2008) female friendship and solidarity; and Touré (*Confidences* 2011) the register of personal confessions. These novels probe the various facets of success and failure in personal growth and development, which is also true of Samira Al Ayachi's *La Vie rêvée de Mademoiselle S* (2009), set outside of Lille, and also of Beyala's literary return to the *banlieue* context with *Le Roman de Pauline* (2009).

Another notable twenty-first-century trend has been toward figurative and prospective writing, while holding the *banlieues* in balance.[29] Kaoutar Harchi's *Zone cinglée* (2009) served as a shock wave in its science-fiction perspective on a *cité* in which a war pits an army of mothers against an army of children as they differ over the demographic reality and future of their *cité*. The mothers seek to raise a new generation of children who will be exclusively protected from the negative influences of drugs and crime. It has since been characterized as a dystopian novel and studied alongside Disiz's *René* as a novel of anticipation.[30] In other cases, this adjustment to possible futures speaks to the current sociopolitical climate in France, including the rise of the Front National and tribalism gaining currency. Notable here are Sabri Louatah's *Les Sauvages* (2011) and Insa Sané's *Gueule de bois* (2009), the second of which produces an alternate history around President Barack Obama's being assassinated shortly after his election.[31] More recently, Karim Amellal published *Bleu Blanc Noir* (2016), which imagines the immediate future after another presidential election, in this case one produced after a woman extreme-rightest president won the 2017 elections.

Another generic turn that *banlieue* literature has taken is toward the thriller with writers such as Karim Madani and Santaki. One of the most interesting and innovative writers in this regard is Jilali Hamham, who got himself an appointment in Rivages Noirs editor and director François Guérif's office by posing as a journalist only to hand Guérif the completed manuscript to *MachiAdam* (2012), his first novel.[32] Hamham's second novel, *93 Panthers* (2017), moves between Seine-Saint-Denis and Angers and between two groups of terrorists—the first, a cell declaring the independence of Seine-Saint-Denis; and the second, originating in Vendée, seeking representation for its far-right political views. Neither group, each of which is radicalized and extreme, wins nor can claim victory. What is at stake once again intersects with the changing sociopolitical climate in France at present: the rise of the Far Right, the instrumentalization of religious ideology, political representation and the people who represent the electorate, collusion, and so on. We are back to the notion of *banlieue* literature today containing social experiments in fiction, "would-be, could-be" scenarios that themselves point to possible futures, in most cases possible futures that would have extreme and sometimes dire consequences. Here we can return to and affirm Prieto's assessment that *banlieue* literature can be seen to hold "laboratories of social and cultural innovation."[33] But now these laboratories are more futuristic and dystopian.

It is hard to know if all the above continue to cohere into the category of *banlieue* literature, one that has never been neat and that is much less so at present. There is no agreed-upon "canon" of *banlieue* literature; some writers might say they partake in it, while many others would say that they do not. On the one hand, salient traits do characterize *banlieue* literature: it can still be defined as consisting of place-based narratives whose primary geo-location is the *banlieues*; it continues to predominantly address a young-adult readership and to convey a decided social angle and interest on the part of writers. On the other, the normal evolutionary movement of literary and cultural forms leads them to diversify following the movement of history and ideas, and *banlieue* literature has multiplied and divided accordingly and will continue to diversify until it is no longer integral. As there is presently huge diversity within what has been called *banlieue* literature, it may well be that *banlieue* literature is coming to the end of its natural life. Today, there are no one center to *banlieue* literature, no one form, and no one name for it. It is now prospective and retrospective, male and female-authored, inner-looking and outer-facing. Whereas early *banlieue* literature centered on the Parisian *banlieues*, now *banlieues* surrounding Lille, Strasbourg, or Angers are in evidence. Now plotlines move between locations (whether intra- and extra-muros, or France and another country altogether) and inhabit the *banlieues* as the cities (not just as *cités*) that they are. In newer writing, the *banlieue*-scape is sometimes literal and sometimes figurative. This is all to say that despite the fact that *banlieue* literature has largely been contained from without, it has undergone a high level of experimentation and change, has defied getting fixed down, and today it is decidedly heterogeneous, or, we could say, de-centered.

3. Why *BanLit* Matters for the Global Literary Ecology

A cautionary note has been sounded by a range of writers, theorists, critics, and philosophers, including some of the writers featured here, who see danger in a single, homogenized story. One such writer is Chimamanda Adichie in her "The Danger of a Single Story," in which she holds that "stories matter. Many stories matter."[34] When a single story predominates, lives and places are rendered flat and incomplete. A single story is particularly dangerous when it speaks authoritatively about a group or place, thus subjecting them to stereotyping, as is the case of Africa for Adichie and the *banlieues* here. In this respect, *banlieue* literature has worked against the single story, and at the same time its own "center" had shifted.

If one function of the global literary ecology is creating greater proximity among people and experiences through the literary imagination, then shrinking views on the world and single stories are in turn a threat to it. And if the preferred future is a "non-homogenous global literary ecology,"[35] one in which English does not become a hegemon and in which novels do not become monocultural—what Tim Parks has referred to as "The Dull New Global Novel"—then it stands to reason that the global literary ecology needs the French language, literary languages, and literatures in all their diversity. As we have already seen, the French language matters to the global literary ecology in part as a counterweight or counterbalance to English—as Beecroft sees it, French is the only other sui generis language in the global literary ecology, without which we would head further in the direction of a monolingual and monocultural literary future. It stands to reason, however, that the diversity of French should also matter: the more a language diversifies, the more flexible and inclusive it becomes, and the more it stands to endure challenges and ensure sustainability, as is the case in any ecosystem. In this regard, language variations within the French national ecosystem, including "langue de banlieues," should not be disregarded. Rather, they should be seen to contribute to helping French be a global idiom in the dual sense of encompassing its own diversity and having reach in the world.

One of Beecroft's primary preoccupations is how conditions can be made favorable for "greater interconnection without greater homogenization" (279) in the global literary ecology of our shared literary future. To provincialize *banlieue* literature and to exclude its mention in discussions of "world-literature in French" is to thwart this. In an authentic global literary ecology, a "world-literature in French" should not be divided into different and unequal spheres or worlds. Instead, *banlieue* literature should be seen to matter to the French national ecosystem, which, in turn, matters to the global literary ecology. In fact, an argument could be more straightforwardly made that *banlieue* literature matters to the global literary ecology. As place narratives that provide the deep texture of a context with great complexity, they are anything but flat. Over time, *banlieue* literature has challenged uniformity, whether through nonstandard literary language or by countering the single story that has been all too often told on the *banlieues*. As it has evolved, *banlieue* literature has become more invested in thinking big and imagining big: the "would-be, could-be" scenarios that have risen to the fore in the last few years extend well beyond the *banlieue* context in France and invoke a shared future. Finally, if there has been one constant across *banlieue* literature, it has been the rejection of the monocultural and monocentric. In this way, this literary corpus holds diversity itself at its core. For its own best possible future, the global literary ecology needs precisely this type of literature to be one dimension of the globalness of French-language literature.

Notes

1 See Bill Marshall, "Cinéma-monde? Towards a concept of Francophone cinema," *Francosphères* 1, no. 1 (2012): 35–51.
2 See Charles Murphy, "The Postcolonial Manifesto: Partisanship, Criticism and the Performance of Change," in *Transnational French Studies: Postcolonialism and Littérature-Monde*, ed. Alec G. Hargreaves, Charles Forsdick, and David Murphy, 67–86 (Liverpool, UK: Liverpool University Press, 2010); Stève Puig, "Littérature-monde et littérature urbaine: deux manifestes, même combat?" *Nouvelles francographies* 2, no. 1 (2011): 87–95; Laura Reeck, "The World and the Mirror

in Two Twenty-first-Century Manifestos," in Hargreaves, Forsdick, and Murphy, *Transnational French Studies*, 258–73.

3   It goes without saying that the *banlieues* are themselves not one and the same. In this chapter, *banlieues* (used in the plural) refers to urban areas also called *banlieues défavorisées* or *banlieues populaires*.

4   On these biological relationships, see Elsa E. Cleland, "Biodiversity and Ecosystem Stability," *Nature Education Knowledge* 3, no. 10 (2011), https://www.nature.com/scitable/knowledge/library/biodiversity-and-ecosystem-stability-17059965 (accessed July 13, 2018).

5   Alexander Beecroft, *An Ecology of World Literature: From Antiquity to the Present Day* (New York, NY: Verso, 2015), 248.

6   Beecroft, *An Ecology*, 259.

7   Beecroft, "World Literature Without a Hyphen: Towards a Typology of Literary Systems," *New Left Review* 54 (November–December 2008), 99.

8   Beecroft, *An Ecology*, 247.

9   The classification into "peripheral," "central," "super-central," and "hyper-central" in Beecroft derives from Abram De Swaan's typology. See Abram De Swaan, "Language Systems," in the *Handbook of Language and Globalization*, ed. Nikolas Coupland (Hoboken, NJ: Wiley Blackwell, 2010), 56–76.

10 The Académie Française has been one of the most vocal bodies to oppose enshrining regional and minoritarian languages into the Constitution. See "La langue de la République est le français" (http://www.academie-francaise.fr/actualites/la-langue-de-la-republique-est-le-francais [accessed June 2, 2019]) for a June 12, 2008, consensus statement against an amendment to Article 1 of the Constitution.

11 Former president François Hollande made a campaign promise to write a provision for the charter into the French Constitution so that it could be ratified, but his attempts to do so failed and reignited a long-standing debate about the indivisibility of French as the lone national language. See Geoffrey Roger and Julia DeBres, "Langues de France et Charte européenne des langues régionales et minoritaires: inventaire critiques des arguments anti-ratification," *Sociolinguistic Studies* 11, no. 1 (2017): 131–52.

12 Most recently, the Académie Française has grappled with calls for gender-inclusive writing in the French language. Proponents argue that there is no gender neutral in French, namely, that gender neutral is set to a masculine default. Academicians view this as an ideological and politicized battle. See statement by Academician Michel Serres at http://www.academie-francaise.fr/la-bataille-ideologique ("La bataille idéologique," April 6, 2018, accessed June 2, 2019). On the flip side, linguist Maria Candea makes a compelling argument against the continued exclusivity of the French language. See a relevant interview with Candea at https://www.revue-ballast.fr/maria-candea-langage-politique/ ("Le langage est politique," interview by *Ballast*, September 8, 2017, accessed June 2, 2019).

13 Each of these coinages confers a different status to this new linguistic form, implying in some cases a spoken language and in others a written language. For my part, I have chosen to use "langue de banlieues."

14 For one of the most compelling examples of inclusion of "la langue des Gitans," see Jilali Hamham's *MachiAdam* (2011), first set in a *banlieue* outside of Angers.

15 Albert Valdman, "La Langue des faubourgs et des banlieues: de l'argot au français populaire," *The French Review* 73, no. 6 (May 2000): 1190.

16 Somewhat paradoxically, in *Le Gone du Chaâba* (1986), Azouz Begag provides dictionaries to assist the reader with the diglossic nature of spoken language in the novel. He supplies one for his young narrator, "Petit dictionnaire des mots azouziens," and two for the narrator's Algerian immigrant father, "Petit dictionnaire de mots bouzidiens" and "Guide de la phraséologie bouzidienne." See Daniel Delas, "Les parlers jeunes dans deux romans littéraires d'Azouz Begag à Thierry Jonquet," *Le Français aujourd'hui* 4, no. 143 (2003): 89–96.

17 Nadia Duchêne, "Langue, immigration, culture: Paroles de la banlieue française," *Meta* 47, no. 1 (March 2002): 33.

18 Rachid Santaki, Interview with Pierre Labainville, "Quel statut pour le parler des banlieues?," *On parle média*, July 4, 2017, https://onparlemedia.wordpress.com/2017/07/04/quel-statut-pour-le-parler-des-banlieues/ (accessed July 13, 2018).

19 For a fuller discussion on "abstract individualism" in relation to idealized French citizenship, see, for example, the introduction to Joan Wallach Scott's *The Politics of the Veil* (Princeton, NJ: Princeton University Press, 2007), 1–20.

20 About *banlieue* novels and films, Eric Prieto writes: "They portray their protagonists as explorers on the cutting edge of French social evolution—innovators who are deeply, and sometimes successfully, engaged in the search for new solutions to the ongoing social malaise of the *banlieues*." See Prieto's *Literature, Geography, and the Postmodern Poetics of Place* (New York, NY: Palgrave, 2013), 116.

21 Mohand Mounsi, *Territoire d'outre ville* (Paris, France: Stock, 1995), 47.

22 Kaoutar Harchi, Interview with Lauren Bastide, "Les Savantes," FranceInter.fr, July 28, 2018, https://www.franceinter.fr/emissions/les-savantes/les-savantes-28-juillet-2018, 15:15 (accessed November 21, 2018).

23 Rachid Djaïdani, Interview with lemagazineinfo, April 8, 2007, http://www.lemagazine.info/?Interview-Rachid-Djaidani (accessed December 4, 2018).

24 Harchi, Interview, 16:43.

25 Collectif Qui fait la France?, *Chroniques d'une société annoncée* (Paris, France: Stock, 2007), 8.

26 Fabrice Pliskin, "Un nouveau mouvement littératire, Qui fait la France? Nous!," *Le Nouvel Observateur*, September 6, 2007, https://bibliobs.nouvelobs.com/actualites/20070919.BIB0087/qui-fait-la-france-nous.html (accessed December 3, 2018).

27 Collectif Qui fait la France?, *Chroniques*, 12–13.

28 Forms, too, have changed and include *bande dessinée* (e.g., Farid Boudjellal, the Gargouri sisters), pamphlet-writing such as *La Guerre des banlieues n'aura pas lieu* (Abd Al Malik 2011), *Place de la République* (Abd Al Malik and Wallen 2015) and *La France de demain* (Brahim Chikhi and Rachid Santaki 2015), and novels including a soundtrack (e.g., Insa Sané, Kaoutar Harchi, Rachid Santaki).

29 For a review of *banlieue* literature from 2000 to 2015, see Christina Horvath, "Écrire la banlieue dans les années 2000-2015," in *Banlieues vues d'ailleurs*, ed. Bernard Wallon (Paris, France: CNRS Editions, 2016), 47–67.

30 See Rebecca Blanchard, "Carceral States in Kaoutar Harchi's *Zone Cinglée*," *Romance Studies* nos. 1–2 (2018): 63–75; Stève Puig, "Banlieue et dystopie en littérature urbaine: Les cas de *Zone cinglée* et *René*," *Itinéraires: Littérature, Textes, Culture* 3 (2016), https://journals.openedition.org/itineraires/3546 (accessed December 4, 2018).

31 Insa Sané deserves particular mention here for his "Comédie Urbaine" spanning five novels from *Sarcelles-Dakar* (2006) to *Cancres de Rousseau* (2017), the last of which

serves as a prequel to the other four novels. With it, he invokes Balzac's "Comédie Humaine," using the *banlieues*, namely Sarcelles, as his contemporary microcosm.

32 See Chrystel Chabert, "'93 Panthers': Jilali Hamham conjugue violence et élégance du verbe," *Culture Box*, last updated March 7, 2017, https://culturebox.francetvinfo.fr/livres/policier/93-panthers-jilali-hamham-conjugue-violence-et-elegance-du-verbe-25330920 (accessed December 3, 2018), for more on how Hamham got an initial meeting with Guérif.

33 Prieto, *Literature*, 116.

34 Chimamanda Adichie, "The Danger of a Single Story," filmed July 2009 for TEDGlobal, video, 17:55, https://www.ted.com/talks/chimamanda_adichie_the_danger_of_a_single_story?language=en (accessed December 15, 2018).

35 Beecroft, *An Ecology*, 250.

7

As the World Falls Apart: Living through the Apocalypse in Christian Guay-Poliquin's *Le poids de la neige* and Catherine Mavrikakis's *Oscar de Profundis*

Vincent Gélinas-Lemaire

> Everything lived had already tumbled into nothingness, but some prose would survive. Maybe that was how things were mostly meant to be enjoyed. (*Tout le vécu avait déjà basculé dans le néant, mais de la prose allait survivre. C'était peut-être surtout comme cela qu'il fallait apprécier les choses.*)
>
> —Antoine Volodine, *Dondog*

Québec literature enjoys a long, meandering history defined by a diversity of literary voices and by their unstable appropriation of the national past. Culturally balanced between Europe and America but protective of their distinct identities, these authors have always been aware of a wavering distance between their microcosm and the struggles and contests of the rest of the world. As such, it is no surprise that contemporary Québécois writers would address, through fiction, the strengthening pull of a globalized society with its dominant rules, codes, products, languages, and appetites. However, despite its sensitivity to outside contexts, Québec literature has not yet echoed widely beyond its national borders. Few of its authors have succeeded in taking a seat at the big table of World Literature, be that defined by Johann Wolfgang von Goethe, Pascale Casanova, or David Damrosch. In *Le roman sans aventure*, where she recently addressed this very question, Isabelle Daunais asserts that Québec's quiet history, with its centuries of peace beyond the reach of most wars and natural catastrophes, has compelled the region's writers to craft tales steeped in a state of enduring contentment. For this reason, the protagonists of Québécois novels are not prone to facing, enduring, and overcoming experiences capable of transforming them viscerally or of reshaping their worldview in a radical and lasting manner. They are too firmly anchored to the conditions of what Daunais names *l'idylle*. "This term, I believe," writes Daunais, "perfectly defines the Québécois experience of the world.

That is because *l'idylle* does not here designate a pure and marvelous world, expunged from all worry, from all adversity or from all hardship, but, more modestly or more concretely—and at the same time more terribly—the state of a world that is pacified, of a world without combat, of a world that rejects adversity."[1]

One of the most recognizable symptoms of this peculiar isolation is the desire of innumerable protagonists of Québécois novels to remain cloistered in their homes and, oftentimes, to retreat further still into the reassuring confines of their bedroom. From the snowed-in cabins of the rural novel to the intimate insurgencies of the *Révolution tranquille* all the way to computerized cocoons in the present, these characters find comfort, growth, and meaning by looking inwards, behind closed doors. This peculiar spatiality is now taking on new shapes and a new meaning as it molds itself after the rising trend of apocalyptic and postapocalyptic fiction. While end-of-days scenarios are not unknown to the Québécois literary corpus—tales of wintry isolation and of twisted family tragedies abound—contemporary authors now work with codes explicitly borrowed from foreign fiction. Studying their take on the genre will allow us to observe how they negotiate the assimilation of a global, but ever closer, cultural movement into the national literary tradition, with its own geographies, characters, doubts, drives, and memories.

1. Contemporary Québécois Literature in Context

If, indeed, Québec literature remains unfamiliar to many foreign readers, it should help as we delve into the novels that will be at the center of this chapter to recall some essential moments of this literature's history and provide some significant points of reference. A first key period extends from the beginning of the British occupation of Nouvelle-France—sanctioned by the 1763 Treaty of Paris—to the first decades of the twentieth century. French Canadian literature was then focused on a local readership and on its desire to process the historical shock of regime change. Some authors would thus peer backward to outline the defining traits of a sturdy and noble, albeit lost, primeval society. Thus, *Les Anciens Canadiens* (1863) by Philippe Aubert de Gaspé, one of the most popular works of its time, reenacted with nostalgia the routine, the cultural frame, and the beliefs of the pre-Conquest era. Other defining titles of this period, such as Patrice Lacombe's *La Terre paternelle* (1846), Antoine Gérin-Lajoie's *Jean Rivard, le défricheur canadien* (1862), and Louis Hémon's *Maria Chapdelaine* (1913), sustained the appeal of a traditional way of life while proposing an ethos centered on the diligence of their protagonists in taming the Canadian wilds and in establishing a life centered on family, the Catholic faith, and the survival of the French language in the Americas.

The following generations would be enmeshed in the pursuit of a just cultural distance from France and, to a lesser degree, the United States, eventually engaging in a radical shift in the 1960s. Spurred by the urban fictions of Gabrielle Roy, the tormented poetry of Anne Hébert, and the radical artistic and political claims of the *Refus global*, a new wave of authors shunned most traditional literary expectations. Some reclaimed the unique sounds and phrases of working-class Québécois speech, *joual*, and brought it to theater, while others sought to invent a novel freed from its established forms and codes. Hubert Aquin, notably, wielded an oneiric prose to take the political cause of French Canada's independence to the waters of Lake Geneva, inventing a Wolof spy to support and incarnate the narrator of his first novel, *Prochain épisode*. This gesture echoed the call made by Aquin in his manifesto, "La fatigue culturelle du Canada français" (1962), for a renewed posture on national identity, a posture he shaped with the help of essays by Léopold Senghor, Cheikh Anta Diop, and Aimé Césaire, challenging the innocuousness of cultural "universalism" and interrogating the preconditions of certain literary works' global appeal. Reflecting on the national context, he states that

> the problem is not to write stories that take place in Canada, but to assume fully and painfully the whole difficulty of one's identity.... The French Canadian denies his center of gravity, desperately looking elsewhere for a center as he wanders in all the labyrinths he may encounter. Neither hunted nor persecuted, he nonetheless relentlessly holds his country at a distance through an exoticism that never fulfills him.[2]

The same challenge was tackled, although differently, by two other major novelists of this period of intense cultural and political transformation in Québec, the *Révolution tranquille* (the Quiet Revolution). Both would stage characters faced with the choice of retreating within the confines of their homes or going out into the wider world: Marie-Claire Blais had her protagonists look outwards but find suffering and death whether they left or stayed; Réjean Ducharme preferred to have his hunker down and craft their private little microcosms. In the contemporary era, too, Québec literature and popular culture remain markedly aware of their origins, echoing a certain nostalgia for the tales of old and for such "simpler times" as were fantasized in the snow-blanketed forests of the *romans du terroir*. This self-referentiality was also reinforced by the development of the academic field of Québec studies and by its marked influence on the teaching of literature at all levels of the public curriculum. Simultaneously, the field was shaped by migrant authors who gave new roots, new poetic forms, and new expectations to the national corpus. Coming from an array of Francophone countries, authors such as Naïm Kattan, Régine Robin, Dany Laferrière, Ying Chen, and Kim Thúy have taken their place in the public and scholarly definitions of Québec literature. These definitions are now increasingly acknowledging the voices of writers from Québec's First Nations, such as those of the novelist Naomi Fontaine and of the poets Joséphine Bacon and Natasha Kanapé Fontaine, who belong to the Innu community.

Attached to these new configurations and faced with the drives and mechanisms of the contemporary world, the Québécois novel negotiates its perennial hesitation between tradition and the influence of outside forces in ways that works such as

Nicolas Dickner's *Six degrés de liberté* tackle directly. The novel follows two friends from a rural community south of Montreal as they scheme to transform an intermodal container into mobile living quarters. One character remains cloistered in his room because of his agoraphobia, hacking his way into foreign transit systems, while the other travels the world from the inside of her windowless cube, drifting along international trade lanes: squaring the circle, the novel adapts to a changing world and extends the reach of its story beyond national borders while at the same time shutting its reader out of the landscapes and cultures waiting outside the characters' padded rooms.

This chapter will allow us to study this encounter between tradition and globalization in the narrower but perhaps more acute context of present-day apocalyptic novels. The genre—I use the category quite flexibly—possesses its own referential networks, borrowing from the postapocalyptic wave gripping the Anglophone sphere today, a movement energized by Cormac McCarthy's *The Road* (2006) and that now extends to all forms of popular culture, from television series and Hollywood cinema to video games and zombie walks coordinated between metropolises. Tales of broken worlds have also become a defining feature of contemporary French literature, with such varied works as Jonathan Littell's *Carnets de Homs* (2012), Jean-Yves Jouannais's *L'usage des ruines: Portraits obsidionaux* (2012), Michaël Ferrier's *Fukushima: récit d'un désastre* (2012), Elsa Boyer's *Heures creuses* (2013), Antoine Volodine's *Terminus radieux* (2014), and Jean Rolin's *Les Événements* (2014). Many such titles weave in overt political, historical, and social commentary, showing the influence of anthropological thinkers such as Henri Lefebvre, Guy Debord, Michel de Certeau, Marc Augé, and Paul Virilio on the literary representation of a globalized future.

Some of the most influential end-of-days scenarios from the Québécois national corpus would include Dany Laferrière's *Éroshima* (1987), Dickner's *Tarmac* (2009), as well as Wajdi Mouawad's theatrical opus, marked by a brutal imaginary that oscillates between Québec, war-torn Lebanon, and the allegorical landscapes of Greek myths, and full of viciousness, anger, and godly punishment.[3] Another important example, Gaétan Soucy's *La jeune fille qui aimait trop les allumettes* (1998), attracted much popular and critical attention, with its gender-bending protagonist, eerie atmosphere, and unexpectedly dark twists. The book revolves around two siblings who live within the strict limits of their father's property, their world closed off from society by a stretch of pine trees. Since the narration is focalized on the perception of the most candid sibling, we are led to picture an environment reminiscent of the idealized rurality of the *romans du terroir*, settled on the *limes* of farm and forest and neighboring a village whose characters have legible motivations and desires. The snow and the cold, as well as the colloquial expressions used by the children, indeed suggest a Québécois setting, but the lack of place names and the family's Southern French accent confound our sense of localization. While *the* world does not come undone in the novel, the family's own world, thick with secret places and buried memories, is torn asunder by the death of the father, the madness of the brother, and the belated incursion of the villagers—it is through their eyes that we can finally grasp the dystopic bent of the children's accepted normalcy. Soucy's novel sets the stage for an encounter between tradition and modernity, a confrontation that happens not only in the clash of the family with the outside world but also within the novel's own generic identity, in that the book's obvious nods to tradition serve to frame the reader's expectations, which can then be shattered by the plot's apocalyptic developments. As such, *La jeune fille qui aimait trop les allumettes* can be considered a direct precursor to the two novels I will be addressing below.

The first, *Le poids de la neige* (2016) by Christian Guay-Poliquin, also borrows its setting from such recognizable classics as *Maria Chapdelaine* and *Kamouraska*, for it mostly takes place in a rudimentary shelter beset by snow and devoid of electricity and modern modes of communication. The second, *Oscar de Profundis* (2016) by Catherine Mavrikakis, paints a catastrophe of planetary proportions, but with an insistent awareness of Québécois culture and history, if only to outline how they were lost. My goal is to pursue the generic convergence of two otherwise fundamentally different works, especially in regard to their relationship to the national tradition and to a wider Western cultural frame. Thus, I ask: Why do these two authors decide to portray a society built on the ruins of our present?[4] Does this destruction serve to expose the value of what is lost, or rather to open up new possibilities? Do the authors propose a way forward, or are their literary experiments picturing a catastrophe with no remedy? In order to answer these questions, I will survey four aspects of both novels: the spatial and social structures of their universes; the physical and mental imprisonment of their characters; the impossible or overbearing relationship of these characters with an outside world; and the leitmotiv of high culture and erudition.

2. *Le poids de la neige*

Both writers hold a double position as novelists and academics, which may explain a distinctly intertextual—and sometimes critical—dimension of their works. Guay-Poliquin, for instance, helps situate his reflections on the literary representation of survival and of the apocalypse in essays that include an MA thesis dedicated to Volodine, Pavel Hak, and Marc Villemain, as well as an article centered on *White Hunger* (2012) by the Finnish writer Aki Ollikainen, which depicts a poor family's demise during a catastrophic wintry famine.[5] He touches on literary works such as Primo Levi's *If This Is a Man*, Albert Camus's *La peste*, Michel Tournier's *Vendredi ou les Limbes du Pacifique*, and McCarthy's *The Road* and dwells on extreme fictional situations such as one's forced regression to an animal state or "to the time of origins, of beginnings," one's visceral calling to social life after long periods of isolation, or the embodiment of a group's destiny in an individual subject.[6]

The unnamed narrator of *Le poids de la neige*, Guay-Poliquin's second novel, is coming back to his village to visit his sick father, whom he is hoping to see one last time. But his car flips over, a short distance from the destination, crushing his legs and leaving him at the mercy of the villagers' help. The scenario appears to follow the oedipal conclusion of Guay-Poliquin's first novel, *Le fil des kilomètres* (2013), in which the narrator crosses a continent beset by a power outage and rising unrest only for his car to collide with his father, who is roaming the road, we are told, as the Minotaur roamed its labyrinth.[7]

While the novel is not explicitly labeled as apocalyptic or postapocalyptic, many central aspects of the setting invite such a perception. First, we notice the absence of numerous staples of contemporary life, most notably electricity and running water, while food, gas, and medical supplies are rationed by the villagers—survival, rather than comfort, progressively becomes the driving force of the characters. They have also lost all means of communication with the outside world, and as the village becomes increasingly snowed-in, they become radically isolated from any possible help and from any source of information regarding the unfolding of a vague global catastrophe. Second, the danger of the situation is amplified by the narrator's dire wounds and by the initial hesitation of the villagers to rescue him, owing to their limited resources. They find a place for him on the veranda of a secluded house and put him in the care of Matthias, a well-read old man who desperately wants to return to the city to take care of his dying wife. If the two characters are not, strictly speaking, prisoners in the village, they are certainly forced into a growing sense of claustrophobia. Third, an eerie ambience permeates the novel because of the characters' names, which are artificially limited to two initials: the "M" of Matthias and Maria (the beautiful veterinarian), and the "J" of José (her sinister husband), Joseph (the supportive watchman), and of a secondary cast consisting of Jude, Jacques, Jonas, Jacob, Jérémie, Judith, Jean, and Jannick. That being said, because the protagonists never starve nor lack medicine, the novel rarely flirts with the extreme sentiments—horror, desolation, paranoia—found in many apocalyptic novels. One macabre exception, the narrator's discovery of a dead old woman, is tempered by her pacifying burial.

As was the case in *La petite fille qui aimait trop les allumettes*, the spatial context of the novel remains indeterminate. It would nonetheless be recognizable to most readers as a rural Québec community of the present or the recent past. The most obvious clues lie in the close proximity of a river and wild forests and in the ever-thicker snow blanket. Not only does the story itself echo the constraints of snowfall, the characters losing the ability to travel and feed themselves without trouble, but Guay-Poliquin also labels each of the short chapters with the gradations of the snow gauge Matthias has planted in front of a window. As the narrator gazes through the frost-covered pane, immobilized by his broken legs, he conjures the figure of the young national poet Émile Nelligan, who famously describes such an experience in his poem "Soir d'hiver":

> Oh! how snow has snowed!
> My window is a garden of frost.
> Oh! how snow has snowed!
> What is the spasm of living
> To the pain I hold, I hold.[8]

For most of the novel, the narrator is a prisoner of his fragmented body, the image of which he sometimes discovers on a windowpane or on the glass surface of an unpowered television. He evades this reality by retreating into a silence that lasts for a quarter of the book and by readily slipping away into sleep. Matthias, although he can move freely, also feels increasingly trapped by the nursing role foisted on him. As the season progresses, he is compared to "a snowbank withering under the late winter rains," and it is said that he rusts under his forced immobility.[9] With time passing, the pressure inside the veranda becomes unbearable for the two men, but their microcosm is equipped with a safety valve that the narrator can use as he starts healing. This release takes the form of a spatial reach that incrementally extends to the deserted house, to the village, and then to a nearby lake and its abandoned dwellings. Each location provides new scenes and new supplies, relieving the boredom and hunger of the characters. While they always remain tethered to a single room—which makes for a challenging literary constraint—their growing health and focus allow them to orbit further away from this center. In the process, the narrator and Matthias are forced to learn and adopt fundamental survival tools, some of which are tied to the basics of rural life, some borrowed from native methods—such as the preparation of the pemmican, a hearty bread fortified with meat—while others are based on tactics dating back to the draft dodgers of the world wars. As such, the novel takes shape as a northern variation on Daniel Defoe's *Robinson Crusoe* and on its classic adaptation to the Québécois context in *Jean Rivard, le défricheur canadien*.

The apocalyptic texture of the novel also depends on the construction of a larger context surrounding the protagonists' microcosm. The eerie sentiment caused by the characters' peculiar names is also fueled by the absence of toponyms in the novel's cartography, these being replaced by antonomasias such as "the village" and "the city." While this poetic choice can serve to simulate a certain matter-of-factness—for there would be only one city nearby—it also imbues the narrative with an allegorical veneer that gives the story a global scope: *the* village would stand for all villages and *the* city for all cities. Furthermore, with the rising snow preventing most travel and communication, the sense of isolation in the village becomes acute, and so does the polarization of the outside world between zones of danger and salvation: a string of rumors—inexplicable, as the village is in a state of armed defense and autarchy—allows for a superficial representation of the place's surroundings. On the side of danger, the characters agree that the roads must be rife with ambushers and other desperate figures poised to steal the food and fuel of anyone reckless enough to drive to the city. This vague threat serves to keep everyone corralled as long as possible, most notably Matthias, whose expedition to the city is considered to be almost criminal as it implies his willingness to break his pact with the villagers and abandon the narrator to his fate. His attempts fail pathetically, until he finally receives the narrator's blessing. On the side of salvation, the narrating character's imagination is fixated on his uncles' hunting camp, where his family retreated after leaving him behind because of his fragile state. He repeatedly pictures life inside the cabin, focusing his gaze on the X inscribed on the vast swath of forest of his topographical map:

> At this instant, they must be loudly discussing next to the wood-burning stove. In the chaos of tangled voices and exclamations, they are probably pouring themselves a little of the strong alcohol that they preciously brought so as to

remain warm. They talk about their day out hunting or perhaps tell anecdotes from years past. They joke, mostly, interrupting and stoking one another. It is so. It is always so. And this tumult of tales, of banter and bursts of laughter certainly sweetens winter. (75)

The cabin distills the fantasy of an idealized Québécois past whose form is immediately recognizable from any number of folk tales and *romans du terroir*, with its deliberate simplicity and its hearty mode of life. Such nostalgia markedly points to the *uncles'* hunting camp, just as the villagers reminisce about how "our fathers and uncles" (150) would practice handling weapons, while women were tasked with making the shelter homely and hospitable. This gendered vision of the *good ol' days* certainly is not indifferent to the narrator's final choice at the close of the novel: having gone through a symbolic rebirth by plunging into the frozen waters of the lake, he chooses not to return to the uncertain remnants of modernity, preferring to delve into the wild forest and into his yearnings for the past.

This nostalgic withdrawal is partially counterbalanced by Matthias's own dedication to world literature. The narration, fashioned by the main character's perspective, alludes to Homer, Hesiod, Dante, Jules Verne, Samuel Beckett, and Gabriel García Márquez, while at other times underlining them clearly, as if to invite the reader to enrich the novel's frozen landscapes with bright otherworldly touches and to endow the stunted movements of its characters with an heroic scope. But Matthias's most cherished book, and one of the novel's central references, remains the Bible, a reminder of the strict Catholic tradition that defined the Québec of old. The novel nods to Noah's Ark and to the parable of the prodigal son, but it creates its most striking parallel with the story of the Nativity: in a hopeful but unresolved episode, Maria the veterinarian escapes the village with Joseph, whose carpentry skills helped preserve the protagonists' shelter from the weight of the snow. The reader will also notice that every section of the book is prefaced by a monologue—of Daedalus to his son Icarus—which has been cut into seven staggered fragments. This extradiegetic poetic layer resonates with the two main characters, Matthias serving as a father figure to the narrator. Matthias tells him of his own father's work as a *draveur* (a log driver), with a wink to the famous tale of the *chasse-galerie*, in which lumberjacks beset by snow make a pact with the devil in exchange for a flying canoe, echoing Icarus's foolhardy gamble. If Guay-Poliquin makes such marked use of intertextuality in his novel, it is not only to expand the book's scope and implications but also as a means to hybridize local legends and weave them into a larger Western context.

Together, these observations on *Le poids de la neige* point to the crucial tension of the novel. On the one hand, the novel composes a nostalgic longing for the loss or for the fantasy, rather, of a traditional way of life of rural Québec. The "end of the world" allows for a renewed sense of solidarity, musters and reactivates a lost heritage, and liberates the character from a modern world in which "we would all be watching television, with a cold beer and a frozen meal warmed in the microwave" (117). On the other hand, the author's care in erasing all toponyms and in developing his novel's intertextual network points to a certain allegorical temptation: he offers the reader the opportunity to extend the novel beyond the frame of Québécois literature and situate it in a broader, more elastic, and more widely shared tradition.

3. *Oscar de Profundis*

Catherine Mavrikakis's vision of the apocalypse in *Oscar de Profundis* is markedly darker and starker. Indeed, her novel strongly resonates with the refined, cruel, and cannibalistic fantasies of Lautréamont's *Chants de Maldoror*, with the twisted worlds of Antoine Volodine's *Dondog* (2002) and *Terminus radieux* (2014), with the gothic affectation of Marilyn Manson, with Jean Genet's delicate crimes, and with Hervé Guibert's frank relationship with disease and death. Its first lines sketch the irreversibility of the world's end:

> That night, the big, pale Moon had moved still further from the Earth. Its chilliness had obviously intensified. She appeared to shiver in the extinguished sky. For years, the planets had been distancing themselves. In their course, they were accentuating an increasingly obvious gap, as if the world here below could not seduce the cosmic immensity anymore. The young stars had disappeared. In secret, the celestial bodies were getting the hell out. . . . Only the sun still came to flirt with the horizon, all the while threatening it with an imminent, terrible rape and with infernal ardors.[10]

Nodding explicitly to the cosmic machinery of Lars von Trier's film *Melancholia* (2011), Mavrikakis immediately establishes that her narrative will not be negotiating with notions of hope or restoration: apocalyptic rather than postapocalyptic, it is set in an ongoing process of human extinction. Nevertheless, the novel reveals the lingering vitality of two contrasting groups. The first, a small number of *gueux*, of derelict outcasts, is faced with an outbreak of the "black disease," a plague seemingly engineered to kill off the miserable citizens corralled at the heart of the world's metropolises. The clan is led by one Cate Bérubé, a former doctor renowned for her ruthlessness and recognizable by the sparrow hawk flying above her head. These *gueux* must navigate a world of total misery structured by the authorities so as to deny the inhabitants any comfort or safety, with soldiers arbitrarily turning swaths of the city into no-man's-lands where they can kill without warning. On the other side, Oscar de Profundis, an acclaimed star singer and all-around cultural icon, lives the life of an aesthete, traveling the world with his large entourage. The story takes place during his reluctant return trip back to Montreal, his native city, where he is forced to confront his memories of the kidnapping and murder of his younger brother. Indifferent to the plight of the diseased, he tries to soothe himself into sleep with a mix of drugs and Wagnerian music.

One strikingly uncanny aspect of this universe lies in the way most cultural fields have been either eradicated or corralled for the pleasure of a happy few. Following international breakdowns of the Internet in 2054 and 2055, the World Government puts the blame on the "Front de libération de la Terre"—a name that resonates with that of the Front de libération du Québec, a separatist faction active in the province in the 1960s and 1970s—and convinces its citizens to double down on their use of virtual media, in a supposed effort to curb the environmental impact of book printing. In the novel's present, professors and intellectuals have thus become anachronistic shadows haunting the halls of the few remaining universities. Mavrikakis also plays with an enduring anxiety of the Québécois in having the World Government replace the use of French with that of globalized English. She makes this dissolution tangible in a few instances of quoted speech by Cate Bérubé who, despite being recognized as a superior speaker of French, weaves her Québécois expressions with a large measure of English: "*Tant pis pour eux*. I can't do anything, Mo . . . You know . . . I can't change them, now . . . *Juste une bande d'épais. Câlice . . . Ça mérite peut-être de mourir ces gens-là.*"[11] Remarkable also is the erasure of history, especially that of the generational trauma carried over from Auschwitz and the beaches of Normandy, a trauma that ripples obsessively in Mavrikakis's *Fleurs de crachats* (2005), *Sous le ciel de Bay City* (2008), and *Omaha Beach* (2008). The Holocaust and its science of death are still present in *Oscar de Profundis*, but their memory is not actively carried by the characters and their families; it is rather embodied in the full breadth of the world's driving urges and mechanisms. Children, indeed, are nowhere to be seen—the *gueux* do not procreate, and Oscar does not think beyond himself, his fame, and the commodification of his music.

The spatial context of *Oscar de Profundis* appears, in turn, easily recognizable to any reader familiar with Montreal's cultural district, its landmarks, and its streets, all of them being identified explicitly in the novel. As for the central location of the story—the mansion where Oscar and his crew hole up during the quarantine—its identity is only superficially veiled, the factual "Maison Notman" becoming the fictional "Maison Ormund." Despite this apparent precision, the city remains superficially described, allowing its representation to become overwhelmed by a recurring material lexicon of mud, rain, snow, stone, stiff soldiers, hunched masses, and corpses coated in blue disinfectant powder. On a larger scale, urban spaces are firmly divided between those of the *gueux* and those of their better peers, who are now settled in the suburbs and in protected pockets in the city. This frame, because it replicates a planetary model of tightly policed metropolises, has the effect of diluting the reader's sense of place—these suburbs are not those of Montreal but, rather, an abstraction of *the* suburb as a bastion of the bourgeoisie, a class now willfully out of touch with the sinister sides of capitalism and globalization. These competing spatial codes force the reader into an admittedly uncomfortable position, for one has to negotiate the familiar and the prospective, to weave between Montreal as a historical city—its memory maintained by a fictional avatar of the architectural activist Phyllis Lambert—and its dilution in the litany of cities on Oscar's world tour. Space, as such, enters in resonance with history, language, and culture and allows Mavrikakis to set her universe right in the middle of its dissolution into formless oblivion.

As was the case in *Le poids de la neige*, a strong claustrophobic feeling permeates *Oscar de Profundis*, affecting all characters. Hounded by the government and the plague, the *gueux* retreat into ever-tightening areas of the city until the idea of intimacy becomes unthinkable to them. Oscar, also shut in by the quarantine—albeit in the safety and luxury of the Maison Ormund—simmers among his obsessions and his ghosts. Such confinement, voluntarily or not, has become a defining trope of Québec novels, but this particular setup also bears a close affinity with des Esseintes's fabricated sensory laboratory in Joris-Karl Huysmans's *À rebours*. Cozily installed in his white box of a room, Oscar becomes, however, increasingly pulled inwards, toward his most intense and troubled memories. Chief among them is the murder of his brother in a convoluted scenario meant to replicate the kidnapping of Charles Lindbergh's son, a trauma Oscar had worked to sublimate into his artistic projects. On many occasions, he is tempted to leave his refuge with an armed escort to visit the graves of his brother and his mother at the cemetery, but he systematically prefers to wallow in a state of masochistic contentment, which he sustains with the help of a virtual-reality system and powerful anesthetics. Oscar's staunch narcissism and solipsism appear, in fact, to be the fundamental principle of his success and of his endurance inside Mavrikakis's harsh fiction: one's attachment to outside beings and institutions, to a culture and its language, and, worst of all, to the poetic notion of an everlasting humanity would constitute fatal liabilities at this stage of the world's disintegration.

Moving now from the scope of the city to that of the larger, global structure of this world, we observe such dystopic scenarios as were conceived by those anthropologists who, after Debord and Lefebvre, prophesized that Western societies would become ever more constrained by hierarchies of money and class inscribed in the concrete permanence of streets, barriers, towers, highways, and airports. While globalization would appear to work, on a superficial level, as an equalizer of opportunity, it would ultimately serve, it has been argued, to concentrate all symbolic and effective power in a few hands. Mavrikakis does not give us a clear image of the political elite of her fictional universe, choosing rather to present Oscar as a pop emperor, oblivious to the roots and stakes of his domination but decidedly invested in reaping all of its benefits. While the *gueux* are absolutely tethered to the city center, which has been sucked dry of most of its cultural patrimony and of the tools necessary to appreciate it, Oscar's own relationship with the outside world is one of absolute availability: his brand has a global reach, and he owns a private plane, travels without restrictions, and remains beholden only to a tour schedule set up by a close confidante. Investing the money made off his branding contracts, Oscar also absorbs vast swaths of the world's artistic patrimony, including famous American architectural landmarks such as the Château Marmont in Los Angeles, the Biltmore Hotel in Arizona, and Frank Lloyd Wright's Taliesin West, a famous desert retreat favored by the architect. These locations, along with other properties in Michigan, Louisiana, and Texas, serve as repositories for private collections of books and movies tailored to Oscar's tastes, allowing these artifacts a reprieve from governmentally mandated erasure. The narration, closely attached to his fantasies, indulges in the sensual experience of his exclusive ownership of classics, relishes in his performative erudition, and toys with the reader's own expected fondness for high culture. One can easily come to admire Oscar's absolute embodiment of a dandy's camp ideals, his resistance against the disappearance of whole art forms, and his retreat from society and into aesthetic sublimation. But the reader, keeping a measure of distance from the protagonist, will remain aware of the terrifying, willful blindness necessary to this mode of life and will recoil from the cultural eugenics underpinning Oscar's targeted conservation project. Simultaneously, such a character cannot fail to become laughable in his autocratic, delirious, and plaintive devotion to his personal cult, a satirical aspect that Mavrikakis acknowledges in an interview: "I laughed a lot because, for me, Oscar is a ridiculous person. It is a character in which I could concentrate all my neuroses."[12]

We discover further depths to Oscar's narcissistic project when we learn that he is developing an underground necropolis on his Michigan property. Indeed, as the World Government starts emptying cemeteries in order to gain usable space on an overpopulated planet, he is allowed to take his pick of famous corpses before they are incinerated. As one would stock a bookshelf with rare manuscripts, Oscar giddily collects the remains of "Baudelaire, Banville, Aloysius Bertrand, Honoré Champion, Cioran, Charles Cros, Marie Dorval, Charles Garnier, Joris-Karl Huysmans, Pierre-Jean Jouve, Pierre Louÿs, Man Ray, Maupassant, Marie-Laure de Noailles, Tristan Tzara, Ossip Zadkine[, as well as] Volodine, for whom Oscar had a unique admiration."[13] To this group imported from the Montparnasse cemetery, Oscar adds many great German, Austrian, and Russian figures, but none from Asia, as the continent had long been hesitant to sell the remains of its greatest creators. Oscar's collection, which plays with Mavrikakis's own habit of inventing literary and psychoanalytical necropolises, outlines the refined, although old-fashioned, tastes of an aesthete trained in the academic canon and who is careful to balance the sacred, the obscure, and the controversial.[14] But a more revealing list, perhaps, would be that of the figures absent from Oscar's repertory. Indeed, readers aware of Mavrikakis's literary and essayistic oeuvre and of her areas of expertise as a professor of literature would notice a glaring dearth of female, Francophone, and American writers—of a sizeable proportion, in short, of the field of World Literature as it has evolved since the era of Erich Auerbach and Leo Spitzer. If, in an issue of *Lettres québécoises* dedicated to her works, Mavrikakis composes her literary lineage around figures such as des Esseintes, Marcel Proust's Charlus, and Genet's Divine, she also includes characters from the works of Elfriede Jelinek, Marguerite Duras, Anne Hébert, Réjean Ducharme, and Claude Gauvreau.[15] This contrast emphasizes Oscar's absolute lack of interest in Québécois writers, with the exception of Nelligan, to whom he is related on his mother's side. Just as the French language stands forgotten and the humanities are excised from higher education, the national corpus appears to have no place in this particular vision of the future. Thus, Mavrikakis takes aim at the deep-seated anxiety the Québécois have of seeing their culture silenced or absorbed by overwhelming outside forces.

Here lies a defining paradox of *Oscar de Profundis*: the national context does not become a crucial issue here because it is brought to the fore but, rather, because it has been almost entirely obscured. Its last authentic presence lies in Cate's rare monologues, which binds the disappearance of the Québécois language to her death in a failed revolt of the underclass. As for Oscar, he has long turned away from his roots in his desire to escape the overwhelming burden of their memory. Mavrikakis orchestrates her vision of the apocalypse in the crude and violent chaos of the streets, in her characters' imprisonment, and in the unopposed rise of a totalitarian government, but something more subtle is also lost in this dystopian future: the shaping of a surviving culture has been left in the hands of a protagonist with an intensely masculine and Western perspective, uninterested in any local literary heritage or in any voice—too popular or too foreign—that escapes the grasp of his own contrived narrative. While some readers will give the nod to his refined taste, others will grind their teeth.

4. Conclusion: Remaking the *Idylle*

The two authors, through vastly different means, follow some common threads in their invention of an apocalyptic novel adapted to the Québécois context. Both sustain a particular version of the *idylle*, as described by Daunais, in that they allow their protagonists to live out the end-of-days from the relative comfort of their bedrooms rather than have the heroes embark on a perilous and potentially life-altering journey through the wastelands. This stability, while it constricts the spatial scope of the stories, allows the characters to dwell on the structure of their lives, on family and community, and on their culture and their roots. It also elicits meandering reflections on literature and art, offering the two men meaningful ways to retreat from the bleak reality. Thus, while Matthias reconfigures his frozen landscapes with the help of epics and fables, Oscar delights in works of high culture and in his ability to meld them into his own identity. Regarding the novels' connection to the Québécois literary context, this tie is clearly legible in Guay-Poliquin's staging of a forced but ultimately embraced return to traditional crafts, hierarchies, and temporalities. As for the poetic voice and violent world of Mavrikakis, they recall the determination of some major novelists of the *Révolution tranquille* to mercilessly rebuke a pastoral vision of the national past. *Oscar de Profundis* echoes, most clearly perhaps, the dreary world of Marie-Claire Blais's *Une saison dans la vie d'Emmanuel* with its soulless and submissive farmers, its impotent poet, its murderous priest, its maimed children, its lustful nun, and its hopeless escapes.

Both novels also give a privileged position to their male figures; few of their female characters remain in control of their destiny. But if the apocalypse is a men's club, each novel's main character is strikingly different. Guay-Poliquin's protagonist, overcoming his initial vulnerability, achieves his rebirth by plunging into the wilds to connect with a fabled lineage of lumberjacks, log runners, and *coureurs des bois*; Mavrikakis's remains a fluid, ambiguous figure who deliberately constructs his superstar persona around the monstrous models of Lautréamont, Huysmans, and Oscar Wilde rather than the raw male *id* of the roving bands of the *gueux*. What these two contrasting models of masculinity share, though, is their strong control over their society's legacy, the protagonists being endowed with the license to select what cultural forms shall endure beyond their phase of the apocalypse.

The intersection of the global trend of apocalyptic fiction with the Québécois context appears fitting, especially as it relies on various moments of the national literary history to imagine a future surviving on the values and means of a distant past, or one emptied of its memory, its language, and its hope. The two books appear, indeed, to earn a place in Daunais's peculiar take on the Québécois novel. As she follows its generational developments, observing its enduring reliance on the protective properties of the *idylle*, of a retreat from the world's worst dangers, she comes to define a second crucial term, *la planque*:

> In fact, if I had to designate with a single word the physical and most of all mental relationships that [the characters] maintain with the world that they observe from a distance, it would be, if one were to remove the term's pejorative meaning, that of *planque* which would appear to me the most fitting. These characters who live in a turbulent era, who see yesterday's frozen society put in motion and who should then logically throw themselves into this world that was finally "shaken up," rather distance themselves, break off all ties, shelter themselves from it, and do so ever so easily, ever so naturally that no one around them is surprised by it or holds them accountable.[16]

The characters' *planque*, their shelter, their hideout, is what allows them to weather the storm and survive the apocalypse. They do not fight the worldly menace, nor do they try to repair the damage or to reestablish society as it was. In fact, the end of the world is no cause for an adventure. It is, rather, an opportunity to retreat ever deeper inward.

Notes

1 Isabelle Daunais, *Le roman sans aventure* (Montreal, Canada: Boréal, 2015), 18. All English translations in this chapter are mine. They are meant to convey a word-for-word rendition of the original text rather than an author's personal voice.
2 Hubert Aquin, "La fatigue culturelle du Canada français," *Liberté* 4, no. 23 (1962): 320.
3 For a more detailed history of apocalyptic literature in Québec and its development in the contemporary period, see Élisabeth Nardout-Lafarge, "En finir avec la guerre? *Fleurs de crachat* de Catherine Mavrikakis," and Ursula Mathis-Moser, "L'Apocalypse sur le mode de la dérision: Nouveaux enjeux de la littérature québécoise," in *Que devient la littérature québécoise? Formes et enjeux des pratiques narratives depuis 1990*, ed. Robert Dion and Andrée Mercier (Montreal, Canada: Nota bene, 2017), 37–54 and 55–74.
4 This question was raised, notably, by the contributors of the collective *Writing Beyond the End Times? The Literatures of Canada and Quebec*, ed. Ursula Mathis-Moser and Marie J. Carrière (Innsbruck, Austria: Innsbruck University Press, 2017).

5   Christian Guay-Poliquin, *Au-delà de la "fin": mémoire et survie du politique dans la fiction d'anticipation contemporaine. Sociocritique de* Dondog *d'A. Volodine,* Warax *de P. Hak, et* Je dirai au monde toute la haine qu'il m'inspire *de M. Villemain* (M.A. dissertation, Université du Québec à Montréal, Canada, 2013).
6   Christian Guay-Poliquin, "Espoirs et épuisements: Persistances de l'imaginaire de la survie," *L'Inconvénient* 69 (2017): 18.
7   Christian Guay-Poliquin, *Le fil des kilomètres* (Chicoutimi, Canada: La Peuplade, 2013).
8   Émile Nelligan, "Soir d'hiver," in *Poésies complètes* (Montreal, Canada: Fides, 1952), 82.
9   Christian Guay-Poliquin, *Le poids de la neige* (Chicoutimi, Canada: La Peuplade, 2016), 167. Further citations of this text will be given parenthetically.
10 Catherine Mavrikakis, *Oscar de Profundis* (Montreal, Canada: Héliotrope, 2016), 9.
11 Mavrikakis, *Oscar de Profundis*, 108.
12 "J'ai beaucoup ri parce que pour moi, Oscar est une personne ridicule. C'est un personnage dans lequel j'ai pu concentrer toutes mes névroses." Interview fragment from "Alice Michaud-Lapointe dans l'univers de Catherine Mavrikakis: La fleur même du macadam," *Les Libraires* 96 (2016): 14.
13 Mavrikakis, *Oscar de Profundis*, 91.
14 Regarding an in-depth inquiry into this topic, see Sarah-Anaïs Crevier Goulet, "Du théâtre au cimetière: l'image de la '*nécro-polis*' dans *Omaha Beach* de Catherine Mavrikakis," in *Littératures québécoise et acadienne contemporaines: Au prisme de la ville* (Rennes, France: Presses Universitaires de Rennes, 2014), 215–28.
15 Catherine Mavrikakis, "Je ne renierai jamais la femme qui me hante: Autoportrait," *Lettres québécoises* 166 (2017): 6–7.
16 Daunais, *Le roman sans aventure*, 162.

8

Poetry in the World: Aimé Césaire, Édouard Glissant, and the Language of Landscape

Jane Hiddleston

Intensely debated over the last twenty years, the concept of World Literature must be one of the most discussed and disputed paradigms in modern literary criticism. Pioneered by David Damrosch's celebrated series of studies and anthologies, Goethe's original *Weltliteratur* has been reinvigorated and transformed into a new epithet for comparative literature, foregrounding the cultural dialogue facilitated by the circulation of texts beyond their origins into new contexts of reception.[1] The resulting resurgence of studies of World Literature has, on the one hand, triggered a salutary recognition of the importance of literary works outside the Euro-American canon, a productive attention to the effects of literary translation and circulation, and an enriching foregrounding of texts as potentially composite networks incorporating, as Ngũgĩ Wa Thiong'o describes them, "different streams and influences from different parts of the globe."[2] On the other hand, however, the universalizing sweep of World Literature has also provoked a good deal of criticism, as a number of critics have complained that the "world" of World Literature promises diversity but actually turns out to be constructed from the point of view of the European and American academy and produced by a neoimperialist publishing market tethered to the inegalitarian workings of global capitalism. For the Warwick Research Collective, for example, "world literature" is inevitably a product of the capitalist "world-system," and the term's attempted global reach only masks the persistent inequalities of the system as they are manifested in the world literary market.[3] Aamir Mufti's comprehensive critique in *Forget English!*, published in 2016, traces the genealogy between "world literature" and Enlightenment-era intellectual and literary practices and argues that the category is "fundamentally a concept of exchange, or, in other words, a concept of bourgeois society predicated on the rise of English as the global vernacular."[4] Mufti's study, as the title suggests, perceives the emphasis on works in English, but also in other hegemonic languages including French and Spanish, as symptomatic of the collusion between World Literature and the international division of labor. While the book ostensibly offers a critique of the Anglocentrism of World Literature, then, Francophone World Literature is evidently no less bound up in neocolonial politics.[5]

One of Mufti's central questions in *Forget English!* is, "Where in the world is world literature?" and, indeed, the parallel questions of "which world?" and "whose world?" are ones that have also troubled critics of the *littérature-monde* movement spearheaded by Michel Le Bris and Jean Rouaud in France.[6] The implication is that the "world" of World Literature is a partial one and defined by the agendas of the dominant Euro-American literary economies. While this attention to the power relations and cultural bias at work in the concept of World Literature is no doubt crucial, there has been less discussion of the ways in which the world affirmed here tends to be conflated with the human world and is assumed to refer to the interaction between different human cultures, but not to the mutual interpenetration of humans and the nonhuman world. The concept of the "world-system" with which World Literature is necessarily imbricated, however, is one that rests not only on economic injustice but also on environmental management and, eventually, destruction. We need, then, to reflect on the ways in which World Literature can testify not only to diverse cultural activity across the world but also to the ways in which human beings interact with the landscape and the physical world. Certain forms of writing might not only dramatize cultural circulation and transfer but also situate our "world-making" in relation to the ecosystems that necessarily shape our cultural practices and thought. World Literature would from this point of view also record and indeed contest the assumed sovereignty of the human world over the nonhuman environment within the capitalist system.

A few critics have started to engage with the question of the environment in ways that help to probe and uncover some of the normative assumptions buried in World Literature. Alexander Beecroft's 2015 *An Ecology of World Literature*, also discussed by Laura Reeck in this volume, calls for a better understanding of the "ecology" of literary production, that is, of the ways in which literature is shaped by its "ecological relationship to other phenomena—political, economic, sociocultural, religious—as well as to the other languages and literatures with which it is in contact."[7] Beecroft's study, then, helpfully expands the scope of World Literature by situating it within various "ecosystems" of thought and culture, but the ecological vocabulary of *An Ecology* is for the most part used metaphorically to give a more nuanced account of the conditions of emergence and dissemination of particular literary cultures rather than to offer a developed reflection on the relationship between World Literature and the nonhuman environment. Michael Niblett's work, however, has offered a significant intervention through its insistence on the complicity between the capitalist "world-system" and the "world-ecology" that has been so dramatically destroyed and reorganized by the world economy, and his idea of World Literature is therefore one that comprises works that testify to this domination over and sapping of resources.[8] Moreover, in a recent volume on *The Caribbean* coedited with Chris Campbell, Niblett has shown how the Caribbean is a region that has experienced the most devastating environmental transformation, and how Caribbean literature—as World Literature—has produced a particularly challenging response to that transformation. Caribbean literature testifies, according to Campbell and Niblett's volume, to the destructive effects of the world economy and world ecology and can contribute to a reconfiguration of the human interaction with and integration into "the world."[9]

This chapter will follow Campbell and Niblett's example in focusing on Caribbean World Literature and will use the examples of poetry by the highly experimental Francophone authors Aimé Césaire and Édouard Glissant to show how "Francophone Literature as World Literature" can use aesthetics to think differently about the ecological world. Moreover, I want to explore not so much the depiction of ecological damage, but rather the ways in which Césaire and Glissant construct the relationship between human and environment so as to resist the ideology of management and exploitation, at the same time as they invent a language better able to give expression to a nonhuman world that speaks to human cultures. Césaire's and Glissant's world literary poetic texts not only represent the violence of the world ecological system but also exploit aesthetic form in such a way as to encourage us to rethink our perception of the nonhuman world. Their poetic language can be seen to accomplish an alternative form of communion with "the world," another form of "world-making" that would resist the capitalist discourse of dominance and the exploitation of the land.

My approach at the same time draws on Pheng Cheah's critique of World Literature in his groundbreaking volume *What Is a World?* Cheah usefully rehabilitates the concept of World Literature here by looking beyond its production and circumscription within Euro-American academic discourses and publishing markets and by arguing that world literary texts are not merely reactive; rather, World Literature is "a force of world-making," "an active power in the making of worlds, that is, both a site of processes of worlding and an agent that participates and intervenes in these processes."[10] In a subtle reading of Martin Heidegger that extends and develops his thought to theorize the "worlding" operated by literary texts, Cheah demonstrates how this "worlding" could contest the degradation of the world by socioeconomic forces and argues that "literature uncovers the world and opens up other possible worlds, thereby giving us resolve to respond to modernity's worldlessness and to remake the world according to newly disclosed possibilities."[11] From this point of view, World Literature would be not merely reflective of the inequalities of the world-system but could be a powerful site of resistance, too. In Cheah's account of Heidegger, this is also because literature offers a space for the construction of alternative temporalities that contest the temporal model of capitalist modernity and its insistence on constant productivity and progress.

Cheah's conceptualization of the world-making force of literature also leans on both Hannah Arendt and Jacques Derrida to demonstrate the role of narrative and of the telling of stories in this creative space. Drawing, however, on Cheah's conception of literary texts as active producers of "world-making," I want to move away from the focus on narrative and address more explicitly the twofold potential of poetic form to create a language beyond that of mimesis and to convey the forms of expression and alternative temporalities of the nonhuman world. Césaire and Glissant do not merely record the devastation of the Caribbean environment by the plantation system; they do not just reflect back mimetically the injustices of the ecological reorganization of the

Caribbean. Rather, they call for an entirely new vision of and mode of communication with the world, one that also bears affinities with Heidegger's anti-capitalist "world-making" and with Derrida's "coming of the new." It is in this sense that they can be construed as World Literature authors: they speak to as well as alongside another "world," and they also imagine a relationality that contests the exploitative activity of the world-system while seeking to capture the expressiveness of the Caribbean surroundings both with and beyond the trauma of the plantation system.

Césaire and Glissant demonstrate that poetry can give expression to the Caribbean landscape in the wake of its mismanagement so as to convey nature's larger force, using rhythm and musicality, lexical diversity, and experimental syntax in highly testing ways. Thus, they can be associated with what Jonathan Bate has evocatively called "ecopoetry," a form that both captures and is immersed in "the song of the earth," one that does not simply describe the ecological world from an external perspective but that dwells in dialogue with it. Bate argues that

> the rhythmic, syntactic and linguistic intensifications that are characteristic of verse-writing frequently give a peculiar force to the *poiesis*: it could be that *poiesis* in the sense of verse-making is language's most direct path of return to the *oikos*, the place of dwelling, because metre itself—a quiet but persistent music, a recurring cycle, a heartbeat—is an answering to nature's own rhythms, an echoing of the song of the earth itself.[12]

Bate takes as one of his examples Césaire's Caliban in *Une Tempête*, who communicates with the voices of the island, but it is Césaire's later collections of verse, and in particular *i, laminaria . . .* , that performs the poet's most linguistically challenging and also self-reflexive conversation with the landscape. The languages of Césaire's and Glissant's poetic exchanges with the nonhuman world also testify to an encounter with both the power and the unpredictability of the ecosystem as the latter impacts on and far exceeds human framing in a way that seems to transcend Bate's more reassuring and harmonious "song of the earth." Both also give expression to a communality related to Heideggerian dwelling, but they are also more self-conscious about the power of poetic language and more cognizant of the violence inflicted both on and by the landscape. Césaire's and Glissant's poetry can at the same time be conceived to resist the temporality of the world-system in ways that chime with, but also exceed the scope of, Cheah's analyses of narrative: chronological time is for Césaire, for example, subtended by "le Grand Temps," the vast landscape of cosmic time, figured, as Jean Khalfa describes, through "a confrontation with rocks, not at all as inert beings, but rather as éclats, bursts, sparks and splinters, signs or residues of the extraordinary creation of which they are a part."[13] Césaire's poetry seeks to capture, and is itself figured as, a cosmic movement, the scope of which far exceeds the measurements of human time.

Césaire consistently affirms the integration of the human with the land and the embrace rather than the domination of the elemental and ecological world throughout his poetry and thought. In *Notebook of a Return to the Native Land*, the black man's renewed bonding with the earth is crucial to the reclaiming of his freedom and acts as a force of resistance to the slave owner's brutal appropriation and management of the land by means also of his exploitation of the black body. The climactic closing of the poem beseeches to "bind my black vibration to the very navel of the world," as if the black man's work of resistance will take place through a sort of fusion with the belly of the earth, man and earth joined together in their challenge to centuries of exploitation and damage.[14] Notably, in the essay "Poésie et connaissance," first printed in *Tropiques* in 1945, Césaire explicitly links poetry with the cosmos, and the poet is imagined as taking on the role of speaking with the natural world and communicating its movements to the rest of humanity.[15] The poet converses with the nonhuman world, and, by means of his privileged language, is able to capture the richness of this world and allow it to speak through him. A little later, in "Lost Body," first published in a volume of the same title in 1950, the poet seeks a more developed identification with a multiplicity of forces of nature, as if his poetry both voices the power and the extraordinary diversity of the natural world and is somehow constructed out of them:

I who Krakatoa
I who everything better than monsoon
I who open chest
I who lailaps
I who bleat better than cloaca
I who outside the musical scale.[16]

Here, the volcano, which resonates throughout Césaire's poetry, figures the poet himself, as if the poem too surges forth from the earth with an energy that is not only destructive but also productive in its announcement of movement and change. As Jean Khalfa suggests, the volcano is a constant and recurrent figure for Césaire's *ars poetica*; it presents "a jolt of matter before life and often against life," a surging that precedes or interrupts chronological time, again, in a way that speaks to Cheah's vision of literature's "world-making."[17] The poet also attributes to himself powers greater than those of the monsoon, compares himself to a racing hound, to the Zambezi river, a rhombus (an instrument using the wind to make a sound), and a cannibal, before relinquishing his position of leadership to descend into the living matter of the earth. The anaphora emphasizes the poet's transformation as he reimagines himself and his art as elemental forces working with the energy of the land and the cosmos.

It is striking, however, that "Lost Body" ends with an affirmation of the preeminence of the poet: "I shall command the islands to exist."[18] While earlier he sought to "lose [him]self falling / into the living semolina of a well-opened earth," here he summons the islands into existence as if from a position of mastery. Césaire's aesthetic is still one of resistance, in the sense that the islands are brought to life rather than subjugated by the plantation holders, yet the poetic self is both participant in and leader of the land's rebirth. Césaire's late collection *i, laminaria . . .* , however, goes the furthest in its endeavor to fuse with the nonhuman world, to give voice to it, as well as to conceptualize its own force in dialogue with this world. Although, as we shall see, Césaire's foregrounding of the poet's voice distinguishes his poetry quite clearly from that of Glissant, *i, laminaria* . . . seems to move closer to Glissant's relational aesthetic than it might at first appear. From the start, the title of the volume couples the poetic voice with the ecological world, as "laminaria" designates a long, flat seaweed that attaches itself to the rock, as well as a thin flow of winds. The juxtaposition of the poetic self with seaweed and wind announces a close association with the plant world as it becomes one with, and is shaped by, the elements, while the ellipsis also suggests not a fixed correlation but the promise of further associations.[19] Moreover, the volume's preface situates the verse again within a larger cosmic temporality patterned by geographical diversity, as "non-time imposes on time the tyranny of its spatiality" (651). The poems will move through this dynamic nonhuman space in tune with a different temporality, "between sun and shadow, between mountain and mangrove, between dawn and dusk, stumbling and binary" (651).

The opening poem, "lagoonal calendar," provides an apt example of this aesthetic immersed in the world, and the poet's position here is crucially rather less heroic than that invoked by the *Notebook* or by earlier volumes, as well as by "Lost Body." The title, which was only added later, indicates something of the poet's increased uncertainty about his status and craft—promising both a movement through the changing seasons of the calendar and in the environment of the lagoon—and at the same time a lack, as the French "lagunaire" is also suggestive of "lacunaire." First, then, the poetic voice here does not command but more passively inhabits, and this immersion is both an acceptance of historical devastation and a reckoning with environmental forces. The poet claims to live with "a sacred wound" and "imaginary ancestors," but also, returning to the image of volcanic eruption, "i inhabit not a flow of basalt / but the tidal wave of lava / that runs back up the gulch at full speed / and burns all the mosques" (653). Here, the straining of the syntax against the verse form mimics the surging forth of words like "lava," in a way that contrasts with the more staccato anaphora of "i inhabit" and the invocation of historical destruction that shapes the first lines of the poem. The "fiery whirlwind / ascidium like no other for dust / of wayward worlds" also announces an embrace of movement, a whirlwind of fire, and a pouring out of the dust of wandering worlds, as if the poet both conjures and mimics this elemental energy. The shifting here between shorter and longer lines also buffets the reader in an uneven rhythm, as if we are subjected to this irregular yet continual movement that shapes humanity but that we cannot control. At the same time, the poem seeks to touch the materiality of the animal and plant worlds, as the poet inhabits suckling goats, the argan tree, the octopus, and sea kelp, "uncoiling myself like a porana" (a type of plant thought to have anticoagulant properties). In her reading of "lagoonal calendar," Carrie Noland draws attention to Césaire's use of scientific botanical terms (as opposed to local terminology) and maintains that one of the achievements of the poem is to deploy these names to celebrate the biological diversity that monocultural production relegates to obscurity.[20] Not only, however, does Césaire use this lexical diversity to mine what he calls "the untapped space," but he also at once inserts the poet into its sensory universe and conceptualizes the poem's movement as part of the dynamic activity of the elemental and ecological environment.

Noland's uplifting reading of "lagoonal calendar" emphasizes the text's assertion of voice and lexical virtuosity rather than its conceptualization of the communication between poet and world, and yet this latter aspect of Césaire's reflection is not unproblematically celebratory. The imagery of immersion is coupled here with confessions of disillusionment, as if the mounting of energy contained both in the elements and in the history of the landscape surrounding the poet exerts a painful pressure on the poet: "the atmospheric pressure or rather the historic / immeasurably increases my pains / even as it renders sumptuous certain of my words."[21] The poet's words, then, are infiltrated and enriched by the cosmic and historical changes of landscape and ecology, but he also knows that their force exceeds the frame of the poem. The echoing in the French original between "mots" (words) and "maux" (pains) betrays a sense of anxiety toward the poetic project, as if the poet's attempt to inhabit the world through his poetry also leads to frustration. Once again, however, this frustration is a crucial part of the poet's statement of resistance: the historical suffering the poem inhabits is that of the unforgettable legacy of the slave trade, evoked by the "three-hundred-year war." The poet's desire to connect with the soil is also the result of this history of uprooting and dispossession, and his stretching of the lexicon, turbulent rhythms, and ultimate uncertainty about the power of his words ("i remain with my loaves of words and my secret minerals") trace both his aspiration toward a better communion with the land and his difficulty in achieving it given the land's traumatic history. Césaire both responds in this way to the devastation of the Middle Passage and the plantation system and calls for an alternative relationship with the land, while also remaining wary of ascribing too much power to his own language.

Some of the other poems in *i, laminaria . . .* explicitly invoke a fusion between language and landscape. In "annunciations," a promise of change is uttered through elements of the landscape: "the good news shall have been brought to me through the throng of yellow and red stars in bloom for the first time by a flight of drunken flies" (657). The imagery of the poem also stresses connections between the cosmos, flora, and fauna, with the movement envisaged being precipitated, once again, by the eruption of the volcano. Refreshing change is brought about, then, by communication within the ecosystem, not by attempted dominion through human concepts and language. In "sentiments and resentments of words," Césaire expands on his vision of "le Grand Temps," a mythic time that transcends and surpasses chronological time, whose "archangels," "ambassadors swarmed out of the Turbulence," again bring about change (669). Yet the poetic voice also wonders about the efficacy and compliance of his own words in the face of this larger expression, as his utterances seem to emanate from mythological creatures, but these are ones that are destructive to humans: "the word thunderbird / the word dragon-of-the-lake / the word strix / the word lemur / the word touaou" (671).[22] In "macumba word," Césaire celebrates the magical powers of language, however, as if the poet could now use language to navigate the landscape in a way that mimics nonhuman life: "with the word *couresse* one can cross a river swarming with caimans" (701).²³ "Macumba" refers to a set of Brazilian religions, and latterly, to witchcraft, suggesting in the poem a fantasy of linguistic alchemy where words conjure and take on the properties of the animal world. And yet, despite both this attentiveness to the language of the elements and this visionary expansion of the poet's own language, *i, laminaria* . . . never returns to the heroic rhetoric of the *Notebook*, and the landscape is also apt to hinder the poet. As we saw in the preface, the volume constantly shifts between shadow and light, hope and despair, and the poet's attempt to communicate with the world is always punctuated with admissions of his failings, as human language necessarily falters and struggles to overcome the history of alienation and rupture against which Césaire writes.

If Césaire's late poetry nevertheless reaches toward this integration between the poet and the nonhuman world, Glissant's poetic work embraces the land and, more comprehensively, in particular the ecosystem of the Caribbean archipelago. Although he frequently mentions Césaire and in his final theoretical volume *Philosophie de la relation* pays him due homage, Glissant was for a long time skeptical of the former poet's fantasized return to Africa, and he also eschews Césaire's introspective focus on the poet as subject and voice. Most strikingly, while for Césaire, at least in *i, laminaria* . . . , poetry is a forum in which the poet contemplates his place and that of his art within the world, for Glissant the poet himself is no longer a centralizing force. Glissant is indeed well known for his theory of relation, a notion that throughout his work articulates not only the continual, buzzing interconnection and movement between cultures but also an ecological relationality, a communication between the people and the Antillean landscape, which in turn is conceptualized as a dialogue both with history and between islands and sea. Glissant's novels, moreover, focus on a community, on a range of characters, and his poetry foregrounds not a "je" but a "nous," including multiple voices in an effort to puncture the myth of the poet as master figure. The rest of this chapter will analyze some sections from Glissant's *Dream Country, Real Country*—first published in 1985, only three years after *i, laminaria* . . .—to explore how the verse form accomplishes, in Glissant's entire corpus, the most aesthetically complex engagement with the world in all its relationality.

Dream Country, Real Country is the volume most explicitly focused, as the title suggests, on the relationship between the physical landscape and the human imagination and therefore speaks directly to my essay's concerns. As with Césaire, however, a dialogue with the landscape has been central to Glissant's thinking throughout his career. "Antillanité," as it is conceived in *Caribbean Discourse*, is created out of the layering of history and geography, and in *The Poetics of Relation*, Glissant calls for an alternative way to conceptualize the relationship between human and nonhuman world, as he notes the stultifying legacy of the plantation system and the need for an opening out of man's apprehension of the environment (the "entour") and the elements. A number of critics have conceptualized Glissant's thinking on the human and nonhuman world in ways pertinent to the present discussion. Sylvia Wynter's philosophical reckoning with Glissant's thought demonstrates how he expands and challenges "the Word of Man," a notion of humanity Wynter traces back to the sixteenth century with the movements of global expansion and ultimately the plantation structure.[24] Wynter emphasizes Glissant's anti-universalism in her reading, and yet this critique of the "Word of Man" is revealing in that it also raises questions about the position of "Man" in relation to the nonhuman over which, historically, he has attempted to reign. More recently, Jana Evans Braziel situates Glissant's critique in dialogue with contemporary ecocriticism, showing how he undermines the discourses of capitalist development as well as of an exoticized tourist paradise, both of which "subordinate nature to cultural dominion."[25] Celia Britton's article on Glissant's "parole du paysage" goes furthest in its conceptualization not only of Glissant's environmental critique but also of his vision of a language spoken by the landscape.[26] Glissant's late volume *Une Nouvelle région du monde*, argues Britton, conceives landscape as inherently expressive, and indeed, the astonishing opening passage of the work seeks to evoke the shapes, shadows, and textures in which the dramatic Diamond Rock, south of Fort de France, expresses both its geological and biological materiality and its historical overlaying.[27] More particularly still, the poetic form of *Dream Country, Real Country* performs the relation between human history and the nonhuman environment in its highly challenging use of imagery, syntax, and verse and accomplishes through its aesthetics a "world-making" whose understanding, I would contend, intersects with Césaire's and Cheah's worldviews in revealing ways.

While the volume's title promises a reflection on the relationship between the real landscape and a landscape of the imagination, the poems themselves demonstrate the blurring and layering between them. The "dream country" refers ostensibly to a mythic Africa while the "real country" is that of Martinican lived experience, though the "country of before" is also that which bears the mark of the slave past. This layering of different moments augurs, as in Césaire, an alternative temporality, one that maps human history onto a broader scale and eschews linear chronology with its associations with industrial progress, again anticipating Cheah's vision of "world-making." History and geography mutually shape and inform one another, as Glissant sketches a poetics that records the dialogue between the human and the nonhuman as this conversation has unfolded in particularly dramatic and destructive ways in the Caribbean. However, unlike in Césaire's *i, laminaria . . .* , where the poetic voice is relatively constant, in Glissant's *Dream Country, Real Country* different sections are attributed to different characters, with Ichneumon the storyteller, Milos the blacksmith, and Laoka, an African goddess, as invented "placeholders," as Noland calls them, for African gods, and Thaël, Mathieu, and Mycéa as protagonists from Glissant's novels reflecting contemporary Martinique.[28] These different voices also weave together references to past, present, and future and testify to the at once traumatic and regenerative encounter between character and landscape without at any point assuming a position of mastery. Experiments in verse also indicate that a new linguistic form is required to trace this complex layering. Hugues Azérad has demonstrated how Glissant's placing of the caesura and discordant manipulation of syntax in relation to verse constitute a sort of counter-poetics, as if another history can then emerge, trembling, out of the ruptures and anti-rhythmic structures of the verse.[29] Moreover, Noland has shown how the use of names of plants and trees proper to the Caribbean environment serves as an antidote to the people's sense of alienation from the land, while the echoing of syllables and phonemes across words connects landscape and history in ways that are often not immediately apparent.[30]

The first two series of verses, entitled "Country" and "Country of Before," convey the silencing imposed by the destructive history of the Middle Passage and the plantation system but also call for another language that would both reconnect the Martinicans with their landscape and give voice to the traumas the people have suffered and to which nature bears witness. The opening stanzas conjure the cries of the slaves as they are transported across the sea ("we spelled our herd of cries from the wind") as if the wind carries their testimony even as the verse refrains from speaking of the colonizers' guilt.[31] While the lines lament the fracturing and oppression of past voices, a "you" is addressed who is called upon to access the trace of their suffering as it is recorded in the environment: "you who know how to read around the landscape of words where we wandered," and "hail the trace of our feet." Furthermore, the "mild senseless speech" evokes both the irrational cries that resist ordinary forms of communication and the opening of another expression, falteringly emerging from the disjointed syntax with references to the "reddish stars / Between stones of water and green of depths." At the end of the initial section, this combination of allusions to past silencing and the call for a new language resonates through the lines, "we crack the country of the past in the fetter of this country / We moor it to this mangrove that feigns memory / We go back up the stream of exhausted love and discover man and woman / Bound together by an iron chain of clearly forged rings."[32] The imagery of cracking suggests an opening to the "country of before" out of the shackles of the present, which will also be rebound with the mangrove, a figure that in turn currently only simulates a memory of the past. The French term "amarrons" (moor), moreover, carries connotations of the binding of sugarcane and the liberation of "marronnage," in a richly layered image that again both gives voice to the past destruction of the land and encourages the generation of a fuller form of expression. The section finishes with an image of the movement of the earth—"the earth of yesterday stirs up rocks and itching within us"—but also with a reference to the forgetting of past methods for tying up corn and to the healing plant "*à-tous-maux*" (184).

The "country of before" section is again littered with references to the sea, rocks, trees, and plants, and Glissant's imagery appears to want to prize open these materials to reveal both past traumas and the remnants of an ancestral heritage. "We are born from this sifting of sea water / From the single imperceptible flank of the earth like corn" evokes the sea both as the site of the Middle Passage and as a source offering rebirth, and the "imperceptible flank" refers to the silencing of the land's past destruction (185). Laoka the African goddess as well as Milos the blacksmith are referenced in this section too, as "Milos / Sends the word, so between the heights of branches rises / Straight up, beneath his hand, our mother the moon," suggesting that these mythical figures also serve to reconnect the community with the trees and the moon (186). Packed with references to flora, fauna, and the elements as if to release their presence into the history of silence, syntactically rich and complex lines are then surprisingly concluded with a much more lucid verse affirming that "we who are not poets or mad singers speak clearly / Our voice scowls at the folds of the blue mahoganies" (187). The voice of the community tentatively emerges, then, from the fabric of the mahogany tree, which resonates, as in the novel of that name, with "mahogony," a word containing the "agony" of the past. The lines "There is no connection O storyteller / Between name and earth or wind / And cinders" convey the sense of a rejection of the atavistic language of affiliation and of the assumption that a word or name can be straightforwardly rooted in the land. The verses of the whole section suggest, instead, a chaotic network of sounds linking history and geography in more allusive and transversal ways.

The verses recounted by the mythical figures of the "dreamed country" are also constructed out of the history of silencing and of cries while at the same time calling for the landscape to speak out. The section "For Laoka" seems to address another spirit, embedded in the material environment and marked by past violence while promising another language, more fully resonant with the changes wrought by history on both the people and the environment: "You are the other reason, which makes its way within, where the muds / Are red with our cries and the grease in our hair winks / You are the hidden taste we give to our words / In the night when straw budges and bamboo cracks" (191). The lines invoke a language of hidden meaning, capturing not only the stain of spilled blood and the echoing of cries but also the rustling of straw and bamboo. The stanza finishes, moreover, with a reference to the ocean, which encapsulates the ambivalent symbolism of the sea throughout Glissant's work: it carries the chains of the slaves of the Middle Passage, and yet it is the algae's dwelling place, which symbolizes the people's breath. The "Song of Thaël and Mathieu" conveys, though, an even stronger sense of desperation, of disorientation and uncertainty: a string of negatives serves to obliterate the markings that the speaker seeks, leaving an overriding impression of alienation from the land and sea at the end. The final stanza in the section also conjures "our ancestors lying all along the spreading grass" as if the ancestral past is housed by the grass, and "we turn into the country" suggests an attempt at reintegration (195). Once again, Glissant maintains the ambivalent juxtaposition of silencing with the promise of an opening for new forms of expression, as "dévirons" in French is very close to "dérivons," hinting at "marronnage" and liberation but also at the memory of the slave past.

It is the section "Pour Mycéa" that offers the most impassioned address to the land, however, and that attempts most explicitly to access or give expression to the secrets held by the nonhuman environment. The opening stanza of the section issues a call to the land, alluding both to the opaque night of slavery and to a new language of regeneration:

O earth, if it is earth, O all-illuminated into which we have come. O plunged into the brightness of water and the plowed word. See that your words have liberated me from this long dream where so much blue has mixed with so much ochre. (196)

Here, the prose form, one used alongside various verse forms throughout the collection, promises flexibility, as if the language of the land brings a kind of liberation: in French, "déhalé" suggests both the hauling of a ship, possibly a slaver, but also a sense of emergence from a past colored by the mingling of blue waters with rusty chains.

While Mycéa, on the one hand, repeatedly figures the expressivity of the landscape as a form of textuality, on the other hand, she also imagines that her own language might somehow achieve a renewed bonding beyond the rupture caused by slave history. She addresses the earth: "I named you Unpossessable and All-fleeting," and "I write in you the music of every branch, grave or blue / With our words we illuminate and tremble," as if her poetry both embraces the ungraspable history and force of the landscape and somehow translates into her own writing the sonority and color of the trees. Throughout the section, references to the elements and to flora and fauna are associated with words, sounds, textures, and colors, and though the history of the stultifying domination of landscape and people is also embedded in the imagery, the poetic voice claims here more affirmatively than elsewhere a form of communication between the "I" and the wider "us," on one side, and, on the other, the material features of the environment as they emerge from the trauma of the past.

Both Césaire and Glissant seek to embrace the nonhuman world in their poetry at the same time as they imagine giving expression to a geographical environment damaged by history even as the force of this natural world transcends human management. Glissant's aesthetic is more consistently focused on the locus of the Caribbean with its history of ecological devastation and seeks a more relational communication between the people, the sea, the soil, and vegetation, while Césaire is more concerned with the voice of the poet, immersed in the elements, reaching a geological time that far transcends a human history that is nevertheless mapped onto this much extensive temporality. In both cases, however, "the world" is a material presence in poetry, and the poets reflect extensively on the ways in which their poetic language might capture that materiality, as well as on the extent to which they might convey the forms of expression—sounds, textures, forces, and movements—of the nonhuman world. At the same time, the nonhuman world here is never conceptualized as a purely autonomous realm that could be imagined in isolation from the human. Rather, history and geography, space and time mutually shape one another, and Césaire and Glissant are concerned with the dialogue between human and nonhuman expressiveness in relation to the history of the Middle Passage and the plantation system, as well as to geological movements. Their "poetry in the world" constitutes a kind of World Literature in that it promises an aesthetics of the bonding between human and nonhuman world in the Caribbean and, indeed, the cosmos. Their poetics are constructed of languages immersed in and listening to the world, and both acknowledge the gaps in these languages and express a powerful aesthetics of resistance to the violence of capitalist world ecology.

Notes

1. The first of these was David Damrosch's *What Is World Literature?* (Princeton, NJ: Princeton University Press, 2003).
2. Ngũgĩ Wa Thiong'o, *Globalectics: Theory and the Politics of Knowing* (New York, NY: Columbia University Press, 2012), 49.

3 Warwick Research Collective, *Combined and Uneven Development: Towards a New Theory of World-Literature* (Liverpool, UK: Liverpool University Press, 2015).
4 Aamir Mufti, *Forget English! Orientalism and World Literatures* (Cambridge, MA: Harvard University Press, 2016), 11.
5 Françoise Lionnet's critique of the *littérature-monde en français* movement spearheaded by Jean Rouaud and Michel Le Bris anticipates Mufti's more comprehensive study in that Lionnet too points out that Rouaud and Le Bris's manifesto serves to shore up the hegemony of French letters. See Françoise Lionnet, "World Literature, *Francophonie*, and Creole Cosmopolitics," in *The Routledge Companion to World Literature*, ed. Theo D'Haen, David Damrosch, and Djelal Kadir (London, UK, and New York: Routledge, 2012), 325–35.
6 See, for example, Charles Forsdick, "'Worlds in Collision': The Languages and Locations of World Literature," in *A Companion to Comparative Literature*, ed. Ali Behdad and Dominic Thomas (Chichester, MA: Wiley Blackwell, 2011), 473–89.
7 Alexander Beecroft, *An Ecology of World Literature: From Antiquity to the Present Day* (London, UK: Verso, 2015), 19.
8 Michael Niblett, "World-Economy, World-Ecology, World Literature," *Green Letters* 16, no. 1 (2012): 15–30.
9 Chris Campbell and Michael Niblett, "Introduction," in *The Caribbean: Aesthetics, World-Ecology, Politics*, ed. Chris Campbell and Michael Niblett (Liverpool, UK: Liverpool University Press, 2017), 1–14.
10 Pheng Cheah, *What Is a World? On Postcolonial Literature as World Literature* (Durham, NC: Duke University Press, 2016), 3, 2.
11 Cheah, *What Is a World?* 129.
12 Jonathan Bate, *The Song of the Earth* (London, UK: Picador, 2000), 75–6.
13 See Aimé Césaire, *i, laminaria . . .* , in *The Complete Poetry of Aimé Césaire*, trans. A. James Arnold and Clayton Eshleman (Middletown, CT: Wesleyan University Press, 2017), 108. See also Jean Khalfa, *Poetics of the Antilles: Poetry, History, and Philosophy in the Writings of Perse, Césaire, Fanon, and Glissant* (Bern, Switzerland: Peter Lang, 2016), 103–4.
14 Aimé Césaire, *Notebook of a Return to the Native Land*, in *The Complete Poetry of Aimé Césaire*, trans. Arnold and Eshleman, 61.
15 Aimé Césaire, "Poésie et connaissance," in *Aimé Césaire: l'homme et l'œuvre*, ed. L. Kesteloot and B. Kotchy (Paris, France: Présence Africaine, 1973), 119.
16 Aimé Césaire, "Lost Body," in *The Complete Poetry of Aimé Césaire*, trans. Arnold and Eshleman, 497. According to Arnold's notes, "lailaps" refers to a storm, vortex, or whirlwind.
17 Khalfa, *Poetics of the Antilles*, 98, 103.
18 Césaire, *The Complete Poetry of Aimé Césaire*, trans. Arnold and Eshleman, 499. Further citations of this text will be given parenthetically.
19 For more on the resonance of the title, see both Khalfa, *Poetics of the Antilles*, and Gregson Davis, *Aimé Césaire* (Cambridge, UK: Cambridge University Press, 1997).
20 Carrie Noland, *Voices of Negritude in Modernist Print: Aesthetic Subjectivity, Diaspora, and the Lyric Regime* (New York, NY: Columbia University Press, 2015).
21 Césaire, *The Complete Poetry of Aimé Césaire*, 655.
22 According to Arnold's notes, "touaou" is the bridled tern of the French West Indies.

23 According to Arnold's notes, "macumba" is a syncretic Afro-American religion of Brazil. "Couresse" is a grass snake endemic to Martinique.
24 Sylvia Wynter, "Beyond the Word of Man: Glissant and the New Discourse of the Antilles," *World Literature Today* 63, no. 4 (1989): 637–48.
25 Jana Evans Braziel, "Caribbean Genesis: Language, Gardens, Worlds (Jamaica Kincaid, Derek Walcott, Édouard Glissant)," in *Caribbean Literature and the Environment: Between Nature and Culture*, ed. Elizabeth DeLoughrey, Rénée Gosson, and George Handley (Charlottesville, VA, and London, UK: University of Virginia Press, 2005), 110–26.
26 Celia Britton, "La parole du paysage: Art and the Real in *Une Nouvelle Région du monde*," *Language and Literary Form in French Caribbean Writing* (Liverpool, UK: Liverpool University Press, 2014).
27 Édouard Glissant, *Une Nouvelle Région du monde* (Paris: Gallimard, 2006). For a full reading of the passage on Diamond Rock, see also Carine Mardorossian, "'Poetics of Landscape': Édouard Glissant's Creolized Ecologies," *Callaloo* 36, no. 4 (2013): 983–94.
28 See Carrie Noland, "Édouard Glissant: A Poetics of the *Entour*," in *Poetry After Cultural Studies*, ed. Heidi R. Bean and Mike Chasar (Iowa City, IA: University of Iowa Press, 2011), 143–72.
29 Hugues Azérad, "Poétique/politique de la césure dans la poésie d'Édouard Glissant," *Esprit créateur* 55, no. 1 (2015): 152–66.
30 Noland, "Édouard Glissant: A Poetics of the *Entour*."
31 Édouard Glissant, *The Collected Poems of Édouard Glissant*, trans. Jeff Humphries and Melissa Manolas (Minneapolis, MN: University of Minnesota Press, 2005), 183.
32 Glissant, *The Collected Poems of Édouard Glissant*, 183. Further citations of this text will be given parenthetically.

Part III

Relational Identities: Sex, Gender, and Class in Francophone World Arenas

9

World Literature, *littérature-monde*, and the Politics of Difference

Thérèse Migraine-George

Contemporary scholars' renewed interest in the idea of *Weltliteratur*, introduced by Goethe in 1827, points out not only their belief in the limiting and distorting effect of treating literature within nation-based frameworks but also their skepticism toward a conception of world literature as a level playing field where all texts enjoy equal opportunities. Such a flattening conception of world literature conceals the persistent control exerted by certain cultural and linguistic centers as well as what Emily Apter has called "the politics of untranslatability." "I invoke untranslatability," writes Apter, "as a deflationary gesture toward the expansionism and gargantuan scale of world-literary endeavors."[1] The writers of *littérature-monde* in French similarly contribute to a transnational view of literature that must remain aware of its own politics of production and circulation. However, here I argue that the notion of *littérature-monde* can counter some of the risks posed by the globalizing impetus of world literature in English and by the potentially homogenizing thrust of translation into English as "incontestably the lingua franca of neoliberal capitalism."[2] Indeed, *littérature-monde* is made of works that culturally touch on multiple parts of the world but are written in French—albeit in a variable and translingual French.[3] The politics of difference at stake within *littérature-monde* can therefore break away from the narrow identity politics of multiculturalism by fostering what the authors of the 2007 manifesto call a "constellation" (de)structured around multiple and shifting centers.[4] As Charles Forsdick notes, "*World-Literature in French* can thus encompass works written in the same language but produced across multiple countries and continents, and may also acknowledge what Bakhtin called (almost a century ago) the 'heterology' of the apparently monolingual text—or what Jacques Derrida tellingly dubbed the 'monolingualism of the other.'"[5]

More specifically, *littérature-monde* fosters a politics of hospitality that can be used to leverage further diversity and inclusion within the so-called "one and indivisible" French Republic and beyond. This politics, I maintain, is particularly illustrated by the former French minister of justice Christiane Taubira's use of multiple literary references during the debate about the legalization of same-sex marriage (or *mariage pour tous*, as it was dubbed) in France in 2012–13. By looking at how the paradoxical relation between French Republican universalism, on the one hand, and the acknowledgment of diversity, both ethnic and sexual, on the other hand, was negotiated through Taubira's numerous literary examples, I simultaneously question, in what follows, the equally paradoxical conviviality between unity and multiplicity, or the "centrifugal and centripetal gestures" in the heart of a *littérature-monde en français*.[6]

1. World Literature and *littérature-monde*

During the last two decades, the study of world literature—born in nineteenth-century Europe and developed in Anglo-American academia with the goal of broadening the aesthetic conception of literature and the field of comparative literature beyond its Eurocentric focus—has been fueled by postcolonial criticism and the new reflections prompted by globalization. As Carl Niekerk notes, "The notion that needs to be questioned is not just the global dimension of 'world literature' but also its literary aspect. It is a mistake to think that 'literature' exists in every culture in more or less the same form. At least to some extent the term 'literature' itself is an 'untranslatable.'"[7]

The conversation between Gayatri Chakravorty Spivak and David Damrosch at the 2011 American Comparative Literature Association Conference, a dialogue dedicated to discussing "Comparative Literature/World Literature," foregrounds some of the issues debated by scholars in this field. For Damrosch, what matters most is to offer more languages and language studies, more collaborative scholarship and teaching, and a "great deal of pluralism" to resist a superficial promotion of diversity and the nationalistic tendencies underlying the discipline of comparative literature.[8] Spivak, on the other hand, stigmatizes Damrosch's "populist" conception of world literature; for her, fostering a multicultural environment in a US classroom has very limited and limiting impact, as does expanding the canon of traditional literature for the sake of linguistic and cultural relativism. What need to be critically unearthed and examined, she contends, are the epistemological and ideological underpinnings of world literature as a discipline.[9]

The various issues discussed by Damrosch and Spivak pointedly reflect those raised by world literature scholars, including the institutionalizing, assimilationist, and exclusive effects of a so-called literary canon; the necessary reformation of a cultural center and (an) exotic periphery/ies produced by this canon; the ethnicization of texts written by nonwhite writers in contrast to the aestheticization of works written by white, Western writers, who are held to superior standards; and the reinstated dichotomy between literature produced in the western hemisphere and world literature by writers from the southern hemisphere. Following scholars such as Spivak and Pascale Casanova, who articulate the unequal relationship between national literatures within an ethnocentric world republic of letters, Apter notes that "*littérature-monde*, like World Literature paradigms in general, either reinforces old national, regional, and ethnic literary alignments or projects a denationalized planetary screen that ignores the deep structures of national belonging and economic interests contouring the international industry."[10]

Recent studies share this assessment. For Aamir R. Mufti, "*World literature has functioned from the very beginning as a border regime*, a system for the regulation of movement, rather than a set of literary relations beyond or without borders,"[11] and according to Baidik Bhattacharya, "The idea of world literature—especially in its recent reincarnation through the works of critics like David Damrosch, Franco Moretti, and Pascale Casanova—has always and already been embedded in colonial/postcolonial histories. Postcoloniality is indeed the prehistory of this present celebration of world literature."[12] Many students of world literature have therefore called for what various scholars of *Francophonie* and *littérature-monde* have also demanded: the shattering of cultural comfort and certainty; the decentering, defamiliarizing, or "unhoming" of all texts; the importance of stressing both the potentially global "value" of literary works, on the one hand, and their local specificities and incommensurability, or untranslatability, on the other; and the study of the aesthetic resistance of literary works, which cannot be equated to ethnographic documents.[13] In his presidential address to the 2011 ACLA Conference, Haun Saussy thus calls somewhat humorously for the study of an "interplanetary literature" leading "toward an investigation of multiple worlds or planets."[14]

Like world literature, *littérature-monde* illustrates what Achille Mbembe identifies as "the irreversible entanglement and intertwining between cultures, beings, and things."[15] For Derrida, "home" necessarily borders on exile and homesickness:

> *To inhabit*: this is a value that is quite *disconcerting* and equivocal; one never inhabits what one is in the habit of calling inhabiting. There is no possible habitat without the difference of this exile and this nostalgia.... But it does not follow that all exiles are equivalent. From this shore, yes, *from this* shore or this common drift, all expatriations remain singular.[16]

Despite its own potential biases and the controversy that has followed in the wake of the publication of the 2007 manifesto, the notion of *littérature-monde* creatively highlights writers' transnational mobility against the constricting or "homey" notion of "Francophone" literature that performs only a partial decentering of literary and cultural categories. Instead, *littérature-monde* welcomes what Mbembe views as "a multiplicity of times, trajectories, and rationalities that, although particular and sometimes local, cannot be conceptualized outside of a world that is, so to speak, globalized."[17]

Similarly, *littérature-monde* can be described, to use the Haitian poet René Depestre's terms, as a "*métier à métisser*" that thrives on translinguistic polyphony.[18] Such humanistic (*mé*)*tissage* was also in the heart of Léopold Sédar Senghor's founding vision of *Francophonie* and in what he envisioned as its cultural, political, and even economic mission. Although his definition of *Francophonie* as "this *integral Humanism*, which weaves itself around the earth," has often been derided for its stylistic hubris, Senghor himself believed in both the centripetal and centrifugal strands of "*enracinement* [rootedness]" and "*ouverture* [opening]," or in what he also called *"notre authenticité de métis culturels."*[19] Significantly, the text in which Senghor celebrates *Francophonie* as "this *integral Humanism*" opens with his mention of a speech he made in 1937 in Dakar, in front of both white and black people, and in which he unabashedly criticized assimilation and called for a return to "negro-African languages." This speech, Senghors notes, created "a success of scandal more, in fact, amongst Africans than Europeans."[20] Although Senghor is rightly remembered as a founding father of *Francophonie*, he also shares the iconoclastic spirit of the champions of *littérature-monde* because of the inextricably aesthetic and political role that he attributes to literature. As he further declared in the mid-1960s, "We think that the development of our economy demands people first and, second, some capital. This is the reason why I came to the idea of *Francophonie*."[21] In a similar vein, Stephen Klemm contests a conventional view of Goethe's *Weltliteratur* and emphasizes its continued relevance to a more nuanced and complex conception of a global(ized) literature by noting that

> counter to the standard humanist interpretation of *Weltliteratur*, Goethe's anthropological project sought to understand literatures in their uniqueness as emerging and entangled in specific histories, geographies, and languages with their own meaning structures and standards that cannot be applied universally. Thinking about the untranslatable aspects of language and culture is, in other words, part and parcel of Goethe's anthropological project.[22]

Just as they seek to deconstruct entrenched dichotomies between the center and the periphery and between a standard French and an "other" French, the proponents of *littérature-monde* reclaim literature as a space of absolute hospitality whose "task," in the words of the manifesto, is to give "a voice and a visage to the global unknown—and to the unknown in us," a space in which the "other" is always already here and the distinction between the "guest" and the "host" becomes largely moot.[23] If, as Klemm points out, literatures in their "uniqueness" should be understood as opaque and "untranslatable"—"as emerging and entangled in specific histories, geographies, and languages with their own meaning structures and standards that cannot be applied universally—then "home" and "hospitality" themselves become highly mobile, fluid, and reversible. As Mireille Rosello indicates, "The very precondition of hospitality may require that, in some ways, both the host and the guest accept, in different ways, the uncomfortable and sometimes painful possibility of being changed by the other."[24] *Littérature-monde* in French thus shows that a language freed from a nation and shaped by differences, rather than forceful unity, can provide a "home," albeit a changing and provisional one, for such reciprocal hospitality. In other words, and if, as Derrida puts it, "An act of hospitality can only be poetic," such poetic hospitality necessarily breaks down the literary and cultural barriers of the Francophone territory.[25] Indeed, the notion of *Francophonie* assumes a "one and indivisible" host language and literature, on the one hand, and exogenous guest contributors invited and/or welcomed, more or less conditionally, to partake in the French metropolitan literary feast—in what

Mabanckou terms "the grand banquet of the universal"—on the other hand.[26] Even more importantly, an epistemological reformulation of French/Francophone literatures into *littérature-monde* testifies to the centrifugal development of a world literature in which languages themselves can ultimately be seen as porous boundaries. If writing is always a form of translation, then literary works can always lend themselves, whatever their linguistic or cultural origins, to multiple forms of passage, visit, translation, deterritorialization, and reappropriation.

2. *Littérature-monde* and the Politics of Difference

The controversy that surrounded the legalization of marriage and adoption for same-sex couples in France during 2012 and 2013 prompted the unraveling of a tangled web of social, cultural, and political issues pointing at the ideologically fraught conceptualization of difference in the "one and indivisible" Republic posited by the French Constitution. Although the debate focused mainly on the question of "marriage for all," as it was "euphemistically" titled, some iconic moments during the period when the text of the law was being discussed in the Parliament and Senate highlight a multivalent correlation between racial and sexual issues in the French body politic today.[27] One of them was the by now quasi-legendary speech given at the French National Assembly on January 29, 2013, by the black, French Guyanese-born minister of justice Christiane Taubira, who offered a passionate defense of marriage and adoption for same-sex couples and concluded her speech with a reference to the work of the Guyanese poet Léon-Gontran Damas, one of the forefathers of the Négritude movement. In that speech, Taubira offered an extensive survey of the laws that have historically informed and regulated marriage in France, pointing out that various groups such as Jews, Protestants, and comedians were at some point excluded from the institution of marriage and connecting the progression in marriage laws and, in particular, the institution of a civil and secular marriage, to the progression in women's and children's rights. Toward the end of her speech, Taubira declared: "Marriage, which has been an exclusionary institution, will finally become, through the inclusion of same-sex couples, a universal institution."[28] This address, which received a standing ovation from left-wing political representatives, made numerous headlines that compared Taubira to political pioneers such as Simone Veil, a former French minister of health who fought for the legalization of abortion in the 1970s, and Robert Badinter, who served as a French minister of justice in the 1980s and advocated for the abolition of the death penalty. It was also widely hailed in the French LGBTQ community as a breakthrough in public discourses about the legitimacy of gay rights and relationships in the French civic space.

Although the universalistic rhetoric deployed by Taubira and other proponents of the law can be seen as highly problematic in its assimilationist tendencies, such constant reference to core French Republican ideals can be interpreted as a calculated strategy aiming both at creating consensus and at deconstructing such ideals by highlighting their persistent discriminatory inadequacies. Assimilation in France has been traditionally seen as a social and cultural cornerstone and has been deemed incompatible with the promotion of "identitarian micro-communities" based on ethnicity, sexual orientation, or gender.[29] Such fear of communitarianism, perceived as a divisive avatar of American multiculturalism, has been a staple in French Republican history and has largely contributed to the uneasy tension between Republican unity and the promotion of diversity, creating in the process what Catherine Raissiguier has called "impossible subjects of the French Republic."[30] Collecting statistics on race, ethnicity, or religion is therefore proscribed in a supposedly color-blind French Republic that claims secularism as one of its main principles. As Mbembe comments, "The perverse effect" of "this radical indifference to difference" "is thus a relative indifference to discrimination." Thus, Mbembe sees "French universalism," in its paradigmatic "masking" of racial difference, as the very "product of racial theory."[31]

Many other left-wing political representatives who defended the law invoked universalism as a cornerstone of the French Republic—a universalism that is itself "seen as intimately bound up with the universal revolution of 1789"—and therefore as a foundational rationale for marriage equality.[32] During the debate at the French National Assembly following Taubira's speech, the minister for family (*Ministre déléguée à la Famille*) Dominique Bertinotti further said that

> the Republic must recover its universal vocation. . . . No one should be clandestine in society, clandestine in the Republic. . . . Just as we fight against sexism, . . . against racism, just as we must still fight against homophobia, this reform aiming at opening marriage and adoption to same-sex couples is consistent with other laws fighting all forms of discrimination.[33]

For the opponents to marriage for all, by contrast, the legalization of marriage and adoption for same-sex couples would doom the Republic to fragmentation, dissolution, and to its ultimate demise rather than lead toward the teleological epiphany of national unity invoked by proponents of the law. The fear of communitarianism was thus often agitated as the ultimate threat to Republican unity.

Throughout her staunch advocacy for marriage equality during this critical period, Taubira thus consistently referred to equality and to a form of positive assimilation within a Republican space that would be respectful rather than repressive of such differences as the main justifications for the legalization of marriage and adoption for same-sex couples. As she put it, "The fight against discrimination is demanded by the Republican Pact. It is the responsibility of public powers to watch out for this."[34] In her closing speech after the law was adopted by the Senate on April 12, 2013, Taubira addressed senators by stating that "by voting for this text . . . you have consolidated and reinforced the Republican pact. The Republican pact, the res publica, . . . the common good, and what is more precious as a common good than our institutions? By opening this Republican institution to same-sex couples we simply recognize their full citizenship."[35]

Before becoming the minister of justice in former president François Hollande's government and being propelled to political stardom by her vehement speeches during the marathon debates that took place in January and February 2013 over marriage and adoption "for all" at the French National Assembly, Taubira already had a long record of political and intellectual commitment to issues of diversity. A *conseillère régionale* of the French overseas territory Guyana, whose autonomy she militated for at the beginning of her political career, she was also the driving force behind a 2001 French law, named after her, that recognizes the Atlantic slave trade and slavery as a crime against humanity. She is also the author of several books including *L'esclavage raconté à ma fille* (2002), in which she argues that slavery, even if it was officially abolished over 150 years ago, continues to have a deep and destructive impact on contemporary societies.[36] In an interview given on May 11, 2013, just two days after then president Hollande ruled out reparations for France's role in the colonial-era slave trade, Taubira called on the French government to consider ways to redistribute land in its Caribbean overseas territories to favor the descendants of slaves.[37]

In the landmark speech that she gave at the French National Assembly on January 29, 2013, Taubira concluded with the following impassionate statement and quote from Léon-Gontran Damas:

> We . . . are so proud of what we are doing. . . . We are so proud of this that I would like to define it through the words of the poet Léon-Gontran Damas: what we are going to accomplish is "beautiful as a rose whose petals the besieged tower at dawn finally sees blooming." It is "grand as the need for a change of scenery." . . . It is "strong as the high-pitched scream of a voice in the long night."[38]

Taubira, who is known for her frequent and eclectic references to French and Francophone writers such as Émile Zola, René Char, Aimé Césaire, and Gisèle Halimi, made numerous such literary and philosophical references illustrating her commitment to both sexual and ethnic equality in her various interventions at the French National Assembly.[39] In February 2013, she addressed Hervé Mariton, a particularly vehement right-wing opponent of the legalization of marriage and adoption for same-sex couples, by stating that difference could not be used as a pretext for the inequality of rights and quoting again a poem from Damas's poetry collection *Black-Label*: "We the wretches / we the nothing / we the little / we the dogs / we the skinny / we the Negroes / What are we waiting for / What are we waiting for to be silly / to take a leak / to our heart's content / against the life / stupid and beastly / that was given to us?"[40] Finally, on February 12, 2013, and after the official vote of the French National Assembly in favor of the law on *mariage pour tous*, Taubira received another standing ovation for a talk in which she praised this historic vote and concluded with a quote from the philosopher Emmanuel Lévinas: "To think otherness falls under the irreducible worry for the other. This is what we have done throughout this debate."[41]

One speech Taubira delivered on the work of Damas highlights with particular clarity, albeit indirectly, five years before Taubira became a public advocate for same-sex marriage, her commitment to Lévinas's call for a necessary ethics of alterity. I am referring here to the talk, as masterful as her January 29 landmark speech, that she gave in January 2008 at the Université des Antilles-Guyane as part of a conference on Damas.[42] In that lecture, Taubira recalled that Damas, who is especially known as one of the three founding fathers of Négritude with Léopold Sédar Senghor and Aimé Césaire, whom Damas met in Paris in the early 1930s, dedicated his life to denouncing the alienating effect of colonial assimilation and oppression. Taubira further pointed out that Damas's best-known collection of poems, *Pigments*, was in fact censored in 1939 by the French government for "attempt against the established order."[43] Damas, Taubira also explained, wanted his words (*sa parole*) to break into the bastions of conservatism, through the pillars and walls of the status quo, inequalities, and injustices. She quoted Damas: "Since then how many ME, ME, ME have died" in a binary world dominated by a black and white discourse that "forever prevents him from being human."

In the course of her presentation, Taubira also insisted on the anti-conformist relevance of Damas's thinking in regard to what she called today's *interrogations profondes*. A poet but also a politician who became a deputy of Guyana in the French National Assembly in the late 1940s and early 1950s, Damas experienced an essential "*conscience d'être*" that made him intensely aspire to what he called "the mass-organized escape from inferiority." Damas, Taubira said, refused to let himself be "stuck in past determinations"—in Frantz Fanon's terms—and his entire work is a long manifesto, an injunction to rise up and impose one's human quality to "this world that is mine against my will." Because he smashed all poetic conventions to pieces, Damas was a poet not just rebellious but also subversive. According to Taubira, indeed, "Subversion is richer. It is not content to oppose, like rebellion; it dissects, it pierces, and it shows all the insufficiencies, all the abuses of a power that pretends to obedience and respect." And she quoted Damas again: "It is less about restarting than continuing to be against Western morality and its parade of precepts preconceptions pre-notions pretentions prejudices."

In many ways, this 2008 talk can therefore be said to contain the seeds of her 2013 speech on *mariage pour tous*. Taubira's long-standing determination to "think otherness" and its accompanying "irreducible worry for the other," as well as her tireless fight for human dignity and equality, thus encompass racial and sexual diversity in a broad visionary redefinition of difference as a universal right. It is in this sense, and because she too stands against entrenched prejudices and conservatism, that Taubira's speeches and actions can be seen as being not only rebellious but also deeply subversive. Taubira's oratory can be further analyzed as rather fascinating tours de force in this tightrope walking exercise between Republican unity and universalism, on the one hand, and a celebration of diversity and differences, on the other. Many of the most prominent French poststructuralist and postmodern intellectuals who, in turn, largely contributed to the rise of postcolonial and other fields of study focusing on minority issues in the Anglophone world developed their own thinking within such a universalistic and humanistic perspective. As Derrida reminds us in *Monolingualism of the Other*, "It is in the form of a thinking of the unique, precisely, and not of the plural, as it was too often believed, that a thought of dissemination formerly introduced itself as a folding thought of the fold."⁴⁴ In other words, asserting the otherness of the same is not tantamount to celebrating multiplicity and differences but, and much more radically, to questioning the homogeneity of the self by showing it as being intimately divided or "folded." This does not mean that all differences are collapsed within one undifferentiated category: it is also in this *pli* of difference within homogeneity that, according to Derrida, a delicate articulation between the universal history and the particular story, "between transcendental or ontological universality, and the exemplary or testimonial singularity of *martyred* existence," can take place.⁴⁵

Various contemporary French and Francophone critics have continued to rethink notions of difference and diversity in the line of this historical, cultural, and intellectual heritage. In his extensive 2009 study *Un Humanisme de la diversité: Essai sur la décolonisation des identités*, Alain Renaut, for example, draws on the writings of Derrida and Kwame Anthony Appiah, among many other scholars, to examine the ethical dimensions of a humanism that recognizes and supports cultural, ethnic, and sexual diversity and that criticizes what Renaut terms the "*fétichisation*" of supposedly homogeneous identities.⁴⁶ Such humanism thereby opposes the assimilationist and putatively color-blind brand of universal humanism traditionally championed by French Republicanism and celebrates instead what Serge Gruzinski calls a "*pensée métisse*."⁴⁷ Finally, for Mbembe, one of the most prominent postcolonial critics today, notions of humanism and universalism do not need to be discarded but radically questioned and reworked in a much more concrete, personal, and inclusive fashion:

> The question of the relationship between democracy and difference can never be resolved by a purely abstract conception of both humanity and universalism. A citizen is someone who can personally answer the question, who am I? . . . Of course, speaking in the first person does not suffice to exist as a subject. But there can be no full citizenship when such a possibility is purely and simply negated. . . . The abstraction of our fundamental differences is not a condition sine qua non of a conscious belonging to a common humanity or, in the case at hand, to a multicultural democracy based on the obligation of mutual recognition as a condition for convivial life. . . . Recognizing difference—and mutuality—is therefore hardly incompatible with the principle of a democratic society. Such an acknowledgment does not signify that society proceeds without common ideas and beliefs. To the contrary, this recognition is the very condition for these ideas and beliefs to become truly common. And the recognition of this difference by others is precisely the mediation through which we become the same (*semblable*). It appears, then, that a communion of singularities is indeed prerequisite for a politics of similarity and an ethics of mutuality.⁴⁸

I would argue that a remarkable "folding" of concrete differences into universalism happened through the voice of Christiane Taubira, in particular when she quoted Damas, a poet and critic of colonial racism and oppression, to end her passionate plea for *mariage pour tous*. Moreover, her reliance on various poetic, literary, and philosophical references can be interpreted as a means to demonstrate the multilayered semantics of discrimination in French history and society. According to Mbembe once again, an "authentic human encounter" "must begin through reciprocal disorientation. This vital disorientation, in turn, requires the elaboration of forms of thought that are at once profoundly historical and philosophical, sociological, hermeneutical, and ethical—memory and antimemory, militant and antimilitant, political, anti-political, and poetic."[49] For Mary Gallagher also, "poetics," which she describes as "the dominant mode of francophone postcolonial discourse," is a central feature in the writings of many Francophone writers addressing "the question of the interface between culture on the one hand and empire, globalisation, colonialism or imperialism on the other": "This means that francophone thinking on 'empire and culture now' is often more mediated, more embedded, more dense, more oblique, and thus less easily translated or applied than thought that is not articulated as, or in relation to, a poetics: that is, writing in which literary values of expression and form, including values of semantic richness, of infinite levels of meaning, of aesthetic resonance and ethical depth are— often both theoretically and performatively—central and pre-eminent."[50] Rather than having a purely ornamental function, Taubira's many poetic references can therefore be viewed as a both aesthetic and political strategy that points out, through its "dense" and "oblique" polysemy, the universal ethics and imperative of difference in contemporary France.

My analysis of Taubira's historical and political use of transnational literary references thus uncovers ways in which *littérature-monde* and world literature more generally can rethink notions of a shared humanity, a common good, and a global world through the lenses of difference and diversity. As Pheng Cheah argues, postcolonial world literature "attests to literature's continuing pertinence, not only as an expression of humanity's ideals or sufferings, but as an active force for the emergence of new subjects in the world. In opposition to the calculative appropriation of time that sustains contemporary global capitalism," Cheah also notes apropos of the works he discusses, "the novels I have considered propose revolutionary time and worldly ethics as alternative temporalities."[51] Similarly, relocating literary works within the global frame of *littérature-monde* highlights both writers' and critics' aesthetic, ethical, and political commitment to the humanizing powers of writing, translating, and interpreting the many voices and strands of literary creation.

Notes

1 Emily Apter, *Against World Literature: On the Politics of Untranslatability* (New York, NY: Verso, 2013), 3.
2 Aamir R. Mufti, *Forget English! Orientalisms and World Literatures* (Cambridge, MA: Harvard University Press, 2016), 17.
3 See Jacqueline Dutton, "État Présent: World Literature in French, *Littérature-Monde*, and the Translingual Turn," *French Studies* 70, no. 3 (2016): 404–18. As Dutton notes, "Whether French studies embraces translingualism as a conceptual framework, not just to examine creolization in African texts or stylistic devices adopted in

post-Soviet writers in France, but to rethink the unity and diversity of the French language, remains to be seen. What is clear is that before the *littérature-monde* manifesto burst on to the literary scene, thrusting itself into academic discourse, contemporary understanding of world literature in French was evolving more calmly out of the various strands of postcolonial, francophone, transnational, transcultural, and world literature studies. The catalysing force of *littérature-monde*, in spite of its inherent lacunae, sparked a new disciplinary turn towards translingual studies" (417–18).

4 Muriel Barbery et al., "Pour une 'littérature-monde' en français," *Le Monde des Livres*, March 16, 2007, https://www.lemonde.fr/livres/article/2007/03/15/des-ecrivains-plaident-pour-un-roman-en-francais-ouvert-sur-le-monde_883572_3260.html (accessed June 1, 2018). Unless otherwise indicated, the translations from French are mine.
5 Charles Forsdick, "*World-Literature in French*: Monolingualism, Francopolyphonie and the Dynamics of Translation," in *Translation and World Literature,* ed. Susan Bassnett (Abingdon, UK, and New York, NY: Routledge, 2019), 36.
6 Christopher Miller describes this contradiction as the "centrifugal and centripetal gestures" combined in the expression "world literature . . . in *French*." See his article "The Theory and Pedagogy of a World Literature in French," *Yale French Studies* 120 (2011): 41.
7 Carl Niekerk, "World Literature without Goethe: On Pramoedya Ananta Toer's Labour Camp Memoirs *The Mute's Soliloquy*," *Seminar: A Journal of Germanic Studies* 54, no. 2 (May 2018): 249.
8 Gayatri Chakravorty Spivak and David Damrosch, "Comparative Literature/World Literature: A Discussion with Gayatri Chakravorty Spivak and David Damrosch," *Comparative Literature Studies* 63, no. 4 (2011): 463.
9 Spivak and Damrosch, "Comparative Literature/World Literature," 473.
10 Gayatri Spivak, *Death of a Discipline* (New York, NY: Columbia University Press, 2003); Pascale Casanova, *The World Republic of Letters*, trans. M. B. DeBevoise (Cambridge, MA: Harvard University Press, 2004); Apter, *Against World Literature*, 177.
11 Mufti, *Forget English!*, 9.
12 Baidik Bhattacharya, *Postcolonial Writing in the Era of World Literature: Texts, Territories, Globalizations* (London, UK, and New York, NY: Routledge, 2018), 1.
13 Mireille Rosello, "Unhoming Francophone Studies: A House in the Middle of the Current," *Yale French Studies* 103 (2003): 123–32.
14 Haun Saussy, "Interplanetary Literature," *Comparative Literature* 63, no. 4 (2011): 438.
15 Achille Mbembe, "Pièce d'identité et désirs d'apartheid," in *Je est un autre: Pour une identité-monde*, ed. Michel Le Bris and Jean Rouaud (Paris, France: Gallimard, 2010), 115.
16 Jacques Derrida, *Monolingualism of the Other: Or, The Prosthesis of Origin*, trans. Patrick Mensah (Stanford, CA: Stanford University Press, 1998), 58.
17 Achille Mbembe, *On the Postcolony* (Berkeley, CA: University of California Press, 2001), 9.
18 René Depestre, *Le Métier à métisser* (Paris, France: Stock, 1998). As Roland Barthes puts it, "The grouping of codes, as they enter into the work, into the movement of the

reading, constitute a braid (*text, fabric, braid*: the same thing); each thread, each code, is a voice; these braided—or braiding—voices form the writing; when it is alone, the voice does no labor, transforms nothing; it *expresses*; but as soon as the hand intervenes to gather and intertwine the inert threads, there is labor, there is transformation" (*S/Z*, trans. Richard Miller [New York, NY: Hill and Wang, 1974], 160).
19 Léopold Sédar Senghor, *Liberté I: Négritude et Humanisme* (Paris, France: Seuil, 1964), 363.
20 Senghor, *Liberté I*, 358.
21 Maryse Bray, "Une approche plurielle," in *Regards sur la Francophonie*, ed. Marc Gontard and Maryse Bray (Rennes, France: Presses Universitaires de Rennes, 1996), 25.
22 Stephen Klemm, "Historicism, Anthropology, and Goethe's Idea of World Literature," *Seminar: A Journal of Germanic Studies* 54, no. 2 (May 2018): 150.
23 Barbery, "Pour une 'littérature-monde' en français."
24 Mireille Rosello, *Postcolonial Hospitality: The Immigrant as Guest* (Stanford, CA: Stanford University Press, 2001), 176.
25 Jacques Derrida, *Of Hospitality: Anne Dufourmantelle Invites Jacques Derrida to Respond*, trans. Rachel Bowlby (Stanford, CA: Stanford University Press, 2000), 2.
26 Alain Mabanckou, "Immigration, *Littérature-Monde*, and Universality: The Strange Fate of the African Writer," trans. Donald Nicholson-Smith, *Yale French Studies* 120 (2011): 85.
27 Bruno Perreau, "The Political Economy of 'Marriage for All,'" *Contemporary French Civilization* 39, no. 3 (2014): 354.
28 "Assemblée nationale, XIVe législature, Session ordinaire de 2012-2013, Compte rendu intégral, Deuxième séance du mardi 29 janvier 2013," http://www.assemblee-nationale.fr/14/cri/2012-2013/20130118.asp (accessed December 2, 2018).
29 Naomi Schor, "The Crisis of French Universalism," *Yale French Studies* 100 (2001): 52–3.
30 Catherine Raissiguier, *Reinventing the Republic: Gender, Migration, and Citizenship in France* (Stanford, CA: Stanford University Press, 2011), xii.
31 Achille Mbembe, "Provincializing France?," trans. Janet Roitman, *Public Culture* 23, no. 1 (2011): 93, 101.
32 Schor, "The Crisis of French Universalism," 43.
33 "Assemblée nationale."
34 Christiane Taubira, "Le mariage civil est désormais universel," *Le Huffington Post*, April 23, 2013, http://www.huffingtonpost.fr/christiane-taubira/vote-mariage-gay_b_3137872.html (accessed December 3, 2018).
35 "Mariage pour tous." *Ministère de la justice*, 12 avril 2013, http://www.justice.gouv.fr/la-garde-des-sceaux-10016/archives-2013-c-taubira-12869/mariage-pour-tous-30062.html (accessed December 5, 2018).
36 Christiane Taubira, *L'esclavage raconté à ma fille* (Paris: Bibliophane, 2002).
37 Laurent Valdiguié, "Taubira: 'Des terres pour les descendants d'esclaves,'" *Le Journal du Dimanche*, May 11, 2013, http://www.lejdd.fr/Societe/Justice/Actualite/Taubira-Des-terres-pour-les-descendants-d-esclaves-606801 (accessed December 3, 2018).
38 "Assemblée nationale."
39 Laurène Daycard and Maxime Pargaud, "Christiane Taubira, bonne amie de la poésie," *Le Figaro*, February 8, 2013, http://www.lefigaro.fr/culture/2013/02/0

8/03004-20130208ARTFIG00351-christiane-taubira-bonne-amie-de-la-poesie.php (accessed December 4, 2018).
40 Quentin Girard, "Qu'attendons-nous pour jouer aux fous, pisser un coup, tout à l'envi?," *Libération*, February 6, 2013, http://www.liberation.fr/politiques/2013/02/0 6/qu-attendons-nous-pour-jouer-aux-fous-pisser-un-coup-tout-a-l-envi_879838 (accessed December 5, 2018). Léon-Gontran Damas, *Black-Label* (Paris, France: Gallimard, 1956). Noting that Léon-Gontran Damas in fact vehemently criticized assimilation, Hélène Ferrarrini questioned Taubira's choice of literary references in her passionate plea for gay marriage: "In Guyana, Damas could notice that the gap between the proclamation of equality and the reality of social, economic, cultural situations is sometimes wide. While we are interrogating the concrete form of equality that marriage for all can create between homosexual and heterosexual couples, especially as it pertains to adoption, the work of the Guyanese poet carries a meaning more complex than shown in the few verses quoted by Christiane Taubira." Hélène Ferrarini, "Léon-Gontran Damas, l'étrange choix poétique de Christiane Taubira," *Slate.fr*, February 1, 2013, http://www.slate.fr/story/67853/etrange-choix -poetique-de-christiane-taubira (accessed December 8, 2018).
41 "Taubira accueille le mariage pour tous avec humour et poésie," *Le Monde*, February 12, 2013, http://www.lemonde.fr/politique/video/2013/02/12/taubira-accueill e-le-mariage-pour-tous-avec-humour-et-poesie_1831484_823448.html (accessed December 8, 2018).
42 "Léon-Gontran Damas par Christiane Taubira," *Dailymotion.com*, January 31, 2008. http://www.dailymotion.com/video/x481pa_leon-gontran-damas-par-christiane-t _news#.UUINFDf4JK0 (accessed December 7, 2018).
43 Léon-Gontran Damas, *Pigments* (Paris, France: Présence Africaine, 1962).
44 Derrida, *Monolingualism of the Other*, 26.
45 Derrida, *Monolingualism of the Other*, 27.
46 Alain Renaut, *Un Humanisme de la diversité*: *Essai sur la décolonisation des identités* (Paris, France: Flammarion, 2009), 434–5.
47 Serge Gruzinski, *La Pensée métisse* (Paris, France: Fayard, 1999).
48 Mbembe, "Provincializing France?" 117–18.
49 Mbembe, "Provincializing France?" 117.
50 Mary Gallagher, "Postcolonial Poetics: L'exception francophone?" *Modern and Contemporary France* 18, no. 2 (2010): 257–8.
51 Pheng Cheah, *What Is a World? On Postcolonial Literature as World Literature* (Durham, NC, and London, UK: Duke University Press, 2016), 330.

10

Queer Desire on the Move: Resistance to Homoglobalization in World Literature in French

Jarrod Hayes

In the late 1990s, several conferences and, then, anthologies were devoted to the relation between globalization and homosexuality, representing not just a global turn in LGBTQ studies but also the ongoing queering of postcolonial theory.[1] In this chapter, I would like to consider a connection between the debates that these conferences elicited and the recent phenomenon within "Francophone" studies that has consisted in a rejection of the very term "Francophone"—with its implied ghettoization, according to the proponents of this rejection—in favor of a *littérature-monde*. To do so, I will look at examples of writings by queers, queer writing, and even the queer in writings by the not-so-queer from Québec, Africa, and the Caribbean to provide an overview of the intersection between World Literature in French, on the one hand, and sexuality studies, on the other; to explore the tension between the globalizing tendencies of Western homosexuality (if one could speak of such a thing in the singular) and local resistances to it in the form of culturally specific instances of same-sex desires and sexual behavior; and to examine ways of queering Francophone studies and opening up multicultural approaches to queer French studies. I use the term "queer" here because "lesbian," "gay," and "homosexual" often do not pass muster outside of the Western contexts in which these terms arose. When appropriate, I will also rely on the expressions *men who have sex with men* and *women who have sex with women* (MSM and WSW), which scholars and activists have employed to avoid complicity with the very globalizing pressures under consideration. My point here is not to provide an encyclopedic treatment of queerness and/or MSM/WSW in world literatures in French; rather, by highlighting a handful of texts from across the most commonly acknowledged regional divisions of Francophone studies, I hope to offer ways both to include questions of gender and sexuality in the *teaching* of French studies from a global perspective and to suggest modalities of teaching gender and sexuality studies from a global and therefore less Eurocentric perspective.

While for the Western reader, Québec/French Canada, with a significant number of its most canonical writers openly identifying as lesbian or gay, is the region whose sexual cultures share the most similarities with those of the United States, in the other Francophone regions as well, representations of MSM and WSW are far from uncommon. Queer passages may be harder to find in the French literature of sub-Saharan Africa, but they are by no means nonexistent. And while Guadeloupe and Martinique are French departments, Haiti nonetheless offers some of the most explicit examples of MSM. In these regions, French words like *homosexuel(le)*, *gay*, and *lesbienne* often compete with a more "local" vocabulary that can be read as part of a resistance to the sexual globalization described earlier. Interestingly, this tendency is just as real in Caribbean departments that are administratively a part of France to this very day as it is in now-independent sub-Saharan countries. The Maghreb stands out in its own way, since it can also draw on precolonial traditions of homoeroticism in Arabic literatures. Rather than arguing for an increasingly globalized lesbian or gay identity, however, I will focus on the resistance to this globalization offered by more "local" paradigms of same-sex desire. In addition, I will seek to extend an assertion I made in *Queer Nations: Marginal Sexualities in the Maghreb* to other regions of the French-speaking world:

> While Maghrebian novels articulate critiques of the sexually normative moves of Maghrebian nationalisms, *Queer Nations* also allows these works to cast a critical glance back on the West. Tendencies of imposing Western theoretical frameworks on "postcolonial" literature are well enough known, as is the Western critic's privilege of questioning his/her cultural Others without being questioned by them. "We" do not have a monopoly on queering; through our readings of Maghrebian novels, "we" might also be queered by them.[2]

Whereas the proponents of *littérature-monde* group the literatures in French of the various geocultural regions where French is spoken, read, and written into a single category, comparative and global approaches to "sexuality" studies have the potential to highlight differences in local practices and manifestations of desire. In the end, I hope that readers of this chapter will find within it a practical starting place from which to develop more multicultural approaches to queer French studies as well as more queer-friendly approaches to Francophone studies, and this even in the realm of curriculum development. For the purposes of this discussion, as I move from one of the four major geocultural regions of Francophone studies to another so as to get at some of these differences, I will supply an overview of the general state of queer studies in relation to that region and briefly survey the texts (including films) that one might look to in order to further queer studies in that region, focusing more intensively, after that, on a literary work or two for each geographical area. So while my contribution will cover a broad array of geocultural zones, close reading will not be foregone as an important methodology for queering Francophone literature as a world literature. I would like to start with the region whose LGBTQ cultures may be more familiar to

Western readers, namely, Québec. Then I will move to places where representation of MSM and WSW are fewer and farther between. Finally, I will bring my discussion back to Québec in a move that I hope will carry out the promise of allowing Africa and its diaspora to queer the West.

1. Québec

In 2014, the American Council for Québec Studies held its biennial conference in Montreal and issued a separate call for papers for a Queer Québec colloquium, which offered at least one queer panel for every session.[3] The very existence of this colloquium demonstrates that Queer Québec studies is so well integrated into a more general Québec studies that the number of book-length works may not best indicate the strength of the field. Consulting monographs on the best-known lesbian and gay writers—like Michel Tremblay, Nicole Brossard, Marie-Claire Blais, and Michel Marc Bouchard—might be a better place to start. Even a comprehensive list of such writers would be beyond the scope of this study. Essays such as Jane Moss's 1992 "Dramatizing Sexual Difference: Gay and Lesbian Theater in Quebec" and Alain-Michel Rocheleau's 1996 "Gay Theater in Quebec: The Search for an Identity" attest to the wealth of queer literary production in single genres. Likewise, Québec boasts a lively queer cinema of which perhaps the most renowned recent newcomer is the *Wunderkind* Xavier Dolan, whose films have obtained international acclaim.[4]

More generally known for bringing *joual*, the working-class French of Montreal, to the Québec stage, Tremblay has also written an entire series of drag-queen plays. One of these, *Damnée Manon, sacrée Sandra* (1976),[5] is indeed a play of contrasts as its opening makes clear:

> *In her completely white kitchen, Manon, a devout woman dressed entirely in black rocks back and forth. In her completely black booth, Sandra, a transvestite dressed entirely in white, does her nails.*
>
> MANON The solution for everything . . . is the good Lord.
> SANDRA No matter who, no matter when, where, why, the answer is always sex (le cul).[6]

The contrast here between the play's two eponymous characters, its only characters, is thus literally black and white. Manon personifies Québec's religious history and the cultural importance of the Catholic Church in the preservation of the French language and Québec identity, and Sandra personifies a certain sexual freedom that came with the secularization brought about by the Quiet Revolution. As an embodiment of the nation, Sandra also represents a nonnormative gender and sexual identity. Yet, as early as these opening lines, this contrast is articulated in formulas so parallel that the oppositeness of the characters can be read as a similarity as much as a difference.

Indeed, as each character elaborates on her opening line, and Manon tells the story of purchasing a giant rosary at the Saint Joseph Oratory, the excesses of her religious zeal come to seem less normative as well, for although she is often mistaken for a nun, her devotion exists outside of any religious institution. In a dream that Manon recounts, a statue of the Virgin Mary "has green lips and fingernails," the same color as the lipstick with which Sandra has fantasized about covering her naked Martinican boyfriend (298). In the narration of this dream, Manon says, "She stroked me with her hands as I had stroked the body of Our Lord, and then she softly whispered, 'Do you like that, Manon? Do you like that? It's nice, eh? Do you want me to stroke your body with my lips, over all your skin?" (299). The play later ends with a kind of ecstatic ascension for Manon, which Sandra envies, stating: "If Manon hadn't existed, I would have invented her" (305). This ending, a sort of marriage between an unorthodox Catholicism and sexuality, recalls a statement by Doctor Sanregret about barely dressed children in the annual Corpus Christi parade in Tremblay's 1980 novel, *Thérèse et Pierrette à l'école des Saints-Anges* (Thérèse and Pierrette at the School of the Holy Angels): "There is something sexual about this masquerade that stuns me each year. Just look at these children offered up, immobile, forced to pose, and admired for hours on the verge of a trance. The unconscious is truly the mother of all religious ceremonies."[7]

I have always taught *Damnée Manon, sacrée Sandra* as a national allegory for this reason, and it is useful to compare it with another play, Tremblay's earlier *Hosanna* (1973), whose eponymous drag queen removes her makeup and attire after a night of humiliation at the annual Halloween ball. The ever-so-bitchy Hosanna had prepared an elaborate costume to impersonate Elizabeth Taylor's version of Cleopatra, thereby hoping that her appearance on stage would be as triumphant as Cleopatra's entry into Rome. When she walks out on stage, however, she notices that all the other queens have conspired (with the complicity of her boyfriend Cuirette) to dress as the same character, and they are even more glamorous than she. When she hesitates, they shout in mocking unison: "Dare, Anna, Dare [*Ose, Anna, ose*]!" in a play on her very name.[8] The play ends with her removing the last articles of clothing and saying, "Ain't I a man!" [*Chus-t-un homme!*] (185). Many analyses of this play have engaged in an allegorical reading in which a nude Hosanna (at this point more Claude—her "boy name"—than Hosanna), stripped of her costume and makeup, represents an authentic, that is, decolonized, Québec. More recent readings, however, have questioned the transphobic implications of such an understanding of drag as inauthentic.[9] The nation allegorized in such readings would therefore be one founded on gender normativity. By contrast, what rereading *Hosanna* back through the more fractured nature of national identity allegorized by *Damnée Manon, sacrée Sandra* can tell us is that queerer allegories of the nation are also possible. In short, while representations of queer desire in Tremblay's plays may seem familiar to readers from other Western countries (especially if they are aficionados of drag performance like myself), as national allegories they are nonetheless attentive to the specificities of Canada's colonial history, especially as experienced by its French-speaking minority.

2. Maghreb

While the Maghreb's literatures may contain fewer examples of queer representation, queer Maghrebian studies is arguably just as established as Queer Québec studies. My own *Queer Nations* was published in 2000. Other scholarly queer work in Maghrebian scholarship followed bit by bit as the field quietly gained steam until the 2010s, which then became *the* decade of queer Maghrebian studies, with new work just as likely written in French as in English. In 2013, Claudia Gronemann and Wilfried Pasquier published their collection *Scènes des genres au Maghreb: Masculinités, critique queer et espaces du féminin/masculin* (Scenes of Gender in the Maghreb: Masculinities, Queer Critique, and Masculine/Feminine Spaces). Also in 2013, Jean Zaganiaris's *Queer Maroc: Sexualités, genres et (trans)identités dans la littérature marocaine* (Queer Morocco: Sexualities, Genders, and (Trans)Identities in Moroccan Literature) came out. In 2014, one of France's strongest presses largely devoted to Francophone literatures and studies, L'Harmattan, published Khadija El Achir's master's thesis on Rachid O. Finally, in 2017, the field seemed to explode with two important book-length studies: Mehammed Amadeus Mack's *Sexagon: France, Muslims, and the Sexualization of National Culture* and Denis M. Provencher's *Queer Maghrebi French: Language, Temporalities, Transfigurations*.[10]

These developments coincided with the arrival onto the literary scene of Francophone Maghrebian writers who openly proclaimed their same-sex desires and sexual histories, beginning with Rachid O. in 1995 and Eyet-Chékib Djaziri in 1997, whom Nina Bouraoui and Abdellah Taïa followed in 2000. Yet the Maghreb certainly did not have to wait for such writers to read representations of queer desires. As I wrote in *Queer Nations*, "Rare indeed is the Maghrebian writer who does not deal with male homoeroticism or same-sex sexual behavior in at least one novel, and a number of prominent writers deal with these topics in many works."[11] If more recent scholarship has understandably gravitated toward writers who may be more identifiable as something like lesbian or gay, I am still convinced that other writers are still offering representations of "queer" deeds and thoughts that we should not neglect. A recent novel that confirms this conviction is Mohamed Leftah's posthumously published 2011 novel, *Le dernier combat du Captain Ni'mat* (The Final Battle of Captain Ni'mat).

Leftah tells the story of a retired air force officer who falls in love with his Nubian domestic servant named Islam after having an erotic dream about him. A physical relationship ensues behind the back of Ni'mat's wife, and they even end up living together before Islam must flee because of threats issued by self-styled neighborhood morality agents. The sexual contact between them begins when Ni'mat asks Islam to massage him, and in the end, the latter inserts his finger into the former's anus. When Islam, shocked, voices his dismay to his uncle Samir, the latter suggests that Ni'mat may have needed the "internal massage" because of his aging prostate. Even at the novel's beginning, therefore, being fingered by another man is no cause for concern on the part of the novel's older characters.

Worth considering in some detail are the novel's first three mentions of the word "homosexuality." The first is in a description of the transformations Ni'mat undergoes while coming to terms with his newfound love and desires. This passage describes "a transformation in the way he dressed . . . and . . . a more discreet, specific, and intimate hygiene," as well as the way Ni'mat transforms his bikini underwear into G-strings

> so as to be permanently aware *of* and in touch *with* his body, with what he had become, which he wanted to come to terms with and take full responsibility for [*qu'il voulait assumer pleinement*]. At least in the depths of his physical and mental being, because in this society of his, publicly admitting that he was a homosexual was out of the question.[12]

The use of the word "assumer" here is quite significant, since it means to accept, take responsibility for, almost to choose in the existentialist sense. In *Queer Maghrebi French*, Denis Provencher details even a French difference from the Anglo-American notion of coming out signified by a frequent preference for the verbs *assumer* and *s'assumer* over French equivalents of the more Anglo alternative of *coming out*. In short, homosexuality is *not* what Ni'mat is laying claim to in this passage.

The second and third mentions of homosexuality occur in a discussion of Cairo's Queen Boat incident:

> Homosexuality was considered a grave, extreme perversion that threatened the foundations of religion and society, an insulting defamation of Egyptian masculinity. . . . The hunt for homosexuals could open up an abyss for a man like Captain Ni'mat, who had served in the institution charged with defending the country.[13]

And again, homosexuality here is more something that might cause a problem for Ni'mat than something with which he might want to identity. That these two mentions occur in response to an actual historical event resulting in the arrest of Egyptian MSM is worth detailing, for this incident provoked a good deal of outrage on the part of Western activists, an outrage that Joseph A. Massad critiqued in his 2007 *Desiring Arabs* as representative of what he calls the Gay International—Western gay rights organizations that, in the name of defending the rights of non-Western sexual minorities, engage in Orientalist efforts contributing to the imposition of a hetero/homo binary. Massad's book as a whole "is decidedly *not* a history of 'Arab sexuality,' whatever that is, but an intellectual history of the representation of the sexual desire of Arabs in and about the Arab world and how it came to be linked to civilizational worth."[14] In his account of what he also calls the "*heterosexualizing* of a world that is being forced to be fixed by a Western binary," rather than essentializing an Arab *difference* as some have claimed, he instead stresses, "Ironically, this is the very process through which 'homosexuality' was invented in the West."[15]

I have been arguing for some time now that queer Maghrebian studies can only benefit from, and indeed become even queerer, by taking seriously Massad's assertions and assessing what they might contribute to our field. And one way of reading Leftah's novel is as an allegory of the very transformations Massad details. This aspect of the novel is especially noticeable in an explicit sex scene with the following "conclusion": "Captain Ni'mat's flesh weakened, melted, became nothing more than gratitude for this sublime, loving sodomization that took him to the heights of a double pleasure, made him ejaculate at the same time as his marvelous horseman shot off [*déchargeait*] in him, while holding onto his hips and drawing him even closer."[16] The word I translate here as "horseman" (*cavalier*) refers also to the Arabic word Ni'mat uses throughout to label himself: *khawala*, "*celui qui se laisse chevaucher*," as he defines it in French, he who lets himself be straddled or ridden like a horse. In short, although the word *homosexualité* is not banished from the novel, in the term *khawala*, one finds as much resistance to a Westernizing, homosexualizing reading as an affirmation of one.

3. Sub-Saharan Africa

While queer Francophone studies may not have produced works like Neville Hoad's 2007 *African Intimacies: Race, Homosexuality, and Globalization* and Brenna M. Munro's 2012 *South Africa and the Dream of Love to Come: Queer Sexuality and the Struggle for Freedom*, queer African studies in general has always included literature in French. Two essays on the topic were published as early as the 1980s: Daniel Vignal's "L'homophilie dans le roman négro-africain d'expression anglaise et française" (Homophilia in Black African Novels of English and French Expression) and Chris Dunton's "'Wheyting Be Dat?' The Treatment of Homosexuality in African Literatures," both of which consider both French and English examples as if, otherwise, there would not have been enough material for an article-length study. Even as recently as 2013, Chantal Zabus's *Out in Africa: Same-Sex Desire in Sub-Saharan Literatures and Cultures* took a similar approach. This was certainly the thinking that guided my own chapter on sub-Saharan Africa in *Queer Roots for the Diaspora: Ghosts in the Family Tree*, "Queer Roots in Africa," in its own inclusion of literary texts in both English and French.

If many studies like Vignal's and Dunton's do not consider work by writers that are arguably queer, this is especially true for the works in French. In fact, in many cases, the main question asked in such work has been whether this or that representation could be considered homophobic. In many ways, therefore, the treatment of MSM and WSW in sub-Saharan literature in French may seem "under-developed," if I might risk a cliché saturated with colonial implications. By contrast, however, Francophone African cinema has "led the way" in the representation of queer desire, as may be seen in the examples of Mohamed Camera's 1997 *Dakan* (Guinea), Laurent Bocahut and Philip Brooks's 1998 *Woubi chéri* (Côte d'Ivoire), Joseph Gaï Ramaka's 2001 *Karmen*

Geï (Senegal), and Marthe Djilo Kamga's 2017 *Vibrancy of Silence: A Discussion with My Sisters* (Belgium). Interestingly, three of these four films deal with WSW, of which even France-based Zabus gives no French examples. Nonetheless, in her 2017 essay, "States of Emergence: Writing African Female Same-Sex Sexuality," Brenna M. Munro writes that

> Francophone African writing of the lesbian has taken different directions [than Anglophone ones], with diasporic writers such as Calixthe Beyala (Cameroon-France) and Frieda Ekotto (Cameroon-United States) producing controversial, experimental novels that challenge taboos of multiple kinds; Ekotto's 2005 *Cuchote Pas Trop* (*Whisper Not Much*), for example, depicts incestuous, intergenerational, and interracial relationships in a narrative of multiple chronologies and narrators.[17]

In the interest of bringing less-known texts to the attention of a wider readership, I would like to follow up on Munro's suggestion in relation to Ekotto's more recent 2010 novel, *Portrait d'une jeune artiste de Bona Mbella* (Portrait of a Young Artist from Bona Mbella), which takes place in the neighborhood named in its title, a poor area in the Cameroonian city of Douala. In a series of vignettes, Chantou, this novel's female narrator, remembers a youth shared with other female characters known collectively as the Bona Mbella Girls, who circulate while emanating queer desire: "Abroad, as soon as they come together, they recognize each other, they signal each other with signs like *la sape*, cruising, coins, in short the look-at-me [le m'as-tu-vu] characteristic of torrid girls."[18] And during their adolescence in Bona Mbella, they underwent an apprenticeship of queer desire so well detailed by the novel:

> Leaning against a pole, two young girls are working at the play of seduction. They try out the first kiss. I contemplate them in absolute silence. They kiss on the lips, touch each other, and then draw in close. They are completely turned on by their body heat. Desire intensifies. They whisper love me, love you. Their faces light up, both disturbing and joyful. Time and space belong to them; nothing moves around them. The wind transmits echoes of their daring, but they lack the experience of real girls in love. (23)

Love, desire: these are always a matter of apprenticeship, but lacking queer models for such an apprenticeship, these young female characters must rely on their own collective experimentation in what I would argue is quite a refreshing difference from their American or European counterparts. For Western coming-out narratives often stress the (often male) narrator's feeling of being isolated, of being the only boy in the world who desired other boys. In Ekotto's novel, however, the apprenticeship of queer desire is always already collective.

Her novel is also quite unique among world literatures in French for its detailed and often extensive discussion of WSW, as in the following passage, in which the narrator's cousin Munyengue Kongossa, "sorcière du bavardage" (sorceress in the art of banter), and one of the novel's most self-confident and adventurous characters, reveals her sexual proclivities:

> According to her, whitey likes downtown [*le* whity *aime le* downtown], which he regularly visits. With an air of defiance, Munyengue Kongossa suggests to her best girlfriend [*sa meilleure amie*] that they proceed to the act itself. No thanks, the other answers, I don't like being licked as if by a dog. Come on, girl! Don't be such a heavy [*quelle lourdeur*], relax, chick [*petite*], it's delicious, I promise. Munyengue Kongossa insists and proceeds to demonstrate. For whitey, cunnilingus is there for those who want to use it. Every time he visits downtown, he enriches his business with unbelievable interest. "No," says the Bona Mbella Boy, "*I* refuse the practice of visiting the Netherlands." "You mean downtown," MK corrects with confidence. "I prefer uptown, where I perform better," answers the other. "Why ask for the impossible?" he counters. "Downtown cunnilingus is no longer part of my skill set [*n'est plus de mon ressort*]." (18–19)

Notable here is the mapping of the cityscape onto the female body. When desire circulates, it does so across both city and body. Furthermore, another request for queer experimentation is embedded within a discussion of interracial hetero sex, which, especially "downtown," is considered nonnormative by the African male character in the passage. Again, the novel does not shun the word "homosexuality"; in one passage, the very same Muyengue Kongossa, who has returned from France to visit the neighborhood she grew up in, says to the narrator, "I am proud of you, you live your life, you embrace your homosexuality [tu assumes ton homosexualité]. That's so cool" (33). Yet, even here, homosexuality remains, as in Leftah's novel, something to be *assumé*, not what one arrives at after leaving the "dark continent" of a closet behind.

4. The Caribbean

At first glance, it might seem difficult to find examples of queer representation in the Francophone Caribbean. Thomas Glave's 2008 anthology *Our Caribbean: A Gathering of Lesbian and Gay Writing from the Antilles* contains just one author (out of thirty-seven) from a Francophone country, Haitian Assotto Saint, and he was an English-language writer, whereas the single island of Puerto Rico and its diaspora have an entire GLQ literature anthology devoted just to themselves.[19] Such studies as Lawrence La Fountain-Stokes's *Queer Ricans: Cultures and Sexualities in the Diaspora* and Mark Padilla's *Caribbean Pleasure Industry: Tourism, Sexuality, and AIDS in the Dominican Republic* have no counterparts in the French-speaking Caribbean even though some islands are administratively part of France.

In the first chapter of *Queer Roots*, "Looking for Roots among the Mangroves," I examined the Creole figure of the *makoumè* or sissy faggot in the literatures of Martinique and Guadeloupe, from the famous footnote in Fanon's *Peau noire, masques blancs* (*Black Skin, White Masks*), in which he denies the existence of homosexuality in Martinique only to go on to describe the presence of the *makoumè* there, to the deployment of the same term in the novels of Raphaël Confiant and Patrick Chamoiseau, as well as in Maryse Condé's *Traversée de la mangrove* (*Crossing the Mangrove*). Whereas in the Créolistes' novels, supermale characters often engage in verbal jousts during which they try to outdo each other in the realm of masculinity by calling each other *makoumè*, in Condé's novel, the *makoumè* is used as a figure to queer the notions of Caribbean roots, identity, and cultural origins. Yet even in the novels of Confiant and Chamoiseau, a careful reading of the role of the *makoumè* can lead to a deconstruction of the very masculinity that many of their male characters must work so hard to claim.

In the second chapter of her *Creole Renegades: Rhetoric of Betrayal and Guilt in the Caribbean Diaspora*, "Maryse Condé's *Histoire de la femme cannibale*: Coming Out in the French Antilles," Bénédicte Boisseron carries a number of these ideas forward in relation to a wider body of Condé's work. But first, in a section titled "From *Débarqué* to *Macoumè*" (64–8), she situates her reading of Condé in relation to a survey of other representations of MSM and WSW, including Fanon's as mentioned earlier. She then goes on to give a list of Condé's novels containing representation of MSM and WSW.[20] In an interview, Boisseron also gets Condé to discuss her gay son who died of AIDS.[21]

Prior to my own work on Guadeloupe and Martinique, Michel Magniez had already published "Le héros homosexuel dans les récits en Haïti" (The Homosexual Hero in Haitian Narratives), which highlights three Haitian novels that prominently feature MSM: Claude Fignolé's 1999 *La dernière goutte d'homme* (Man to the Last Drop), Jean-Euphèle Milcé's 2004 *L'alphabet des nuits* (Night Alphabet), and Kettly Mars's 2005 *Vents d'ailleurs* (Winds from Elsewhere). Set in Port-au-Prince, Milcé's novel is especially useful for my purposes here. Its narrator, Jeremy Assaël, is a third-generation Jewish immigrant and shop owner who has two male lovers over the course of the novel. The first mentioned is Lucien, Jeremy's security guard and "passive lover," who is shot by a police officer and dies on page 21.[22] Right away, therefore, the political violence of a number of Haiti's recent regimes comes to the fore in relation to the novel's representation of queer desire.[23] More broadly, the wider political context frequently "intrudes" into the narrative in the form of passages in italics that represent such "texts" as (often violent) news broadcasts, official government proclamations, missionary discourse, and human-interest stories.

After Lucien's death, Jeremy reconnects with his boyhood friend and lover Fresnel, who also disappears, but not before lots of childhood memories are brought back: "My love relation with Fresnel was ten years old. In spite of the passion and desires of our adolescence, we never displayed them in public. Our secret has the advantage of distancing us from school by the magic of our journeys" (51). In Western narratives, this childhood secrecy would be considered an infantile phase to be followed by a coming out. While the question of negotiating between dissimulation and disclosure does come up from time to time in Milcé, homosexuality as an identity predicated on a past coming out is never unequivocally embraced. In a conversation with a homophobic American missionary, Jeremy expresses a certain discomfort with being called a homosexual: "It would bother me less if you considered me a homosexual person rather than saying I was a homosexual [je me sentirais moins gêné si vous me traitiez de personne homosexuelle au lieu de dire que je suis un homosexuel]" (76–7). Whereas my English translation might be less clear as regards Jeremy's reticence, in French the difference between an adjective that assigns one attribute among many to a whole person and the same word as a noun that names a person as essentially defined by that one attribute is clearer.

After Fresnel's disappearance, Jeremy goes on a quest to determine Fresnel's fate. This quest occurs in three stages, starting with the homophobic missionary. Then Jeremy seeks assistance from Zaccharias, a functionary who "also admitted to being homosexual" and whose function is not clear, though he seems to have fingers in lots of pots and to extract payments for greasing the gears of bureaucracy (96). The third and final stage of this quest involves consulting the *lwa* or vaudou divinities with the assistance of Ebner, an *houngan* or vaudou priest. After Ebner is unable to find signs of Fresnel in the afterlife, he contacts a dead Lucien, who informs them that Fresnel is in Florida awaiting political asylum. The novel even suggests that Jeremy might join him. When he finally receives a letter from Fresnel, the latter writes, "My immediate project is you, and then I would write a book, a novel about exile and migration [traverse]" (137).

From its passages in Creole (especially in relation to vaudou) to its reflections on Jewish history to even its acknowledgment of the oddity of a Jew seeking succor from the vaudou *lwa*, *L'alphabet des nuits* is indeed a novel about queer diaspora. In fact, the connection between a traditional Jewish understanding of diaspora and the making of an African one is driven home in one of the many italic intrusions mentioned earlier, an excerpt from the *Journal officiel de la République d'Haïti* (Official Journal of the Republic of Haiti) in the eightieth year of independence: "Foreign nationals belonging to the Muslim Jewish [!] community are forbidden entry into Haitian territory.... Mobile and immobile goods [Les biens meubles et immeubles] belonging to those affected by this measure will be auctioned off and funds collected will be disbursed to the former owners minus any taxes or fees owed" (97). This proclamation not so subtly echoes two aspects of the 1685 Code noir governing the treatment of slaves in the French Caribbean, including Haiti: the first article expelling Jews from islands in French possession, and the declaration that slaves are *meubles* (normally furniture, but here movable property). By rereading the history of slavery through the experiences of a homosexual Jew, Milcé creates a queer allegory of the Nation of the sort we also saw in Tremblay.

5. French-Kissing World Literature in French

In the primary texts that I have considered for each region, we have seen how the diversity of local manifestations of MSM and WSW can come to challenge various

Western homosexualizing assumptions about same-sex desire. In Leftah and Ekotto's novel, use of the French verb *assumer* offers an alternative to Anglo coming-out models. Ekotto's and Milcé's novels highlight the possible critical contributions that we might make when considering the importance of the circulation of desire. I would now like to end this chapter by allowing the empire to write back, so to speak, by bringing, that is, the insights garnered through my readings of literary texts from Africa and its diaspora back to Québec where I started. Although this reading strategy runs the risk of giving the West the last word, it nonetheless allows for the decentering of Eurocentrism that can happen when the West is forced to follow and take after Africa and the Caribbean. It is appropriate that the "novel" *French kiss: Étreinte/exploration*, by poet, novelist, and feminist theorist Nicole Brossard be chosen for such a final look, since she once appeared on a panel with Ekotto at the Rhetoric of the Other conference held at the Université du Québec à Montréal in May 2000, and since this novel is about, more than anything else, the circulation of desire.

Yolande Villemaire's "critical presentation" of the novel's first edition remains one of the best readings of it:

> *French kiss* is a stupefying novel that gets you stoned and turns you to stone [*Qui stone et méduse*] because everything dances around in it. . . . At the blank center of this novel "it's so hot, one mixes up its words." As if one mixed up the exploring tongues/languages in the embrace of mouths, during a French kiss that occurred on 30 October 1973.[24]

Villemaire goes on to summarize its plot in the simplest of ways: "Two men and three women working at exploring their bodies, their city" (8). Brossard herself writes a summary of the novel's plot into its text: "Following Sherbrooke Street from one end to the other. From east to west. Historic, geographic merry-go-round" (15). Indeed, and as in Ekotto's novel, Brossard's city and body become so intertwined as to become almost indistinguishable: "One mixes up the words *body* and *city*, maps/cards [*cartes*] on the table, anatomic illustrations, systems" (13).

Translated into English as *French Kiss; or, A Pang's Progress*, the novel's title alone merits close reading. With its first part seemingly in English and meaning kissing with the tongue, the title is not necessarily in English given that the *Dictionnaire de la langue québécoise* offers an entry for "French kiss," which it defines as follows: "A kiss involving the penetration of one's tongue into one's partner's mouth."[25] But since *tongue* can double as language, the title can also mean to kiss in and through language. Given that the second part of the title names the text as an embrace and an exploration, an exploration *qua* embrace, French kissing becomes a critical maneuver as well, one that I would relate to queering. Indeed, meaning itself becomes lesbian in a lexical "Sapphic/semantic chain" (98). This "text that doubles as a vibrator . . . slows down in one's mouth and salivates words and love letters to . . . kiss/fuck [*baiser*] fragments of fiction" (17, 80). This *French kiss* thus brings together "fictive lips" as sex itself becomes a form of textual production: "Juices slide: the tongue licks from left to right as one strikes through or erases" (15, 23). If the French kiss swipes left to right across the text of desire, it serves as a kind of going-back-over of the movement of the lavender queer car of desire (their mauve Plymouth) from east to west or right to left. Brossard's novel can thus serve as an allegory of reading of the sort that allows us to read and theorize queer desire on the move in world literatures in French.

Notes

1. See Cindy Patton and Benigno Sánchez-Eppler, eds., *Queer Diasporas* (Durham, NC: Duke University Press, 2000); John C. Hawley, ed. *Postcolonial, Queer: Theoretical Intersections* (Albany, NY: SUNY Press, 2001); Arnaldo Cruz-Malavé and Martin F. Manalansan IV, eds., *Queer Globalizations: Citizenship and the Afterlife of Colonialism* (New York, NY: New York University Press, 2002); Eithne Luibhéid and Lionel Cantú, Jr., eds., *Queer Migrations: Sexuality, U.S. Citizenship, and Border Crossings* (Minneapolis, MN: University of Minnesota Press, 2005).
2. Jarrod Hayes, *Queer Nations: Marginal Sexualities in the Maghreb* (Chicago, IL: University of Chicago Press, 2000), 20.
3. Some of the papers delivered as part of this colloquium were gathered into a two-part special dossier of *Québec Studies* edited by Charles R. Batson and Denis M. Provencher. See especially Batson and Provencher's introductions to each part: "Feeling, Doing, Acting, Seeing, Being Queer in Québec: Michel Marc Bouchar, Rodrigue Jean, and the Queer Québec Colloquium," *Québec Studies* 60 (2015): 3–22; and "Queer (Again) in Québec" 61 (2016): 111–14.
4. For a good place to start for queer films, students, teachers, and scholars might look at Bill Marshall, "Sex and The Nation," in *Quebec National Cinema* (Montreal, Canada: McGill-Queen's University Press, 2001), 103–32.
5. This title is hard to translate. "Damné" means "damned," and "sacré" means "sacred," but the latter can also be a curse word, and the verb "sacrer," which means to consecrate a king in French, means to curse in Québec French.
6. Michel Tremblay, *Théâtre I* (Montreal, Canada: Leméac, 1991), 287. Unless otherwise indicated, all translations of the texts under discussion are my own. Further citations of this text will be given parenthetically.
7. Michel Tremblay, *Thérèse et Pierrette à l'école des Saints-Anges* (Montreal, Canada: Bibliothèque Québécoise, 1991), 59.
8. Tremblay, *Théâtre I*, 153.
9. See for example the shift from Robert Schwartzwald's 1991 "(Homo)sexualité et problématique identitaire" (in *Fictions de l'identité au Québec*, ed. Sherry Simon, Pierre L'Hérault, Robert Schwartzwald, and Alexis Nouss, 115–50 [Montreal, Canada: XYZ, 1991]) to his 1992 "From Authenticity to Ambivalence: Michel Tremblay's *Hosanna*" (*American Review of Canadian Studies* 22, no. 4 [1992]: 499–510) to his 2008 "'Chus t'un homme': Trois (re)mises en scène d'*Hossana* de Michel Tremblay" (*Globe* 11, no. 2 [2008]: 43–60).
10. For more details on these two studies, see my double review of their works, "'Queeriser' le Maghreb, un Maghreb qui 'queerise,'" rev. of Mehammed Amadeus Mack's *Sexagon: Muslims, France, and the Sexualization of National Culture* and Denis M. Provencher's *Queer, Maghrebi, French: Language, Temporalities, Transfiliations*, *Nouvelles études francophones* 33, no. 1 (2018): 160–8.

11 Hayes, *Queer Nations*, 18.
12 Mohamed Leftah, *Le dernier combat du Captain Ni'mat* (Paris, France: La Différence, 2011), 99.
13 Leftah, *Le dernier combat*, 99.
14 Joseph A. Massad, *Desiring Arabs* (Chicago, IL: University of Chicago Press, 2007), 49.
15 Massad, *Desiring Arabs*, 188–9.
16 Leftah, *Le dernier combat*, 106–7.
17 Brenna M. Munro, "States of Emergence: Writing African Female Same-Sex Sexuality," *Journal of Lesbian Studies* 21, no. 2 (2017): 189.
18 Frieda Ekotto, *Portrait d'une jeune artiste de Bona Mbella* (Paris, France: L'Harmattan, 2010), 17. Further citations of this text will be given parenthetically. *La sape* is a Congolese fashion phenomenon often defined by the style donned by the men who embrace it, one that involves ostentatious elegance of the sort dandies engaged in. Ekotto herself, in another passage, defines its practitioners, *sapeurs*, as "redoutables bluffeurs des nanas, un monsieur Gigolo, en somme," or "chick bluffers to be reckoned with, in short, Sir Gigolo" (27).
19 David Caleb Acevedo, Moisés Agosto Rosario, and Luis Negrón, eds., *Los otros cuerpos: Antología de temática gay, lésbica y queer desde Puerto Rico y su diáspora* (San Juan, Puerto Rico: Tiempo Nuevo, 2007).
20 Bénédicte Boisseron, "Maryse Condé's *Histoire de la femme cannibale*: Coming Out in the French Antilles," in *Creole Renegades: Rhetoric of Betrayal and Guilt in the Caribbean Diaspora* (Gainesville, FL: University Press of Florida, 2014), 68–9.
21 Bénédicte Boisseron and Maryse Condé, "Intimité: Entretien avec Maryse Condé," *The International Journal of Francophone Studies* 13, no. 1 (2010): 131–53.
22 Jean-Euphèle Milcé, *L'alphabet des nuits* (Orbe, Switzerland: Bernard Campiche, 2004), 14. Further citations of this text will be given parenthetically.
23 Although the novel is structured almost as entries in a journal or diary, the lack of years in the constant dating and timing of these entries makes its historical setting difficult to pinpoint, but it does seem to be more recent than the Duvalier dictatorships.
24 Nicole Brossard, *French kiss: Étreinte/exploration* (Montreal, Canada: Les Quinze, 1974), 7. Further citations in text.
25 Léandre Bergeron, *Dictionnaire de la langue Québécoise* (Montreal, Canada: VLB, 1980), 235.

11

Locations of Identity: *Littérature-mondaine* and the Ethics of Class in Evelyne Trouillot's *Le Rond-point*

Régine Michelle Jean-Charles

In July 2018, the Haitian government announced a 51 percent increase in gas prices, which led to a wave of protests throughout Port-au-Prince. The incident, which circulated on social media under the hashtag #gazmonte, resulted in widespread demonstrations in the lower parts of the city as well as in the more affluent Pétionville. The fallout from the rise in prices and the subsequent demonstrations inspired the creation of the Kòt Kob Petrocaribe movement, led to the resignation of several ministers, and eventually culminated in more massive protests and demands for Haitian president Jovenel Moise to step down in 2019.[1] Responding to the chaos during the summer of 2018, Haitian novelist and academic Evelyne Trouillot wrote a social media post about the rampant inequality in twenty-first-century Port-au-Prince. Her critique is worth citing at length:

> We must mourn the losses, for the sake of those who have invested and have lost, especially the small and medium-sized business owners who had to struggle to set up shops and keep them running under such difficult and precarious conditions. We must mourn the losses for the entire country, for we are all going to suffer the consequences. But in this great swell of lamentations, let's especially not forget those who have truly lost [*dans cette grande mouvance de lamentations n'oublions surtout pas les vrais perdants*]. . . . To chalk [the] movement up to political manipulation is a complete denial. An age-old denial of the other who suffers, who is hungry, who can't send his children to school, who lives in unsanitary housing, who, when he does go to school, comes out half-illiterate, who can't find work, who knows that his future is a big question mark without an answer, who sees life as a vast desert in which he has no place, who thinks his only choice is to leave this country that offers him nothing, who becomes filled with frustration, anger, and resentment, who goes to church, lifts his hands to God, the spirits, the Virgin and her saints, who knows some places are off-limits to him, who

encounters discrimination and injustice every day, who doesn't always recognize his true enemies and sometimes lashes out in desperation, who learns to lie, to steal in order to survive, who wanders the streets in his despair with a fake smile and wild eyes, who dies because he cannot pay for medical care or medication, who falls victim to bullets in a no-go zone or elsewhere, who eats badly and very little or not at all, who runs to catch an already overflowing bus, who sweats under a blazing sun to arrive on time at the factory where she makes terrible wages, who has to fight off the fondling of a perverted boss, who sometimes resigns herself to it all because she knows life isn't on her side, who fights nevertheless to stay alive, who spends her days in front of a hot stove waiting for buyers, who roams the streets with her merchandise on her head to earn a few cents, . . . who knows the State has forgotten her, that her fate doesn't interest the officials, that those who have money and live well don't even look at her, that her life will not change, . . . who . . . who. . . . The ones we forget, whom the president has once again forgotten in his statements after the protests, don't need encouragement to join in pillaging. You can't buy off people to get them to act frustrated and angry when they already are.[2]

I begin with Trouillot's post because of the way she forcefully indicts class disparities here as an omnipresent and too often neglected problem in Haiti. Trouillot's admonishment to "not forget those who have truly lost" is a warning to Haitians of the middle and upper classes as well as to those in the diaspora. The repetition of "who" reminds us that the list goes on because the injustice to which the poor are subject is unremitting. As the lines above make clear, for Trouillot class divides are one of the most pressing challenges of contemporary Port-au-Prince. This visible concern with the daily lives of people who make up the poor, working poor, and poor middle class is also reflected in her fiction, in which class structure is a social, cultural, political, and ethical problem.

Trouillot's attention to this issue gives rise to a preoccupation with what Michel-Rolph Trouillot calls the "everyday."[3] Building on the elder Trouillot, Martin Munro argues that Haitian literature should be seen through the lens of *littérature-mondaine*, or worldly literature, rather than *littérature-monde*, the term that famously rose to prominence in 2007 as a number of authors writing in French sought to resist and reframe the label "Francophone." Munro frames Haitian literature as at once the precursor and the successor to *literature-monde*, proposing that a worldly literature is to a large extent a literature of the everyday, of humankind interrogating itself on its own terms, alone in the universe and largely unbound by religious thought. It is, he adds, also sophisticated in terms of its style and philosophical and political content; it is not falsely naïve or tentative in its representation of its subjects or their relation to the world.[4]

Taking this definition seriously, in this chapter I examine Evelyne Trouillot's *Le Rond-point* (2015) as a worldly text in which class division is central to imagining the everyday. As I show here, Trouillot's approach to class evidences the characteristics of *littérature-mondaine* described earlier. Indeed, the novel is concerned with daily existence, reveals humankind interrogating itself, and is never falsely naïve in its representation of class as a social and ethical problem. I argue that Trouillot's use of narrative devices such as multiple points of view and lengthy interior monologues highlights the complex relational dynamics of class in modern-day Port-au-Prince. By writing class differences into and through her narrative techniques, Trouillot puts pressure on a contentious social topic, revealing the depths of the cleavages and inviting us to ask ethical questions about how these divisions manifest in society. What does it mean to live side by side yet never interact with people of vastly divergent status? How does one make sense of social inequities from a philosophical perspective? In raising these questions, Trouillot also gestures toward a broader global issue, that of class and class disparity as a problem throughout the Global South.

Set during the early 2000s, *Le Rond-point* follows the daily lives of Sorel, Titi, and Dominique, each from different socioeconomic backgrounds. The inequalities between their disparate worlds are reflected in the narrative structure—the narrators alternate in each chapter, which has the effect of containing their stories, and thus their worlds, within a chapter. This material division of isolated chapters reflects how rigidly class functions. Given the lack of social mobility, class hierarchies can be viewed as fixed and easily maintained. When examined from the perspective of the protagonist's reflections about class barriers, the individual chapters display insightful social commentaries specific to the main characters' social positions: Sorel, a young man from a poor background, is struggling to make ends meet; Titi, an eleven-year-old boy from a modest working-class milieu, is uneasy about his place in society; and Dominique, a woman from the elite upper class, is increasingly uncomfortable with what her life has become. The novel's second epigraph is excerpted from Victor Hugo's 1872 collection of poems, *L'année terrible*, in which he points out the relationship of interdependence between people from different social strata.[5] In the collection, Hugo laments the conditions of life in nineteenth-century France. The verse quoted in the epigraph reads: "Alas! How long will it be necessary to tell you again that they should be given their share of the city? That your blindness produces their blindness." The poem's message is clear: the rich and the poor are mutually dependent upon one another, and the rich should have an obligation to the poor. At the very least, the wealthy should understand that the lavish lives they live relate directly to the problem of social inequality. The intertextual reference to Hugo is noteworthy—no other writer in France devoted such sweeping and pointed attention to the negative effects of class division. In fact, Hugo emblematizes thoughtful and nuanced care for the dynamics of class. In many ways, *Le Rond-point* provides a twenty-first-century example of how this kind of careful attention to class—one that considers the perspectives of characters from distinct parts of society and places them in social interactions—offers insight into social inequality. Nowhere is class division more evident in *Le Rond-point* than in the use of three narrators to tell the story. Accordingly, I structure the following analysis around each protagonist and his or her perception of how class operates.

1. Sorel, or Centering the Poor Majority

For *Le Rond-point*'s protagonists, class governs social interactions and takes up a significant amount of their mental space. In Sorel's case, material concerns restrict his life and drive him to make decisions with negative consequences. As a part of the working poor, he is barely able to subsist on what he makes daily: "How to get by on this minimum wage? You can barely survive on what you earn while your debts increase[. You owe] the seller of fried food, or the girl who looks after her mother's banana trade."[6] Almost rhetorical in nature, the question is put to the reader and demands an answer. It is an ethical question. How can anyone survive on the low wages offered to people like Sorel, who make up the poor majority in Port-au-Prince? Moreover, it also raises policy issues, pointing a finger at the government's culpability in maintaining the social inequality that governs life in Haiti.

Nonetheless, Sorel realizes that his situation is not the worst in the city. Recognizing how many others struggle like him, he acknowledges that his reality is not isolated from that of his neighbors. Often, he makes use of the French word *les gens* (people) to indicate belonging and non-belonging: "But people like you [*les gens comme toi*] have to count every gourd, every penny of their pitiful salary, so they don't just buy in small quantities, but rather drop by drop. The moral of the story is that the rich will remain" (69). *People like you.* There are others. Whenever "people" is used in the novel, it usually connotes difference. There are *these* people and *those* people. The distinctions, which the French articles make clear, denote either distance or proximity. Furthermore, Sorel's use of the term here conveys scale. Namely, people like him make up the greatest number. For this majority, survival is the foremost concern: "Here, people are all busy surviving [*Ici, les gens sont tous occupés à survivre*], not raising the number of anonymous corpses, insignificant and multiple deaths in a city where human life passes like clear water between the cracks of the toes" (77).

Trouillot may emphasize Sorel's point of view because he represents the impoverished masses. The centrality of his voice and perspective highlights Trouillot's commitment to rendering thoughtful portraits of the poor. For Sorel, the ordinary and everyday bring misery and privation. Recounting the details of his daily experience is essential to laying bare how he got to the point of opting for a life of violence and crime. With Sorel at the center, *Le Rond-point* becomes a story about class discrepancies, one that is invested in the implications of social inequality for the poor. By privileging Sorel's vantage point, Trouillot invites the reader to inhabit his world more closely, more deeply. This kind of intimacy is achieved, more specifically, through the use of the second-person voice. Sorel constantly raises questions about class that ask the reader, the "you," to contemplate its ethical implications. His assessment of Port-au-Prince as a universe made up of two worlds—the rich and the poor—articulates one of the basic premises of the novel:

> This country is the same. It's not a single country, it's a lot of different movies playing simultaneously. Some are shown in incredibly rich and beautiful places, and you [*tu*] do not even try to recognize them. Like those well-kept gardens that you sometimes see on the sly in the instant it takes for a vehicle to pass through the

gate before it closes again and blocks the view of the flower beds, an instant where you're speechless and find yourself back in your place in a brutal, ugly world. You know that in your film, you will never be the main actor, the one who gets around the bad guys, the hero who carries the girl in his arms out of a building in flames. You just don't want to die stupidly, like those black people who regularly get killed in the first fifteen minutes in American gangster movies, as if a black person always has to be shot for the action to start. (70)

The point of view elaborated here, that people of different classes are worlds apart, is reflected in the novel's narrative structure, as noted above. Similarly, the use of the film metaphor in this passage offers a revealing comparison. It exposes the sharp disparity between the classes, as well as the way subject positioning is informed by the particular social milieu you belong to. According to this logic, one's worth is based on one's proximity to privilege. Consequently, one's humanity becomes linked to one's class. The two environments are characterized by stark contrasts: "incredibly rich and beautiful places" stand in opposition to "a brutal, ugly world." Here, this world makes up one part of an internally divided Haiti, "this country" that is "a lot of different movies playing simultaneously." But Sorel's musings about American films end on a note that also acknowledges inequality in global terms, beyond the borders of the nation. Explaining that his cousin who migrates to the United States in search of a better life must eventually return with "the lights out in his eyes and fear in his belly," Sorel effectively debunks the myth that migration is the solution to poverty (70–1).

Victimized by the class structure, Sorel has very limited life choices in terms of both access and mobility. This experience develops in him a heightened awareness, an ability to see with his "third eye" and interpret these social dynamics. Having lived two weeks in Cité Soleil, he understands how the poorest of the urban poor live:

> And since that day, in spite of yourself, at every corner you saw the children in the city. The six-year-old boy going at dawn to fetch water from the fountain who was mowed down one fine morning by the car of a gang on the run.... The nine-year-old girl raped by a policeman. The HIV-positive baby thrown naked into a gutter. (72–3)

These grim, everyday scenes inform Sorel's vision of inequality as a bleak and omnipresent backdrop. The poor, he reminds us, just as Trouillot's social media post does, are the ones who suffer the most from such cleavages.

Another key aspect of the lived destitute experience that Trouillot brings out in her novel is the temporality of the torment. Sorel's economic situation is perpetually precarious. He repeatedly describes in vivid detail the difficulty of being poor, emphasizing the way in which time stretches out. His reflection on Haiti's poor is rooted in his own, first-hand knowledge:

> A country where hunger never falls asleep. Hunger—you've known her for a long time, you've been sleeping next to her, and when the night comes, she goes right into your dreams and makes fun of you by sending you visions where you eat

all you want. In the morning, she is still there and greets your awakening with a painful pinch. (158)

Sorel's story is about how to survive in a society where there is no room for him to exist. It is especially noteworthy that of all the characters' voices, only Sorel's is personalized for the reader. Narrated in the less frequently used voice of the second person, his tale registers most intimately. Positioning the reader as an onlooker, second-person narration connotes more proximity than the third person but more distance than the first-person voice. Typically, second-person narration is "not defined by who is speaking but by who is listening."[7] In *Le Rond-point*, the use of "you" underscores Trouillot's ethical preoccupation with the situation of the masses. Her concern with class divides is manifestly informed by the way in which, in the story, the poor are left out of consideration, or, when they are indeed considered, how they are cast as violent and abject. Thus, the use of this particular narrative mode becomes a powerful example of how second-person narration can be most effectively deployed. As Matt Del Conte notes, this mode "manifests in narrative technique the notion that someone or something outside of yourself dictates your thoughts and actions . . . the inclusiveness of the you pronoun lumps the readers and the protagonist together."[8] For example, when Sorel explains his decision to join a gang, the reader must put herself in his mind, forcing her to imagine what his decision to take part in the planned kidnapping attack must be like. In sum, through this technique, Trouillot's depiction of class division poignantly conveys the extent of the rift and reveals how harmfully present this gulf is for Sorel and others daily.

2. Titi, the Youth, and Class Division

Read through the perspective of young Titi, *Le Rond-point* also exposes the impact of social inequality on the youth of the lower middle classes. As someone from the working poor or precarious middle class, Titi goes to school, where he interacts with people of different social backgrounds. Yet rather than serving as an equalizer that grants him access to mobility, school becomes a place where inequality is magnified. Interacting with children more privileged than him alerts Titi to what he does not have, making him painfully aware of how inequity operates. The trope of invisibility becomes the main way through which readers apprehend and understand his relationship to social class. For Titi this invisibility manifests itself in two registers: as an awareness of how he is seen by others and as a learned behavior that becomes a mode of survival. "Gradually," the narrator relates, "he learned not to shine, to imitate voices and gestures, to slip among them, to become even more invisible" (31). Throughout the novel, the language of visibility and invisibility is often deployed specifically in conversations about class division. The poor are acutely aware of their invisibility to those of higher class status than theirs. Invisibility is a subject position shaped by upper-class attitudes, as well as a survival strategy necessitated by the social dynamics. The logic of invisibility demonstrates a deeper truth about how people are classed: different social groups *become* invisible based on their class status. As an ocular logic, invisibility is integral to the maintenance of class division. As long as the poor masses are unseen, their humanity will continue unrecognized, and there will be no moral impulse to assist them. The trope of invisibility recurs throughout the novel but is only used in reference to Titi and Sorel, making it clear that social disappearance exists as a problem only for the poor and working class.

As Trouillot points out in her impassioned post, the rage of the underprivileged is an essential ingredient of violent unrest. But how does one represent the cyclical movement from inequality to poverty, anger, and violence, without presenting those who perpetrate that violence as morally abject? In *Le Rond-point* we witness the mounting anger of a young boy as he becomes increasingly attuned to the inequity of the world around him and to how he himself figures in. Charting the escalation of Titi's rage from the beginning of the novel to the end, we can see how social inequity informs the growth of his frustration. Class awareness inspires and intensifies his anger the more he realizes that he is helpless against these circumstances: "Titi wipes his face angrily as rage, spite and sorrow still simmering in him. He hates what he feels, did not know you could feel so bad, to the point of wanting to take his own flesh in his hands and hit it to get the pain out" (58). A confusion of several simultaneous emotions overcomes him. His visceral anger links directly to his social position. As a boy on the cusp of puberty, Titi is acutely aware of how masculinity functions; he feels his emotions are a cause of shame and must be hidden from those around him. How Titi responds to these emotions is just as important as the emotions themselves. The frequency with which "anger [*colère*]" and "rage" are associated with the boy effectively communicates the degree of his frustration.

Titi's awareness about class comes primarily from his family and schoolmates. His cousin Mireille constantly reminds him that he should be thankful for what he has. As she comments, "At your age, many boys have to let old perverts fiddle with them you know where, to eat their fill" (136). The sexual implications of her statement remind the reader that the mechanics of inequality are sexed and gendered, too. His mother's job as a domestic worker also reveals the effects of class division and economic disparities to Titi. He regularly contemplates what her experience is like, and how the people she works for must look down on her. When his mother shares how well she is treated by her bosses, he thinks to himself, indicating his wariness, "As if the bosses could treat the servants well!" (32). At school, he encounters children of varying means. Even in the smallest social interactions with his classmates, he is mindful of these distinctions. For example, as the group discusses the need for children to have more play spaces in Haiti, he sits back to listen to what his classmates have to say only because he knows that they, unlike him, have travelled abroad: "Titi did not say much, and he let others who have more advantages than him speak. Curiously they were the ones who had the most to say, the ones who naturally found themselves in this priest's school without it being because of their mothers' employers" (137). After family and school, the third source of Titi's class consciousness comes from his encounters with the Calvins, the family his mother works for. "Whenever Titi visits the Calvins," recounts the narrator, "he plunges into another world, as if he had crossed through the TV screen and entered a magical land" (171). In this passage, we notice the importance of visibility again. Titi is keenly aware of how this wealthy family perceives him. He feels his otherness through their gaze: "The outrageously artificial face they put on told the young boy clearly that he did not belong to their world" (182). To be poor, his story makes clear, is to understand how one appears to others. This ability to see oneself through the eyes of others is a form of class double consciousness that is at work for all of the characters who are not part of the elite. The novel shows emphatically that those outside the upper class are fully aware of how their economically and socially privileged neighbors look (or do not look) at them.

Titi reveals as much when he sums up his interaction with Claude P. Séverin, the man he believes to be his father. This moment, when Titi sees himself through the eyes of this possible parent, becomes a final breaking point: "His anger has reached its climax" (102). This anger has two sources. First, his father abandoned him, and second, in his current state, he is invisible to his father: "The fact is that this Claude P. Séverin had not really even looked at him. He had seen a kid who didn't belong to his world and had immediately stuck him in a box: street child, beggar-in-the-making, or budding little thug" (138). Even though he has a home, while his mother works, and he attends school, to Séverin he is invisible. Clearly, Titi is cognizant of the way others view him, and that for them, he could be any child from the streets. The fact that he does not look like a child from the elite upper class suffices in their mind to write him off as a future hoodlum. Once again, the logics of visibility and invisibility are revealed to play an operative role in class division. Who is seen? Who is not seen? Who gets to be seen? Who wants to be seen? The logics of visibility, understood well by those who are not members of the privileged elite, underscore how class inequality results in the creation of two worlds.

3. Dominique, or the Obsessions of the Rich

Constant references to class in the characters' interior monologues suggest that this social reality is simultaneously hypervisible and invisible. That is to say, class is not often explicitly discussed but is regularly contemplated by all regardless of their social status. From their various subject positions, Sorel, Titi, and Dominique all consider the intricacies of class division. When these protagonists reflect and comment on inequality, their conclusions are astute, unflinching, and precise. Interestingly, perhaps no other character ponders the gulf between the classes more than Dominique, whose privileged status still does not afford her the luxury of not having to think about it. Much of Dominique's mental space, as evidenced by her interior monologue, is occupied by ruminations on the reality and effects of class discrepancies. When analyzed for its ethical implications, though, a close reading of this monologue reveals her callousness. That is to say, while one might expect someone who reflects so regularly on class and social inequalities to behave differently, Dominique does not.

The baggage that comes with Dominique's class does cause her to constantly question the actions of those around her. She is keenly aware of the social hierarchies of Haitian society, even if she is unwilling to do anything about it. For instance, on a rare occasion in which Dominique discusses the class divides in Port-au-Prince *with* her friends, she paints a stark picture: "'On one side famine, on the other, opulence. Orchid exhibitions and luxury-goods fairs versus food riots and hordes of ragged children.

The contrasts in this country never cease to throw me off guard," admits Dominique to her two friends" (161). Of course, given the context of the 2000s, when Port-au-Prince was racked by a series of kidnappings, it makes sense that Dominique would begin to think more deeply about class division, since her privileged and protected life in the suburbs of Port-au-Prince is actually in jeopardy. Her new awareness only emerges when she begins to perceive her pampered existence as threatened.

Still, at times Dominique contemplates social gaps with remorse and culpability. It even seems that conspicuous consumption by people of her status irks her: "How much money must a human being accumulate before he feels safe? But she makes no criticism, not out of unconditional acceptance but out of laziness and a need for mental comfort" (131). On the one hand, she hates the fact that the poor have become invisible to people like her, but, on the other hand, she recognizes that she too refuses to see them: "Dominique is aware that in reality, she does not look at others, that she is only interested from afar" (151). Dominique is mindful that she lives in what she describes as "an unequal world, where those running on short legs will never catch up with the tall ones" (152). Still, her knowledge and disdain for how class operates do not inspire her to engage with the world differently. Dominique's interior monologue reveals the contradiction in her views of social class: there are many barriers and symbols of inequality that she critiques, but she is comfortable with the basic structures remaining intact. Furthermore, when we compare her musings about class with her anxieties about her safety, Dominique's disinclination to do anything more than ask moral questions about how social hierarchies remain in place becomes even more apparent.

When Dominique observes that "hunger is the scourge [*le fléau*] against which we should fight, but these people do not care, too busy walking from the beach, to the supermarket, to luxury restaurants," she identifies hunger as a source of contagion that is corrupting the society (161). Her thoughts about class regularly focus on what divides people, on the creation of distinct worlds, and on the idea of separation: "Here more than elsewhere, people seem to evolve in different worlds but so close that sometimes Dominique thinks she's in the zone of the fantastic, in a surreal and unpredictable world" (43). Dominique is actually quite critical of her neighbors' opulence without seeming to even notice the poor that surround them or the enormous chasm between the rich and the destitute in Port-au-Prince. During a party, she goes so far as to ask herself, "In what country did they live? Did they not realize that coexistence was becoming more and more difficult, that they were evolving like mad ants, each one running after booty for itself, indifferent to the fate of others?" (86). She is not fond of these kinds of conventional class trappings, and even seems to be suspicious of them. Yet Dominique's reflections on the ideological and ethical problems posed by her position occur largely in isolation from her social interactions. That is to say, while she thinks about these questions on her own, she never deigns to bring them up to anyone else for discussion. As a result, her admonishment rings hollow when viewed in the context of her own behavior. Dominique's class identity consolidates around her understanding of what her status affords her in terms of comfort, lifestyle excess, and access.

For people like Dominique, kidnappings pose a constant threat. The number of references to kidnapping in Dominique's interior monologue as well as in her conversations with friends shows the extent to which it is one of the upper class's main preoccupations. Her obsession with the topic and the fear it inspires in her serves as another marker of her social class. Take, for example, the statement that "her best friend was kidnapped last year," which immediately signals to the reader that she is a part of the group for whom kidnapping is an ever-present danger (40). Dominique's concerns about kidnapping are aggravated by a recent incident in which a close family friend was taken at gunpoint and held for a period of weeks. She confesses the extent to which this event impacted her emotional health: "I am traumatized, I do not know how Jean-Paul can endure the sight of these streets, of this space where he was attacked" (110). That she associates his remaining in Port-au-Prince with the lavish conditions in which he is fortunate to live reminds readers of the global implications of class division. In other words, rich, elite Haitians may not necessarily enjoy such status in the other countries where they might live in diaspora.

Despite these glimpses of her troubled emotions, what we see most often from Dominique is that she is able to relativize the pain and the poverty that she observes around her. When she muses to herself about the condition of the world, it is merely as a way to comfort herself that the injustice in Port-au-Prince is not peculiar to Haiti but, in fact, a universal problem: "From Gaza to Beirut, from Bogotá to Athens, men kill each other, the big ones eat up the little ones, and injustice and violence reign" (151). Through this global link to other countries, the author reminds us that Haiti does not have a monopoly on suffering. We can note here that someone of Dominique's class status needs to justify the existence of suffering so as to assuage her own culpability in maintaining social inequalities. Furthermore, the fact that Dominique moves so quickly from her own emotions to the suffering of those around her suggests that she is unable to grasp the difference between the systemic and structural suffering of the poor and her own concerns as a privileged woman. The emotional labor she exerts worrying about her life pales in comparison to that of Port-au-Prince's poor majority. There is also, in Dominique's case, a sense of resignation pervading her interior monologue. On one side, she sees kidnappings upset the comforts of the upper class, but on the other, these attacks are just one more in a list of difficulties that they must endure for having chosen to live in Port-au-Prince: "It is necessary to accept this world, to deal with the insalubrity of the streets, administrative corruption, and the annoyances of an increasingly unpredictable daily life, and now the kidnappings" (109). As the linchpin of Dominique's social anxiety, the kidnappings present the paradox of the rich: they are threatened because of their lavish lifestyles, yet they refuse to leave Port-au-Prince because they enjoy those lifestyles so much. By deploying these strategies to represent the characters' consciousness, the author unveils the inner workings of their minds, judgments, assumptions, fears, and anxieties.

In his study of class dynamics in African American fiction, Rolland Murray posits that "novelists rewrite class division as form, ideology, and epistemology."[9] As we have seen, Trouillot's exposition of such a division inscribes this chasm in narrative form, beginning with her use of multiple narrators, each contained within his or her own chapter, and continuing with her focus on the interior lives of these characters, which further emphasizes their social cleavages as we witness what divides and unites them. The novel's structure interrogates the construction and maintenance of class differentiation in order to expose the deleterious effects of these intervals on all members of society. Ultimately the novel unveils between rich and poor a gaping chasm that is both local and global. Form, ideology, and epistemology are all integral to Trouillot's approach to the operation of class in the everyday lives of Haitians. The ethical nudge she gives her readers prompts them to ask themselves to what end this division is, and what it will come to.

Le Rond-point's rapid dénouement, where the worlds of these characters quite literally clash, uncovers the possibility of a disastrous ending that looms in the future of Haitian class relations.[10] In the final chapters, the narration shifts to reflect the overlap and collision of the characters' lives (194). This change is an aesthetic choice that mirrors the action of the plot. As the suspense picks up in a culminating chapter in which the three perspectives alternate within this single section in a more condensed form, suddenly we see what happens when the classes crash into one another. The disaster that strikes in the novel's conclusion offers, at best, a pessimistic interpretation of the cost of social division. Haitian society's stratification is such that people live in the same space without ever interacting with one another. At the same time, *Le Rond-point*'s leitmotif highlights this moment of contact. This also recalls Nadève Ménard's argument, in "The Impact of Fleeting Encounters," that Trouillot does not allow class divide to remain unperturbed. Describing several short stories in which brief encounters hold tremendous weight for the characters in question, Ménard writes:

> One might be tempted to read these brief texts by Trouillot as commentary on the enduring divide between social classes in Haiti. . . . Especially since in popular representations and scholarly discourse Haiti is often depicted as a space where separation between classes cannot be breached at all. In these stories, Trouillot reveals that in fact the separations are themselves quite fragile and subject to being torn down at any moment.[11]

Likewise, *Le Rond-point* also reminds us that although these characters exist metaphorically in different worlds, they actually live in the same city, in the same country, and that class disparities *are* responsible for many of the conflicts between them. By giving us characters who eventually must *see* each other and who demand interaction across the division dictated by social inequality, she offers another path forward. In the clear-eyed bluntness of its assessment, the novel's closing pages thus evince, and embody, the concept of *littérature-mondaine*, disabusing us of the naivete of the belief, whether implicit or explicit, that social inequality can be so easily overcome. The conflicts created by class tensions manifest differently for each character, yet all are united in their affective responses, which range from frustration and fear to anger. These protagonists show that, despite how different they are in terms of socioeconomic background, they operate within a similar emotional register. The end result—and what lies at the heart of Trouillot's ethical project in *Le Rond-point*—is a thoughtful interrogation of humankind that transcends social differences even as it exposes class division.

Notes

1. The question "Kote Kòb Petwo Karibe'a?" (Where is the Petrocaribe money?) became wildly popular and led to an anti-corruption movement when Haitian writer and filmmaker Gilbert Mirambeau posted a video on social media asking about the funds from Haiti's participation in the oil-sharing program created by Venezuelan oil company Petrocaribe.
2. Nicole Simek's translation of Evelyne Trouillot, "Dans cette grande mouvance de lamentations n'oublions surtout pas les vrais perdants," Facebook, July 10, 2018 (accessed July 10, 2018).
3. See Michel-Rolph Trouillot, "The Odd and the Ordinary: Haiti, the Caribbean, and the World," *Cimarrón: New Perspectives on the Caribbean* 2, no. 3 (1990): 3–12.
4. Martin Munro, "Haiti's Worldly Literature," *Small Axe* 14, no. 3 (2010): 69.
5. Victor Hugo, "L'année terrible," in *Œuvres complètes de Victor Hugo* (Paris, France: Alexandre Houssiaux, 1869–85).
6. Evelyne Trouillot, *Le Rond-point* (Port-au-Prince, Haiti: L'Imprimeur, 2015), 68. All translations from the novel are my own. Further citations of this text will be given parenthetically.
7. Matt Del Conte, "'Why You Can't Speak': Second-Person Narration, Voice, and a New Model for Understanding Narrative," *Style* 37, no. 2 (2003): 204.
8. Del Conte, "'Why You Can't Speak,'" 205.
9. Rolland Murray, "The Time of Breach: Class Division and the Contemporary African American Novel," *Novel: A Forum on Fiction* 43, no. 1 (2010): 16.
10. With regard to the plot, toward the end of the novel, more such connections become clear when we learn that Magda works for Gabrielle, who is Dominique's cousin (Trouillot, *Le Rond-point*, 165).
11. Nadève Ménard, "The Lasting Impact of Fleeting Encounters in Evelyne Trouillot's Fiction," *Palimpsest: A Journal on Women, Gender, and the Black International* 8, no. 1 (2019): 11–14.

Part IV

Francophone Literature and Planetary Intertexts

12

Writing French in the World: Transnational Identities and Transcultural Ideals in the Works of Michel Houellebecq and Boualem Sansal

Jacqueline Dutton

1. Introduction: Declinism and World Writing

French-language literatures have never been entirely confined to a Francophone bubble. However, the twenty-first century has produced new paradigms that influence where writing in French is read today and how we find out about it. Digital editions apparently allow instantaneous access to e-books anywhere in the world, but in reality, pirated copies are easier to download than official editions due to national publishing embargos. According to the Organisation Internationale de la Francophonie (OIF), literacy in French continues to rise throughout the world, but it is nearly impossible to record readership of literature in French, as books are frequently photocopied and circulated widely in Africa and elsewhere, often with the clandestine blessing of their authors.[1] Although said bubble is clearly not Hexagonal, the highest sales of literatures in French are still reported in France, extending then to Belgium, Luxembourg, Switzerland, and Québec. Another factor impacting the place of French-language literatures in any reading environment is the promotion of English-language literatures via the Internet and global streaming services like Apple TV, Netflix, and Amazon, thus increasing the footprint of blockbuster films and series such as *The Girl on the Train / La Fille du train* (Paula Hawkins, translated into French by Corinne Daniellot in 2015), which was among the top ten best-selling books in France in 2017.[2] Australian author Karen Viggers's phenomenal and unexpected success—with over 500,000 books sold to date in France—materialized when influential bookseller and television host Gérard Collard promoted the 2011 novel *The Lightkeeper's Wife* (translated into French by Isabelle Chapman as *La Mémoire des embruns* in 2016) as the book of the summer in 2016.[3]

Outside the *francosphère*, there are other challenges. Declining numbers of translations into English over the past fifty years have effectively reduced the range and reach of many authors writing in French. Even a Nobel Prize in Literature can only partially resuscitate the desire to translate J. M. G. Le Clézio's novels: whereas his first seven works were immediately published in English from 1964 to 1975, in the wake of Anglophone interest in Jean-Paul Sartre, Albert Camus, Françoise Sagan, and the New Novel, his 2008 Nobel has only produced four more translations, including one retranslation.[4] When the Nobel went to another French writer in 2014, the English newspaper headlines were practically identical to those announcing Le Clézio's win: "Patrick Modiano: the Nobel prize-winner nobody had read."[5] Translations of Modiano have been marginally more successful, potentially due to his engagement with a universal and increasingly fashionable preoccupation—war—as in *The Occupation Trilogy* (*La Place de l'Étoile*, *The Night Watch*, and *Ring Roads*) republished by Bloomsbury in 2015.

Before either of these national treasures cum French Nobel laureates were named, there was a turning point in the twenty-first-century French literary landscape when, in 2006–07, a series of mainstream press articles changed wider perceptions of writing French in the world. After five of France's major literary prizes were awarded to writers who were not typical representatives of Franco-French culture in 2006, there was open debate on the state of French literature in every form of media.[6] Mobilizing the "Étonnants Voyageurs" festival partisans,[7] Michel Le Bris and Jean Rouaud assembled forty-four signatories to the 2007 *Manifeste pour une littérature-monde en français* to defend the capacity of French-language literatures to "*dire le monde*."[8] The impact and longevity, as well as the lacunae and flaws, of this manifesto have been amply documented in articles and conferences all over the world. On the other side of the Atlantic, Donald Morrison declared "The Death of French Culture" in his November 2007 article in *Time* magazine,[9] for which he was pilloried, and responded in 2010 by coauthoring with Antoine Compagnon a book of the same title.[10] In fact, Morrison laid out similar claims regarding French literature as those outlined earlier, namely, that demand for and distribution of French fiction is waning with fewer and less popular translations into English, and that 30 percent of fiction sold in France is translated from English.

Despite this potent combination of rallying cry and low blow, the crisis of confidence in French literature in 2006–07 has resulted neither in a renewed interest in French writing in general nor in a fuller embrace of world literatures in French among English-language translators, publishers, and readers. There are of course still great examples of contemporary French literature in translation, including those short-listed for the French-American Foundation's prestigious translation prize,[11] and of the ten French novels recommended by Mira Kamdar in the *New York Times* in 2017, half of them are written by authors with heritage that is at least bicultural.[12] But this does not constitute a resurgence, much less a renaissance, and critics note instead a continuing "decline" in French society and literature, with "declinism" described as an "obsession" and a "booming industry" in Rachel Donadio's *New York Times* article citing the success of Michel Onfray's writing among others.[13] Hugh Schofield interviewed several best-selling French authors for *BBC News Magazine* including Marc Lévy and Marie Darrieussecq, in an attempt to find out why French books are not selling abroad, suggesting the answers may lie in stereotypes perpetuated around fundamental differences in book cultures, with the French perceived as intellectual and inaccessible, and the Anglo-Americans as storytellers in the style—ironically—of the nineteenth-century French social realists.[14]

While this theory has anecdotal and ethnographic merit, Gisèle Sapiro's quantitative and qualitative analyses of the causal interplay between globalization and transnational publishing industries influencing translation of French literature into English demonstrate conclusively that there are also world economic systems and field-theory factors at stake.[15] Her data set—literary titles translated from French in the United States between 1990 and 2003—confirms many of the "death of French culture" claims. It shows that past achievements constitute French symbolic capital with 60 percent of the translations being "classic" literature—from the seventeenth century to modern postwar titles, while the remaining 40 percent of translations, published essentially by small independent publishers or university presses, reveal increased diversity in terms of gender and ethnicity of authors.[16] There is a clear correlation between the "grandeur and decadence" mainstream hypothesis and the empirical academic evidence that underscores the historical prestige of the Hexagon and the contemporary scattering of smaller-scale status among French-language literatures from all over the world.

Declinism and national depression are therefore not just journalistic buzzwords for French-bashing; scholarly books and articles are also tackling the same issues. In *How the French Think: An Affectionate Portrait of an Intellectual People*, Sudhir Hazareesingh laments the loss of French intellectual dynamism, describing a culture of inward-looking consolation oriented toward a national provincialism.[17] Sarah Waters attributes the French narrative of national decline to the 2008 economic crisis, signaling this perception's use value for nationalists as a symbol of the inevitable fall and rebirth of a strengthened nation-state.[18] In her groundbreaking study of the neglected field of Middlebrow French literature, Annamma Varghese determined that best-selling fiction published during the Sarkozy years (2007–12) can be divided into three distinct categories:

> escapist "lowbrow" narratives, by writers such as Marc Levy and Guillaume Musso, where a French expatriate finds salvation abroad thanks to a relationship with an Anglophone character; secondly, "highbrow" narratives of failure (by Michel Houellebecq and Marie Ndiaye) where the protagonist's relationship with a foreigner increases anxiety or is abandoned; thirdly, "Middlebrow" narratives of recovery (by Muriel Barbery, David Foenkinos, and Anna Gavalda) where the French protagonist falls in love with a foreign character within France and is rehabilitated.[19]

Varghese's categories and conclusions foreshadow the need to develop identities and ideals that traverse national and cultural boundaries in order to overcome French declinism and national depression. Writing French in the world today presents new challenges and new opportunities to react in more original, innovative, and creative ways. In this chapter, I want to explore the transnational identities and transcultural ideals of Michel Houellebecq and Boualem Sansal as writers of world literature in French, focusing on their 2015 novels *Soumission* and *2084: La Fin du monde*, respectively. Selected for their current influence and status as best-selling authors in French, Houellebecq and Sansal represent the intersection of critical success, consecrated by literary awards and prizes, and popular fiction. The immediate translation of their 2015 works into English, as well as into many other languages, attests to their relevance in the global thinking space and marketplace. After briefly describing the background and content of *Soumission* and *2084*, I will seek to expose the intratextual, intertextual, and extratextual factors that enhance the global mobility of these two exemplary authors and their works. In this way, I hope to show that the relative impact of writers today can be traced to their capacity to "*dire le monde*"—as Le Bris suggested in his *littérature-monde* manifesto—and even "*prédire le monde*," as they are less constrained by national networks and more influenced by global, social, and virtual realities.

2. Michel Houellebecq's *Soumission* and Boualem Sansal's *2084: La Fin du monde*

Houellebecq is well known to anyone interested in contemporary French literature, having garnered the Prix Goncourt in 2010, written six novels, five collections of poetry, and several essays, and participated in art exhibitions, films, and other public representations. His controversial, even scandalous reputation as a misogynistic, anti-Islamic, and pornographic writer broke the bounds of literary circles to make global headlines when his face appeared on the cover of the French weekly newspaper *Charlie Hebdo* on January 7, 2015. The apparently random confluence of events that occurred that day included the release of Houellebecq's new novel *Soumission*, which predicts in fictional form an Islamic future for France, and the killing of twelve *Charlie Hebdo* employees in a terrorist attack at the paper's office in Paris's eleventh arrondissement by Islamic extremists Cherif and Said Kouachi. The upsurge of support for the victims, their families, and freedom of speech represented by the paper and by extension France itself took shape in the slogan, logo, and hashtag "Je suis Charlie" that entered mainstream culture as a meme[20] and was the subject of academic conferences and special issues of journals.[21]

Houellebecq's *Soumission* became a confusing symbol of anti-Islamic sentiment, interpreted as a cynical speculation on the forthcoming presidential elections (2017), with its "dystopian" scenario depicting the rise of the Muslim Brotherhood political party in France and the appointment of its candidate, Mohammed Ben Abbes, as president in 2022. Critics related it to other "Great Replacement" precursor texts (in which, typically, France is invaded, overrun, or insidiously colonized by culturally differentiated migrants), such as Jean Raspail's *Le Camp des saints* (The Camp of the Saints) (1973) and Renaud Camus's *Le Grand Remplacement* (The Great Replacement) (2011).²² This collective, public narrative frames the intimate, individual story of the main hero's intellectual and religious trajectory toward Islam. François, the protagonist, is a moderately successful professor at the University Paris III—Sorbonne, specialized in the work of Joris-Karl Huysmans. His life is bereft of meaningful relationships, inspiration, or even purpose. He is eventually seduced by the Islamic way of life and faith as presented in the novel, for this mode of existence provides elite professional roles and young submissive wives to men like François without denying them the pleasures of alcohol or other Western indulgences. While his conversion seems ostensibly a means to keep his job and indeed improve his status, it also implies a pathway leading to a more meaningful spiritual life.

Sansal is just as controversial and scandalous in his home country of Algeria as Houellebecq is in France and the rest of the world, primarily due to his outspoken stance on the country's official observance of Islam and its repressive regime. His novels, short stories, and essays have been bestsellers in France and Europe. But *2084*, which appeared in August 2015, is the most mediatized, undoubtedly in part because of *Soumission*'s notoriety earlier in 2015, and potentially because the public was fired up by the Bataclan and Saint Denis attacks on November 13, 2015, which killed 137 people. Nominated and/or short-listed for seven literary prizes, including the Goncourt, *2084* won the Grand Prix du roman de l'Académie française 2016, and the English translation was released in 2017.²³ Houellebecq said in an interview with Laurent Ruquier that Sansal went much further than *Soumission* in its projections and predictions,²⁴ providing excellent publicity for *2084*. There are also some mitigated responses to this novel, though reviews are mainly positive.²⁵

Published between Sansal's two polemical essays, *Gouverner au nom d'Allah: Islamisation et soif de pouvoir dans le monde arabe* (2013) and *L'impossible paix en Mediterranée* (2017), the novel follows a narrative arc similar to George Orwell's *1984*.²⁶ Sansal describes future sociopolitical, cultural, and linguistic innovations, which are essentially an Islamist society where Mohammed is replaced by Abi (or Bigaye), Allah by Yölah, and the Koran by the Gkabul. Unlike Orwell's protagonist Winston, Sansal's hero Ati does not experience the heights of a passionate love affair or the depths of painful torture. He is recovering from tuberculosis in a sanatorium when he begins to question his faith and the foundations of his existence, based not on his own memories of better times but on the stories gleaned from pilgrims and caravans and the enlightenment of a delirious dream. After leaving the sanatorium and while slowly making his way back to his town, Qodsabad, he meets Nas, a civil servant who has discovered evidence in archaeological excavation that there was a world before Abistan where Yölah's religion coexisted with others. This means that 2084 was not the beginning of civilization when the Abistanis won the Holy War and disproves Abistani history upon which religion, the endless war, power, and enemies are founded. Ati returns home, meets a fellow subversive Koa, who follows him to

Kiiba, the Holy City, to find Nas. What they discover is the remains of Paris, complete with relics of the Louvre, and an enclave of privileged rulers who control knowledge, power, and ultimately the minds of the Abistanis. Koa is killed, and Ati is saved by Toz, an influential dissenter with a nostalgia for the twentieth century, who is nonetheless tolerated by the regime. The epilogue, composed of various newspaper reports and missives, indicates that Ati has been granted his final wish, to be taken back to the mountains near the sanatorium.

These preliminary descriptions of the authors and their novels already indicate the intertextual and extratextual factors that can impact distribution, circulation, translation, and reception of the texts. *Soumission*'s intertextuality ranges from Joris-Karl Huysmans to Raspail; *2084* reprises Orwell and cannot avoid responding to Houellebecq himself—all of these references attract new and old readers, in France and elsewhere. The horrific terrorist attacks on French soil in 2015, the looming presidential elections, the rise of Far Right political parties in France, as well as the intractable government in Algeria, with its hardline Islamic policies making world news, present clear extratextual reasons to be interested in representative voices from the literary front. Such linkages into imaginary and real networks enhance the novels' ability to traverse more diverse terrain and permeate more markets. A closer look at the transnational identities and transcultural ideals that underpin *Soumission* and *2084* allows for deeper understanding of the complexities at play when writing French in the world.

3. Transnational Identities

Widely used in the social sciences,[27] history,[28] and literary studies[29] to describe oscillations beyond and exchanges across (national) boundaries, "transnational" has also been attached to identity research, notably in migrant and diaspora studies.[30] Both Houellebecq and Sansal were born into transnational identities and have further developed this tendency through their residential decisions, social affiliations, and writing. Their original transnationality is less ethnic than statal, though subsequent movements emphasize the tensions between heritage and exile.[31] The role of transnational identities for successfully writing French in the world will be underscored through reference to these authors as well as to their literary progeniture.

In 1956, Houellebecq was born on Réunion Island, an overseas department of France, where his Algerian-born mother with Corsican heritage, Lucie Ceccaldi, was working as an anesthetist and living with her French ski instructor husband René Thomas. Symbol of France's extended outreach into the Indian Ocean, Réunion is the most ex-centric point of European lands, a vestige of French colonization and a haven of creolization. But for Houellebecq, Réunion was just a name on his birth certificate and a place his mother called home—he never knew or belonged to this island, and yet it has remained and forged part of his transnational identity. When his mother offloaded him as an infant first to his maternal grandparents in Algeria, then to his paternal ones in a small town in northern France, he finally set foot in the metropole and put down roots there, living somewhat centered for a time. During these formative years in France, he followed a traditional French education. Unusually, his grandparents were not religious, so Houellebecq researched, then rejected Catholicism on his own, attending catechism, contemplating baptism, then leaving religion behind when he discovered philosophy through Pascal at the age of fifteen.[32]

From these border-crossing beginnings, where France's colonial outposts were burdened with often irreconcilable transnational identities, Houellebecq drifted to the Parisian center, where his literary fortune was made. Le Bris, Rouaud, and the signatories of the *littérature-monde* manifesto point out the ingrained injustices of this center-periphery hierarchy, yet Paris was a necessary stopover for Houellebecq on the way back out to even more estranged territories. After the success of *Extension du domaine de la lutte* (*Whatever*) (1994) and *Les Particules élémentaires* (*Atomised*) (1998), the author moved to Ireland's west coast in 2000, avoiding income tax and spending his summers under the Spanish sun in Andalusia. The autofictional projection of Michel Houellebecq into *La Carte et le territoire* (*The Map and the Territory*) (2010) depicts the author entrenched but bored in his Irish home, then when he returns to the French countryside and his transnational identity is minimized, he is brutally murdered by a thief who wants to steal a simulacrum—his million-dollar portrait. Daniel, the comic protagonist whose clones (simulacra) populate *La Possibilité d'une île* (*The Possibility of an Island*) (2005), moves from Paris to Lanzarote, an ex-centric Spanish island equivalent in some senses to the Réunion Island of Houellebecq's birth, where his transnational identity enables him to transcend the vicissitudes of life in Paris.

The continual reshaping of Houellebecq's transnational identities in his life and work accounts not only for the author's cosmopolitan competence but also for his ability to render fiction in French accessible and enticing to a wider world of readers. Though his descriptions, anecdotes, and humor seem to require knowledge of contemporary French high and low culture, his writing does not exclude non-French readers—he has clear appeal across cultures, as one of the bestselling French authors in translation in the world today. Houellebecq himself has declared that everywhere he went to promote *Soumission*, responses were the same:

> *Revue des Deux Mondes*—You're currently promoting your book outside France. Are the journalists' questions and their understanding of the book the same everywhere you go?
>
> Michel Houellebecq—Let's say that it's more relaxed outside France. But it's still the same things that interest them every time: it's a European book. There's not much difference; when I think about it, the similarities are more striking to me.[33]

However, Joseph Voignac boldly contradicts the author, categorizing media reactions to *Soumission* according to French or English-language reporting and suggesting that while reactions to the novel in France focus on integration, insecurity, and

Islamophobia, the Anglophone press brings out the author's "real" themes: the moral and sexual misery of a world without religion and France's place in the world.³⁴ This interpretation raises important questions about the worldviews of both the author and the reviewers/readers and about how the author's transnational identity influences his writing and its subsequent circulation, translation, and appreciation.

Soumission's characters present a fascinating array of transnational identities, though François is resolutely French with some "exotic" tastes in food and women. As his name suggests, he *is* France, a product of the French education system, specialized in the work of a nineteenth-century French writer—Huysmans—and working in the most French of educational institutions—the Sorbonne. His confidants—Marie-Françoise and Alain Tanneur—are also French; indeed, Alain represents the essence of national interest, for he is a member of the political police. The young woman with whom François is in love, Myriam, is the perfect figure of the transnational Jewish-French citizen who has grown up in France but flees with her family to Israel in fear of persecution in France from either Far Right or Muslim Brotherhood power bases. Her transnational identity is incompatible with the new Muslim political regime, yet the new Sorbonne president Robert Rediger's Belgian nationalism—he has never become French despite living in France for twenty years—seems to belong in a France that rewards such an evangelical proselyte of Islam.³⁵ In *Soumission*, transnational identities only function in France if conjoined to transnational networks of Islam, such that Myriam may even be replaced in François's affections by French-Moroccan prostitute Rachida.³⁶

Like Houellebecq, Sansal was born in a transnational zone, a French colony where two nations and several different ethnic identities were vying for dominance. Another shared experience was being raised by an extended family rather than his mother: after his birth in Theniet El Had in 1949, Sansal was brought up by the wealthy sister of his grandmother before rejoining his mother in Algiers.³⁷ A nonobservant Muslim who declares never to have believed in God, Sansal grew up with transnational French-Arab traditions, enjoying the occasional flirtation with other religions like Jehovah's Witness, which apparently managed to convert many Algerians momentarily after independence.³⁸ He pursued engineering studies at the École Polytechnique d'Alger, then in Paris at the École Nationale Supérieure des Télécommunications, and also completed a doctorate in economics. Sansal moved to Boumerdès in 1972, when it was a university town with around fifteen research institutes and a transnational community of researchers from Canada, America, Russia, and elsewhere, financed by the Algerian oil industry.³⁹ In June 1972, Sansal travelled to Prague on a university exchange and met Anicka, who became his first wife in 1974. Their child Nanny was born in 1976, but they did not stay long as the situation became more difficult for mixed couples—Anicka was Christian—so she returned to Prague and the family eventually dissolved. After the oil crisis in 1986, cosmopolitan Boumerdès collapsed into a transnational depot for unwanted Islamist professors from other countries:

> To replace the professors, [the state] brought just about anybody in from Lebanon, Iraq, Syria. These countries used the opportunity to get rid of their own Islamists,

who all arrived at the same time, with their false qualifications. This damaged the scientific and cultural standards, coinciding as well with the Arabisation policy. In three months, the system went from completely French to completely Arab. But we spoke Arabic very badly whereas they mastered it perfectly.[40]

After working as a teacher, consultant, and company director, Sansal became a high-level civil servant, "directeur général de l'industrie et la restructuration" in the Ministry for Industry in 1995. As the Islamists exerted more political and social control, writers like Tahar Djaout were assassinated, provoking Sansal to find his own voice and start writing. His first novel, *Le Serment des barbares*, was published by Gallimard in 1999, and the international press began to seek his commentary on Algerian affairs. He spoke out against President Bouteflika, Islamists, and anything he believed was corrupt or unjust. In 2003, he was asked to leave the Ministry of Industry by Bouteflika, but he has remained in town with his second wife. Despite the fact that some of his books are banned in Algeria, they still seem to circulate, and he has a dedicated following. He also receives hate mail and death threats from various people enraged by his critical discourse on Islamism but is not persecuted by the government nor stopped from traveling. As one of the few successful French-language authors who has not relocated to France, Sansal lives a transnational life: his work is mostly sold in France, while his time is mostly spent in Algeria.

Yet the country which contributed to Sansal's original transnational identity is now determinedly nationalistic. Speaking of his bestselling semiautobiographical novel *Rue Darwin* with Dinah Assouline Stillman, Sansal stated:

> The Algeria of history (deeply embedded in that of the western Mediterranean entity) does not exist anymore. There is a new Algeria, born in convulsion and pain. This is a fake Algeria, rootless, without veritable links to the Western world (object of myth to some, and of disdain to others) or to the Oriental world (an Orient of fairy tale, extremely idealized).[41]

His transnational identity is now an anomaly in his country. The transnational present that is taken for granted in France and the rest of the world, extrapolated to negative ends in Far-Right identity politics as well as in Houellebecq's *Soumission*, is markedly absent from Sansal's account of Algeria, both in this interview and in his futuristic novel *2084*. His writing is anchored in an Algeria under 132 years of French colonization, a socialist country struggling with independence, and an Islamist lockdown that blocks intellectual enquiry and any search for authenticity other than that to be found in fundamentalist Islamism.

Unsurprisingly, there is little sign of transnational identities in *2084*. In fact, there seems to be no end to the sprawling nation of Abistan. Only those who oppose the regime or try to subvert it show even an awareness of otherness—like Ati, Toz, Nas, and Koa—but this does not translate into a sense of belonging to another nation or into negotiations between competing identities. In an empire where people are not meant to stray from their province, pilgrimages are the only possibility for mobility, yet the pilgrims are like lost souls, "comme des réfugiés oubliés" (forgotten refugees).[42] Like soldiers in the perpetual wars, they are apparently doing God's work:

> No one, not one single worthy believer, ever thought for an instant that these perilous pilgrimages might be an effective way to rid the cities of their teeming masses and offer them a beautiful death along the road to fulfillment. Similarly, no one ever thought that the Holy War might have been waged for the same purpose: to transform useless, wretched believers into glorious, lucrative martyrs. (18)

It is Abistan that represents the transnational entity, bringing together sixty provinces in fundamentalist misery, but its stronghold is so tight and intolerant that there can be no real diversity within its past, present, or future. There is no real distinction between nations—either historical or geographical—that can be recognized or even understood. In this way, Sansal's *2084* mirrors Orwell's *1984*. Winston, the dissident lead hero in *1984*, ends up like a brainwashed zombie in Orwell's Soviet-styled dystopia, with the only evident transnationalism being the fabricated alliances with Eurabia and/or Eurasia in their continual wars. In *2084*, Sansal's own dissident protagonist Ati is last sighted on a mountain in search of the "Frontier" to cross into a pocket of life where the repressive regime of Abistan does not reach, and where its rulers Abi and Yölah have no influence: "I would like Ram to leave me off somewhere in the Sîn mountains, in the Ouâ range . . . in a place where that Border has one chance in a million of existing. And if, by miracle, it does exist, I'll find it and cross it, and I'll see with my own eyes that twentieth century you so faithfully reconstructed . . ." (246). This hypothetical Frontier emphasizes the global domination of Abistan, for it is the only transnational crossing left.

Both Houellebecq and Sansal understand transnational identities through lived experience and have managed to mediate this extratextual reality in their fictional writing using both intratextual and intertextual techniques. Houellebecq's vision of France and Europe in 2022 predicts the coming transnationalism as overwhelmingly Islamic, hegemonic, yet perceived by his protagonist as positive. It is a panacea to the French secular nation's struggles with multicultural interventions; it is a solution to Belgium's conflict between nationalist Flemish and Wallon parties; it brings the northern and southern Mediterranean together. Some transnational identities must fall away for the dominant transnational dynamic to change France and Europe in the future. Sansal's vision functions as an extrapolation on Houellebecq's transnational identities, demonstrating that such hegemonic transnationalism results in nationalistic and homogenizing regimes intolerant of identities that require consultation or arbitration. While there is ultimately little hope for transnational identities in either of these novels, Houellebecq and Sansal, through their own transnational identities and their engagement with related themes in their fiction, do attempt to speak to and of the world—"*dire le monde*." By writing about their visions in a futuristic mode, they also seek to predict or project so that others might see where the present may lead—"*prédire le monde*." Examining how their transcultural worldviews influence their ideals exposes more hopeful prospects in their novels and potentially enhances their relevance to a globally oriented readership.

4. Transcultural Ideals

Soumission and *2084* have most often been described as dystopias in the mainstream press and in critical scholarship. While they may depict "an inverted, mirrored or negative version of utopia, the imaginary bad place as opposed to the imaginary good place,"[43] or a "non-existent society painted in considerable detail and normally located in time and space that the author intended a contemporaneous reader to view as considerably worse that the society in which that reader lived,"[44] they are first and foremost "uchronias"—projections of imagined societies in the future.[45] As such, they emphasize the protagonists' dissatisfaction not with the *present*, but with the *future* status quo. Accordingly, descriptions of an inherently dystopian society fill most of the pages, and the prospect of a better option for the future is introduced only toward the end of each of the novels.

There are nonetheless transcultural ideals that permeate the texts as positive symbols of cultural outreach, attempts to understand other cultures that allow glimmers of hope in the gloom. Tom Moylan sees these features as contributing to a literary construction he defines as "critical dystopia," which is essentially negative in its depiction and may be mistaken for declinist but maintains, nevertheless, a promise of change for the better if one knows where to look for it.[46] The ways in which Houellebecq's and Sansal's transcultural ideals are integrated and interpreted in the novels show the extent to which cultural crossings are valued or devalued and thereby determines whether solutions to society's future malaise may be found in contact zones with other cultures.[47] It is noteworthy, in this vein, that in *Soumission*, Parisian society in 2022 is not clearly distinguishable from the Paris of 2015. The main difference is the degree to which society has become transcultural, ranging from the cultural diversity of students at the Sorbonne to the cuisine François consumes from all around the world. However, there are many signs that these transcultural ideals have changed Paris for the worse. There is plenty of gunfire, car-burning, and commentary that Chinatown is and will be the safest place in the future due to Chinese repulsion of blacks and Arabs: "If the ethnic fighting spreads within Paris itself, the Chinese will stay out of it. Chinatown may be one of the last safe neighbourhoods in the city."[48] The refusal of transcultural ideals seems to have added value in Paris of 2022, resulting in considerable support for Marine Le Pen's Far-Right political party, "Indigènes de France."

Houellebecq's François also explores transcultural ideals in the form of religion, departing from the agnostic stance of the author and the official secular ethos of the state. A discussion with Tanneur about the future of religious transculturalism under

Muslim Brotherhood president Ben Abbes predicts that tolerance will be possible though the goal will be a religious monoculture via conversion to Islam:

> The real enemy—the thing they fear and hate—isn't Catholicism. It's secularism. It's laicism. It's atheist materialism. They think of Catholics as fellow believers. Catholicism is a religion of the Book. Catholics are one step away from converting to Islam—that's the true, original Muslim version of Christianity. (127)

This religious transcultural ideal is therefore also dismissed, and although François himself explores the cultural otherness of Catholicism in Rocamadour at Tanneur's recommendation, he too is disillusioned, and so another avenue for future happiness closes. The only transcultural ideal that persists is the seduction of Islam, which is presented as a valuable cultural crossing. After the new statutes of the Islamic university of Paris-Sorbonne determine that non-Islamic staff are not allowed to continue working there, and François along with most of his colleagues is retired from his duties, he is invited to the reinvestiture of Jean-François Loiseleur, who has converted to Islam. The striking transformation of this disheveled and dirty professor into a well-dressed representative of the faith, with a new young wife, is an obvious marker of value. The promotion of Rediger to president of the university and the trappings of his wealth and power are equally revealing of a positive interpretation of this religious transcultural ideal (214–20). For François himself, conversion to Islam also becomes an ideal, expressed in the subjunctive and conditional tenses,[49] as a crossing over into another culture and another dream (250).

François's conversion in *Soumission* is the opposite of Winston's conversion (or submission) in Orwell's *1984*; the transcultural ideal is clearly alive in the former, whereas in the latter, physical and psychological torture are required to force the protagonist to abandon his nonaligned ideals. Interestingly, there is no conversion in Sansal's *2084*, nor are there really many transcultural ideals, valued or not, as the absolute ignorance of the people, along with their blind submission to belief without any knowledge of the history or textual foundations of their existence, makes it practically impossible to recognize any options outside the seemingly irredeemable dystopia of Abistan. However, when they enter the ghetto of Qodsabad, Ati and Koa experience a subversive quarter that moves them in unfamiliar ways:

> There was a sort of spirit, a culture of resistance, an economy of making do, an entire relentless little beehive of activity that found a way to survive and to hope. Life was just passing by, seeking, clinging, inventing, confronting all sorts of challenges, then starting over again as much as was humanly possible. There would be a lot to say about the ghetto, about its reality and its mystery, its assets and its vices, its tragedies and its hopes, but in fact the most extraordinary thing about it, something no one had ever seen in Qodsabad, was this: the presence of women in the streets, women who could be recognized as human and not fleeting shadows: in other words, they wore neither mask nor burniqab, and clearly no bandaging

beneath their smocks. . . . Ati and Koa were so moved when a woman came up to them hawking some item that they lowered their eyes and began trembling all over. It was as if life had been turned upside down; they didn't know how to behave. (101–2)

This filthy dark ghetto inhabited by semi-liberated humans represents the "other side" of life in Abistan, but it is far from valued as a transcultural ideal. There is still another side of society that is revealed in the novel—a conspiracy of powerful people called "Démoc" (171), who are plotting to overthrow the current rulers but not create any real change. Only these "Honorables" in the city that has replaced Paris, la Cité de Dieu, have the key to the future, because they alone understand that a past and other cultures existed before 2084. Yet they do not wish to acknowledge or bridge cultural difference—their ideal is simply to perpetuate the ignorance of atemporal nationalism.

Among this ruling class, there is an individual who does display transcultural ideals that are accepted and even valorized. Toz, together with a few elite companions, pays homage to the past in his "musée de la Nostalgie" (240), which is located in the preserved temple of the Louvre. He invites Abi and Koa to play his game in the museum: "To get into the next room, the next episode in life, the key had to be found, and there wasn't all the time in the world, life is movement, it doesn't wait" (232). It is a metaphor for the need to take from the past what is needed in the present; as we gather, the key to access the present can only be found in the past. However, outside the museum, in Abistan, all repairs are lost because not only has History been modified but a new geography has also been invented, one that nobody contests because nobody travels and returns with news of other nations or cultures (257–8). So Toz's transcultural ideal is simply to retreat into the colonial past of his museum and into the luxuries of twentieth-century life such as trousers, cakes, and cigarettes, and thus he constructs his future happiness based on the past.

In their efforts to predict what the world might become, Houellebecq and Sansal present the relative successes and failures of transcultural ideals in their future fictional societies. The only examples with any value attached are conversion to Islam in *Soumission* and covert nostalgia in *2084*. As in the case of transnational identities represented in the novels, Sansal's society seems like an extrapolation on Houellebecq's scenario: if everyone succumbed to Islamic pressure and adopted François's transcultural religious ideals, there would no longer be any transcultural ideals at all, except those, like Toz's, harking back to a long-buried past.

5. Conclusion: Worlding Uchronia

Once more, writing French in the world is both less and more challenging than it used to be. On the one hand, publishing, distribution, translation, and reception are less constrained by national networks and more influenced by global, social, and virtual realities. Yet authors still need to pass through national networks before those global, social, and virtual realities can impact their success. Houellebecq and Sansal are prime examples of authors whose own transnational identities have served them well, offering them opportunities to access the Parisian publishing networks and to express perspectives that resonate beyond the borders of France. Their 2015 novels represent a complementary pair of texts that draw on transnational identities and transcultural ideals to enhance their global appeal and pertinence.

Whereas Houellebecq builds a uchronia in Paris 2022 that offers Islamic transnational and transcultural solutions to a splintered and uncontrolled transnational secular state, Sansal's projection of a uchronia in *2084* condemns the Islamist empire, which is clearly neither transnational nor transcultural. Each author employs techniques borrowed from critical dystopias, which provide pathways for the protagonists to escape the dire situations portrayed in society. In *Soumission*, François is saved by a transcultural step into a new religious life: "I'd been given another chance; and it would be the chance at a second life, with very little connection to the old one. I would have nothing to mourn" (250). In *2084*, Ati takes a transnational step over the frontier into a space of relative freedom from Islamist indoctrination, which may be interpreted as resembling a precolonial Algeria—a life of freedom in the mountains:

> The helicopter merely circled here and there and eventually left a man off on a plateau; he was carrying mountaineering equipment. Every day thereafter the guards saw him, spotted him, caught a glimpse; he was dressed in a very odd way, shall we say old-fashioned, and he hurried here and there and yonder, as if he were looking for something—a lost trail, a legendary ruin, a secret passage, the forbidden road, perhaps. (257)

Novels like these write French into world literature today because they can *"dire le monde"* and *"prédire le monde."*

Notes

1 Around sixty million sub-Saharan African and Indian Ocean students enrolled in French-language education in 2018—contributing 75 percent of those undergoing this type of instruction outside France—up 126 percent since 2014. Of the 300 million people in the world who speak French, 59 percent live in sub-Saharan Africa and the Indian Ocean area, with predictions that this proportion will rise to nearly 80 percent by 2070. See Organisation Internationale de la Francophonie, "La langue française dans le monde: Synthèse 2018," http://observatoire.francophonie.org/2018/synthese.pdf (accessed November 10, 2018).

2 Statista: The Statistics Portal, "Book Titles Ranked by Unit Sales in France in 2017," March 2018, https://www.statista.com/statistics/420806/book-best-sellers-france/ (accessed November 20, 2018).

3 Viggers has just sold the French world rights for her forthcoming book *The Orchardist's Daughter* (2019). Books and Publishing, "Viggers Novel Sold to France, Following 'Remarkable' Sales," May 31, 2018, https://www.booksandpublishing.com.au/articles/2018/05/31/108527/viggers-novel-sold-to-france-following-remarkable-sales/ (accessed November 20, 2018).
4 Association des lecteurs de J. M. G. Le Clézio, "Les traductions en anglais des œuvres de J. M. G. Le Clézio," https://www.associationleclezio.com/ressources/les-traductions-des-oeuvres-de-j-m-g-le-clezio/les-traductions-en-anglais-des-oeuvres-de-j-m-g-le-clezio/ (accessed November 20, 2018).
5 Duncan White, "Patrick Modiano: The Nobel Prize Winner Nobody Had Read," *The Telegraph*, July 18, 2015, https://www.telegraph.co.uk/culture/books/11741343/Patrick-Modiano-the-Nobel-Prize-winner-nobody-had-read.html (accessed November 20, 2018).
6 The Goncourt and the Grand Prix du roman de l'Académie française went to Jonathan Littel for *Les Bienveillantes* (*The Kindly Ones*); the Renaudot to Alain Mabanckou for *Mémoires de porc-épic* (*Memoirs of a Porcupine*); the Femina to Nancy Huston for *Lignes de faille* (*Fault Lines*); and the Goncourt des lycéens to Léonora Miano for *Contours du jour qui vient* (Contours of the Coming Day).
7 Étonnants Voyageurs, "Festival international du livre et du film," http://www.etonnants-voyageurs.com/ (accessed November 20, 2018).
8 Muriel Barbery et al., "Pour une 'littérature-monde' en francais," *Le Monde*, March 15, 2007, https://www.lemonde.fr/livres/article/2007/03/15/des-ecrivains-plaident-pour-un-roman-en-francais-ouvert-sur-le-monde_883572_3260.html (accessed November 20, 2018).
9 Donald Morrison, "The Death of French Culture: In Search of Lost Time," *Time*, November 21, 2007, http://www.time.com/time/magazine/article/0,9171,1686532,00.html (accessed November 20, 2018).
10 Donald Morrison and Antoine Compagnon, *The Death of French Culture* (Cambridge, UK: Polity, 2010).
11 This prize has been awarded since 1986. French-American Foundation, "Translation Prize," https://frenchamerican.org/initiatives/translation-prize/ (accessed November 20, 2018).
12 Mira Kamdar, "10 French Novels to Read Now," *The New York Times*, October 10, 2017, https://www.nytimes.com/2017/10/10/books/review/10-french-novels.html (accessed November 20, 2018).
13 Rachel Donadio, "France's Obsession with Decline is a Booming Industry," *The New York Times*, February 3, 2017, https://www.nytimes.com/2017/02/03/books/france-michel-onfray-decadence.html (accessed November 20, 2018).
14 Hugh Schofield, "Why Don't French Books Sell Abroad?" *BBC News*, December 9, 2013, https://www.bbc.com/news/magazine-25198154 (accessed November 20, 2018).
15 Gisèle Sapiro, "Translation and Symbolic Capital in the Era of Globalization: French Literature in the United States," *Cultural Sociology* 9 (2015): 1–27.
16 Sapiro, "Translation and Symbolic Capital."
17 Sudhir Hazareesingh, *How the French Think: An Affectionate Portrait of an Intellectual People* (London, UK: Allen Lane and New York, NY: Basic Books, 2015).
18 Sarah Waters, "The 2008 Economic Crisis and the French Narrative of National Decline: Une causalité diabolique," *Modern & Contemporary France* 21, no. 3 (2013): 335–54.

19 Annamma Varghese, "From Crisis to Comfort: Contemporary Bestsellers and the French Middlebrow's Narrative of Recovery," *Belphégor* 15, no. 2 (November 2017), http://journals.openedition.org/belphegor/965 (accessed November 20, 2018).
20 Mukul Devichand, "How the World Was Changed by the Slogan 'Je Suis Charlie,'" *BBC News*, January 3, 2016, http://www.bbc.com/news/blogs-trending-35108339 (accessed November 20, 2018).
21 Isabel Hollis-Touré, ed. "Special Issue: Charlie Hebdo," *French Cultural Studies* 27, no. 3 (2016).
22 See my forthcoming chapter "Transnational Utopianism in French Futuristic Fiction: From Mercier's *L'An 2440* (1771) to Houellebecq's *Soumission* (2015)," in *Transnational French Studies*, ed. Charles Forsdick and Claire Launchbury (Liverpool, UK: Liverpool University Press, 2020).
23 Only three of Sansal's seven novels have been translated into English to date.
24 Michel Houellebecq, "Michel Houellebecq—On n'est pas couché 29 août 2015," interview by Laurent Ruquier (YouTube video), August 29, 2015, https://www.youtube.com/watch?v=UyGX14yz-8w (accessed November 20, 2018).
25 Nadia Ghanem, "Why Algerian Novelist Boualem Sansal's '2084' is a Sensation in France," *Arabic Literature (In English)*, October 6, 2015, https://arablit.org/2015/10/06/2084/ (accessed November 20, 2018) and Bruce Fudge, "The Failure of Sansal's '2084': Its Essential Optimism," *Arabic Literature (In English)*, October 21, 2015, https://arablit.org/2015/10/21/sansals-2084/ (accessed November 20, 2018).
26 There have been many books, video games, and films that take the title 2084, extrapolating on Orwell's premise, but Sansal's is now the most well received. Kamel Saoud's Goncourt winner *Meursault: Contre-enquête* (2013) and Salim Bachi's *Le Chien d'Ulysse* (2001) are two other recent examples of Algerian authors rewriting classic texts from postcolonial perspectives.
27 In his 1999 article "Conceiving and Researching Transnationalism" from *Ethnic and Racial Studies* 22, no. 2, 447–62, Steven Vertovec summarized recent research into six categories influenced by transnationalism: social morphology, consciousness, cultural representation, avenues of capital, political engagement, and reconstructing place.
28 Akira Iriye, *Global and Transnational History: The Past, Present and Future* (Basingstoke, UK: Palgrave Macmillan, 2013).
29 Yogita Goyal, "Introduction: The Transnational Turn," in *Cambridge Companion to Transnational American Literature*, ed. Yogita Goyal (New York, NY, and Cambridge, UK: Cambridge University Press, 2017), 1–17. Paul Jay, *Global Matters: The Transnational Turn in Literary Studies* (Ithaca, NY: Cornell University Press, 2010).
30 Cristina Bradatan, Adrian Popan, and Rachel Melton, "Transnationality as a Fluid Social Identity," *Social Identities* 16, no. 2 (2010): 169–78.
31 Katherine Verdery suggests this distinction between statal and ethnic transnationalism in "Beyond the Nation in Eastern Europe," *Social Text* 38 (1994): 1–19.
32 See Houellebecq, "La religión en las novelas de Houellebecq," interview with Agathe Novak-Lechevalier, *La Térmica*, June 12, 2017, https://www.youtube.com/watch?v=i1DFEW09dvU&feature=share (accessed November 20, 2018) and "Nobody Will Make Us Do Yoga: A Conversation with Michel Houellebecq," interview with Christian Lorentzen, *Garage Magazine*, June 12, 2017, https://www.vice.com/en_us/article/qv43a7/michel-houellebecq-interview (accessed November 20, 2018).

33 My translation from Michel Houellebecq, "Michel Houellebecq: 'Dieu ne veut pas de moi,'" interview with Valérie Toranian and Marin de Viry, *Revue des Deux Mondes* (July–August 2015): 27.
34 Joseph Voignac, "Michel Houellebecq: Le Monde Anglophone réagit à *Soumission*," *Revue des Deux Mondes*, October 29, 2015, http://www.revuedesdeuxmondes.fr/michel-houellebecq-le-monde-anglophone-reagit-a-soumission/ (accessed November 20, 2018).
35 Boualem Sansal, *2084: La Fin du monde* (Paris, France: Gallimard, 2015), 247.
36 Sansal, *2084: La Fin du monde*, 197.
37 Boualem Sansal, "Boualem Sansal: '2015 marquera peut-être le début de la troisième guerre mondiale,'" interview with Julien Bisson, *Lire*, December 1, 2015, http://www.lexpress.fr/culture/livre/boualem-sansal-2015-marquera-peut-etre-le-debut-de-la-troisieme-guerre-mondiale_1747284.html (accessed November 20, 2018).
38 Boualem Sansal, "Boualem Sansal: 'Le mauvais islam continue à avancer,'" interview with Grégoire Leménager, *BiblioObs*, October 14, 2011, https://bibliobs.nouvelobs.com/romans/20111011.OBS2224/boualem-sansal-le-mauvais-islam-continue-a-avancer.html (accessed November 20, 2018).
39 David Caviliogli, "Boualem Sansal: Le kamikaze," *BiblioObs*, September 14, 2015, https://bibliobs.nouvelobs.com/romans/20150911.OBS5690/boualem-sansal-le-kamikaze.html (accessed November 20, 2018).
40 "Pour remplacer les enseignants, il [l'État] a fait venir n'importe qui du Liban, d'Irak, de Syrie. Ces pays en ont profité pour se débarrasser de leurs islamistes, qui sont tous arrivés en même temps, avec de faux diplômes. Ça a cassé le niveau scientifique et culturel, d'autant que ça a coïncidé avec la politique d'arabisation. En trois mois, on est passé du toutfrançais au toutarabe. Mais nous le parlions très mal, alors qu'eux le maîtrisaient parfaitement." Caviliogli, "Boualem Sansal: Le kamikaze."
41 Boualem Sansal, "A Rustle in History: Conversations with Boualem Sansal," interview with Dinah Assouline Stillman, *World Literature Today*, September 2012, https://www.worldliteraturetoday.org/2012/september/rustle-history-conversations-boualem-sansal-dinah-assouline-stillman-0 (accessed November 20, 2018).
42 Boualem Sansal, *2084: The End of the World*, trans. Alison Anderson (New York, NY: Europa Editions, 2017), 16–17. Hereafter references in text will refer to this edition.
43 Gregory Claeys, "News from Somewhere: Enhanced Sociability and the Composite Definition of Utopia and Dystopia," *History* 98, no. 330 (2013): 155.
44 Lyman Tower Sargent, "The Three Faces of Utopianism Revisited," *Utopian Studies* 5, no. 1 (1994): 9.
45 Louis-Sébastien Mercier's *L'An deux mille quatre cent quarante: Rêve s'il en fut jamais* (1771) was the first uchronia, as confirmed by Paul K. Alkon in *Origins of Futuristic Fiction* (Athens, GA, and London, UK: University of Georgia Press, 1987), 115–17, but other futuristic novels preceded its publication, such as Jacques Guttin's *Epigone, histoire du siècle futur* (1659) and Samuel Madden's *Memoirs of the Twentieth Century* (1733). Though Mercier was the first to practice "uchronia," Charles Renouvier coined the term in his text *Uchronie (L'Utopie dans l'histoire). Esquisse historique apocryphe du développement de la civilisation européenne tel qu'il n'a pas été, tel qu'il aurait pu être* (Paris, France: Bureau de la Critique Philosophique, 1876).
46 Tom Moylan, *Scraps of the Untainted Sky: Science Fiction, Utopia, Dystopia* (Boulder, CO, and Oxford, UK: Westview Press, 2000).

47 Mary Louise Pratt's theories of the contact zone, where cultures meet and evolve through exchange, were elaborated in *Imperial Eyes: Travel Writing and Transculturation* (London, UK: Routledge, 1992).
48 Michel Houellebecq, *Submission*, trans. Lorin Stein (London, UK: Penguin Random House, 2015), 50. Hereafter references in text will be to this edition.
49 Agathe Novak-Lechevalier posits that François does not necessarily convert, given the conditional tense in "Soumission: La littérature comme résistance," *Libération*, March 1, 2015, http://next.liberation.fr/culture/2015/03/01/soumission-la-litterature-comme-resistance_1212088 (accessed November 20, 2018).

13

Literature's Purchase: Remaking World Economic Relations in Crusoe's Footsteps

Nicole Simek

In 2012, Martinican writer, social worker, and anti-capitalist critic Patrick Chamoiseau published a retelling of Daniel Defoe's *The Life and Strange Surprising Adventures of Robinson Crusoe*. *L'Empreinte à Crusoé*, or "Crusoe's Print," is one of hundreds of Robinsonades and rewritings inspired by Defoe's 1719 novel, a text whose opening paragraph alone could provide all the material necessary for a year's work, as Jacques Derrida says in his last seminar, *The Beast and the Sovereign*.[1] Following so many earlier engagements with the tale, including Michel Tournier's *Vendredi ou les Limbes du Pacifique* and Saint-John Perse's writing on the subject, Chamoiseau himself admits that he struggled to find a path into this rich material that would bring it to life in new ways. Yet, driven by the fascination and "intense emotion" he had felt ever since reading the book as a child, he affirms having "always known that, at some moment or another, [he] would create [his] own Robinson."[2] Moreover, in the challenge of the impasse that *Robinson Crusoe* presents lies what Chamoiseau has identified as literature's most important task today: to do something with nothing, to confront the void or the static until it begins to open up.

How might literature come to serve as an antidote to a world impasse? Under what circumstances does the "literary"—a term that takes on universalist valences in Chamoiseau's recent work—come to have weight within particular, historically defined struggles over the economic organization of life? The figure of Robinson Crusoe, or the Robinson scenario, frequently reemerges in world discourses about economics, credit, debt, and obligation, and Chamoiseau's adaptation seizes on this aspect of Defoe's material in an effort to elucidate what he describes as an "individuation disease" plaguing global neoliberal culture in general and the French Caribbean in particular.[3] Yet beyond a better understanding of the world as it currently exists, what Chamoiseau seeks in rewriting *Robinson Crusoe* is to engage, through poetics, with "the unspeakable, the unthinkable, the impossible" dimensions of the Crusoe story in such a way as to forge new modes of relationality in the world. The novel thus seeks to re-world *Robinson Crusoe*, to harness the normative, world-remaking force of literature and participate in fostering a new "ethicopolitical horizon," to use Pheng Cheah's terms.⁴ To read Chamoiseau's *L'Empreinte à Crusoé* and, with it, Defoe's own *Crusoe*, as world literature is thus, I propose, not just to examine a book's "circulation"⁵—how, as a commodity, it moves from one geographic space (England) to others (the French metropole and Martinique, one of France's overseas departments). Rather, what also matters here, following Cheah, is to attend to the novel's "world-forming" capacity.⁶

In focusing on the specific ways in which Chamoiseau reengages with the figure of Robinson, or with what economists sometimes refer to as the "Robinson Crusoe scenario," as well as with the discourses of obligation, responsibility, and power that this castaway plot has nourished, the principle issue I would like to raise is not so much whether or not Defoe's *Crusoe*, or literature itself, can be said to have purchase, to have leverage within political struggles, as if this question could be answered simply "yes" or "no" and translated into a calculable political tactic to be applied repeatedly across time and place. Instead, I would like to consider *how* the perhaps overly familiar tale has come to prompt new, strange meanings and imaginations at certain points in history, at "one moment or another," to take up Chamoiseau's words again. Finally, then, in what ways, in our current "moment," might rewriting a novel so often taken as a portrait of quintessential *homo economicus* constitute a worlding operation offering an alternative mode of being-in-the-world, a way out of or through the economic relationships marking contemporary global life?

1. Uncanny Returns

The persistent return of Crusoe as a figure and reference point for cultural production might itself be described as uncanny. It has become something of a commonplace for the novel's commentators considering the remarkable and enduring popularity of the text to evoke its "charm" in the strong sense of a mysterious, gripping appeal. The novel's "scenario" and style have resonated with a wide range of publics including writers, economists, philosophers, children, and scholars of all stripes. Notably, the book has been translated into more than one hundred other languages and has remained continuously in print since its first publication in 1719. That year alone, six authorized editions were published, and the story immediately began to circulate in a variety of forms: pirated editions, chapbooks, and, of course, adaptations or rewrites. The text's appeal lies in part in its blending of the familiar and the strange; *Crusoe* makes the familiar strange, but also the strange familiar. Contemporary readers were already acquainted, for example, with the premise itself, which had served as the subject of other true-life accounts and tales previously: a man, stranded alone on a deserted island, survives the harsh environment for years through luck, wit, and physical exertion. Similarly, Defoe's text also employs elements of spiritual biography, and so the plot's progression from desperate loss to sudden restoration of riches (plus interest) echoes that of the story of Job. As Teresa Michals has shown, abridged versions of the text that circulated in chapbooks disproportionately emphasized this theme and the happy economic ending, devoting long pages to the exact details of the goods and profits that flow to Crusoe after he is rescued.[7]

The premise itself has certainly played a major role in *Crusoe*'s reception and has continually struck a chord with very different audiences both for its elements of adventure and its capacity to serve as an allegory submitting various human experiences and questions to reflection—questions of nature and animality; of solitude, social contact and social contract, sovereignty and finitude; and of the meaning of productivity. Ian Watt's 1951 essay "*Robinson Crusoe* as a Myth" cites as one important factor in the novel's persistent popularity the "vast ignorance that separated production and consumption in the London of Defoe's day, an ignorance," he asserts, "that has enormously increased since then, and that surely explains much of the fascination we find in reading the detailed descriptions of Crusoe's island labors."[8] For Chamoiseau, the appeal of Robinson's story similarly lies in its reconnection of consumption to production, but also in its questioning of both, in the promise it holds out of rethinking and rebuilding economic and social relations anew. "Defoe's Robinson fascinated people," he writes in the workshop notes included at the novel's end, "because he could re-envision everything from the starting point of the self—everyone's secret dream . . . the challenge of our day."[9] In a globalized world of intense "relational flux," an intensity "fed by the world's digital cortex, technoscientific accelerations, the contaminations of the market economy, [and] planetary mobility," social strictures and structures, argues Chamoiseau, have become somewhat archaic, playing less of a role in world experience than the "processes of individuation that allow each individual to build his or her own *person*."[10] Not only does *Crusoe* allow readers to imagine themselves constructing themselves differently in a space where social guardrails have fallen away, but it requires that readers in capitalist consumer society look at themselves full in the face, undistracted and unaided by the fast-paced occupations of work and consumption ruling the majority of their lives and blotting out other possibilities.[11]

The plot itself has proven at once strikingly memorable but also subject to selective amnesia, and this mnemonic malleability may also account for its success at specific stages in history or, in other words, for its worlding force; the novel has been made to speak, more or less faithfully, to a range of problematics concerning readers located in very different historical conjunctures. If classical economists had little use for Crusoe, whose exceptional situation did not seem pertinent to the sorts of dynamic, macroeconomic relationships that interested them, neoclassical thinkers, as William S. Kern has noted, frequently invoked Crusoe and the "Robinson Crusoe Economy" as illustrative examples in their work. This predilection for the solitary Crusoe making decisions within a fairly stable, given set of constraints, Kern suggests, stemmed from a shift to a microeconomic approach that focused on allocation and optimization of a relatively fixed set of resources and conditions and also relied heavily on natural science methods of isolation and idealization.[12] Neoclassical economists frequently took the novel to be presenting man in his most essential, stripped-down condition, and argued that social relations, which are absent for much of the novel, could merely be added on to this model without changing the basic facts of economic operations. Karl Marx was one of the first to critique this deployment of Crusoe as a figure for the isolated, independent, laboring individual and of the novel as an illustration of actual social relations of production.[13] Feminist and postcolonial critics have since turned the novel back on itself, finding within it not just an unrealistic fantasy of independence but also a revealing glimpse of instrumentalist attitudes and structures of desire underpinning paternalist and imperial projects.

Beyond its plot, however, early admirers often located the book's peculiar appeal in its style, and more precisely in its knack for bringing familiar elements together into something new—the text was said to harmonize instruction and entertainment, abstract spiritual lesson and realistic, idiosyncratic detail in surprising and pleasant ways. Modern readers have taken an interest in the novel's form as well, which relies heavily on doubling and echoing devices—a retrospective narration that hints at troubles to come; warnings from Robinson's father that foolishly abandoning stable middle-class life would lead to a life of misery; a first shipwreck that seems to confirm these predictions but ultimately does not dissuade Robinson from making another, ill-fated voyage; and finally, dreams that foreshadow future events. This self-reflexivity has made the novel particularly adaptable to the ends of writers like Tournier or J. M. Coetzee, whose retellings of *Robinson Crusoe*, as Christian Moraru demonstrates, participate in a broader postmodern practice of rewriting that critiques "the sociohistorical ambience—values, ideas, formations, cultural mythologies—within which rewriting is undertaken or within which the reworked text was produced."[14] Defoe's text offers a wealth of pliable structural resources for such reworkings, and creates suggestive interpretive ambiguities that seem almost to beg for new readings and applications. While anticipating major developments and thus rendering them familiar once they occur, for example, *Robinson Crusoe* is also punctuated by unexpected, obtrusive details and abrupt turns whose significance or arbitrariness is unclear. The most famous of these is Robinson's sudden discovery of a single footprint in the sand one day, whose appearance, years after Robinson's arrival and years before any other humans are spotted on the island, is never explained.

Such intrusions cast the predictable and familiar in a new, uncanny light, while also prompting attempts to domesticate and neutralize the strange and singular. Crusoe's conception of self is constantly challenged—his exceptionality as human distinct from other animals, his relation to God and nature, his morality and responsibilities to self and other cannot be taken for granted in his situation, and his daily tasks and responses to crises aim to reproduce that self or to reform and restore it to an ideal image. Crusoe himself expends a great deal of time managing his fears and anxieties through planning, building fortifications, accounting for his supplies and projects, and counseling himself through depressive and murderous thoughts. One famous episode that attracts Derrida's attention occurs just after Crusoe sets out to sail around the island, or, as he puts it, "to view the Circumference of my little Kingdom."[15] Having nearly been dragged out to sea by a strong current, he forces his way back to shore, and falls into a deep, exhausted sleep. He is awakened, however, by a voice calling, "Poor

Robin Crusoe, Where are you? Where have you been?" (104). He reports being "at first dreadfully frightened," before realizing that the speaker is his parrot, Poll:

> Even though I knew it was the Parrot, and that indeed it could be no Body else, it was a good while before I could compose my self: First, I was amazed how the Creature got thither, and then, how he should just keep about the Place, and no where else: But as I was well satisfied it could be no Body but honest *Poll*, I got it over; and holding out my Hand, and calling him by his Name *Poll*, the sociable Creature came to me, and sat upon my Thumb, as he used to do, and continu'd talking to me, *Poor Robin Crusoe*, and *how did I come here?* and *where had I been?* just as if he had been overjoy'd to see me again; and so I carry'd him Home along with me. (104)

Whether or not Robinson succeeds in his mind in domesticating the *unheimlich*, the unhomely—by literally taking it home, as he claims in this passage—the trace of the uncanny remains for readers, who have alternately followed Robinson in reestablishing order or halted in front of what becomes a stumbling block, an unsolved variable in the sorts of calculations or rationalizations Robinson is making. In observing that *a voice + a parrot—the presence of other bodies = ventriloquized speech*, Robinson seems to solve the puzzle but leaves traces drawing readers to other possible explanations: superhuman intervention in the form of divine Providence (or perhaps malevolent forces) is considered possible elsewhere in the narrative, though apparently ruled out here, while the "just as if" at once excludes but authorizes speculation on Poll's agency. Moreover, as Derrida has pointed out, this self-enclosed, autonomous form of speech—this self-naming and "auto-interpellation" mechanically reproduced and circularly returned to Robinson by the parrot prosthesis—exists in the text alongside a "counter-narcissistic," self-destructive, or autoimmune drive that also comes from within but undermines the self as sovereign master.[16]

Equivocal moments such as these become fertile examples for particular readings of the text or interpretive dilemmas prompting renewed fascination. These episodes, which have appealed the most to readers, also often revolve, however, around the very question of equivalency and how the latter is to be determined. Is Poll more than animal, or is Robinson less than human? Are uncanny repetitions exact reproductions of the same or rather instantiations of distinct events, echoes whose differences from the original are as important as their similarities? How are we to understand Robinson's credit and debit bookkeeping, his reckonings, and accounts, which have famously built his reputation as a "true-born Briton," as Marx put it disparagingly, and as an economic agent endowed with rational choice?[17] Most importantly for our topic, how are we to read what amounts not just to a restoration of Robinson's wealth, but the compounded returns he receives from the Brazilian plantation and savings tended to by friends during his twenty-six-year absence?

This redemptive ending on one level appears to illustrate the benefits of trade and venture capitalism. Crusoe leaves England with £40 worth of "Toys and Trifles" (14) and ends up with £5,000 of money on hand and a productive tobacco plantation in the Brazils generating £1,000 pounds a year.[18] This return is not the product of a single investment; rather, as Stephen Hymer has shown well, the £40 travels through various circuits of money, commodities, and labor, with Crusoe's gains depending in part as well on his appropriation and sale of others' property (he steals a boat to escape captivity, for example, and later sells it, along with a slave who had escaped with him and whom he appropriates as a sellable good). Though the novel makes no secret of these details, many economists and economic textbooks have set aside the frame narrative and seized instead upon the island episode, or rather, upon a selectively remembered vision of the island economy. As Michael V. White has observed, to approach *Crusoe* through a neoclassical lens, to read Crusoe himself as a rational economic agent and the island as an example of an originary state of nature, requires specific assumptions and some interpretive leaps: it entails interpreting the terms "use" and "value" in particular ways; assuming Crusoe is motivated by a desire to maximize profit rather than to satisfy a divine plan or fulfill moral obligations; ignoring moments when Crusoe "wastes" time or fails to calculate; and, crucially, failing to connect the island economy and his behavior during his stay there to larger markets.[19] This means losing sight, for example, of what Stephen Hymer has described well as Crusoe's "large store of embodied labor,"[20] that is, the significant stockpile of goods and tools that the hero salvages from the shipwreck and without which he likely would have starved to death. For later readers ostensibly opposed to slavery, it also means reading Robinson's relationship to his captured servant, Friday, as an abstraction illustrating how exchange functions essentially, rather than as a concrete example of how hierarchical relations of power and exploitation function historically.

These caveats and precisions draw us closer to uncovering the more troubling moral dimensions of credit, debt, obligation, and justice that permeate the novel and particularly mark its ending, moral dimensions that Crusoe himself alludes to when he remarks: "I might well say now, indeed, That the latter End of Job was better than the Beginning" (205). Crusoe's happy fate echoes Job's in that the losses of Defoe's protagonist are revealed to be temporary and his recompense larger than the assets with which he began. This restoration of wealth can be read as a sign of divine mercy and celebrated as such; within a Christian framework, it is possible to view these material comforts as symbols or promises of the more significant eternal rewards of paradise. Yet these material goods, which are described in precise detail, also seem to erase in a disturbing way the prolonged period of torment as well as the singularity of the loved ones that death takes away from Job and Crusoe. Crusoe's losses are arguably less dramatic than Job's, but, like Job's, raise the troubling question of equivalence: Can immaterial loss be quantified and compensated by money or goods?

2. Stranded Assets

Importantly, Crusoe's odyssey does not end with his rescue from the island, and the interlude between his discovery and the sudden influx of wealth he receives provides a brief but generative depiction of economic exchange that nuances the value of these material gains. The ending may come as a surprise in a novel stressing the contingency of value, the uselessness of coin to a marooned Crusoe, and the way in which needs and wants become redefined as social relations change. Crusoe himself, who becomes ill with joy when he learns of the resources now at his disposal, nearly dies from shock at this sudden reversal. The news of his wealth comes only after he has returned to England to find himself "as perfect a Stranger . . . as if [he] had never been known there," since most of his family has died, and no inheritance has been provided for him (200). Although he has, in some sense, been delivered, without social ties or adequate funds to provide for himself, he is stranded once again; as he puts it, "In a Word, I found nothing to relieve, or assist me" (200).

This return to England is related rapidly and in a fairly matter-of-fact style, but the terms in which Crusoe's subsequent attempts to find a foothold in his new life are described give some indication of the precariousness of his situation and of the instability of credit-debt economies more generally. The dramatic recovery of his assets depends on a remarkably high level of trust, honorable stewardship, and reliable government documentation of titles and holdings. Those in a position to sell off Crusoe's property have, despite his long absence, kept clear records of all profits and transactions in the event he should return and immediately turn over the accounts and possessions to him—the procuration proceedings last only seven months, including the time it takes to communicate the affidavit to Brazil and return shipments of account records and payments in gold and tobacco. Crusoe comments effusively on the fairness, honesty, and affection his remaining friends and business partner show him when they learn he is alive, and it is notable that this period of reacquaintance is marked not merely by impersonal transactions but also by gift-giving: Crusoe receives leopard skins from his partner and takes pains to reward an old captain friend who had rescued him from his first mishap. As Crusoe states, once in possession of his estate,

> The first thing I did was to recompense my original Benefactor, my good old Captain, who had been first charitable to me in my Distress, kind to me in my Beginning, and honest to me at the End. I shew'd him all that was sent to me, I told him, that next to the providence of Heaven, which disposes all things, it was owing to him; and that it now lay on me to reward him, which I would do a hundred-fold. (205)

The bonds between Crusoe and the captain are built on credit; each one, at different points in the narrative, shows charity toward the other by providing money and assistance in times of need. The trust between them is built as much on disclosure as on successful repayment itself. In fact, the captain has just related that he is indebted to Crusoe because he had had to use some of Crusoe's funds during hard times; despite his own misfortunes, he offers Crusoe the money he has on hand and title to his ship as a sort of promissory note that can be cashed in when his son returns from a trading voyage. Crusoe is moved nearly to tears by the captain's hardships and by his honesty, which is described in terms of disclosure when the protagonist tells us that "the old Man *let me see* that he was Debtor to me 470 Moidores of Gold, besides 60 Chests of Sugar, and 15 double Rolls of Tobacco" (203; emphasis added). Crusoe responds in kind by "shew[ing] him all that was sent [to him]" (205), that is, by acknowledging an even greater debt, one that is to be repaid by ensuring that the captain, as well as his son, will have a steady income henceforth.

If this ending is taken as a description of market relationships, it reads as a fantasy: credit, in the sense of faith or belief, is abundant, and debts are honestly admitted and repaid. Nor do we need to recall here that Defoe was an advocate for bankruptcy reform who had himself spent time in debtors' prison to see the appeal of such a vision, where long-term faithfulness and bureaucratic efficiency triumph over short-term interests.[21] Yet what is displayed here are not only specific sums of money and goods but also a relationship of obligation that is not in fact fully quantifiable. The exchanges that take place between these two men hover closer to the region of the gift than to that of the loan, in that debts are repaid—or counter-gifts offered—at intervals determined by necessity and abundance rather than by fixed terms and interest rates. The friend who has, gives, even when he has little himself, and recipients renew the bond by offering more than they had received. If loans carry the obligation of quantifiable repayment, gifts imply the obligation of relation—once repaid, lending relationships cease to exist and the parties involved separate; gifts, on the other hand, call not for repayment but for counter-gifts, for renewed obligation. The open-ended temporality of the gift is most visible in this case in the way Crusoe ensures a living for the captain's son, offering the captain himself lifelong peace of mind.

That Crusoe falls ill when he learns of his wealth signals an ironic recognition and enactment of the social relationships to which he has returned: in the moment, he becomes vulnerable and dependent on the people around him, who pull him through by fetching cordials and a doctor. His reinsertion into social relationships comes with both the risk of obligation and joys unparalleled by solitary self-sufficiency. In short, he exchanges the emptiness of debt-free solitude—the emptiness of an illusory immunity to the outside—for the passion, in the sense of pain and pleasure, of relation, of social contagion. As Derrida puts it, such a relation must "start from compassion in impotence, and not from power."[22]

3. Underwater on Dry Land

Returning in this concluding section to our present moment and the larger question at issue—the relationship between literature and our neoliberal world impasse—I would like to look more closely at what Patrick Chamoiseau describes as "*une maladie de l'individuation*," or an "individuation illness": the particular modes of competition, egoism, and isolation that he takes as the subject of his adaptation of Defoe's material and that seem at times to pose an insurmountable impasse to reform or revolution.[23] The island, like the prison cell, becomes in his novel a figure for deadlock and immobility, and the solitary Robinson an ill subject, one who has mistaken self-sufficiency for plenitude.[24]

Chamoiseau's Crusoe suffers from amnesia and takes his name from the engraving on a sword he finds lying next to him on the shore when he comes to. His sojourn on the island is one that carries him from instrumental exploitation of his natural surroundings and desire for mastery and murderous fear of the other through a period of longing where he unsuccessfully searches for the owner of the mysterious footprint and slowly rediscovers the island through new eyes. Discovering that his own foot fits the print, he lapses into a despair only broken when he begins an internal dialogue with Sunday, his intimate other. Finally, having traversed two periods of growth—that of the "Idiot" obsessed with exposure, autonomy, and security and that of the "Young Person" thirsty for discovery and searching for aid outside the self—Crusoe passes into a new phase, the phase of the "Artist," a state of intense lucidity and attentiveness, free of illusions, which he describes as a sort of "brute availability" or "raw openness" (*disponibilité crue*) to whatever may come, to the "infinity of the possible," without constraints of particular expectation but with a readiness to engage, to "sustain an open relationality" (204, 218).

This is a highly meditative novel whose progression takes the form of a spiral—an exploration that circles around one main question, namely, of how to construct a self without the "corsets" of social norms, without "the crutches of community and the standards of civilization" (247). It is one that asks a new question by rethinking the opposition between relational subjectivity and self-sufficiency as a problem of healthy and unhealthy individuations. The book takes aim at what Chamoiseau has described elsewhere as the "desiccation" of life lived through an economic reductionist lens[25]— the desiccation, that is, of a life under water or at risk of sinking, reduced to quantifiable calculations and the tyranny of basic needs, as well as to the isolationism of every-man-for-himself doctrines. To such a reduction he opposes the poetic: an approach that does not deny the needs of bare life but that ceases to subordinate fulfillment to biological survival.[26]

In shifting the terms of the debate away from the oppositions of self versus society, or individual liberty versus sacrifice of self for the common good, Chamoiseau joins Derrida in aiming to open up a space in which individuation serves as the basis for solidarity with the other rather than its antagonist. Individuation might best be understood here as a process of becoming singular, un-repeating and un-repeated—an island in an archipelago, both irreducibly singular yet cohabiting with others, in relation to others. This move involves not the total abandonment of prior models—even in his amnesia, Crusoe retains language and habits of thought traceable to various European and African traditions—but rather a kaleidoscopic decontextualization and recombination of these models, perhaps best figured in the book by the washed-out fragments of writing by Parmenides and Heraclitus that Crusoe sets into dialogue with one another. Like Derrida, who describes such a self as "a divided, differentiated 'subject,' who cannot be reduced to a conscious, egological intentionality,"[27] a subject whose freedom serves as the condition not for an impenetrable autonomy but instead for relationality with the other,[28] Chamoiseau's Crusoe describes his subjectivity as

> an errant availability densifying every day; nothing was happening, but an adventure was unfolding without my understanding a bit of it; nothing was wrong with my mental life or the health of my mood; no melancholy dimmed my eye; neither order nor disorder; neither ascendancy nor conquest, neither indifference nor attachment: my only a priori principle was *the going forward* openly [*l'aller qui se fait disponible*]; this is what I want to name: a freedom without concessions that no longer confined me to anything at all, but which offered me up to myself and to my surroundings; *an entering-into-relation*. (214)

Such a relation "brings [him] closer" to everything around him "without clarifying anything"; in other words, he continues, it puts him into intimate contact with the "irremediable opacity with which I had to come to terms," or, literally, with the opacity with which he has *to compose* (*composer*), to make do with and also to make—cocreate—with (215).

Crusoe's individuation passes through and with others, then—or rather with the other, construed broadly, for otherness encompasses human and nonhuman worlds in this novel. Crusoe is both indebted to his interlocutors, textual and living, and is also a donor who gives the gift of mobility, of unhinging practice and projecting new possibilities. "At the end of twenty-five years of motionless adventure," says Crusoe to the Capitan and crew who land on the island, "I was about to close the final gap with you in the circle of this immense encounter" (221). His final, directly reported words describe him in this moment as carried along by a "plenitude," further qualified as "spherical" and "powerful," a state that "accompanies" every "surge of beauty" he experiences; it is a state of both fullness and mobility, but one that is "neither blissful, nor anxious" in itself (221). This plenitude is a condition rather than an end, a condition of contact and openness to the unpredictable. The novel thus advocates a form of self-reflexivity and malleability that passes through both an aesthetic experience freed of the dictates of utility and a necessary encounter with strangeness outside the self.

Unpredictability entails vulnerability, however, and Crusoe does not survive the novel: as we learn in the final pages, the man calling himself Crusoe is an erudite African sailor, believed to be named Ogomtemmêli, who had accompanied Captain Robinson Crusoe on a number of slave-trading voyages before an accident causes him to lose his memory and to begin to question the social system around him. Fearing the impact of his agitation on their trade, Crusoe and his men assault Ogomtemmêli and abandon him to fend for himself on the island. Returning years later to see what had become of this man, Captain Crusoe and his crew listen to his story of survival—the spiraling tale we have been reading—and recognize the transformative impact of his experience on him, but they remain unable to comprehend his invitation to relation, his ecological (and non-egological) consciousness. When cries begin rising from the hold of the ship, Ogomtemmêli becomes combative again, demanding that the crew release the captive slaves; unable to conceive of his agitation as anything other than derangement, and faced with his uncommon physical strength and determination, Crusoe and his men shoot him at long range rather than risk losing their living cargo. It is only when Crusoe himself is shipwrecked, in an apparent twist of justice, that he comes to rethink his position, dedicating the first lines of his journal to the man he had killed, begging his pardon and hoping to follow his example. Chamoiseau's novel then ends where Defoe's Crusoe's journal begins: "*September* 30, 1659. I poor miserable Robinson Crusoe, being ship-wreck'd, during a dreadful Storm . . . ."[29]

The debt that remains at the end of this novel—Robinson's debt to Ogomtemmêli, but also Chamoiseau's debt to his own predecessors—is one that cannot be repaid but only honored. Robinson does this honor here through a gift of writing and leaves us, readers, to ask what sort of response or gesture we owe that writing. If the aesthetic itself—and the individuated but open modes of relationality it calls forth—is the response to be made to the flattening forces of economic reductionism, we come away from the novel both encouraged and warned: encouraged that literature's spectral worlding, its uncanny haunting, cannot so easily be exorcised from economic life, but warned that literary returns have no fixed term.

Notes

1 Jacques Derrida, *The Beast and the Sovereign*, vol. 2 (Chicago, IL: University of Chicago Press, 2011), 2:25.
2 Bernard Liger, "Chamoiseau: 'L'objet de la littérature n'est plus de raconter des histoires,'" *L'Express*, March 6, 2012, http://www.lexpress.fr/culture/livre/pat rick-chamoiseau-l-objet-de-la-litterature-n-est-plus-de-raconter-des-histoires_1 089728.html#pZsGBjlpGpPLxAOv.99 (accessed June 23, 2015). Unless otherwise indicated, all translations of French texts in this chapter are my own.
3 Patrick Chamoiseau, *L'empreinte à Crusoé* (Paris, France: Gallimard, 2012), 247. Further citations from this text will be given parenthetically.
4 Pheng Cheah, *What Is a World? On Postcolonial Literature as World Literature* (Durham, NC, and London, UK: Duke University Press, 2016), 5.
5 Cheah, *What Is a World?*, 3.
6 Cheah, *What Is a World?*, 116.
7 Teresa Michals, *Books for Children, Books for Adults: Age and the Novel from Defoe to James* (New York, NY: Cambridge University Press, 2014), 37. Cambridge Evidence Based eBooks, doi:10.1017/CBO9781107262201.003.
8 Ian Watt, "*Robinson Crusoe* as a Myth," in Daniel Defoe, *Robinson Crusoe: An Authoritative Text, Contexts, Criticism*, 2nd ed., ed. Michael Shinagel (New York, NY: W. W. Norton and Company, 1994), 293.
9 Chamoiseau, *L'empreinte*, 240.
10 Patrick Chamoiseau, "L'impensable comme source et comme ressource," *Annales Médico-Psychologiques* 173 (2015): 320.
11 Liger, "Chamoiseau."

12 William S. Kern, "Robinson Crusoe and the Economists," in *Robinson Crusoe's Economic Man: A Construction and Deconstruction*, ed. Ulla Grapard and Gillian Hewitson (New York, NY: Routledge, 2011), 65–6.
13 Kern, "Robinson Crusoe and the Economists," 70.
14 Christian Moraru, *Rewriting: Postmodern Narrative and Cultural Critique in the Age of Cloning* (Albany, NY: State University of New York Press, 2001), xii.
15 Daniel Defoe, *Robinson Crusoe: An Authoritative Text, Contexts, Criticism*, 2nd ed., ed. Michael Shinagel (New York, NY: W.W. Norton and Company, 1994), 100. Further citations from this text will be given parenthetically.
16 Derrida, *The Beast and the Sovereign*, 2:134–7.
17 Karl Marx, *Capital: A Critique of Political Economy*, trans. Edward B. Aveling and Samuel Moore, ed. Friedrich Engels, vol. I, book one, *The Process of Production of Capital* (London, UK: Electric Book, 2001), 1:111, ProQuest Ebook Central.
18 Stephen Hymer, "Robinson Crusoe and the Secret of Primitive Accumulation [1971]," *Monthly Review* 63, no. 4 (2011): 20.
19 Michael V. White, "Reading and Rewriting: The Production of an Economic *Robinson Crusoe*," in Grapard and Hewitson, *Robinson Crusoe's Economic Man*, 21–3.
20 Hymer, "Robinson Crusoe and the Secret of Primitive Accumulation," 23.
21 Michals, *Books for Children*, 34.
22 Derrida, *The Beast and the Sovereign*, 2:339.
23 Chamoiseau, *L'empreinte*, 247.
24 Liger, "Chamoiseau."
25 Liger, "Chamoiseau."
26 Liger, "Chamoiseau." On the poetic, see also Ernest Breleur et al., *Manifeste pour les "produits" de haute nécessité*, co-signed by Chamoiseau (Paris, France: Éditions Galaade, 2009).
27 Jacques Derrida and Elisabeth Roudinesco, *For What Tomorrow . . .: A Dialogue*, trans. Jeff Fort (Stanford, CA: Stanford University Press, 2004), 176.
28 Jacques Derrida and Maurizio Ferraris, *A Taste for the Secret*, trans. Giacomo Donis (Cambridge, UK: Polity, 2001), 27.
29 Defoe, *Robinson Crusoe*, 52. Chamoiseau's novel quotes from a French translation of the book (*L'empreinte*, 232).

14

Worlding *Négritude*, or Aimé Césaire's Global Caliban

Zahi Zalloua

In his critical and inventive adaptation of William Shakespeare's early modern play *The Tempest*, Aimé Césaire illustrates and enacts a non-essentialist, anti-racist aesthetic sensibility. As Césaire puts it, he aims to "demythify *The Tempest*," countering Prospero's "totalitarism," fakeness, unforgiveness, and hegemonic "will to power [*volonté de puissance*]" by telling the story from Caliban's vantage point.[1] Through key alterations to the original literary work, Césaire critically rewrites *The Tempest*, designating Caliban a black slave and Ariel a mulatto slave and introducing Eshu, a black-devil god, into the plot. The significance of these changes has long been debated. If Eshu helps move the play away from a strictly European orbit, the specifications provided for Caliban and Ariel make explicit that the logic that governs the relation between Prospero and his subjects is first and foremost a colonial logic, pitting the master against the slave. Does this mean, then, that Césaire's *A Tempest* is something of a rebuttal to Shakespeare's colonial play? Should we see it exclusively as an antagonistic postcolonial rewrite of Shakespeare's *The Tempest*? In this chapter, I propose to reread Césaire's *A Tempest* as an act of worlding. I draw here from Pheng Cheah, who, in his admirable *What Is a World?*, reorients the discussion of world literature away from "the implications of world circulation for the study of literature" and toward an exploration of "what literature can contribute to an understanding of the world and its possible role in remaking the world in contemporary globalization."[2] As an act of worlding, Césaire's *A Tempest* opens up, I argue, a world that differs from both Shakespeare's racial colonial world and our current global world, disclosing—as well as inciting us to invent—new meanings and alternate imaginings of subjectivity, resistance, and relationality. This world to come is not amenable to a fetishization of identity, where only the self's organic or historically given affiliations matter, and where the self only cares about his own. Rather, Césaire's envisioned blackness opens powerfully, if unexpectedly, to a universalization of difference, to a vision of difference *otherwise than rooted*.

What role, if any, does Césaire's notion of *négritude* play in this act of worlding? *Négritude* is at once backward-looking (a nostalgic and redemptive return to Africa) and forward-leaning (a life-affirming gesture that points to a future where blackness is an object not of derision but of pride). It signals a categorical refusal of assimilation and rejects all literatures that tend to "denegrify the black man [*dénégrifier le nègre*]."³ *Négritude* addresses and redresses the denigration of blacks. How are we to understand its significance in today's global world? Would it be blatantly anachronistic to insist on *négritude* in the twenty-first century, to battle an enemy (European hegemony) that exists no more, a relic of the past not in need of hermeneutic resurrection? Or conversely, is today the right time to revisit this key concept and open it up to new interpretive possibilities, to better ways to address the persistent question of race in today's global—and allegedly post-racial—world? I opt for the latter here and, accordingly, will examine Césaire's Caliban as a global and creolizing figure embodying the pull and needs of both particularity and universality, thereby pointing us toward a paradigm of world literature that holds these concepts in productive tension. For, it seems to me, Césaire's *A Tempest* asks us to negotiate the tensions between its particularist appeal (its staging of a *négritude* sensibility) and its universalizing dimension (its calls for a new humanism). The latter point is especially relevant given the context of Césaire's controversial canonization, or co-optation, as a "great humanist" (worthy of burial in the Pantheon) by then French president Nicolas Sarkozy and others after the writer's death in 2008.⁴ What is at stake here are competing visions of universalism: a universalism deeply embedded in European imperialism and a universalism that politicizes the plight of the historically excluded—the subaltern voices of colonial history.

1. *Négritude* and Its Discontents

Seeing Caliban as a global or, better yet, *world* and creolizing figure is already to conceive of *négritude* beyond its historical framework, to inflect and infuse it with *créolité*—to think Césaire's *négritude* with and against a concept that belongs to the subsequent generation of French-Caribbean writers whose relation to their literary father is at best ambivalent. Thus, Jean Bernabé, Patrick Chamoiseau, and Raphaël Confiant, authors of *In Praise for Creoleness*, acknowledge an important existential and aesthetic debt to Césaire:

> To a totally racist world, self-mutilated by its own colonial surgeries, Aimé Césaire restored mother Africa, matrix Africa, the black civilization. He denounced all sorts of dominations in the country, and his writing, which is committed and which derives its energy from the modes of war, gave severe blows to postslavery sluggishness. Césaire's Negritude gave Creole society its African dimension, and put an end to the amputation which generated some of the superficiality of the so called doudouist writing. . . . Césairian Negritude is a baptism, the primal act of our restored dignity. We are forever Césaire's sons.⁵

Ultimately, however, they see *négritude* as substituting one fantasy for another ("Negritude replaced the illusion of Europe by an African illusion"⁶), as essentialist (in its assumption of the purity of blackness[7]) and ultimately as unhelpful in dealing with the challenges at hand. "Negritude," they insist,

> soon manifested itself in many kinds of exteriority: *the exteriority of aspirations* (to mother Africa, mythical Africa, impossible Africa) and *the exteriority of self-assertion* (we are Africans). It was a necessary dialectical moment, an indispensable development. But it remains a great challenge to step out of it in order to finally build a new yet temporary synthesis on the open path of history, our history.[8]

The exclusive focus on Africa, the three writers also argue, led to a denial of the rich and complex "mosaic-identity"[9] of the Caribbean, to a neglect of its interiority, mixed life, and language (Creole). By remaining so affectively and intellectually attached to Africa, Césaire could not truly embrace the historical needs and challenges of the Caribbean people. The rewards of *négritude* were therefore more than counterbalanced by its lacunae and blind spots, by its failure to overcome the racial hierarchy itself. In short, *négritude* was deficient, amounting to an empty reversal of Europe's binary logic and racial ontology.

The Creolists were of course not alone in their negative evaluation of *négritude*. Earlier, Frantz Fanon critically observed: "There is not *one* Negro—there are *many* black men."[10] Fanon credits *négritude*'s anti-colonial attitude for crucially raising black political consciousness but finds its phantasmatic claims of a "golden past" disconcertingly vague and counterproductive; indeed, "to be locked in the substantialized 'tower of the past'"[11] is detrimental to decolonization and genuine emancipation. In its infatuation with Africa, *négritude* relies on a logic of exemplarity that prevents the Caribbean people from engaging in the necessary work of critical self-fashioning, doing no less damage to them than their prior infatuation with Europe:

> Fifteen years before, they [the West Indians] said to the Europeans, "Don't pay attention to my black skin, it's the sun that has burned me, my soul is as white as yours." After 1945 they changed their tune. They said to the Africans, "Don't pay attention to my white skin, my soul is as black as yours, and that is what matters."[12]

If *négritude* was a necessary "black mirage"[13] to block French cultural assimilation, its emancipatory value has run its course. Maryse Condé similarly questions Césaire's notion of "the black man [*le nègre*]," arguing that it did not exist, that it was an abstraction, or even a European abstraction to regard with caution: "Since it was Europe that created the Black man, claiming this myth as one's true identity, or, worse, taking pride in it, amounts to accepting Europe wholesale, including the most misguided thinking of its culture."[14] Moreover, Condé objects to Césaire's overemphasis on the historical trauma of blacks, even accusing him of "tak[ing] pleasure in the memory of the suffering and humiliation inflicted on our race," hinting at "a dubious masochism."[15]

As did Condé and Fanon, the Creolists rejected Césaire's nostalgic vision of the past (its obsession with ancestral origins), tribalism (black versus with white, Africa versus Europe), and homogenization of black culture (through which the identity and concerns of the Caribbean people are reduced to those of a mythical Africa). What they argued for was an emphasis on the local, on cultural and ethnic difference, and on the concreteness of Caribbean particularism over the abstract universalism of blackness. The answer for the Creolists does not lie "elsewhere" but in the here and now of Caribbean existence. At the same time, in a 1997 interview, Bernabé, Chamoiseau, and Confiant frame *créolité* not as a sectarian movement, ensnared in regionalism (simply and unproductively replacing African authenticity with Caribbean authenticity), but as a global movement. Indeed, for the Creolists, the whole world is in an ongoing process of creolization:

> Creolization has been an uninterrupted process, and . . . it didn't peter out in the first half of the nineteenth century. After Abolition in 1848, many groups, including indentured laborers from India and China, came to the Antilles. We are the first authors to speak about these Syrio-Lebanese, Indian, and Chinese communities. . . . Creolite is all about understanding mosaic, multiple identities. In the Antilles, you can be of any race and yet be Creole.[16]

If *créolité* values rootedness, we might describe it as a fragile rootedness (unlike *négritude*'s flirtation with biological determinism), ill-formed to serve as a stable basis for an exclusive identity.

Césaire's attitude toward the Creolists was likewise mixed. He rejected the charge of essentialism—one leveled repeatedly against *négritude* ever since Jean-Paul Sartre, in "Black Orpheus," proclaimed it "an anti-racist racism"[17]—as a conflation of his position with that of Léopold Sédar Senghor. Senghor, he argued, "tended to construct *négritude* as an essentialism, as though there were a black essence, a black soul, finally something rather metaphysical"; as for himself, he wrote, "I do not believe that there is either a black substance or a black essence."[18] Césairean *négritude* is about history, not biology[19] or ontology (as contrasted with Senghor, who translates Martin Heidegger's "*Da-sein*" into "*Neger-sein*,"[20] "being-in-the-world" into "black-being-in-the-world"). For Césaire, *négritude* is an existentialist premise, not an essentialist one: "I do not in the slightest believe in biological permanence, but I believe in culture. My Négritude has a ground. It is a fact that there is a black culture: it is historical; there is nothing biological about it."[21] Césaire also refers disparagingly to *créolité* as a "department of *négritude*"[22] and to its practitioners as derivatives of his art, lacking in originality. Early on in his literary career, Césaire had expressed suspicion about the idea and ideal of cultural *métissage*, questioning its political commitment to blackness. "According to [Césaire]," explain Roger Toumson and Simonne Henry-Valmore, "the Antillean, no matter whether he has light or dark skin, is a Black man."[23] *Creolité* is guilty of dissolving the singularity of the black experience, of ignoring or obfuscating the primacy of blackness for the Caribbean people. Toumson and Henry-Valmore dismissively define *créolité* as "an exoticism of the divers"—one that acquiesces to French curiosity, pandering to a touristic gaze—which can only result in "a negation of radical alterity."²⁴ Promoting an "ideology of hybridity [*métissage*]"²⁵ and celebrating the mixture of African and European races do little to resolve the alienation of blacks. Only a return to and reinvestment in Africa, in its civilizational resources and its foregrounding of race, can do so.

2. Enacting *Négritude*, or Caliban's Will To Power

Unfortunately, one gets the sense that Césaire and his detractors are speaking past each other in this cross-generational exchange. Perhaps a more productive way to imagine a Creole Caliban is to revisit the ways in which Césaire's work reactivates and engages with Shakespeare's play. While readers attentive to *The Tempest*'s early colonial conditions of production have sometimes taken its representation of Caliban at face value as unflattering, Shakespeare's portrayal of Caliban is far from straightforward, as evidenced by the conflicting interpretations the work has prompted. Césaire and Fanon both rejected Octave Mannoni's psychological reading of the play in *Prospero and Caliban: The Psychology of Colonization*, where he theorizes that the colonized identifies with the oppressor, the father figure of the colonizer, as a result of a "dependency complex." Caliban, even when plotting against Prospero, can only think of serving new masters (Stephano and Trinculo), never desiring freedom itself and never seeking a life without a master. According to Mannoni's reductive reading, all colonized subjects are pathologized Calibans, suffering from a desire for subjugation: "Wherever Europeans have founded colonies of the type we are considering, it can safely be said that their coming was unconsciously expected—even desired—by the future subject peoples. Everywhere there existed legends foretelling the arrival of strangers from the sea, bearing wondrous gifts with them."²⁶ Like Fanon, Césaire dismisses such a reading of Caliban, which amounts to an endorsement of "native inferiority, [and] full-blown cultural dependency,"²⁷ stressing, instead, the inextinguishable hunger of the colonized for freedom and full identification with Caliban.

But what is it exactly that Césaire is valuing in Caliban? Is it his desire to reclaim his "rightful" sovereignty over the island? Is it his refusal to compromise à la Ariel? Is it Caliban's sheer negativity? Answering "yes" to all three questions would not necessarily entail a contradiction, but it would diminish the force of the last question. Césaire's play stages competing expressions or modalities of a "will to power" complete with all its Nietzschean resonance.²⁸ Prospero's colonial will to power manifests itself as will to mastery, will to dominate, and will to subjugate, whereas Caliban's expresses itself primarily as a will to resist. Resistance does take many forms in *A Tempest*. It is easily perceivable in Caliban's desire to regain sovereignty over the island. This reclaiming of the land follows a *négritude* script. Having racialized the colonial situation by equating reified blackness with the colonized, *négritude* can now point a way out of the system: independence from Prospero, reunification with the dynamism of the island.²⁹ This overcoming expresses a particular kind of *négritude*, one that privileges rootedness and authenticity. There is an undeniable symbiosis between Caliban and the island. In a key exchange between Prospero and Caliban over Sycorax, the latter's mother, who was defeated and killed by the former for control of the island, we discover Caliban's desire for independence and sovereignty as well as his organic attachment to the island, refuting the notion of his alleged dependence on Prospero's good will:

> PROSPERO What would you be without me?
> CALIBAN Without you? I'd be the king, that's what I'd be, the King of the Island. The king of the island I inherited from my mother, Sycorax.
> PROSPERO There are some family trees it's better not to climb! She's a ghoul! A witch from whom—and may God be praised—death has delivered us.
> CALIBAN Dead or alive, she was my mother, and I won't deny her! Anyhow, you only think she's dead because you think the earth itself is dead. . . . It's so much simpler that way! Dead, you can walk on it, pollute it, you can tread upon it with the steps of a conqueror. I respect the earth, because I know that it is alive, and I know that Sycorax is alive.[30]

If Prospero's line "thou earth" in Shakespeare's play was meant as an insult (reducing Caliban to a pile of dirt), Césaire's Caliban willingly accepts this association with the earth, with the materiality of the island. Whereas Prospero enjoys the privileges of the mind (a disembodied existence, unconcerned with the demands of the body[31]), Caliban draws his strength from the dynamism of the earth (misrecognized by Prospero as "the Anti-Nature" [52], static and devoid of life).

Caliban also enacts his resistance to Prospero in his will to say no to the master and his faithful servant, Ariel, whom Caliban calls "Uncle Tom," and who opposes any notion of violent struggle (26). But independence does entail a violent struggle, one irreducible to the overthrow of colonial occupying forces. What the struggle aims for is a liberation or decolonization of the mind. Caliban has the opportunity to kill Prospero but declines to do it:

> CALIBAN It's you and me, Prospero!
> PROSPERO Strike! Go on, strike! Strike your master, your benefactor! Don't tell me you're going to spare him! (55)

Césaire's Caliban captures and translates the rebellious nature of Shakespeare's Caliban, who, far from being servile, turns Prospero's teachings against him by using the language he has learned to curse back. In *A Tempest*, decolonizing the mind begins with purging Caliban's body, with forcibly removing all the venom of colonialism and all the traces of Prospero's discourse: "I'd spit you out, all your works and pomps! Your 'white' magic!" (60). *Contra* Mannoni, Césaire's Caliban imagines and desires a world precisely *without* Prospero, *without* a colonial master.

This is the enactment of *négritude* as negativity. Caliban's first word in the play is "Uhuru," meaning "freedom" in Swahili. With it, "Césaire Africanizes Caliban"[32] from the beginning. It is tempting to fold "Uhuru" back into the first expression of *négritude* as a return to Africa, where the island is itself Africanized by Caliban (he is one with the island), becoming a substitute for the missing Africa of black slaves and the colonized. A careful reading of the play, however, complicates such an interpretation. Sycorax is not indigenous to the island. She is North African, originating from Algiers, from where she was banished while pregnant with Caliban. While it is true that Caliban was born on the island, his claim to sovereignty through indigeneity must be qualified: *only the island's spirits are really indigenous—everyone else is to various degrees a newcomer*.[33]

Caliban's *créolité*—as the offspring of Sycorax and the island—opens the path to a different understanding of *négritude* and to a reconfiguration of the universalism/particularism divide. The terms "universalism" and "particularlism" have both been used to designate *négritude*. As the phantasmatic impulse to ontologize or homogenize black experience, *négritude* displays a "particularistic logic."[34] Conversely, in homogenizing black experience, it also conveys a vague universalism: all blacks share a fundamental experience of the world (irrespective of class, gender, sexuality, etc.). Worlding *négritude* is an attempt to concretize this universalism, to universalize without sacrificing the singular. It takes up the challenge of making Caliban global—again, in a wordly or worlded sense—while simultaneously situating him in the dynamic realities of the local.

3. Worlding *Négritude*

To be sure, Césaire himself would not have found the abovementioned examples of *négritude* incongruous, but, as I have been arguing, a *négritude* that reaffirms the link between being and soil always runs the risk of duplicating the racist logic of the colonizer, of producing a kind of racist anti-racism (the Sartrean objection).[35] Are we, however, condemned to choose between a myopic particularism and an abstract universalism, with either option ill-suited for worlding? Is *négritude* redeemable only as a black identity politics, a position that arguably collapses the logic of particularism with the abstract sameness of blackness? I want to turn to Slavoj Žižek for a different approach to universalism, one that might help us retrieve *négritude*'s critical (worlding) energy. Žižek takes his inspiration for concrete universalism from Saint Paul's statement from Gal. 3:28: "There is no longer Jew nor Greek, there is no longer slave nor free, there is no longer male and female; for all of you are one in Christ Jesus."[36] To be clear, what Žižek privileges in Paul is not his religious message (the displacement of Judaism with Christianity), but his formulation as an endless source and locus of negativity. It is Paul's principle of *adiaphora* (ethical indifference toward ethnic and cultural particularities) that Žižek harnesses in his politics of universality.

Fanon practices this kind of *adiaphora* when he sustains critical distance from *négritude* and other similar movements, resisting (while also acknowledging[37]) the affective pull of identitarian politics and the impulse for rootedness, that is, the phantasmatic impulse to ontologize or homogenize black experience. "No," he insists, "I have not the right to be black. It is not my duty to be this or that. . . . I acknowledge one right for myself: the right to demand human behavior from the other.... The black man is not. No more than the white man."[38] The shift from difference as experiential rootedness (the stuff of tribalism and identity politics) to difference as experiential relatedness helps to revive a universalist framework where what ultimately matters is to be treated humanly—Fanon's new humanism. It also might be tempting to read Fanon as offering his own version of Pauline cosmopolitanism: *there is neither white nor black*. But here we must not forget about the material conditions of colonial life. There is no transcendence of race without the dismantlement of the colonial system, and there is no dismantlement of the colonial system without an affective and cognitive transvaluation of the *difference* of the colonized.

Worlding *négritude* responds to Fanon's critique and gestures toward an alternative form of anti-racism—one that is not ensnared in the racist binary logic of the included/excluded or white/black. Worlding *négritude* is at odds with the impulse for rootedness, with the phantasmatic claims of indigeneity—the desire for a return to precolonial reality. It seeks relationality, genuine contact with others, on equal footing, but not at the expense of negativity. Again, the critical force of Césaire/Caliban lies in the will to resist, in the refusal to submit to white supremacy, prefiguring, as it were, the "Black Lives Matter" movement and thereby signaling to the world that black lives count—that they are livable and grievable.[39] The slogan "Black Lives Matter," as Judith Butler puts it, is a "mode of address":[40] *Hey you—Prospero and Western (neo)colonizers—recognize my/our black humanity!* To utter it is to contest European privilege and what we might call black *dis*privilege. European privilege and black disprivilege amount to the same thing, since "it is the racist who creates the inferiorized."[41] Conversely, Ariel, in advocating nonviolence, can be seen as trying to convince Caliban to take a humanist approach, urging him to give Prospero a chance: "I've often had this inspiring, uplifting dream that one day Prospero, you, me, we would all three set out, like brothers, to build a wonderful world, each one contributing his own special thing: patience, vitality, love, willpower too, and rigor, not to mention the dreams without which mankind would perish" (27). From Ariel's perspective, Prospero can be reformed; we are all the same, brothers.

Universal claims—like the putatively humanist chant "All Lives Matter" ironically taken up today on the Right—have "always bolstered racism"[42] and perpetuated privilege. As Angela Davis keenly observes, "any critical engagement with racism requires us to understand the tyranny of the universal."[43] More specifically, calls for universalism—if not deliberately obfuscating structural inequalities—tend at the very least to ignore the links between anti-black racism and European imperialism and to forget the historical specificity of blacks—what *made* black lives not matter in the first place. Against Ariel's ideological universalism, Caliban insists on the enemy: "You don't understand anything about Prospero. He's not the collaborative type. He's a guy who only feels something when he's wiped someone out. A crusher, a pulveriser, that's what he is! And you talk about brotherhood!" (27). He points to an incommensurable gap, to the antagonism between Caliban (and Ariel) and Prospero, between the colonized and the colonizer, and between the Third World and Europe. Again, attentiveness to this antagonism does not necessarily translate into a form of identity politics: one identity (*négritude*) fighting against other (white supremacy). Indeed, one cannot simply denounce the universalist-humanist underpinnings of "All Lives Matter" as ideological and affirm, in its place, the "frozen rigidity"⁴⁴ of black difference—as we find in conventional understanding of *négritude*. I concur with Nick Nesbitt about the possibility of "a universal, non-identitarian Négritude."⁴⁵ In a crucial moment in the play, Caliban tells Prospero of his desire to be renamed "X"—with clear allusion to Malcolm X and the Black Panthers. What Malcolm X accomplished with his own renaming is not a move on behalf of sectarianism. Quite the contrary, as Žižek notes, "when he adopted X as his family name[,] he was not fighting on behalf of the return to some primordial African roots, but precisely on behalf of an X, an unknown new identity opened up by the very process of slavery which made the African roots forever lost."⁴⁶ The move from Prospero's Caliban to Caliban's X is a move toward a "worlded" Caliban.

4. Caliban as a Candidate for the "Part of No-Part"

Worlding *négritude* reframes the antagonism between Prospero and Caliban as an expression of concrete universality. What Caliban stands for is not that of a ready-made, precolonial, or phantasmic identity that a return to Africa promises. He is a candidate for what Žižek, following Jacques Rancière, calls the "part of no-part." On Žižek's account, the "part of no-part" stands for the others who are systematically excluded, disprivileged, and racialized by society's laws and norms, falling outside the liberal and humanist umbrella. As a given order's constitutive outsiders, the "part of no-part" stands for "true universality." Since the interests of the excluded others are not predetermined by their subject positions, when they seek to remedy wrongs, they speak to universal concerns. In this respect, Žižek urges postcolonial critics and other partisans of difference not to settle for a demystification of abstract or ideological universalism and to think more dialectically—bringing about a state where "a properly universal dimension *explodes from within a particular context and . . . is directly experienced as universal*."⁴⁷ Not attached to the status quo in the same libidinal and ideological way as Miranda and Ariel are, Caliban holds the promise of transformative change—of politicizing culture, of enacting politics as such. The question of who counts, and how to relate to his or her universal singularity, animates Fanon's work as well. Fanon's solidarity (his attentiveness to black bodies) is always supplemented by a universalist orientation (his commitment to the "wretched of the earth"); even when accounting for one's own trauma or the trauma of *a* people, Fanon fights hard against the myopic impulse to fetishize that suffering, to reify the singular into the particular, preferring to orient his discussion toward a universalist framework that takes up the plight of the dispossessed, of those who *do not count*, the "part of no-part."⁴⁸ Similarly, Caliban's difference is not a retreat into the particular but refers back to a universalism "grounded in the 'part of no-part,' the singular universality exemplified in those who lack a determined place in the social totality, who are 'out of place' in it."⁴⁹

So, if one version of *négritude* remains overinvested in postcolonial particularity, and thus risks reifying the cultural processes of racialization, another, a worlding *négritude*, keeps, strategically, the space of universality empty. Caliban might be ontologized (blackness = the colonized), but his racialization is also interpreted as incomplete, as the condition for politicizing and concretizing universality. Worlding *négritude* pleads for this image of Caliban—a Caliban who foregrounds his insolent negativity. It takes this image of a Caliban *révolté* as Césaire's most important message. At the same time, we recognize that to remain faithful to this reading of *négritude* requires a certain betrayal of the logic underpinning Césaire's more conventional vision of *négritude* as a return to African roots. In this respect, the Creolists were on the right track, if we take seriously, as more than a rhetorical gesture, their statement, according to which "we can only become authentic sons of Césaire and his thought by remaining wary of him, by deviating from the paths that he forged, precisely in order to respect the poet's fundamental message."[50] Creolizing Caliban—mixing, that is, Caliban's decolonial strategies with those of today's Black Lives Matter movement—takes up the hermeneutic challenge of thinking freedom relationally and globally, as opposed to a narcissistic obsession with black sovereignty, with self-determination as an end in itself, and of thinking relationality after negativity. This is the challenge, and the project, of Third World solidarity, of Black Lives Matter's collaboration with Free Palestine, of the Standing Rock Sioux's protest of the Dakota Access Pipeline, and so on. Creolizing Caliban and worlding *négritude* are one and the same.

Notes

1. Thomas A. Hale, *Les Écrits d'Aimé Césaire: Bibliographie commentée* (Montréal, Canada: Les Presses de l'Université de Montréal, 1978), 464–5. My translation.
2. Pheng Cheah, *What Is a World? On Postcolonial Literature as World Literature* (Durham, NC: Duke University Press, 2016), 5.
3. Qtd. in Ching Selao, "Aimé Césaire: 'L'exécuteur de ces œuvres hautes' 1913-2008," *Spirale* 221 (2008): 48–9, 48.
4. For the politics of appropriating Césaire's legacy, see A. James Arnold, "Césaire Is Dead: Long Live Césaire! Recuperations and Reparations," *French Politics, Culture & Society* 27, no. 3 (2009): 9–18.
5. Jean Bernabé, Patrick Chamoiseau, and Raphaël Confiant, *Éloge de la Créolité/In Praise of Creoleness*, Bilingual ed., trans. M. B. Taleb-Khyar (Baltimore, MD: The Johns Hopkins University Press, 1990), 79, 80.
6. Bernabé, Chamoiseau, and Confiant, *In Praise of Creoleness*, 82.
7. Most critical of Césaire's *négritude* is Confiant, who blames the former for his "fetishization of the Pure and the One" (Raphaël Confiant, *Aimé Césaire: Une traversée paradoxale du siècle* [Paris: Stock, 1993], 164).
8. Bernabé, Chamoiseau, and Confiant, *In Praise of Creoleness*, 82.
9. Bernabé, Chamoiseau, and Confiant, *In Praise of Creoleness*, 112.

10 Frantz Fanon, *Black Skin, White Masks*, trans. Richard Philcox (New York, NY: Grove Press, 2008), 115.
11 Fanon, *Black Skin, White Masks*, 201.
12 Fanon, *Toward the African Revolution*, trans. Haakon Chevalier (New York, NY: Grove Press, 1967), 25.
13 Fanon, *Toward the African Revolution*, 27.
14 Maryse Condé, "Négritude césairienne, négritude senghorienne," *Revue de littérature comparée* 48, nos. 3–4 (1974): 413, my translation.
15 Condé, "Négritude césairienne, négritude senghorienne," 413.
16 Lucien Taylor, "Creolité Bites: A Conversation with Patrick Chamoiseau, Raphaël Confiant, and Jean Bernabé," *Transition* 74 (1997): 150, 153.
17 Jean-Paul Sartre, "Black Orpheus," trans. John MacCombie, in *Race*, ed. Robert Bernasconi (Oxford, UK: Blackwell, 2001), 118.
18 Qtd. Arnold, "Césaire Is Dead," 13.
19 His protests notwithstanding, Césaire's description of *négritude* is at times imbued with biological resonance. For example, in *Le Discours de la négritude*, he says: "Chromosomes matter little to me. But I believe in archetypes"; "I believe in the value of all that is buried in the collective memory [of our peoples] and even in the collective [un]conscious"; "I don't believe that we come into the world with an empty brain in the same way that we come with empty hands. I believe in the [plasmatic virtue of centuries-old accumulated] experience [and in the lived experience] conveyed by cultures" (qtd. in Arnold, "Césaire Is Dead," 13).
20 Léopold Sédar Senghor, "De la négritude," *Liberté V: Le Dialogue des cultures* (Paris, France: Seuil, 1993), 17.
21 Qtd. in A. James Arnold, *Modernism and Négritude: The Poetry and Poetics of Aimé Césaire* (Cambridge, MA: Harvard University Press, 1981), 37. In accordance with an essentialist register, Senghor draws out clear differences between whites and blacks: "Là où la raison discursive, la raison-œil du Blanc s'arrête aux apparences de l'objet, la raison intuitive, la raison-étreinte du Nègre, par-delà le visible, va jusqu'à la sous-réalité de l'objet, pour, au-delà du signe, en saisir le sens. . . . Le Blanc européen est, d'abord, discursif; le Négro-africain, d'abord, intuitif" (Senghor, *Négritude, arabisme et francité: réflexions sur le problème de la culture* [Beirut, Lebanon: Éditions Dar al-Kitab Allubnani, 1967], 7).
22 "Entretien d'Aimé Césaire avec Frédéric Bobin," *Le Monde*, April 12, 1994.
23 Roger Toumson and Simonne Henry-Valmore, *Aime Césaire: Le nègre inconsolé* (Paris, France: Syros, 1993), 55, my translation.
24 Toumson and Henry-Valmore, *Aime Césaire: Le nègre inconsolé*, 230.
25 Toumson and Henry-Valmore, *Aime Césaire: Le nègre inconsolé*, 230.
26 Octave Mannoni, *Prospero and Caliban: The Psychology of Colonization*, trans. Pamela Powesland (Ann Arbor, MI: The University of Michigan Press, 1990), 86.
27 Emily Apter, *Continental Drift: From National Characters to Virtual Subjects* (Chicago, IL: The University of Chicago Press, 1999), 77. Chantal Zabus also observes: "The Calibanic figure of the colonized is shrunk to a helpless, dependent, suckling child in need of parental authority" (Chantal Zabus, *Tempests after Shakespeare* [New York, NY: Palgrave, 2002], 20).
28 The French phrase used is "volonté de puissance"—the accepted translation of Nietzsche's German term, "der Wille zur Macht."

29 Zabus also credits the *négritude* movement for "the racialization of Caliban," for making Caliban both a colonial and racial hermeneutic concern (Zabus, *Tempests after Shakespeare*, 34).
30 Césaire, *A Tempest*, trans. Richard Miller (New York, NY: TCG Translations, 2002), 18. Further citations from this text will be given parenthetically.
31 Prospero does sadistically enjoy torturing others through hunger: responding to Ariel's concern over the punishment of the prisoners ("It's evil to play with their hunger as you do with their anxieties and their hopes"), Prospero says: "That is how power is measured. I am Power" (32).
32 Steven M. Almquist, "Not Quite the Gabbling of 'A Thing Most Brutish': Caliban's Kiswahili in Aime Cesaire's *A Tempest*," *Callaloo* 29, no. 2 (2006): 588.
33 As Steven M. Almquist rightly observes, "*A Tempest* almost entirely elides the fact that Caliban is not in fact native to the island and, therefore, his claim to have inherited the island from his mother, Sycorax, implies a displacement of native peoples" (Almquist, "Not Quite the Gabbling of 'A Thing Most Brutish,'" 594).
34 James Penney, "Passing into the Universal: Fanon, Sartre, and the Colonial Dialectic," *Paragraph* 27, no. 3 (2004): 54.
35 "To leave the historical world for the metaphysics of essences like negritude . . . is to abandon history for essentializations that have the power to turn human beings against each other" (Edward Said, *Culture and Imperialism* [New York, NY: Vintage, 1994], 228–9).
36 Žižek, "A Leftist Plea for 'Eurocentrism,'" *Critical Inquiry* 24, no. 4 (1988): 1002.
37 It is wrong, according to Fanon, to simply dismiss *négritude* at the theoretical level. For example, Jean-Paul Sartre's cognitive explanatory framework—which dutifully discerns the epiphenomenal from the real determinants, the symptoms from the causes—fails to account for the affects of *négritude*, for the movement's impact on the psyche. "When I tried to claim my negritude intellectually as a concept," Fanon writes, "they snatched it away from me. They proved to me that my reasoning was nothing but a phase in the dialectic" (Fanon, *Black Skin, White Masks*, 111). That is to say, subjecting *négritude* to a cold dialectical reading neglected to record the movement's affective appeal, the utter joy "in the intellectualization of black *existence*" (Fanon, *Black Skin, White Masks*, 113, emphasis in original). As James Penney puts it, "Fanon held firmly to the view that racially based identity claims on the part of non-European subjects in colonized situations carried an irreducible, cathartic importance" (Penney, "Passing into the Universal," 56).
38 Fanon, *Black Skin, White Masks*, 203–4, 206.
39 "Negritude imposed itself then as a stubborn will of resistance trying quite plainly to embed our identity in a denied, repudiated, and renounced culture" (Bernabé, Chamoiseau, and Confiant, *In Praise of Creoleness*, 80).
40 George Yancy and Judith Butler, "What's Wrong with 'All Lives Matter'?" *New York Times*, January 12, 2015. Available at http://opinionator.blogs.nytimes.com/2015/01/12/whats-wrong-with-all-lives-matter/ (accessed May 24, 2017).
41 Fanon, *Black Skin, White Masks*, 73.
42 Angela Davis, *Freedom Is a Constant Struggle: Ferguson, Palestine, and the Foundations of a Movement* (Chicago, IL: Haymarket Books, 2016), 87.
43 Davis, *Freedom Is a Constant Struggle*, 87.
44 Said, *Culture and Imperialism*, 214.

45 Nick Nesbitt, *Caribbean Critique: Antillean Critical Theory from Toussaint to Glissant* (Liverpool, UK: Liverpool University Press, 2013), 20.
46 Žižek, *Event: Philosophy in Transit* (London, UK: Penguin Books, 2014), 48.
47 Žižek, *Violence: Six Sideways Reflections* (New York, NY: Picador, 2008), 152.
48 See Fanon, *A Dying Colonialism*, trans. Haakon Chevalier (New York, NY: Grove Press, 1965). "It is inadequate only to affirm that a people was dispossessed, oppressed or slaughtered, denied its rights and its political existence, without at the same time doing what Fanon did during the Algerian war, affiliating those horrors with the similar afflictions of other people. This does not at all mean a loss in historical specificity, but rather it guards against the possibility that a lesson learnt about oppression in one place will be forgotten or violated in another place or time" (Said, *Representations of the Intellectual* [New York, NY: Vintage, 1996], 44).
49 Žižek, *Less Than Nothing: Hegel and the Shadow of Dialectical Materialism* (New York, NY: Verso, 2012), 831.
50 Confiant, *Aimé Césaire*, 38. My translation.

15

From Postmodern Intertextuality to "Decomposed Theater": Matei Vişniec between Romanian and Francophone Literatures

Emilia David

Engaging with the dramatic work of Francophone Romanian writer Matei Vişniec, in particular with his post–Cold War participation in the European network of the theater of the absurd, I focus, chiefly in this chapter's second half, on the author's intertextual dialogue with another kindred spirit, Romanian-French author Eugen Ionescu (Eugène Ionesco).[1] Because I do so over and against the linguistic and cultural-historical backdrop of France's highly consequential presence in East European countries such as Romania throughout modernity, I lead off with an overview of the French influence in Romania, especially in Romanian literary history. As I will briefly show, French language and culture have over the past two centuries or so appealed considerably to Romanian writers, critics, artists, philosophers, and politicians, in effect, to entire social categories including but not limited to the intellectual class, before and after Vişniec's own generation.

Playwright, poet, and novelist, Vişniec was born in Romania but has been living for more than three decades in Paris. After years of systematic harassment by Communist censorship, he left his native land and asked for political asylum in France, whose citizen he became in 1993. What made his name well known in French cultural circles, as well as elsewhere in the world, was first of all his dramatic work, which has been published and performed in Paris and other places, inside and outside France, including the Off d'Avignon Festival. Currently the Romanian dramatist who has been translated and staged the most in recent decades worldwide, as well as the living Francophone Romanian writer most appreciated in the French-speaking world, he became, since his relocation to France, entirely bilingual and bicultural. Yet again, this career reset is hardly unusual for modern Romanian authors, whose fascination with French culture has been so powerful that they have often moved to France and have adopted, sometimes with worldwide success, French as their language of expression.

1. Vișniec and the 1980s Generation

Vișniec started out in Bucharest as one of the major poets of the so-called Generation of the 1980s (*generația '80*), the members of which have brought postmodernism on the scene of Romanian literature since the late 1970s. After publishing three collections of poems, he won a 1985 Romanian Writers' Union Prize for his poetry book *Înțeleptul la ora de ceai* (The Wiseman at Teatime).[2] As with other colleagues with whom he founded the Romanian postmodern movement, Vișniec had initially responded strongly to British and American writing. Before long, however, his distinctively ethical concerns steered him toward French literature. More reflective and self-reflective, more skeptical and abstract in his poetry than other representatives of the Generation, who tended to place stylistic and philological virtuosity at the center of their endeavors, Vișniec was naturally drawn to what one might call, with an older vocabulary, "the French spirit."

As we shall see below, such affinities were not unexpected. But the turn to postmodernism and in particular to its US sources in 1980s Socialist Romania was, all the more so because this postmodern sensibility arose in the country, as it did in other Central and East European literatures around the same time, in the absence of the postindustrial and consumption-oriented type of society characteristic of the United States and Western Europe and whose "logic" postmodernism has been said to echo—hence Romanian critic Mircea Martin's formula, "postmodernism without postmodernity."[3] But the emergence of a postmodern orientation in Cold War Romania is not the exclusive result of external influences. Other "internal" factors to consider here are the widely felt crisis of the modernist aesthetic within the national literature, on the one hand, and, on the other, the growing impact of older writers whose style had been at odds with the modernist mainstream and who, on this ground, would be regarded by the young Romanian postmoderns as their precursors: in poetry, Leonid Dimov, whose poetry is a feast of richly oneiric imagery, and Mircea Ivănescu, creator of minimalist scenarios with a strongly theatrical and intertextual thrust; in prose, Radu Petrescu, Mircea Horia Simionescu, and Costache Olăreanu, authors of ingeniously metafictional experiments.

Having entered into circulation in Romanian criticism belatedly, after the mid-1980s, the postmodern concept has been viewed by some as a literary-historical inevitability.[4] Ion Bogdan Lefter, one of the Generation's most active critics and theorists, has argued that postmodernism inaugurated in Romanian literature a whole new literary paradigm revolving around "a new type of relationship" that "authorial subjectivity"—the author who says "I"—"establishes with the world [and] the text, with life and literature."[5] Essentially, the novelty inheres in the writer's largely unprecedented cultural attitude, we are told, toward his or her surroundings and the profound changes that have marked them in recent times, including the transformations deriving from the rise of mass society and globalization. Identifiable primarily in the style of the literature published both in the West and in Eastern Europe throughout the 1980s and 1990s, Lefter's list of "postmodern symptoms and attitudes" speaks, likewise, to the ways and protocols marking the author's orientation toward reality, more specifically, toward *concrete, immediate* reality: the tendency to "salvage" bits and pieces of this reality, to recycle, "with a difference," elements of the everyday; "irony"; the "expansion of narrativity into genres such as poetry and criticism"; the "overlaying of multiple textual levels"; "polystylistics," or heterogeneity of style; and the "use of cultural references, citation, collage, pastiche, parody, and other forms of intertextuality."[6]

It is true that a major target of the latter is tradition. But, as Lefter and others have insisted, unlike modernism's, postmodernism's relation with the literary archive, in Romania and elsewhere, is less straightforwardly polemical. Instead of rejecting the national patrimony, Vișniec and other young writers of the 1980s recontextualize and reutilize it, albeit often playfully and ironically. Thus, because they were writing about the present by rewriting the past, the most experimental authors at the time of the regime's collapse are best read as intertextual performers. More broadly, their work is performance tout court—the kind involved in "second-degree" writing, or writing "through" or "across" previous writing. Performative in this sense, the poetry of the Generation showcases a theatricality whose conventions represent not only a dominant element in Western contemporary culture,[7] as Michel Benamou has commented, but also, and more specifically, a "unifying form in postmodernism."[8] Built into this performativity are the notion and practice of the work as process, theoretical awareness, and the centrality of play. All of these elements, in turn, also feed into the literary dynamics of intertextuality, hence, again, the dramatic aspect of at least some of the Generation's poetry. Genrewise, one could even point to this body of work's "double nature," one best illustrated in poets like Vișniec, who exercises his unique capacity as a creator of verse while simultaneously availing himself of an entire dramatic repertoire. Beyond the expressive possibilities offered by the language of theater to all the new poets of the 1980s—the predisposition to lyrical farce, the overt use of staging devices, the simulations and disguises of all types, whether geared to literary effects or existential attitudes—what stands out in Vișniec is the habit of directly addressing, in a poem, present or imaginary interlocutors. Sometimes, he involves them in complex and strange poetic spectacles as in the 1982 poetry volume *Orașul cu un singur locuitor* (The Town with a Single Inhabitant) or in Beckettian scenarios in which the lyrical persona performs attired as in a circus or theater show.[9]

Vice versa, this dialogism is articulated intertextually in Vișniec's conversation with authors of the past. In following the legacy of Romanian poets from the second half of the twentieth century such as Nichita Stănescu, Marin Sorescu, and Ivănescu, he develops a multilayered "rapport," so to speak, with a whole array of literary figures, national and international, an entire network of connections, images, and symbols sometimes organized into what elsewhere I have defined as spectacular "intertextual triangles" and "quartets."[10] In this vein, the relation with Franz Kafka— to give just a quick but relevant example—is noteworthy. In addition to "canonical" intertextuality—the usual reference or allusion to Kafka and his oeuvre—in play in Vișniec is also what Jean Ricardou has labeled "restricted intertextuality."[11] The latter's occurrence in the Romanian writer's work speaks to specific situations pertaining to the Vișniec's own biography, writing, and their broader context, for instance to his double (Franco-Romanian) affiliation as a citizen and artist and, of late, to his triple status (poet, playwright, and fiction writer) as a literature author. Joseph K., his *seconde main* character, to recall Antoine Compagnon's formula, is emblematic here, given the kind of poetic investment Vișniec makes in Kafka's solitary protagonist.[12] One could say, in fact, that Vișniec belongs to the Kafka family. Like other kindred spirits, he is reflective and skeptical, admirer of the imaginary worlds of the absurd and existential angst, projecting his visions onto monstrous landscapes in parabolic settings that are both abstract and fantastic, and creating characters who are maladjusted, solitary, and victims of an invisible yet crushing power.[13] A unique literary topos lying in the heart of an entire intertextual constellation of world literature, Joseph K. intrigues Vișniec, too, to say the least. The spell the famous character casts on the Romanian writer initially marks three poems—"Era o zi ploioasă, domnule judecător" (It Was a Rainy Day, Your Honor) and "O meditație" (A Meditation), both included in *Orașul cu un singur locuitor*, as well as "Din viața domnului K" (Tales from the Life of Mr. K.) from the subsequent collection, *Înțeleptul la ora de ceai*—but ends up informing a whole novel.[14] Likewise, a "Messrs K. Quartet" is included in "The Town with Only One Inhabitant," a phrase already present in the title of the poetry book by the same name, then in a monologue from the 1992 *Théâtre décomposé ou l'homme-poubelle* (Decomposed Theater or the Dustbin Man),[15] which postdates the poems by about ten years, as well as in one of the "micronovels" that make up Vișniec's recent "kaleidoscope novel" *Negustorul de începuturi de roman* (The Merchant of Book Openings).[16] Finally, one comes across a "reading-in-the-mirror" of sorts of the aforementioned poems in the novel *Domnul K. eliberat* (Mr. K. Liberated).[17]

Vișniec's repeated returns to Kafka help differentiate, within the Generation, between writers keen—or keener—on explicitly political and ethical issues and authors whose take on such matters was, before the fall of Communism, more "oblique," predominantly philological and hedonistic. This distinction overlaps, at least as far as major figures such as Mircea Cărtărescu, Florin Iaru, and Traian T. Coșovei are concerned, with Lefter's classification. Cărtărescu, Iaru, and Coșovei strike Lefter as "[deliberately] loquacious and prosaic,"[18] virtuosos capable of running the gamut of expressive means and exhausting the potential for intertextual inventiveness; they build ingenious intertextual mechanisms and forefront an awareness of the heterogeneity of the elements flowing into their compositions.[19] Instead, Vișniec is a "proud moralist."[20] Poets like him deem ethics and the unstinting involvement in the everyday the main *raison d'être* of their works, which is why they keep coming back to certain "exemplary" cultural figures, whom they value as moral authorities. At the same time, poets in this category are less preoccupied by the "technical" effects of *seconde main* literature. Therefore, their intertextuality is more subdued. Yet, once again, there is a reason for this. What drives them is primarily ethical and political in nature, and they knew full well that stylistic and intertextual pyrotechnics could both hinder and facilitate a more direct message.[21] Formulating such a message in published poems or in readings at the Generation's Monday Circle meetings moderated by critic Nicolae Manolescu was one of Vișniec's priorities, as Manolescu himself acknowledged.[22]

2. "France Burst into My Life": Vișniec, French Culture, and Francophone Tradition in Romania

To reiterate, the same passion for the ethical, the existential, and, I might add, the strangeness engrained in the quotidian accounts for Vișniec's steadily growing attraction to French literature, in particular to its existentialist writers,[23] theater of the absurd, and avant-garde playwrights such as Samuel Beckett.[24] Vișniec has repeatedly talked about his adoration of French culture, and one of his most revealing confessions paints the picture of an intellectual life oriented by this interest at every step of the way. "France," he tells us,

> burst into my life during my studies at Elementary School N. 4 in Rădăuți, right from first class.... I repeat—I'm still not sure how it was possible in a Communist country for a young boy to find all the beautifully translated classics of French literature in the school library.... Subsequently, as a high-school student, I discovered Camus, Sartre, Lautréamont.... And while Romania became increasingly grim because of the totalitarian regime in control, I was granted "political asylum"—[before actually applying for it officially, later on in France]—in the books of Raymond Radiguet, Proust, Michel Tournier, Patrick Modiano, Louis-Ferdinand Céline, Simone de Beauvoir.... After this, once I had gone to study in Bucharest, I discovered French drama, starting with Molière, continuing with Cocteau and Camus, and concluding with Ionesco.[25]

Quite a few Romanians, be they artists, public figures, or even commoners, would recognize themselves in this excerpt. Throughout modernity, education, becoming literate, and *literacy* overall in the country have had a strong French component, in the sense that up until recently, one did not have to "major" in French (and go to college for that), as we might say today, to learn French and be exposed to the likes of Marcel Proust and Albert Camus. A powerful driving force of modernization in this part of Europe, the French influence in the Romanian principalities of Moldavia and Wallachia may be traced back to the end of the eighteenth century but gained momentum, initially inside the upper class, around the time of the 1848 revolutionary uprisings.[26] Social modernization inhered, simply speaking, in adopting Western institutions complete with their vocabularies. Also roughly put, "Western" meant de facto "French," and the ensuing wholesale Gallicization of Romanian society was geared to countering and ultimately casting aside the political leverage of the Ottoman Empire.[27] The literature of the time, including the plays written around 1840 by Costache Faca and Costache Caragiale, foregrounds the idea that imitating Western cultural models, above all French, constituted the route to progress, both collective and individual, in the socially Darwinist sense in which the lower classes were thought to gain access to the status and privileges of the *élites* through acculturation into the latter's French lifestyle, tastes, mannerisms, and so on. Typical characters in French and Romanian realism alike, the *parvenus* were a social reality, and so was their language, a Franco-Romanian idiolect abundantly present in the melodramatic comedies of the time.

Along with an entire literature, these plays attest to a gradual and multiple transformation of Romanian society and language, especially after the 1848 Revolution. The history buff may remember, however, that, after the 1829 Peace of Adrianopolis (today's Edirne), the Russian presence in the principalities also acts, remarkably enough, as a conduit for France's influence, particularly for the expansion of French. As is well known, Romania, a member of the Organisation Internationale de la Francophonie (OIF), is not the sole country of this part of Europe where French was for a long time not only *the* foreign language but also an idiom extensively used *inside* national borders. But because, unlike the native languages of Russians, Poles, or Bulgarians, Romanian is—as its name suggests—a Romance tongue, the impact of French on it was massive and multiple, so much so that the broad cultural mimesis involved by the country's modernization—to which French was so instrumental—has been described by some as French "colonization" and even deliberate "self-colonization." Be that as it may, Francophonie was and, to a lesser degree today, still is a reality, whether we talk about the learning and employment of French in Romania, both by artists and by laypersons, or about the idiom's use by Romanians who would make up France's Romanian diaspora in the post–Second World War era. A long list of authors, some of them better known than others, comes to mind here, including—for the twentieth century alone—names from Panaït Istrati, Tristan Tzara, Gherasim Luca, and Benjamin Fondane (Fundoianu) to Ionesco, E. M. Cioran, Vintilă Horia, and, closer to our moment, another member of Vişniec's Generation, poet and art critic Magda Cârneci.[28]

3. Networks of "European Theater"

Predating this more recent cluster of writers and, in a sense, paving the way to some of them is Romania's most significant mid-nineteenth-century author, Vasile Alecsandri, who, like most Romanian intellectuals of his time, studied in Paris and did some of his early work in French. A front-ranking cultural figure and politician, Alecsandri was a poet as well as a dramatist whose comedies—some of which incorporated the vaudeville genre—would satirize the very "Gallicization" of Romanian society and, as such, would influence the country's greatest playwright, Ion Luca Caragiale. Portraying the customs and the modus vivendi of the local *bonjourists* and rising bourgeoisie that modeled the demeanor and mannerisms of the French upper classes of mid-late nineteenth century, Alecsandri's and Caragiale's comedies are far more than French imitations. Full of humor and irony, they pay attention to language itself as a symptom of the profound change affecting Romanian society and prove sensitive to absurd situations. A major thread in Romanian literary history, this ironic, sarcastic, and absurdist legacy carries over and gets a modernist-pre-Dadaist upgrade in the caricatural prose of Urmuz (Demetru Demetrescu-Buzău), a writer whose bizarre output—to be titled by his editors posthumously, and aptly, *Pagini bizare* (Weird Pages)—pursued, around the 1920s, the collapse of logic and the overall breakdown of discourse and representation in "fictions" that, in turn, will themselves echo in later authors. One of these authors is Ionesco himself, who acknowledged both Caragiale and Urmuz as his precursors.

So did, to various degrees, Vișniec and his peers in the 1980s. At that point, Caragiale became the Generation's quasi-mandatory point of reference. Vișniec's own drama may be seen, in fact, as a successful attempt to rework, in the political context of the Romanian 1980s and then on the broader stage of the French and world theater, themes and situations that arguably are specific to, or he discovered them first, in his culture of origin and, equally important, in Caragiale's and, later on, Ionescu's kindred dramatic works. Among Vișniec's first plays, the 1985 *Spectatorul condamnat la moarte* (The Spectator Who Was Sentenced to Death) and the 1986 *Caii la fereastră* (Horses at the Window)—all of which would be performed only later on in France—are examples falling into this category even though their specific focus is the devastating effects of dictatorship on individuals and societies.[29] Along with *Le retour à la maison*[30] (2003), *Richard III n'aura pas lieu ou scènes de la vie de Meyerhold* (2001),[31] and *De la sensation d'élasticité lorsqu'on marche sur des cadavres* (2009), they signal an even more emphatic turn to the ethical and political in Vișniec's career.[32] Part and parcel of this shift is the insistent exploration of the war theme, to which the playwright was drawn by the Balkan conflicts of the 1990s, and which he treats in *La femme comme champ de bataille ou Du sexe de la femme comme champ de bataille dans la guerre en Bosnie* (1996)[33] and *Occident Express* (2009).[34] The violence and displacement of war, in turn, were bound up with the cognate problematics of emigration from the Balkans and Eastern Europe in general, a subject also front and center in *Occident Express*, which, I might note, was composed in 2009 and, unlike most of the plays written in France, was done first in Romanian and commissioned by the European Theater Convention within a collaborative project among several EU countries including Romania and its National Theater of Craiova.[35] The ambition of *Occident Express* and of Vișniec's more recent Francophone corpus broadly is to channel meanings that, rooted as they are in an older, Romanian cultural and political history and themes, are recontextualized and, as the directors who have staged these plays in France have recognized, are rendered accessible to world audiences of diverse backgrounds.[36]

This thematics bears witness, however, to Vișniec's affiliation with so-called European theater, that is to say, with a transnational corpus of current drama, the unifying aspects of which were first described by critic and theoretician Michael Corvin. The subjects Corvin identifies as defining this European body of work bring to the fore, one way or the other, the angst-ridden consciousness of individual as well as collective identity. Equally important is, in his opinion, critical reflection on the main sociopolitical events that marked the second half of the twentieth century, starting with the horrors of the Second World War. Based so firmly on historically recognizable topics, this type of drama has given rise, primarily in France, to a style of writing hinging on the centrality of heroes and heroines routinely portrayed in the throes of a crisis and adrift yet whose personal dramas unfold alongside those of a macrohistory viewed as the ultimate source of the contemporary world's conflicts and ills, with the critique of which this kind of writing tasks itself.[37] Characteristic is also a certain handling of textual "blocks" and monologues. Commenting on these dramatic forms in the preface to *Théâtre décomposé ou l'homme-poubelle*, critic Georges Banu glosses on the succession of brief "dramatic modules" and on Vişniec's "modular style" more generally, that is, on the "microtexts" strung up one after another as "drama modules to be assembled."[38] This approach to theatrical composition bodies forth an aesthetic based on research and allowing, at the other end—that of the reader or spectator—for the variable reconfiguration of these "mosaic chips." As Banu has also demonstrated, this sequence of bits and pieces makes up the route or itinerary of a spectator/visitor of a "painting exhibition"—Vişniec's "modular" play—within which each individual text unit is laid out alongside the others as part of a "self-portrait of the artist."[39]

4. Vişniec, Ionesco, and the Theater of the Absurd

The author's long-standing predilection for performance, for "theater within the theater," and for intertextuality is also recognizable in this "Euro-genre" of sorts. But, most notably, plays such as *De la sensation d'élasticité lorsqu'on marche sur des cadavres*,[40] for example, document, beyond this generic affiliation and the wielding of techniques widespread in contemporary French drama, the dialogue with Vişniec's great Romanian and Francophone predecessor, Ionesco, and indirectly—and simultaneously inside and outside the Francophone conversation—with Caragiale and the long-standing Caragiale tradition in Romanian literature. Most intriguing here is the postmodern recontextualization and even transparent recycling of situations, dramatis personae, and prompts from several works by Ionesco, above all the renowned 1950 play, written in French, *La Cantatrice chauve* (The Bald Soprano).[41] It is emblematic that the main stakes of the dialogue with the modernist forerunner remain, as they were in Vişniec's earlier poetry, ethical and political, while the chief thrust of Ionesco's presence, which permeates his heir's text at a remove, "quotationally" or allusively, is the mobilizations of the critical capabilities of the theater of the absurd. More to the point, Vişniec deploys the Ionescian formula to shed light on the absurdity of Romanian dictatorship, which was particularly oppressive during the years in which the play is set. This intertextual relationship with another work is paralleled, inside *De la sensation*, by the dynamic of theater and metatheater, with the characters—prominent Romanian figures detained and persecuted by the Communist regime over many years—improvising theatrical performances in prison. The specific location for the mise-en-scène imagined by Vişniec is Gherla, Romanian totalitarianism's most infamous detention place, where he sets the play's plot, and where the very tortures and political crimes committed against the characters are denounced by the victims themselves, who then restage, in their plays within the play, the unspeakable acts occurring inside the walls of the prison. Gherla thus becomes a metaphor of an entire society imprisoned by the regime, and what takes places in this *univers concentrationnaire* may be seen as a metonymic representation of recent national history.[42] Central to this representation is the scenic expression of the absurd as effectively experienced by Romanian intellectuals, who were, as the author hints, victims of the "rhinoceritis" both affecting and spread by

Communist dictatorship. Indeed, Vişniec transposes *Rhinocéros*' central image into the reality he lived through several decades after Ionesco had captured so memorably its dehumanizing onslaught in the 1959 play.

Because, as suggested earlier, Vişniec's intertextual tack is postmodern, his recuperation of the Ionesco precedent combines the usual techniques of self-distancing from the invoked text, such as parody and irony, with deference and even homage.[43] A "gentleness" if not an outright reverential, "noncompetitive" attitude of the younger writer toward the world-famous master seems to set the tone inside an intertextual agon tempered, I should specify, by particular circumstances: *De la sensation* was composed to celebrate the centenary of Ionesco's birth. It is nonetheless true that, in other places, the "heir"'s references to the classic of the absurd remain largely complimentary, as, for instance, in *Le mot "progrès" dans la bouche de ma mère sonnait terriblement faux* again (2000), where Vişniec uses chairs as metaphors of incommunicability. Feeding off Ionesco's scenic imaginary, the isolation and programmatic display of certain décor items convey here, paradoxically, a shift away from situations involving the external world of objects to characters' inner states.

Le mot "progrès" mines the horrors of the 1990s Yugoslav wars, zeroing in, by means of a carefully assembled set of images and scenic metaphors rather than through sustained narrative, on a family's refusal to make their peace with the idea of the son's death in the absurdly savage conflict. There is no question that the young man is a war casualty, and yet, oddly enough, he continues to be physically present in his parents' modest everyday life and without "haunting" them in the ghostly and terrifying ways in which an ogre of local folklore might. From a director's standpoint, too, Vişniec's solution to the problem posed by the play's tragic plot is quite inspired, helping translate, on one side, an implausible situation into a rational representation that, on the other side, is poetically suggestive of the impossibility of an actual dialogue between the distinct ontologies within which operate the main characters. It is the same unbreakable ontological boundary that marks, within the stage setting, Ionesco's— and now Vişniec's—chairs, which reveal an aesthetic logic driven by the principle of dramatic simultaneity, for the empty chairs concurrently encode the absence of those without whom the protagonists feel they cannot go on.[44] The disappearance of Vibko, the son, and of friends (but who return in several scenes) is just something the mourning family does not get itself to acknowledge, whereas the dead's symbolic, if logically puzzling, status of *presences* bodied forth by a theater that "joins together the visible and the invisible"[45] makes one think of the characters of Dante's limbo and of their own poetic condition.

Venerable as it is, the ploy is not an oddity in recent French drama. One notices the device in the work of Patrick Kermann, for example, a young author who, before committing suicide in 2000, wrote several plays in which some of the main voices heard on stage belong to the deceased. To achieve this "from beyond the grave" effect, Kermann's 1999 *La mastication des morts* borrows from the techniques of the Greek tragics and oratory. Interestingly enough, Vişniec is not indifferent to this technical repertoire either. In *Le mot "progrès,"* the comic and candid, still childish words and gestures of Vibko, who had been forced to become a soldier all of a sudden, are interspersed, in memorable passages, with a funereal choreography whose liturgic moments—grieving wails, ritualic gestures—are meant as vehicles for a theater of the absurd-inflected revisiting of classic tragedy. The comeback of the tragic chorus in Vişniec's work and more broadly in recent "postdramatic" theatrical poetics, as illustrated by Jean-Luc Lagarce in *J'étais dans ma maison et j'attendais que la pluie vienne* (1994) and Olivier Py in *Requiem pour Srebrenica* (1999), documents a more general return of the ceremonial dimension of ancient literature and, more importantly still, enables Vişniec's heroines— whose choral voices index, as elsewhere in his oeuvre, their victimization by history—to act as one body and share their phantasms as such, inside a collective that becomes symbolic of the greater community.[46] The atrocities the latter must cope with feature the war prominently but go beyond it into an exposé of the cynicism surfacing at certain points of abrupt sociohistorical change witnessed by Balkan peoples.

One of these moments is Communism's replacement by a no less violent capitalism under whose auspices an entire sex industry thrives in the West precisely because its recruiting network now reaches deep into Eastern Europe and taps the cheaper workforce of the formerly Communist countries. Vibko's sister, Ida, falls prey to this new phenomenon, but its personal drama helps set up, as well as explain, the play's double ending. Thus, the silence with which the parents invariably "answer" the son's questions, with which *Le mot "progrès"* symmetrically opens and closes, corresponds, in the second ending, to the silent treatment they reserve for Ida, whom they disown after the unfortunate prostitution episode in Paris. Frequent throughout the text, this kind of mute reserve is intertextually eloquent, however, in that it transparently alludes to the Ionescian chairs. A topos par excellence of uncommunicativeness, the chairs are deployed here to accentuate even more emphatically the ambivalence of a tragic and absurd situation. But here, too, Vişniec is careful to deflate some of the metaphysical terror so emblematic of the literature of the absurd and, in so doing, to maintain a critical distance from his model.[47] This double move, through which Vişniec acknowledges others while carving out his own, original space, is highly characteristic of the Francophone Romanian author's self-positioning inside the relationship with Ionesco and the theater of the absurd, on one side, and within the wider network of contemporary European drama, on the other, also accounting for his success in the world's hall theaters and with a broader and broader spectrum of directors and critics.[48]

Notes

1 Whenever I spell "Matei Vişniec"'s name as such (with the Romanian "ş"), I designate the author of works published in Romania. "Matei Visniec" is, by contrast, the author of books that have come out from presses outside Romania.
2 Matei Visniec, *Înţeleptul la ora de ceai* (Bucharest, Romania: Cartea Românească, 1984).
3 Mircea Martin, "D'un postmodernisme sans rivages et d'un postmodernisme sans postmodernité," in the special-topic issue on postmodernism of *Euresis:*

Cahiers roumains d'études littéraires 1-2 (1995): 3-13; reprinted in *Euresis: Cahiers roumains d'études littéraires et culturelles* 1-4 (2009): 11-22, which also focuses on postmodernism.
4 Ion Bogdan Lefter, "Secvențe despre scrierea unui roman de idei," *Caiete critice* 1-2 (1986): 138-52.
5 Ion Bogdan Lefter, "La reconstruction du moi de l'auteur," *Euresis: Cahiers roumains d'études littéraires* 1-2 (1995): 168-71. Romanian scholars as well as some of the poets and critics of the 1980s Generation were aware of Jerome Rothenberg and performance poetry, as Diana Bolcu notes in a 1995 review of the 1994 *Postmodern American Poetry: A Norton Anthology*. Bolcu's text was published in the 1995 *Euresis* issue on postmodernism (the review also refers to the 1960 anthology *The New American Poetry*, ed. Donald M. Allen). On the influence of the Beat Generation on 1980s Romanian poets, see Teodora Dumitru, "Gaming the World-System: Creativity, Politics, and the Beat Influence in the Poetry of the 1980s Generation," in *Romanian Literature as World Literature*, ed. Mircea Martin, Christian Moraru, and Andrei Terian (New York, NY: Bloomsbury, 2018), 271-87.
6 Lefter, "La reconstruction du moi de l'auteur," 168-71. Reissued partially in *Euresis: Cahiers roumains d'études littéraires et culturelles* 1-4 (2009): 99-102. Also see Ion Bogdan Lefter, *Flashback 1985: Începuturile "noii poezii"* (Pitești, Romania: Paralela 45, 2005), 70-92.
7 Richard Schechner, "News, Sex, and Performance Theory," in *Innovation/Renovation: New Perspectives on the Humanities*, ed. Ihab Hassan and Sully Hassan (Madison, WI, and London, UK: University of Wisconsin Press, 1983), 191-208.
8 Michel Benamou, "Presence and Play," in *Performance in Postmodern Culture*, ed. Michel Benamou and Charles Caramello (Madison, WI: Coda Press, 1977), 3.
9 *Orașul cu un singur locuitor* is the title of the second collection of poetry published in Romania by Vișniec (Bucharest, Romania: Cartea Românească, 1982).
10 Emilia David, *Poezia generației '80: intertextualitate și "performance"* (Bucharest, Romania: Editura Muzeul Literaturii Române, 2016), 421-5.
11 Jean Ricardou, "Claude Simon, Textuellement," in *Claude Simon: Analyse, théorie*, ed. Jean Ricardou (Paris, France: U. G. E., 1975), 7-19.
12 Antoine Compagnon, *La seconde main ou le travail de la citation* (Paris, France: Seuil, 1979).
13 Christian Moraru, "The Metamorphic," in Christian Moraru, *Cosmodernism: American Narrative, Late Globalization, and the New Cultural Imaginary* (Ann Arbor, MI: The University of Michigan Press, 2011), 275-93.
14 Matei Visniec, "Era o zi ploioasă, domnule judecător" and "O meditație," in *Orașul cu un singur locuitor*, in Matei Visniec, *Opera poetică*, vol. I (Bucharest, Romania: Cartier, 2011), 171-2 and 162-3; "Din viața domnului K.," in *Înțeleptul la ora de ceai*, in Matei Visniec, *Opera poetică*, vol. II (Bucharest, Romania: Cartier, 2011), 79.
15 Matei Visniec, *Le clochard*, in Matei Visniec, *Théâtre décomposé ou l'homme-poubelle*, preface by Georges Banu, and an "Avertissement" (Paris, Fance: L'Harmattan, 1996), 114-22.
16 Matei Visniec, *Negustorul de începuturi de roman* (Bucharest, Romania: Cartea Românească, 2013), 93-9 and 174-80.

17 Matei Visniec, *Domnul K. eliberat*, with an introduction by the author (Bucharest, Romania: Cartea Românească, 2010). For the French version, see Matei Visniec, *Monsieur K. libéré*, trans. Faustine Vega (Paris, France: Non Lieu, 2013)].
18 Lefter, *Flashback 1985*, 134–5.
19 For an analysis of Mircea Cărtărescu's prose collection, *Nostalgia*, from an intertextual viewpoint, which also touches on a series of themes that are central to the author's overall output, see Christian Moraru's "*Cosmallogy*: Mircea Cărtărescu's *Nostalgia*—The Body, the City, the World," in *Postcommunism, Postmodernism, and the Global Imagination*, ed. Christian Moraru (New York, NY: Columbia University Press, 2009), 47–69.
20 Lefter, *Flashback 1985*, 135.
21 For a discussion of intertextuality as a strategy adopted by some of the 1980s Generation poets as a way of throwing censorship off, see chapters II–IV of Emilia David's monograph *Poezia generației '80*, 59–363.
22 Interview with Nicolae Manolescu, in *Portret de grup cu "generația '80." Interviuri*, ed. Mihail Vakulovski (Bucharest, Romania: Tracus Arte, 2010), 386.
23 Matei Visniec, *Sindromul de panică în Orașul Luminilor* (Bucharest, Romania: Cartea Românească, 2009), 25 and 306. For a French version, see Matei Visniec, *Le syndrome de panique dans la Ville Lumière*, trans. Nicolas Cavaillès (Paris, France: Non Lieu, 2012), 28.
24 Matei Visniec's statement in a dossier of the company Pli Urgent for the play *Le dernier Godot*, Festival Off d'Avignon, 1996, 2.
25 Matei Visniec, *Exilul ca aventură culturală (note și frânturi)*, in *Proiecții ale culturii române în cultura europeană*, ed. Emilia David and Loredana Voicilă (Bucharest, Romania: Editura Muzeul Literaturii Române, 2018), 273. The translation is mine.
26 Alexandru Niculescu, *L'altra latinità. Storia linguistica del romeno tra Oriente e Occidente* (Verona, Italy: Edizioni Fiorini, 2007), 179–180 and 182.
27 Niculescu, *L'altra latinità*, 176.
28 Magda Cârneci, *Le paradis poétique* (Paris, France: Transignum, 2004); *Trois saisons poétiques* (Luxembourg: Phi, 2008); *Peau-ésie*, with Wanda Mihuleac (Paris, France: Transignum, 2008); also see Magda Cârneci, *FEM*, trans. Florica Courriol (Paris, France: Éditions Non Lieu, 2018).
29 Matei Visniec, *Spectatorul condamnat la moarte*, in Matei Visniec, *Teatru: Păianjenul în rană*, vol. I, preface by Mircea Ghițulescu, 2nd ed. (Bucharest, Romania: Cartea Românească, 2007), 191–286. For the French version, see Matei Visniec, *Le spectateur condamné à mort*, trans. Claire Jéquier and Matei Visniec (Paris, France: Espace d'un Instant), 2006]. See also the edition, '*Le spectateur condamné à mort' et autres pièces*, translation by Claire Jéquier (Paris, France: L'Espace d'un Instant, 2013), a volume that includes the plays *Bine, mamă, da'ăștia povestesc în actu' doi ce se-ntâmplă-n actu'-ntâi, Spectatorul condamnat la moarte, Caii la fereastră, Angajare de clovn*, and *Teatru descompus sau omul-pubelă*, the first three of which were translated in collaboration with Claire Jéquier.
30 Matei Visniec, *Le retour à la maison*, in Matei Visniec, *Attention aux vieilles dames rongées par la solitude* (2003) (Carnières-Morlanwelz, Belgium: Lansman, 2004).
31 Matei Visniec, *Richard III n'aura pas lieu ou scènes de la vie de Meyerhold*, with a preface by the author (Carnières-Morlanwelz, Belgium: Lansman, 2005).

32 Matei Visniec, *De la sensation d'élasticité lorsqu'on marche sur des cadavres* (Carnières-Morlanwelz, Belgium: Lansman, 2010).
33 Matei Visniec, *La femme comme champ de bataille ou Du sexe de la femme comme champ de bataille dans la guerre en Bosnie* (followed in the volume by *Paparazzi ou La chronique d'un lever de soleil avorté* [1995]) (Paris, France: Actes Sud-Papiers, 1997).
34 Matei Visniec's *Occident Express* has not been published in French yet.
35 Matei Visniec, *Occident Express*, in Matei Visniec, *Despre senzația de elasticitate când pășim peste cadavre*, with an "Author's Note" (Pitești, Romania: Paralela 45, 2009), 5–70.
36 For the various productions of *Le spectateur condamné à mort* and *Les chevaux à la fenêtre*, see the reception of the play in France during the 1997 and 1998 seasons of the Festival Off d'Avignon, and the seasons 1993, 1996, 2005, 2006, 2007, and 2014, in Emilia David, *Consecințele bilingvismului în teatrul lui Matei Vișniec* (Bucharest, Romania: Tracus Arte, 2015), 348 and 356 and, respectively, 321–3, 340–1, 391–2, 393–4, 401, and 448–9.
37 Michel Corvin, the section, "Le théâtre, vigie de l'Europe: être sur le qui-vive. De l'après guerre à l'an 2000" from the afterword, "Cinquante ans de théâtre francophone mis en perspective dans l'avant et l'ailleurs du siècle," in *De Godot à Zucco: Anthologie des auteurs dramatiques de langue française 1950-2000*, ed. Michel Azama, vol. III. *Le bruit du monde*, foreword by Jean-Claude Lalillas (Montreuil-sous-Bois, France: Éditions théâtrales, 2004), 301–16.
38 Matei Visniec, "Avertissement," in Visniec, *Théâtre décomposé ou l'homme-poubelle*, 11–12.
39 Georges Banu, "Matei Visniec ou de la Décomposition," in Visniec, "Avertissement," 7–9; 8.
40 Visniec, *De la sensation d'élasticité lorsqu'on marche sur des cadavres*.
41 Eugène Ionesco, *La Cantatrice chauve* (Paris, France: Gallimard, 1954).
42 David, *Consecințele bilingvismului în teatrul lui Matei Visniec*, 507.
43 Linda Hutcheon, "Ironie et parodie: Stratégie et structure," translation by Philippe Hamon, in *Poétique* 36 (November 1978): 467–77. See also Hutcheon's essay, "Ironie, satire, parodie," in *Poétique* 46 (April 1981): 140–55.
44 Matei Visniec, *Le mot "progrès" dans la bouche de ma mère sonnait terriblement faux* (Carnières-Morlanwelz, Belgium: Lansman, 2007), 67.
45 Giuseppa Salidu, "'La Romania mi ha dato le radici, la Francia le ali.' Profilo biografico di Matei Visniec," in *Prove di drammaturgia. Rivista di inchieste teatrali*, issue. titled "Il teatro di Matéï Visniec. Impronta dei tempi," 1 (April 2009): 7.
46 Hans Thies Lehmann, "Choral Theatre/Theatre of the Chorus," in *Postdramatic Theatre*, trans. and introduction by Karen Jürs-Munby (New York, NY: Routledge, 2006), 129–33.
47 Gabriella Bosco, "Il meraviglioso al di là del quotidiano, ovvero la poetica teatrale di E. Ionesco," in *L'utile, il bello, il vero*, Quaderni del Seminario di Filologia Francese (Pisa, Italy, and Geneva, Switzerland: Slatkine, 2001), 355–63.
48 David, *Receptarea operei dramatice în Franța*, in David, *Consecințele bilingvismului în teatrul lui Matei Visniec*, 289–455. Among the numerous French and Romanian awards garnered by Vișniec's plays are the "Grand Prix" for radio drama for *L'histoire des ours pandas racontée par un saxophoniste qui a une petite amie à Francfort* (1994);

the "Prix européen" for his entire work (2009), awarded by the Société des Auteurs et Compositeurs Dramatiques, SACD; the "Prix coup de cœur de la presse" at Off d'Avignon 2008 for the play *Les détours Cioran, ou Mansarde à Paris avec vue sur la mort* and the same prize for the play *Le mot "progress" sonnait terriblement faux dans la bouche de ma mère*, in 2009; a 1998 award from the Romanian Academy; the 2002 National Award for Drama given by the Romanian Ministry of Culture; and "Prix de littérature européenne Jean Monnet 2016."

Bibliography

Académie Française. "La langue de la République est le français," June 12, 2008. http://www.academie-francaise.fr/actualites/la-langue-de-la-republique-est-le-francais. Accessed June 2, 2019.

Acevedo, David Caleb, Moisés Agosto Rosario, and Luis Negrón, eds. *Los otros cuerpos: Antología de tematica gay, lésbica y queer desde Puerto Rico y su diaspora*. San Juan, Puerto Rico: Tiempo Nuevo, 2007.

Adichie, Chimamanda. "The Danger of a Single Story." Filmed July 2009. TEDGlobal video, 18:43. https://www.ted.com/talks/chimamanda_adichie_the_danger_of_a_single_story?language=en. Accessed December 15, 2018.

Alexakis, Vassilis. *Foreign Words*. Translated by Alyson Waters. Iowa City, IA: Autumn Hill Books, 2006.

Alexakis, Vassilis. *Les Mots étrangers*. Paris: Stock, 2002.

Alkon, Paul K. *Origins of Futuristic Fiction*. Athens, GA, and London, UK: University of Georgia Press, 1987.

Almassy, Eva. "Emma la Magyare." In Le Bris and Rouaud, *Pour une littérature-monde*, 259–68.

Almquist, Steven M. "Not Quite the Gabbling of 'A Thing Most Brutish': Caliban's Kiswahili in Aimé Césaire's *A Tempest*." *Callaloo* 29, no. 2 (2006): 587–607.

Altbach, Philip G. "Literary Colonialism: Books in the Third World." *Harvard Educational Review* 15, no. 2 (1975): 226–36.

Altbach, Philip G., Amadio A. Arboleda, and S. Gopinathan, eds. *Publishing in the Third World: Knowledge and Development*. Portsmouth, NH: Heinemann, 1985.

Apter, Emily. "Afterword: The 'World' in World Literature." In Hargreaves, Forsdick, and Murphy, *Transnational French Studies: Postcolonialism and Littérature-monde*, 287–95.

Apter, Emily. *Against World Literature: On the Politics of Untranslatability*. London, UK, and New York, NY: Verso, 2013.

Apter, Emily. *Continental Drift: From National Characters to Virtual Subjects*. Chicago, IL: The University of Chicago Press, 1999.

Aquin, Hubert. "La fatigue culturelle du Canada français." *Liberté* 4, no. 23 (1962): 299–325.

Arnold, A. James. "Césaire Is Dead: Long Live Césaire! Recuperations and Reparations." *French Politics, Culture & Society* 27, no. 3 (2009): 9–18.

Arnold, A. James. *Modernism and Négritude: The Poetry and Poetics of Aimé Césaire*. Cambridge, MA: Harvard University Press, 1981.

"Assemblée nationale, XIVe législature, Session ordinaire de 2012-2013, Compte rendu intégral, Deuxième séance du mardi 29 janvier 2013." http://www.assemblee-nationale.fr/14/cri/2012-2013/20130118.asp. Accessed December 2, 2018.

Association des Écrivains de Langue Française. "Grand prix littéraire de l'Afrique noire." http://www.adelf.info/data/documents/HISTORIQUE-GRAND-PRIX-LITTERAIRE-dAFRIQUE-NOIRE-.pdf. Accessed December 9, 2018.

Association des Lecteurs de J. M. G. Le Clézio. "Les Traductions en anglais des œuvres de J. M. G. Le Clézio." https://www.associationleclezio.com/ressources/les-traductions-des-oeuvres-de-j-m-g-le-clezio/les-traductions-en-anglais-des-oeuvres-de-j-m-g-le-clezio/. Accessed November 20, 2018.

Attali, Jacques. *La francophonie et la francophilie, moteurs de croissance durable*. La Documentation française, August 2014. https://www.ladocumentationfrancaise.fr/rapports-publics/144000511/index.shtml. Accessed October 20, 2018.

Azama, Michel, ed. *De Godot à Zucco: Anthologie des auteurs dramatiques de langue française, 1950-2000*. Vol. III of *Le bruit du monde*. Foreword by Jean-Claude Lalillas. Montreuil-sous-Bois, France: Éditions théâtrales, 2004.

Azérad, Hugues. "Poétique/politique de la césure dans la poésie d'Edouard Glissant." *Esprit créateur* 55, no. 1 (2015): 152–66.

Bancel, Nicolas. "Que faire des *postcolonial studies*? Vertus et déraisons de l'accueil critique des *postcolonial studies* en France." *Vingtième Siècle: Revue d'histoire* 115 (2012/2013): 129–47.

Barber, Benjamin. *If Mayors Ruled the World: Dysfunctional Nations, Rising Cities*. New Haven, CT: Yale University Press, 2013.

Barbery, Muriel, Tahar Ben Jelloun, Alain Borer, Roland Brival, Maryse Condé, Didier Daeninckx, Ananda Devi, et al. "Pour une 'littérature-monde' en français." *Le Monde des Livres*, March 15, 2007. https://www.lemonde.fr/livres/article/2007/03/15/des-ecrivains-plaident-pour-un-roman-en-francais-ouvert-sur-le-monde_883572_3260.html. Accessed January 17, 2019.

Barbery, Muriel, Tahar Ben Jelloun, Alain Borer, Roland Brival, Maryse Condé, Didier Daeninckx, Ananda Devi, et al. "Toward a 'World Literature' in French." Translated by Daniel Simon. *Contemporary French & Francophone Studies* 14, no. 1 (2010): 113–17.

Barker, Ronald E. *Books for All: A Study of International Book Trade*. Paris: UNESCO, 1956.

Barker, Ronald E., and Robert Escarpit. *The Book Hunger*. London, UK, and Paris, France: Harrap, Unesco, 1973. https://unesdoc.unesco.org/ark:/48223/pf0000005699. Accessed December 9, 2018.

Barthes, Roland. *S/Z*. Translated by Richard Miller. New York, NY: Hill and Wang, 1974.

Bate, Jonathan. *The Song of the Earth*. London, UK: Picador, 2000.

Batson, Charles R., and Denis M. Provencher. "Feeling, Doing, Acting, Seeing, Being Queer in Québec: Michel Marc Bouchar, Rodrigue Jean, and the Queer Québec Colloquium." *Québec Studies* 60 (2015): 3–22.

Batson, Charles R., and Denis M. Provencher. "Queer (Again) in Québec." *Québec Studies* 61 (2016): 111–14.

Bayart, Jean-François. *Les Études postcoloniales. Un carnaval académique*. Paris, France: Karthala, 2010.

Beecroft, Alexander. *An Ecology of World Literature: From Antiquity to the Present Day*. London, UK, and New York, NY: Verso, 2015.

Beecroft, Alexander. "World Literature Without a Hyphen: Towards a Typology of Literary Systems." *New Left Review* 54 (November–December 2008): 87–100.

Begag, Azouz. "Trafic de mots en banlieue: Du 'nique ta mère' au 'plaît-il'?" *Migrants-Formation*, no. 108 (March 1997): 30–7.

Benamou, Michel, and Charles Caramello, eds. *Performance in Postmodern Culture*. Madison, WI: Coda Press, 1977.

Ben Jelloun, Tahar. "La cave de ma mémoire, le toit de ma maison . . ." In Le Bris and Rouaud, *Pour une littérature-monde*, 113–24.

Benson, Peter. *Black Orpheus, Transition, and Modern Cultural Awakening in Africa*. Berkeley, CA, Los Angeles, CA, and London, UK: University of California Press, 1986.

Bergeron, Léandre. *Dictionnaire de la langue québécoise*. Montreal: VLB, 1980.

Bernabé, Jean, Patrick Chamoiseau, and Raphaël Confiant. *Éloge de la Créolité/In Praise of Creoleness*. Bilingual edition. Translated by M. B. Taleb-Khyar. Baltimore, MD: The Johns Hopkins University Press, 1990.

Bharucha, Rustom. "Peter Brook's 'Mahabharata': A View from India." *Economic and Political Weekly* 23, no. 32 (August 6, 1988): 1642–7.

Bhattacharya, Baidik. *Postcolonial Writing in the Era of World Literature: Texts, Territories, Globalizations*. London, UK, and New York, NY: Routledge, 2018.

Blanchard, Rebecca. "Carceral States in Kaoutar Harchi's *Zone Cinglée*." *Romance Studies*, nos. 1–2 (2018): 63–75.

Blédé, Logbo. *Les interférences linguistiques dans Les Soleils des indépendances d'Ahmadou Kourouma*. Paris, France: Publibook, 2006.

Bobin, Frédéric. "Entretien d'Aimé Césaire avec Frédéric Bobin." *Le Monde*, April 12, 1994.

Boisseron, Bénédicte. "Maryse Condé's *Histoire de la femme cannibale*: Coming Out in the French Antilles." In *Creole Renegades: Rhetoric of Betrayal and Guilt in the Caribbean Diaspora*, 57–89. Gainesville, FL: University Press of Florida, 2014.

Boisseron, Bénédicte, and Maryse Condé. "Intimité: Entretien avec Maryse Condé." *The International Journal of Francophone Studies* 13, no. 1 (2010): 131–53.

Books and Publishing. "Viggers Novel Sold to France After 'Remarkable' Sales." May 31, 2018. https://www.booksandpublishing.com.au/articles/2018/05/31/108527/viggers-novel-sold-to-france-following-remarkable-sales/. Accessed November 20, 2018.

Bosco, Gabriella. *L'utile, il bello, il vero*. Quaderni del Seminario di Filologia Francese. Pisa, Italy, and Geneva, Switzerland: Slatkine, 2001.

Bradatan, Cristina, Adrian Popan, and Rachel Melton. "Transnationality as a Fluid Social Identity." *Social Identities* 16, no. 2 (2010): 169–78.

Brand, Stewart. *Whole Earth Discipline: An Ecopragmatist Manifesto*. New York, NY: Viking, 2009.

Bray, Maryse. "Une approche plurielle." In *Regards sur la Francophonie*, edited by Marc Gontard and Maryse Bray, 21–7. Rennes, France: Presses Universitaires de Rennes, 1996.

Braziel, Jana Evans. "Caribbean Genesis: Language, Gardens, Worlds (Jamaica Kincaid, Derek Walcott, Édouard Glissant)." In *Caribbean Literature and the Environment: Between Nature and Culture*, edited by Elizabeth DeLoughrey, Renée Gosson, and George Handley, 110–26. Charlottesville, VA, and London, UK: University of Virginia Press, 2005.

Breleur, Ernest, Patrick Chamoiseau, Serge Domi, Gérard Delver, Édouard Glissant, Guillaume Pigeard de Gurbert, Olivier Portecop, Olivier Pulvar, and Jean-Claude William. *Manifeste pour les "produits" de haute nécessité*. Paris, France: Éditions Galaade, 2009.

Brillembourg Tamayo, Alfredo, Kristin Feireiss, and Hubert Klumpner. *Informal City: Caracas Case*. Munich, Germany: Prestel, 2005.

Britton, Celia. "La parole du paysage: Art and the Real in *Une Nouvelle Région du monde*." In *Language and Literary Form in French Caribbean Writing*, 154–68. Liverpool, UK: Liverpool University Press, 2014.

Brock-Utne, Birgit, and Malcom Mercer. "Using African Languages for Democracy and Lifelong Learning in Africa: A Post-2015 Challenge and the Work of CASAS." *International Review of Education* 60, no. 6 (2014): 777–92.

Brossard, Nicole. *French Kiss: Etreinte/Exploration*. Montreal, Canada: Les Quinze, 1974.
Bureau international de l'édition française. "Portraits." Promotional Poster, 2017. https://www.bief.org/fichiers/operation/4010/media/9621/PortraitsEditeursFrancophones_Francfort2017Envoi.pdf. Accessed December 9, 2018.
Burnautzki, Sarah. "Penser le pouvoir de racialisation des catégories d'études littéraires." In *Penser les catégories de pensée. Arts, cultures et médiations*, edited by Chloé Delaporte, Léonor Graser, and Julien Péquignot, 67–86. Paris, France: L'Harmattan, 2016.
Bush, Ruth. *Publishing Africa in French*. Liverpool, UK: Liverpool University Press, 2016.
Bush, Ruth, and Claire Ducournau. "La littérature africaine de langue française, à quel(s) prix? Histoire d'une instance de légitimation littéraire méconnue (1924-2012)." *Cahiers d'Etudes Africaines* 3, no. 219 (2015): 535–68.
Calvet, Louis-Jean. "Introduction à la politologie linguistique." 2002. In *Les langues: quel avenir?, Les effets linguistiques de la mondialisation*, 15–40. Paris: CNRS Editions, 2017.
Campbell, Chris, and Michael Niblett. "Introduction." In *The Caribbean: Aesthetics, World-Ecology, Politics*, edited by Chris Campbell and Michael Niblett, 1–14. Liverpool, UK: Liverpool University Press, 2017.
Candea, Maria. "La notion d'accent de banlieue à l'épreuve du terrain." *Glottopol* 29 (July 2017): 13–26.
Candea, Maria. "Le langage est politique." Interview by *Ballast*, September 8, 2017. https://www.revue-ballast.fr/maria-candea-langage-politique/. Accessed June 2, 2019.
Cârneci, Magda. *FEM*. Translated by Florica Courriol. Paris, France: Éditions Non Lieu, 2018.
Cârneci, Magda. *Le paradis poétique*. Paris, France: Transignum, 2004.
Cârneci, Magda. *Peau-ésie*, with Wanda Mihuleac. Paris, France: Transignum, 2008.
Cârneci, Magda. *Trois saisons poétiques*. Luxembourg: Phi, 2008.
Casanova, Pascale. *La langue mondiale. Traduction et domination*. Paris, France: Seuil, 2015.
Casanova, Pascale. *The World Republic of Letters*. Translated by M. B. DeBevoise. Cambridge, MA: Harvard University Press, 2004.
Castaing, Anne, Lise Guilhamon, and Laetitia Zecchini, eds. *La modernité littéraire indienne: perspectives postcoloniales*. Rennes, France: Presses universitaires de Rennes, 2009.
Caviliogli, David. "Boualem Sansal: Le kamikaze." *BiblioObs*, September 14, 2015. https://bibliobs.nouvelobs.com/romans/20150911.OBS5690/boualem-sansal-le-kamikaze.html. Accessed November 20, 2018.
"CEDH, 39426/06 Exposé des faits et Questions aux Parties, 13 octobre 2008, 39426/06." Doctrine. https://www.doctrine.fr/d/CEDH/HFCOMOLD/CASELAW/2008/CEDH003-2503232-2701349. Accessed December 8, 2018.
Césaire, Aimé. *The Complete Poetry of Aimé Césaire*. Translated by A. James Arnold and Clayton Eshleman. Middletown, CT: Wesleyan University Press, 2017.
Césaire, Aimé. "Poésie et connaissance." In *Aimé Césaire: l'homme et l'œuvre*, edited by Lilyan Kesteloot and Barthélémy Kotchy, 112–26. Paris, France: Présence Africaine, 1973.
Césaire, Aimé. *A Tempest*. Translated by Richard Miller. New York, NY: TCG Translations, 2002.
Chabert, Chrystel. "'93 Panthers': Jilali Hamham conjugue violence et élégance du verbe." *Culture Box*. Last updated March 7, 2017. https://culturebox.francetvinfo.fr/livres/policier/93-panthers-jilali-hamham-conjugue-violence-et-elegance-du-verbe-25330920. Accessed December 3, 2018.
Chamoiseau, Patrick. *L'empreinte à Crusoé*. Paris, France: Gallimard, 2012.

Chamoiseau, Patrick. "L'impensable comme source et comme ressource." *Annales Médico-Psychologiques* 173 (2015): 320–3.
Chandra, Sarika. *Dislocalism: The Crisis of Globalization and the Remobilizing of Americanism*. Columbus, OH: Ohio State University Press, 2011.
Cheah, Pheng. *What Is a World? On Postcolonial Literature as World Literature*. Durham, NC: Duke University Press, 2016.
Claeys, Gregory. "News from Somewhere: Enhanced Sociability and the Composite Definition of Utopia and Dystopia." *History* 98, no. 330 (2013): 145–73.
Cleland, Elsa E. "Biodiversity and Ecosystem Stability." *Nature Education Knowledge* 3, no. 10 (2011). https://www.nature.com/scitable/knowledge/library/biodiversity-and-eco system-stability-17059965. Accessed July 13, 2018.
Collectif Qui fait la France?. *Chroniques d'une société annoncée*. Paris, France: Stock, 2007.
Comeau, Germaine. *Laville*. Moncton, Canada: Perce-Neige, 2008.
Compagnon, Antoine. *La seconde main ou le travail de la citation*. Paris, France: Seuil, 1979.
Condé, Maryse. "Liaison dangereuse." In Le Bris and Rouaud, *Pour une littérature-monde*, 205–16.
Condé, Maryse. "Négritude césairienne, négritude senghorienne." *Revue de littérature comparée* 48, nos. 3–4 (1974): 409–19.
Confiant, Raphaël. *Aimé Césaire: Une traversée paradoxale du siècle*. Paris, France: Stock, 1993.
Conseil Constitutionnel [France]. "Décision n° 94-345 DC du 29 juillet 1994." https://www.conseil-constitutionnel.fr/decision/1994/94345DC.htm. Accessed February 24, 2019.
Constitution of 4 October 1958 [France]. https://www.conseil-constitutionnel.fr/en/con stitution-of-4-october-1958. Accessed February 24, 2019.
Costa, Aleixo Manuel da. *Dicionário de literatura goesa*. Panjim, India: Fundação Oriente, 1997.
Coulon, Virginie. *Bibliographie francophone de littérature africaine*. Vanves, France: Edicef, 1994.
Creighton University. "ENG/CNE 120/122: World Literature I Master Syllabus." https://www.creighton.edu/ccas/english/programs/worldliteratureprogram/courses/worldl iteraturei/. Accessed August 13, 2017.
Crevier Goulet, Sarah-Anaïs. "Du théâtre au cimetière: l'image de la '*nécro-polis*' dans *Omaha Beach* de Catherine Mavrikakis." In *Littératures québécoise et acadienne contemporaines: Au prisme de la ville*, edited by Anne-Yvonne Julien, 215–28. Rennes, France: Presses Universitaires de Rennes, 2014.
Cruz-Malavé, Arnaldo, and Martin F. Manalansan IV, eds. *Queer Globalizations: Citizenship and the Afterlife of Colonialism*. New York, NY: New York University Press, 2002.
Daigle, Françoise. *Pour sûr*. Montreal, Canada: Les Editions du Boréal, 2013.
Damas, Léon-Gontran. *Black-Label*. Paris, France: Gallimard, 1956.
Damas, Léon-Gontran. *Pigments*. Paris, France: Présence Africaine, 1962.
Damrosch, David. *What Is World Literature?* Princeton, NJ, and Oxford, UK: Princeton University Press, 2003.
Dasgupta, Gautam. "'The Mahabharata': Peter Brook's 'Orientalism.'" *Performing Arts Journal* 10, no. 3 (1987): 9–16.
Daunais, Isabelle. *Le roman sans aventure*. Montreal, Canada: Boréal, 2015.
David, Emilia. *Consecințele bilingvismului în teatrul lui Matei Visniec*. Bucharest, Romania: Tracus Arte, 2015.
David, Emilia. *Poezia generației '80: intertextualitate și "performance.*" Bucharest, Romania: Editura Muzeul Literaturii Române, 2016.

David, Emilia, and Loredana Voicilă, eds. *Proiecții ale culturii române în cultura europeană*. Bucharest, Romania: Editura Muzeul Literaturii Române, 2018.
Davis, Angela. *Freedom Is a Constant Struggle: Ferguson, Palestine, and the Foundations of a Movement*. Chicago, IL: Haymarket Books, 2016.
Davis, Caroline. "The Politics of Postcolonial Publishing: Oxford University Press's Three Crowns Series 1962-1976." *Book History* 8 (2005): 227–44.
Davis, Gregson. *Aimé Césaire*. Cambridge, UK: Cambridge University Press, 1997.
Davis, Mike. *Planet of Slums*. London, UK: Verso, 2006.
Daycard, Laurène, and Maxime Pargaud. "Christiane Taubira, bonne amie de la poésie." *Le Figaro*, February 8, 2013. http://www.lefigaro.fr/culture/2013/02/08/03004-2013020 8ARTFIG00351-christiane-taubira-bonne-amie-de-la-poesie.php. Accessed December 4, 2018.
Deckard, Sharae, Nicholas Lawrence, Neil Lazarus, Graeme Macdonald, Upamanyu Pablo Mukherjee, Benita Parry, and Stephen Shapiro. *Combined and Uneven Development: Towards a New Theory of World-Literature*. Liverpool, UK: Liverpool University Press, 2015.
Defoe, Daniel. *Robinson Crusoe: An Authoritative Text, Contexts, Criticism*. 2nd ed., edited by Michael Shinagel. New York, NY: W.W. Norton and Company, 1994.
Delas, Daniel. "Les parlers jeunes dans deux romans littéraires d'Azouz Begag à Thierry Jonquet." *Le Français aujourd'hui* 4, no. 143 (2003): 89–96.
Del Conte, Matt. "'Why You Can't Speak': Second Person Narration, Voice, and a New Model for Understanding Narrative." *Style* 37, no. 2 (2003): 204–19.
Délégation générale à la langue française et aux langues de France. "Références 2013: Langue française et traduction en Méditerranée." http://www.culture.gouv.fr/Espace-d ocumentation/Documentation-administrative/References-2013-langue-francaise-et-tr aduction-en-Mediterranee. Accessed January 9, 2019.
Depestre, René. *Le Métier à métisser*. Paris, France: Stock, 1998.
Derrida, Jacques. *The Beast and the Sovereign*. Vol. 2. Chicago, IL: University of Chicago Press, 2011.
Derrida, Jacques. *Monolingualism of the Other: or, The Prosthesis of Origin*. Translated by Patrick Mensah. Stanford, CA: Stanford University Press, 1998.
Derrida, Jacques. *Of Hospitality: Anne Dufourmantelle Invites Jacques Derrida to Respond*. Translated by Rachel Bowlby. Stanford, CA: Stanford University Press, 2000.
Derrida, Jacques, and Elisabeth Roudinesco. *For What Tomorrow...: A Dialogue*. Translated by Jeff Fort. Stanford, CA: Stanford University Press, 2004.
Derrida, Jacques, and Maurizio Ferraris. *A Taste for the Secret*. Translated by Giacomo Donis. Cambridge, UK: Polity, 2001.
De Swaan, Abram. "Language Systems." In the *Handbook of Language and Globalization*, edited by Nikolas Coupland, 56–76. Hoboken, NJ: Wiley Blackwell, 2010.
Devichand, Mukul. "How the World was Changed by the Slogan 'Je suis Charlie.'" *BBC Trending*, January 3, 2016. http://www.bbc.com/news/blogs-trending-35108339. Accessed November 20, 2018.
Diagne, Souleymane Bachir. "Penser de langue à langue." In Mabanckou, *Penser et écrire l'Afrique aujourd'hui*, 72–80.
Diandué, Bi Kacou Parfait. "Histoire et Fiction dans la production romanesque d'Ahmadou Kourouma." Doctoral dissertation, Université de Limoges, France, June 10, 2003.
Diandué, Bi Kacou Parfait. *Topolectes 1*. Paris, France: Publibook, 2005.
Diandué, Bi Kacou Parfait. *Topolectes 2*. Abidjan, Côte d'Ivoire: Baobab, 2009.

Djaïdani, Rachid. Interview with Lemagazineinfo. April 8, 2007. http://www.lemagazine.info/?Interview-Rachid-Djaidani. Accessed December 4, 2018.
Donadio, Rachel. "France's Obsession with Decline Is a Booming Industry." *The New York Times*, February 3, 2017. https://www.nytimes.com/2017/02/03/books/france-michel-onfray-decadence.html. Accessed November 20, 2018.
Drewal, Henry John, and Marilyn Houlberg. *Mami Wata: Arts for Water Spirits in Africa and Its Diasporas*. Los Angeles, CA: Fowler Museum at UCLA, 2008.
Duchêne, Nadia. "Langue, Immigration, Culture: Paroles de la banlieue française," *Meta* 47, no. 1 (March 2002): 30–7.
Ducournau, Claire. *La fabrique des classiques africains*. Paris, France: CNRS, 2017.
Ducournau, Claire. "Qu'est-ce qu'un 'classique' africain? Les conditions d'accès à la reconnaissance des écrivain(e)s issu(e)s d'Afrique subsaharienne francophone depuis 1960." *Actes de la Recherche en Sciences Sociales* 206–7 (2015): 34–49.
Dumitru, Teodora. "Gaming the World-System: Creativity, Politics, and the Beat Influence in the Poetry of the 1980s Generation." In *Romanian Literature as World Literature*, edited by Martin, Mircea, Christian Moraru, and Andrei Terian, 271–87. New York, NY: Bloomsbury, 2018.
Dunton, Chris. "'Wheyting Be Dat?' The Treatment of Homosexuality in African Literatures." *Research in African Literatures* 20, no. 3 (1989): 422–48.
Dutt, Toru. *Le journal de Mlle D'Arvers*. Paris, France: Didier, 1879.
Dutton, Jacqueline. "État Présent: World Literature in French, *Littérature-Monde*, and the Translingual Turn." *French Studies* 70, no. 3 (2016): 404–18.
Dutton, Jacqueline. "Transnational Utopianism in French Futuristic Fiction: From Mercier's *L'An 2440* (1771) to Houellebecq's *Soumission* (2015)." In *Transnational French Studies*, edited by Charles Forsdick and Claire Launchbury. Liverpool, UK: Liverpool University Press, 2019.
Eckermann, J. P. *Conversations with Goethe: Selected, with an Introduction and Annotated Index*. Edited by Hans Kohn. Translated by Gisela C. O'Brien. New York, NY: Frederick Ungar Publishing, 1964.
Ekotto, Frieda. *Portrait d'une jeune artiste de Bona Mbella*. Paris, France: L'Harmattan, 2010.
El Achir, Khadija. *Transgression et identité autofictionnelle dans l'œuvre de Rachid O.: L'Enfant Ebloui, Plusieurs vies, Chocolat chaud et Ce qui reste*. Paris, France: L'Harmattan, 2014.
Escarpit, Robert. *The Book Revolution*. London, UK, Paris, France: Harrap, Unesco, 1966. https://unesdoc.unesco.org/ark:/48223/pf0000003119. Accessed December 9, 2018.
Escarpit, Robert. *La révolution du livre*. Paris, France: Unesco, 1969. https://unesdoc.unesco.org/ark:/48223/pf0000161128. Accessed December 9, 2018.
Estivals, Robert. "Le livre en Afrique noire francophone." *Communication et Langages* 46 (1980): 60–82.
Étonnants Voyageurs. "Festival international du livre et du film." http://www.etonnants-voyageurs.com/. Accessed November 20, 2018.
Fanon, Frantz. *Black Skin, White Masks*. Translated by Richard Philcox. New York, NY: Grove Press, 2008.
Fanon, Frantz. *A Dying Colonialism*. Translated by Haakon Chevalier. New York, NY: Grove Press, 1965.
Fanon, Frantz. *Peau noire, masques blancs*. Paris, France: Seuil, 1952.
Fanon, Frantz. *Toward the African Revolution*. Translated by Haakon Chevalier. New York, NY: Grove Press, 1967.

Fanon, Frantz. *The Wretched of the Earth*. Translated by Richard Philcox. New York, NY: Grove Press, 2004.

Fendler, Ute. "*Un attiéké pour Elgass* de Tierno Monénembo: Une écriture en fugue ou la tresse narrative." In *Litteratures et societes africaines: Regards comparatistes et perspectives interculturelles* mélanges offerts à János Riesz à l'occasion de son soixantième anniversaire, edited by Papa Samba Diop, Hans-Jürgen Lüsebrink, Ute Fendler, and Christoph Vatter, 493–501. Tübingen, Germany: Gunter Narr Verlag, 2001.

Ferrarini, Hélène. "Léon-Gontran Damas, l'étrange choix poétique de Christiane Taubira." *Slate.fr.*, February 1, 2013. http://www.slate.fr/story/67853/etrange-choix-poetique-de-christiane-taubira. Accessed December 8, 2018.

Florida, Richard. "Why So Many Emerging Megacities Remain So Poor." City Lab, January 16, 2014. https://www.citylab.com/life/2014/01/why-so-many-mega-cities-remain-so-poor/8083/. Accessed June 24, 2019.

Florida, Richard, and Benjamin Schneider. "The Global Housing Crisis." City Lab, April 11, 2018, https://www.citylab.com/equity/2018/04/the-global-housing-crisis/557639/. Accessed June 24, 2019.

Fofana, Ramatoulaye. *L'Édition au Sénégal: bilan et perspectives de développement*. Mémoire pour l'obtention du diplôme de conservateur des bibliothèques. Lyon, France: ENSSIB, 2003.

Forsdick, Charles. "*World-Literature in French*: Monolingualism, Francopolyphonie and the Dynamics of Translation." In *Translation and World Literature*, edited by Susan Bassnett, 29–43. Abingdon, UK, and New York, NY: Routledge, 2019.

Forsdick, Charles. "'Worlds in Collision': The Languages and Locations of World Literature." In *A Companion to Comparative Literature*, edited by Ali Behdad and Dominic Thomas, 473–89. Chichester, MA: Wiley Blackwell, 2011.

Foucault, Michel. *Dits et écrits, II*. Paris, France: Gallimard, 1994.

French-American Foundation. "Translation Prize." https://frenchamerican.org/initiatives/translation-prize/. Accessed November 20, 2018.

Fruchon-Toussaint, Catherine. "La France, invitée d'honneur à la Foire du Livre de Francfort." Radio France International, June 22, 2017. http://www.rfi.fr/culture/20170622-france-invitee-honneur-foire-livre-francfort-langue-francaise. Accessed December 9, 2018.

Fudge, Bruce. "The Failure of Sansal's '2084': Its Essential Optimism." *Arabic Literature (In English)*, October 21, 2015. https://arablit.org/2015/10/21/sansals-2084/. Accessed November 20, 2018.

Fyle, Clifford M. "A Continent in Quest of a Publishing Industry." *Unesco Courier* (September 1965): 28–31. https://unesdoc.unesco.org/ark:/48223/pf0000060619. Accessed December 9, 2018.

Gallagher, Mary. "Postcolonial Poetics: L'exception Francophone?" *Modern and Contemporary France* 18, no. 2 (2010): 251–68.

Garnier, Xavier. "Poétique de la rumeur: L'exemple de Tierno Monénembo." *Cahiers d'études africaines* 35, no. 140 (1995): 889–95.

Gassama, Makhily. *La langue d'Ahmadou Kourouma, ou, Le français sous le soleil d'Afrique*. Paris, France: Karthala, 1995.

Gérard, Albert. "Littérature africaine et identité(s) maghrébine(s)." In *The Growth of African Literature: Twenty-Five Years after Dakar and Fourah Bay*, edited by Edris Makward, Thelma Ravell-Pinto, and Aliko Songolo, 79–88. Trenton, NJ: Africa World Press, 1998.

Ghanem, Nadia. "Why Algerian Novelist Boualem Sansal's '2084' is a Sensation in France." *Arabic Literature (In English)*, October 6, 2015. https://arablit.org/2015/10/06/2084/. Accessed November 20, 2018.

Girard, Quentin. "Qu'attendons-nous pour jouer aux fous, pisser un coup, tout à l'envi?" *Libération*, February 6, 2013. http://www.liberation.fr/politiques/2013/02/06/qu-atten dons-nous-pour-jouer-aux-fous-pisser-un-coup-tout-a-l-envi_879838. Accessed December 5, 2018.

Glaeser, Edward. "A World of Cities: The Causes and Consequences of Urbanization in Poorer Countries." *NBER Working Paper Series* No. 19745. National Bureau of Economic Research, 2013.

Glave, Thomas. *Our Caribbean: A Gathering of Lesbian and Gay Writing from the Antilles*. Durham, NC: Duke University Press, 2008.

Glissant, Édouard. *The Collected Poems of Édouard Glissant*. Translated by Jeff Humphries and Melissa Manolas. Minneapolis, MN: University of Minnesota Press, 2005.

Glissant, Édouard. *Introduction à une poétique du divers*. Paris, France: Gallimard, 2013.

Glissant, Édouard. *The Poetics of Relation*. Translated by Betsy Wing. Ann Arbor, MI: University of Michigan Press, 1997.

Glissant, Édouard. "Solitaire et solidaire. Entretien avec Édouard Glissant." With Philippe Artières. In Le Bris and Rouaud, *Pour une littérature-monde*, 77–86.

Glissant, Édouard. *Traité du Tout-monde. Poétique IV*. Paris, France: Gallimard, 1997.

Glissant, Édouard. *Une Nouvelle région du monde*. Paris, France: Gallimard, 2006.

Goyal, Yogita. "Introduction: The Transnational Turn." In *Cambridge Companion to Transnational American Literature*, edited by Yogita Goyal, 1–17. New York, NY: and Cambridge, UK: Cambridge University Press, 2017.

Goytisolo, Juan. "Défense de la hybridité ou La pureté, mère de tous les vices." In Michel Le Bris and Jean Rouaud, *Je est un autre. Pour une identité-monde*, 205–18.

Grapard, Ulla, and Gillian Hewitson, eds. *Robinson Crusoe's Economic Man: A Construction and Deconstruction*. New York, NY: Routledge, 2011.

Gronemann, Claudia, and Wilfried Pasquier, eds. *Scènes des genres au Maghreb: Masculinités, critique* queer *et espaces du féminin/masculin*. Amsterdam, Netherlands: Rodopi, 2013.

Gruzinski, Serge. *La Pensée métisse*. Paris, France: Fayard, 1999.

Guay-Poliquin, Christian. *Au-delà de la "fin": mémoire et survie du politique dans la fiction d'anticipation contemporaine. Sociocritique de* Dondog *d'A.* Volodine, Warax *de P. Hak, et* Je dirai au monde toute la haine qu'il m'inspire *de M. Villemain*. M.A. dissertation, Université du Québec à Montréal, Canada, 2013.

Guay-Poliquin, Christian. "Espoirs et épuisements: Persistances de l'imaginaire de la survie." *L'Inconvénient* 69 (2017): 18–20.

Guay-Poliquin, Christian. *Le fil des kilomètres*. Chicoutimi, Canada: La Peuplade, 2013.

Guay-Poliquin, Christian. *Le poids de la neige*. Chicoutimi, Canada: La Peuplade, 2016.

Guha, Ranajit. *History at the Limit of World-History*. New York, NY: Columbia University Press, 2002.

Gupta, Nolini Kanta. *Collected Works of Nolini Kanta Gupta*. Pondicherry, India: Sri Aurobindo Centre of Education, 1974.

Hage, Julien. "Les littératures francophones d'Afrique noire à la conquête de l'édition française (1914-1974)." *Gradhiva* 2, no. 10 (2009): 80–105.

Hale, Thomas A. *Les Écrits d'Aimé Césaire: Bibliographie commentée*. Montreal, Canada: Les Presses de l'Université de Montréal, 1978.

Halen, Pierre. "Notes pour une topologie institutionelle du système littéraire francophone." https://www.limag.com/Textes/Halen/Riesz.PDF. Accessed May 23, 2019.
Harang, Jean-Baptiste. "Le dernier sango à Paris." *Libération*, September 12, 2002.
Harchi, Kaoutar. Interview with Lauren Bastide. "Les Savantes." FranceInter.fr, July 28, 2018. https://www.franceinter.fr/emissions/les-savantes/les-savantes-28-juillet-2018. Accessed November 21, 2018.
Hargreaves, Alec G., Charles Forsdick, and David Murphy. "Introduction: What Does *Littérature-monde* Mean for French, Francophone and Postcolonial Studies?" In Hargreaves, Forsdick, and Murphy, *Transnational French Studies: Postcolonialism and Littérature-monde*, 1–11.
Hargreaves, Alec G., Charles Forsdick, and David Murphy, eds. *Transnational French Studies: Postcolonialism and Littérature-Monde*. Liverpool, UK: Liverpool University Press, 2010.
Harrell-Bond, Barbara. "Africa Asserts Its Identity. Part 1: The Frankfurt Book Fair." *American Universities Field Staff Reports* 9 (1981): 1–15.
Harrell-Bond, Barbara. "Africa Asserts Its Identity. Part 2: Transcending Cultural Boundaries through Fiction." *American Universities Field Staff Reports* 10 (1981): 1–12.
Hassan, Ihab, and Sally Hassan, eds. *Innovation/Renovation: New Perspectives on the Humanities*. Madison, WI, and London, UK: University of Wisconsin Press, 1983.
Hawley, John C., ed. *Postcolonial, Queer: Theoretical Intersections*. Albany, NY: State University of New York Press, 2001.
Hayes, Jarrod. *Queer Nations: Marginal Sexualities in the Maghreb*. Chicago, IL: University of Chicago Press, 2000.
Hayes, Jarrod. *Queer Roots for the Diaspora, Ghosts in the Family Tree*. Ann Arbor, MI: University of Michigan Press, 2016.
Hayes, Jarrod. "'Queeriser' le Maghreb, un Maghreb qui 'queerise.'" Review of Mehammed Amadeus Mack's *Sexagon: Muslims, France, and the Sexualization of National Culture* and Denis M. Provencher's *Queer, Maghrebi, French: Language, Temporalities, Transfiliations*. *Nouvelles études francophones* 33, no. 1 (2018): 160–8.
Hazareesingh, Sudhir. *How the French Think: An Affectionate Portrait of an Intellectual People*. London, UK: Allen Lane, and New York, NY: Basic Books, 2015.
Hoad, Neville. *African Intimacies: Race, Homosexuality, and Globalization*. Minneapolis, MN: University of Minnesota Press, 2007.
Hollande, François. "France-Afrique: Le texte du discours de Dakar prononcé par François Hollande." *Jeune Afrique*, October 15, 2012. http://www.jeuneafrique.com/173903/politique/france-afrique-le-texte-du-discours-de-dakar-prononc-par-fran-ois-hollande/. Accessed August 3, 2017.
Hollis-Touré, Isabel, ed. "Special Issue: Charlie Hebdo." *French Cultural Studies* 27, no. 3 (2016).
Horvath, Christina. "Ecrire la banlieue dans les années 2000-2015." In *Banlieues vues d'ailleurs*, edited by Bernard Wallon, 47–67. Paris, France: CNRS Editions, 2016.
Houellebecq, Michel. "La religión en las novelas de Houellebecq." Interview with Agathe Novak-Lechevalier (YouTube video), *La Térmica*, June 12, 2017. https://www.youtube.com/watch?v=i1DFEW09dvU&feature=share. Accessed November 20, 2018.

Houellebecq, Michel. "Michel Houellebecq: 'Dieu ne veut pas de moi.'" Interview with Valérie Toranian and Marin de Viry. *Revue des Deux Mondes* (July–August 2015): 8–33.

Houellebecq, Michel. "Michel Houellebecq—On n'est pas couché 29 août 2015." Interview by Laurent Ruquier (YouTube video). https://www.youtube.com/watch?v=UyGX14yz-8w. Accessed November 20, 2018.

Houellebecq, Michel. "Nobody Will Make Us Do Yoga: A Conversation with Michel Houellebecq." Interview with Christian Lorentzen. *Garage Magazine*, June 12, 2017. https://www.vice.com/en_us/article/qv43a7/michel-houellebecq-interview. Accessed November 20, 2018.

Houellebecq, Michel. *Soumission*. Paris, France: Flammarion, 2015.

Houellebecq, Michel. *Submission*. Translated by Lorin Stein. London, UK: Penguin Random House, 2015.

Hugo, Victor. "L'année terrible." In *Œuvres complètes de Victor Hugo*. Paris, France: Alexandre Houssiaux, 1869–1885.

Hutcheon, Linda. "Ironie et parodie: Stratégie et structure." Translation by Philippe Hamon. *Poétique* 36 (November 1978): 467–77.

Hutcheon, Linda. "Ironie, satire, parodie." *Poétique* 46 (April 1981): 140–55.

Hymer, Stephen. "Robinson Crusoe and the Secret of Primitive Accumulation [1971]." *Monthly Review* 63, no. 4 (2011): 18–39.

Interkontinental. "Frankfurt Book Fair 2017." *Interkontinental.org*, October 19, 2017. https://www.interkontinental.org/en/2017/10/19/frankfurt-book-fair-2017. Accessed December 9, 2018.

Ionesco, Eugène. *La Cantatrice chauve*. Paris, France: Gallimard, 1954.

Iriye, Akira. *Global and Transnational History: The Past, Present and Future*. Basingstoke, UK: Palgrave Macmillan, 2013.

Jacquemond, Richard. "Le retour du texte. Jalons pour l'histoire de la traduction arabe de la littérature maghrébine d'expression française." In Nouss, Pinçonnat, and Rinner, *Littératures migrantes et traduction*, 175–86.

Jacquemond, Richard. "Les flux de traduction entre le français et l'arabe depuis les années 1980: un reflet des relations culturelles." In *Translatio. Le marché de la traduction en France à l'heure de la mondialisation*, edited by Gisèle Sapiro, 347–70. Paris, France: CNRS Editions, 2016.

Jay, Paul. *Global Matters: The Transnational Turn in Literary Studies*. Ithaca, NY: Cornell University Press, 2010.

Jeannot, Céline, Sandra Tomc, and Marine Totozani. "Retour sur le débat autour de l'identité nationale en France: quelles places pour quelle(s) langue(s)?" *Revue de Linguistique et de Didactique des Langues* 44 (2011): 63–78.

Jenson, Deborah. "Francophone World Literature (*Littérature-monde*), Cosmopolitanism and Decadence: 'Citizen of the World' without the Citizen?" In Hargreaves, Forsdick, and Murphy, *Transnational French Studies: Postcolonialism and Littérature-monde*, 15–35.

Kamdar, Mira. "10 French Novels to Read Now." *The New York Times*, October 10, 2017. https://www.nytimes.com/2017/10/10/books/review/10-french-novels.html. Accessed November 20, 2018.

Katsakioris, Constantin. "L'Union Soviétique et les intellectuels africains." *Cahiers du Monde Russe* 47, no. 1–2 (2006): 15–32.

Kern, William S. "Robinson Crusoe and the Economists." In Grapard and Hewitson, *Robinson Crusoe's Economic Man*, 62–74.

Khalfa, Jean. *Poetics of the Antilles: Poetry, History and Philosophy in the Writings of Perse, Césaire, Fanon and Glissant*. Bern, Switzerland: Peter Lang, 2016.

Kilito, Abdelfattah. *Je parle toutes les langues, mais en arabe*. Arles, France: Actes Sud-Sindbad, 2013.

Kilito, Abdelfattah. *Le Cheval de Nietzsche. Récits*. Casablanca, Morocco: Le Fennec, 2007.

Kilito, Abdelfattah. *Tu ne parleras pas ma langue*. Essai traduit de l'arabe par Francis Gouin. Arles, France: Actes Sud-Sindbad, 2008.

Klemm, Stephen. "Historicism, Anthropology, and Goethe's Idea of World Literature," *Seminar: A Journal of Germanic Studies* 54, no. 2 (May 2018): 148–65.

Kom, Ambroise, dir. *Dictionnaire des œuvres littéraires négro-africaines de langue française*. Paris, France, and Sherbrooke, Canada: Éditions ACCT/Naaman, 1983.

Koolhaas, Rem. "Pearl River Delta." In *Great Leap Forward*, edited by Chuihua J. Chung and Bernard Chang. Cologne, Germany: Taschen, 2001.

Kotei, S. I. A. *The Book Today in Africa*. Paris, France: Les Presses de l'Unesco, 1981.

Kourouma, Ahmadou. *Allah Is Not Obliged*. Translated by Frank Wynne. Portsmouth, NH: Heinemann, 2006.

Kourouma, Ahmadou. *Monnew: A Novel*. Translated by Nidra Poller. San Francisco, CA: Mercury House, 1993.

Kourouma, Ahmadou. *Quand on refuse on dit non*. Paris, France: Seuil, 2004.

Kourouma, Ahmadou. *The Suns of Independence*. Translated by Adrian Adams. Teaneck, NJ: Holmes & Meier Publishers, 1997.

Kourouma, Ahmadou. *Waiting for the Wild Beasts to Vote*. Translated by Frank Wynne. Portsmouth, NH: Heinemann, 2003.

Krige, John, and Helke Rausch. *American Foundations and the Coproduction of World Order in the Twentieth Century*. Göttingen, Germany: Vandenhoeck & Ruprecht, 2012.

La Fountain-Stokes, Lawrence. *Queer Ricans: Cultures and Sexualities in the Diaspora*. Minneapolis, MN: University of Minnesota Press, 2008.

Le Bris, Michel. "Pour une littérature-monde en français." In Le Bris and Rouaud, *Pour une littérature-monde*, 23–53.

Le Bris, Michel, and Jean Rouaud, eds. *Je est un autre. Pour une identité-monde*. Paris, France: Gallimard, 2010.

Le Bris, Michel, and Jean Rouaud, eds. *Pour une littérature-monde*. Paris, France: Gallimard, 2007.

Lefebvre, Henri. "Le droit à la ville." *L'Homme et la société*, no. 6 (1967): 29–35.

Lefebvre, Henri. *The Production of Space*. Translated by Donald Nicholson-Smith. Oxford, UK: Wiley-Blackwell, 1992.

Leftah, Mohamed. *Le dernier combat du Captain Ni'mat*. Paris, France: La Différence, 2011.

Lefter, Ion Bogdan. *Flashback 1985. Începuturile "noii poezii."* Pitești, Romania: Paralela 45, 2005.

Lefter, Ion Bogdan. "La reconstruction du moi de l'auteur." *Euresis: Cahiers roumains d'études littéraires* 1–2 (1995): 168–71. Partly reprinted in *Euresis: Cahiers roumains d'études littéraires et culturelles* 1–4 (2009): 99–102.

Lefter, Ion Bogdan. "Secvențe despre scrierea unui roman de idei." *Caiete critice* 1–2 (1986): 138–52.

Lehmann, Hans Thies. *Postdramatic Theatre*. Translation and introduction by Karen Jürs-Munby. New York, NY: Routledge, 2006.

"Léon-Gontran Damas par Christiane Taubira." *Dailymotion.com*, January 31, 2008. http://www.dailymotion.com/video/x481pa_leon-gontran-damas-par-christiane-t_news#.UUINFDf4JK0. Accessed December 7, 2018.

Leservot, Typhaine. "From *Weltliteratur* to World Literature to *Littérature-monde*: The History of a Controversial Concept." In Hargreaves, Forsdick, and Murphy, *Transnational French Studies: Postcolonialism and Littérature-monde*, 36–48.
Liger, Bernard. "Chamoiseau: 'L'objet de la littérature n'est plus de raconter des histoires.'" *L'Express*, March 6, 2012. http://www.lexpress.fr/culture/livre/patrick-chamoiseau-l-ob jet-de-la-litterature-n-est-plus-de-raconter-des-histoires_1089728.html#pZsGBjlp GpPLxAOv.99. Accessed June 23, 2015.
Lionnet, Françoise. "Universalisms and Francophonies." In *World Literature in Theory*, edited by David Damrosch, 293–312. Malden, MA: Wiley Blackwell, 2014.
Lionnet, Françoise. "World Literature, *Francophonie*, and Creole Cosmopolitics." In *The Routledge Companion to World Literature*, edited by Theo D'Haen, David Damrosch, and Djelal Kadir, 325–35. London, UK, and New York, NY: Routledge, 2012.
Littérature Africaine Francophone. Database. http://www.litaf.org. Accessed December 9, 2018.
Lobe, Max. "Editeurs africains, mondialisez-vous donc!" *Le Monde*, April 24, 2015. http://www.lemonde.fr/afrique/article/2015/04/24/editeurs-africains-mondialisez-vous-donc_ 4622325_ 3212.html. Accessed August 7, 2017.
Luibhéid, Eithne, and Lionel Cantú, Jr., eds. *Queer Migrations: Sexuality, U.S. Citizenship, and Border Crossings*. Minneapolis, MN: University of Minnesota Press, 2005.
Mabanckou, Alain. "Immigration, *Littérature-Monde*, and Universality: The Strange Fate of the African Writer." Translated by Donald Nicholson-Smith. *Yale French Studies* 120 (2011): 75–87.
Mabanckou, Alain. "La francophonie, oui; le ghetto, non. La littérature francophone n'appartient pas aux lettres françaises." *Le Monde*, March 18, 2006. https://www.lem onde.fr/idees/article/2006/03/18/la-francophonie-oui-le-ghetto-non_752169_3232.h tml. Accessed July 2, 2019.
Mabanckou, Alain. "Le chant de l'oiseau migrateur." In Le Bris and Rouaud, *Pour une littérature-monde*, 55–65.
Mabanckou, Alain, ed. *Penser et écrire l'Afrique aujourd'hui*. Paris, France: Seuil, 2017.
Mack, Mehammed Amadeus. *Sexagon: Muslims, France, and the Sexualization of National Culture*. New York, NY: Fordham University Press, 2017.
Madavane, K. *La malédiction des étoiles ou le Mahabharata des femmes*. Pondicherry, India: Samhita Publications, 1998.
Madavane, K. "'Le geste de l'acteur sur scène est une écriture sur l'eau': Entretien avec K. Madavane." Interview by Jean-Luc Raharimanana. In "Identités, langues et imaginaires dans l'Océan Indien," edited by Jean-Luc Raharimanana. Special issue, *Interculturel Francophonies* 4 (2003): 257–65.
Madavane, K. *Mourir à Bénarès*. Sainte Marie, Réunion: Azalées éditions, 2004.
Madavane, K. "Penser dans la langue de la mère, écrire dans la langue du père, vivre le mythe comme un agent intercultural." In *Ecrire en langue étrangère: interferences de langues et de cultures dans le monde francophone*, edited by Robert Dion, Hans-Jürgen Lüsebrink, and Janos Riese, 505–23. Sainte-Foy, France/Frankfurt, Germany: Nota bene/Iko-Verlag, 2002.
Madavane, K. *To die in Banaras*. London, UK: Picador/PanMacmilan, 2018.
Magniez, Michel. "Le héros homosexual dans les récits en Haïti." In *Ecrits d'Haïti: Perspectives sur la littérature haïtienne contemporaine (1986–2006)*, edited by Nadève Ménard, 213–28. Paris: Karthala.
Mahalakshmi, P. "Ramayana and the Mahabharata Continue to Inspire Writers." *The Times of India*, March 4, 2017. https://timesofindia.indiatimes.com/city/bengaluru/

ramayana-and-the-mahabharata-continue-to-inspire-writers/articleshow/57459220.c ms. Accessed February 2, 2019.

"Mali—Premier Salon de l'écrit et du livre en langues africaines du 03 au 06 décembre 2015." *Afrolivresque*, November 13, 2015. https://www.afrolivresque.com/premi er-salon-de-lecrit-et-du-livre-en-langues-africaines-du-03-au-06-decembre-2015/. Accessed August 10, 2017.

Mani, B. Venkat. *Recoding World Literature: Libraries, Print Culture, and Germany's Pact with Books*. New York, NY: Fordham University Press, 2016.

Mannoni, Octave. *Prospero and Caliban: The Psychology of Colonization*. Translated by Pamela Powesland. Ann Arbor, MI: The University of Michigan Press, 1990.

Mardorossian, Carine. "'Poetics of Landscape': Glissant's Creolized Ecologies." *Callaloo* 36, no. 4 (2013): 983–94.

"Mariage pour tous." *Ministère de la justice*, 12 avril 2013. http://www.justice.gouv.fr/la-garde-des-sceaux-10016/mariage-pour-tous-25267.html. Accessed December 5, 2018.

Marimoutou, Carpanin. "Draupadi aux frontieres: une lecture de *la Malediction des etoiles ou le Mahabharata des femmes* de K. Madavane." In *Draupadi: textures et tissages*, edited by Valérie Magdelaine Andrianjafitrimo, 343–84. La Réunion: Editions K'A, 2008.

Marquès Meseguer, Josep Samuel. "Espai i identitat en l'obra de Jordi Pere Cerdà. Una geografia literària cerdaniana." Doctoral thesis, co-supervised by Joan Petavi Deixona, Université de Perpignan-Via Domitia, France, and Vicent Manuel Salvador Liern, Universitat Jaume I de Castelló de la Plana, Spain, defended in Perpignan, September 5, 2018.

Marshall, Bill. "Cinéma-monde? Towards a concept of Francophone cinema." *Francosphères* 1, no. 1 (2012): 35–51.

Marshall, Bill. *Quebec National Cinema*. Montreal, Canada: McGill-Queen's University Press, 2001.

Martin, Mircea. "D'un postmodernisme sans rivages et d'un postmodernisme sans postmodernité." *Euresis: Cahiers roumains d'études littéraires* 1–2 (1995): 3–13. Partly reprinted in *Euresis: Cahiers roumains d'études littéraires et culturelles* 1–4 (2009): 11–22.

Martin, Mircea, Christian Moraru, and Andrei Terian. "Preface and Acknowledgments." In *Romanian Literature as World Literature*, xiv–xvii. New York, NY: Bloomsbury, 2018.

Martin, Mircea, Christian Moraru, and Andrei Terian, eds. *Romanian Literature as World Literature*. New York, NY: Bloomsbury, 2018.

Marx, Karl. *Capital: A Critique of Political Economy*. Translated by Edward B. Aveling and Samuel Moore. Edited by Friedrich Engels, Vol. I, Book One, *The Process of Production of Capital*. London, UK: Electric Book, 2001.

Massad, Joseph A. *Desiring Arabs*. Chicago, IL: University of Chicago Press, 2007.

Mathis-Moser, Ursula. "L'Apocalypse sur le mode de la dérision: Nouveaux enjeux de la littérature québécoise." In *Que devient la littérature québécoise? Formes et enjeux des pratiques narratives depuis 1990*, edited by Robert Dion and Andrée Mercier, 55–74. Montreal, Canada: Nota bene, 2017.

Mathis-Moser, Ursula, and Marie J. Carrière, *Writing Beyond the End Times? The Literatures of Canada and Quebec*. Innsbruck, Austria: Innsbruck University Press, 2017.

Maurer, Bruno. *Les langues de scolarisation en Afrique francophone: enjeux et repères pour l'action*. Paris, France: AUF, 2010. http://www.bibliotheque.auf.org/doc_num.php?explnum_id=825. Accessed October 26, 2018.

Mavrikakis, Catherine. *Fleurs de crachat*. Montreal, Canada: Leméac, 2005.
Mavrikakis, Catherine. "Je ne renierai jamais la femme qui me hante: Autoportrait." *Lettres québécoises* 166 (2017): 6–7.
Mavrikakis, Catherine. *Oscar de Profundis*. Montreal, Canada: Héliotrope, 2016.
Mavrikakis, Catherine, and Alice Michaud-Lapointe. "Alice Michaud-Lapointe dans l'univers de Catherine Mavrikakis: La fleur même du macadam." *Les Libraires* 96 (2016): 12–15.
Mbembe, Achille. "L'Afrique qui vient." In Mabanckou, *Penser et écrire l'Afrique aujourd'hui*, 17–31.
Mbembe, Achille. *On the Postcolony*. Berkeley, CA: University of California Press, 2001.
Mbembe, Achille. "Pièce d'identité et désirs d'apartheid." In Le Bris and Rouaud, *Je est un autre. Pour une identité-monde*, 115–22.
Mbembe, Achille. "Provincializing France?" Translated by Janet Roitman. *Public Culture* 23, no. 1 (2011): 85–119.
Mbembe, Achille, and Felwine Sarr, eds. *Écrire l'Afrique-Monde*. Dakar, Senegal: Philippe Rey/Jimsaan, 2016.
McDonald, Christie, and Susan Rubin Suleiman, eds. *French Global: A New Approach to Literary History*. New York, NY: Columbia University Press, 2010.
Ménard, Nadève. "The Lasting Impact of Fleeting Encounters in Evelyne Trouillot's Fiction." *Palimpsest: A Journal on Women, Gender, and the Black International* 8, no. 1 (2019): 11–14.
Mérand, Patrick, and Séwanou Dabla. *Guide de littérature africaine*. Paris, France: L'Harmattan/ACCT, 1979.
Michals, Teresa. *Books for Children, Books for Adults: Age and the Novel from Defoe to James*. New York, NY: Cambridge University Press, 2014. doi:10.1017/CBO9781107262201.003.
Migraine-George, Thérèse. *From Francophonie to World Literature in French: Ethics, Poetics, and Politics*. Lincoln, NE, and London, UK: University of Nebraska Press, 2013.
Milcé, Jean-Euphèle. *L'alphabet des nuits*. Orbe, Switzerland: Bernard Campiche, 2004.
Miller, Christopher L. "The Theory and Pedagogy of a World Literature in French." *Yale French Studies* 120 (2011): 33–48.
Miyoshi, Masao. "Turn to the Planet: Literature, Diversity, and Totality." *Comparative Literature* 53, no. 4 (Fall 2001): 283–97.
Mohanty, Satya P. "Literature to Combat Cultural Chauvinism. From Indian Literature to World Literature: In Conversation with Satya P. Mohanty." By Rashmi Dube Bhatnagar and Rajender Kaur. *Frontline: India's National Magazine*, April 6, 2012: 85–92.
Monénembo, Tierno. *Les écailles du ciel: Roman*. Paris, France: Éditions du Seuil, 1986.
Monénembo, Tierno. *Un attiéké pour Elgass: Roman*. Paris, France: Editions du Seuil, 1993.
Monénembo, Tierno. *Un rêve utile: Roman*. Paris, France: Éditions du Seuil, 1991.
Moraru, Christian. *Cosmodernism: American Narrative, Late Globalization, and the New Cultural Imaginary*. Ann Arbor, MI: The University of Michigan Press, 2011.
Moraru, Christian. "The Global Turn in Critical Theory." *symploke* 9, nos. 1–2 (2001): 80–92.
Moraru, Christian. *Postcommunism, Postmodernism, and the Global Imagination*. New York, NY: Columbia University Press, 2009.
Moraru, Christian. *Reading for the Planet: Toward a Geomethodology*. Ann Arbor, MI: University of Michigan Press, 2015.

Moraru, Christian. *Rewriting: Postmodern Narrative and Cultural Critique in the Age of Cloning*. Albany, NY: State University of New York Press, 2001.
Moraru, Christian. "'World,' 'Globe,' 'Planet': Comparative Literature, Planetary Studies, and Cultural Debt after the Global Turn." In *Futures of Comparative Literature: ACLA State of the Discipline Report*, edited by Ursula K. Heise, with Dudley Andrew, Alexander Beecroft, Jessica Berman, David Damrosch, Guillermina De Ferrari, César Domínguez, Barbara Harlow, and Eric Hayot, 124–33. New York, NY: Routledge, 2017.
Moraru, Christian, and Amy J. Elias, eds. *The Planetary Turn: Relationality and Geoaesthetics in the Twenty-First Century*. Evanston, IL: Northwestern University Press, 2015.
Moraru, Christian, and Andrei Terian. "Introduction: The Worlds of Romanian Literature and the Geopolitics of Reading." In *Romanian Literature as World Literature*, edited by edited by Martin, Mircea, Christian Moraru, and Andrei Terian, 1–31. New York, NY: Bloomsbury, 2018.
Moretti, Franco. "A Hundred Years of Solitude." In *Modern Epic: The World-System from Goethe to García Márquez*. Translated by Quintin Hoare. London, UK: Verso, 1996.
Morocco's Constitution of 2011. Translated by Jefri J. Ruchti. William S. Hein & Co., Inc. Constitute.org. https://www.constituteproject.org/constitution/Morocco_2011.pdf?lang=en. Accessed February 24, 2019.
Morrison, Donald. "The Death of French Culture: In Search of Lost Time." *Time Magazine*, November 21, 2007. http://www.time.com/time/magazine/article/0,9171,1686532,00.html. Accessed November 20, 2018.
Morrison, Donald, and Antoine Compagnon. *The Death of French Culture*. Cambridge, UK: Polity, 2010.
Moss, Jane. "Dramatizing Sexual Difference: Gay and Lesbian Theater in Quebec." *American Review of Canadian Studies* 22, no. 4 (1992): 489–98.
Moudileno, Lydie. "Penser l'Afrique à partir de sa littérature." In Mabanckou, *Penser et écrire l'Afrique aujourd'hui*, 137–47.
Mounsi, Mohand. *Territoire d'outre ville*. Paris, France: Stock, 1995.
Mouralis, Bernard. *Littérature et développement*. Paris, France: Silex, 1984.
Mouralis, Bernard. "Qu'est-ce qu'un classique africain?" *Notre Librairie* 160 (December 2005): 34–9.
Moutchia, William. *Le CRÉPLA depuis 1975*. Yaounde, Cameroon: Clé, 2000.
Moylan, Tom. *Scraps of the Untainted Sky: Science Fiction, Utopia, Dystopia*. Boulder, CO, and Oxford, UK: Westview Press, 2000.
Mudimbe, V. Y. *The Invention of Africa: Gnosis, Philosophy and the Order of Knowledge*. Bloomington, IN, and London, UK: Indiana University Press-James Currey, 1988.
Mufti, Aamir R. *Forget English! Orientalisms and World Literatures*. Cambridge, MA: Harvard University Press, 2016.
Mukherjee, Prithwindra. *Le serpent de flames*. Paris, France: Editions Estienne, 1979.
Mukundan, M. *On the Banks of the Mayyazhi*. Translated by Gita Krishnankutty. Chennai, India: Manas, 1999.
Mukundan, M. *Sur les rives du fleuve Mahé*. Translated by Sophie Bastide-Folz. Arles, France: Actes Sud, 2002.
Munro, Brenna M. *South Africa and the Dream of Love to Come: Queer Sexuality and the Struggle for Freedom*. Minneapolis, MN: University of Minnesota Press, 2012.
Munro, Brenna M. "States of Emergence: Writing African Female Same-Sex Sexuality." *Journal of Lesbian Studies* 21, no. 2 (2017): 186–203.

Munro, Ian. "Mapping the Postcolonial Metropolis: Three Recent Novels from Nigeria." In *Representing Minorities: Studies in Literature and Criticism*, edited by Larbi Touaf and Soumia Boutkhil, 38–54. Newcastle, UK: Cambridge Scholars Press, 2006.

Munro, Martin. "Haiti's Worldly Literature." *Small Axe* 14, no. 3 (2010): 69–77.

Murphy, David. "The Postcolonial Manifesto: Partisanship, Criticism and the Performance of Change." In Hargreaves, Forsdick, and Murphy, *Transnational French Studies: Postcolonialism and Littérature-monde*, 67–86.

Murray, Rolland. "The Time of Breach: Class Division and the Contemporary African American Novel." *Novel: A Forum on Fiction* 43, no. 1 (2010): 11–17.

Nandy, Ashish. *The Intimate Enemy: Loss and Recovery of Self under Colonialism*. New Delhi, India: Oxford University Press, 1983.

Nardout-Lafarge, Élisabeth. "En finir avec la guerre? *Fleurs de crachat de Catherine Mavrikakis*." In *Que devient la littérature québécoise? Formes et enjeux des pratiques narratives depuis 1990*, edited by Robert Dion and Andrée Mercier, 37–54. Montreal, Canada: Nota bene, 2017.

National Institute of Statistics of Rwanda (NISR) and Ministry of Finance and Economic Planning (MINECOFIN). *Rwanda Fourth Population and Housing Census*, 2012. *Thematic Report: Education Characteristics of the Population*, 2012. http://microdata.statistics.gov.rw/index.php/catalog/65/download/518. Accessed February 24, 2019.

Nehru, Jawaharlal. *Selected Speeches*. Vol. 5, *1963-64*. New Delhi, India: Publications Division, 1983.

Nelligan, Émile. *Poésies complètes*. Montreal, Canada: Fides, 1952.

Nesbitt, Nick. *Caribbean Critique: Antillean Critical Theory from Toussaint to Glissant*. Liverpool, UK: Liverpool University Press, 2013.

Nganang, Patrice. "Le roman des détritus." *Matatu* 33 (2006): 241–56.

Ngũgĩ wa Thiong'o. *Decolonising the Mind: The Politics of Language in African Literature*. 1986. Oxford, UK, Nairobi, Kenya, and Portsmouth, NH: James Currey-EAEP-Heinemann, 2008.

Ngũgĩ wa Thiong'o. *Globalectics: Theory and the Politics of Knowing*. New York, NY: Columbia University Press, 2012.

Nguyen Phuong Ngoc. "Anna Moï ou la langue migrante comme liberté." In Nouss, Pinçonnat, and Rinner, *Littératures migrantes et traduction*, 55–64.

Niakate, Haby. "Côte d'Ivoire: Le livre de comptes de Dramane Boaré, éditeur et fin gestionnaire." *Jeune Afrique*, January 13, 2016. http://www.jeuneafrique.com/mag/289602/culture/cote-divoire-livre-de-comptes-de-dramane-boare-editeur-fin-gestionnaire. Accessed August 9, 2017.

Niblett, Michael. "World-Economy, World-Ecology, World Literature." *Green Letters* 16, no. 1 (2012): 15–30.

Niculescu, Alexandru. *L'altra latinità: Storia linguistica del romeno tra Oriente e Occidente*. Verona, Italy: Edizioni Fiorini, 2007.

Niekerk, Carl. "World Literature without Goethe: On Pramoedya Ananta Toer's Labour Camp Memoirs *The Mute's Soliloquy*." *Seminar: A Journal of Germanic Studies* 54, no. 2 (May 2018): 247–66.

Nimrod. *Tombeau de Léopold Sédar Senghor*. Cognac, France: Le Temps qu'il fait, 2003.

Nirodbaran. "Correspondence with Sri Aurobindo." https://www.aurobindo.ru/workings/nirodbaran/corresp_1/0004_e.htm. Accessed October 5, 2018.

Noland, Carrie. "Édouard Glissant: A Poetics of the *Entour*." In *Poetry After Cultural Studies*, edited by Heidi R. Bean and Mike Chasar, 143–72. Iowa City, IA: University of Iowa Press, 2011.

Noland, Carrie. *Voices of Negritude in Modernist Print: Aesthetic Subjectivity, Diaspora, and the Lyric Regime*. New York, NY: Columbia University Press, 2015.

Nottingham, John. "Establishing an African Publishing Industry: A Study in Decolonization." *African Affairs* 68, no. 271 (1969): 139–44.

Nouss, Alexis, Crystel Pinçonnat, and Fridrun Rinner, eds. *Littératures migrantes et traduction*. Aix-en-Provence, France: Publications de l'Université de Provence, coll. Textuelles, 2017.

Novak-Lechevalier, Agathe. "Soumission: La littérature comme résistance." *Libération*, March 1, 2015. http://next.liberation.fr/culture/2015/03/01/soumission-la-litterature-comme-resistance_1212088. Accessed November 20, 2018.

Nwosu, Maik. *Invisible Chapters*. Lagos, Nigeria: House of Malaika & Hybun, 2001.

Nwosu, Maik. *Markets of Memories: Between the Postcolonial and the Transnational*. Trenton, NJ: Africa World Press, 2011.

Observatoire de la langue française de l'OIF. "Estimation du nombre de francophones (2018)." http://observatoire.francophonie.org/wp-content/uploads/2018/09/Francophones-Statistiques-par-pays.pdf. Accessed December 10, 2018.

Oluwasanmi, Edwina, Eva Mclean, and Hans Zell. *Publishing in Africa in the Seventies*. Ile-Ife, Nigeria: University of Ife Press, 1975.

Organisation Internationale de la Francophonie. *Charte de la Francophonie*. https://www.francophonie.org/IMG/pdf/charte_francophonie_antananarivo_2005.pdf. Accessed February 24, 2019.

Organisation Internationale de la Francophonie. *La Francophonie dans le monde 2006-2007*. Edited by Christian Valentin. Paris, France: Nathan, 2007. https://www.francophonie.org/IMG/pdf/La_francophonie_dans_le_monde_2006-2007.pdf. Accessed December 10, 2018.

Organisation Internationale de la Francophonie. "La Langue française dans le monde. Synthèse 2018." http://observatoire.francophonie.org/2018/synthese.pdf. Accessed November 10, 2018.

Organisation Internationale de la Francophonie. "Une histoire de la francophonie." https://www.francophonie.org/Une-histoire-de-la-Francophonie.html. Accessed December 15, 2018.

Oustinoff, Michaël. *Traduction et mondialisation*. Edited by Michaël Oustinoff. Paris, France: CNRS Editions, 2011.

Padilla, Mark. *Caribbean Pleasure Industry: Tourism, Sexuality, and AIDS in the Dominican Republic*. Chicago, IL: The University of Chicago Press, 2007.

Patton, Cindy, and Benigno Sánchez-Eppler, eds. *Queer Diasporas*. Durham, NC: Duke University Press, 2000.

Pauvert, Jean-Claude. "Les trois aspects positifs de la conférence d'Addis Abeba." *Bulletin de Liaison de l'Orstom* (December 1961): 7–13. https://core.ac.uk/download/pdf/39893244.pdf. Accessed December 9, 2018.

Pavel, Thomas. *Fictional Worlds*. Cambridge, MA: Harvard University Press, 1986.

Penney, James. "Passing into the Universal: Fanon, Sartre, and the Colonial Dialectic." *Paragraph* 27, no. 3 (2004): 49–67.

Pereira, Felizardo Gonçalves. *Apontamentos para a biographia de Franciso Luis Gomes*. Bombaim, India: Tipografia Anglo-Luisitano, 1892.

Perreau, Bruno. "The Political Economy of 'Marriage for All.'" *Contemporary French Civilization* 39, no. 3 (2014): 351–67.

Pieterse, Edgar, and AbdouMaliq Simone, eds. *Rogue Urbanism: Emergent African Cities*. Auckland Park, South Africa: Jacana Media, 2013.

Pliskin, Fabrice. "Un nouveau mouvement littéraire, Qui Fait la France? Nous!." *Le Nouvel Observateur*, September 6, 2007. https://bibliobs.nouvelobs.com/actualites/20070919.BIB0087/qui-fait-la-france-nous.html. Accessed December 3, 2018.

Polet, Grégoire. "L'atlas du monde." In Le Bris and Rouaud, *Pour une littérature-monde*, 126–7.

Porra, Véronique. "Malaise dans la littérature-monde (en français): de la reprise des discours aux paradoxes de l'énonciation." *Recherches & Travaux* 76 (2010): 109–29.

Pratt, Mary Louise. *Imperial Eyes: Travel Writing and Transculturation*. London, UK: Routledge, 1992.

Prieto, Eric. *Literature, Geography, and the Postmodern Poetics of Place*. New York, NY: Palgrave, 2013.

Provencher, Denis M. *Queer French: Globalization, Language, and Sexual Citizenship in France*. Aldershot, UK: Ashgate, 2007.

Provencher, Denis M. *Queer Maghrebi French: Language, Temporalities, Transfigurations*. Liverpool, UK: Liverpool University Press, 2017.

"Publishing in Africa." Frankfurt Book Fair, Frankfurt, Germany, October 13, 2017.

Puig, Stève. "Banlieue et dystopie en littérature urbaine: Les cas de *Zone cinglée* et *René*." *Itinéraires: Littérature, Textes, Culture* 3 (2016). https://journals.openedition.org.itineraires/3546. Accessed December 4, 2018.

Puig, Stève. "Littérature-monde et littérature urbaine: deux manifestes, même combat?" *Nouvelles Francographies* 2, no. 1 (2011): 87–95.

"Quelles évolutions pour le marché de l'édition francophone?" Frankfurt Book Fair, Frankfurt, Germany, October 12, 2017.

Queneau, Raymond, ed. *Histoire des littératures, III. Littératures françaises, connexes, marginales*. Paris, France: Gallimard, 1958.

Quiñones, Viviana. "La littérature de jeunesse, un art africain: Panorama 2000-2015." In *Takam Tikou, Dossier annuel: La belle histoire de la littérature africaine pour la jeunesse: 2000-2015 (online)*, 2016. http://takamtikou.bnf.fr/dossiers/la-litt-rature-de-jeunesse-un-art-africain-0. Accessed December 9, 2018.

Radio France Internationale. "Burundi: l'anglais officialisé aux côtés du français et du Kirundi," August 29, 2014. http://www.rfi.fr/afrique/20140829-le-burundi-met-ordre-politique-linguistique/. Accessed December 14, 2018.

Raharimanana. "Le creuset des possibles." In Le Bris and Rouaud, *Pour une littérature-monde*, 305–14.

Raissiguier, Catherine. *Reinventing the Republic: Gender, Migration, and Citizenship in France*. Stanford, CA: Stanford University Press, 2011.

Rajchman, John. *The Chomsky-Foucault Debate on Human Nature*. New York, NY, and London, UK: The New Press, 2006.

Rao, Vijaya. *Ecriture indienne d'expression française*. New Delhi, India, and Réunion: Yoda Press/Le GERM, 2008.

Reeck, Laura. "The World and the Mirror in Two 21st Century Manifestos." In Hargreaves, Forsdick, and Murphy, *Transnational French Studies: Postcolonialism and Littérature-Monde*, 258–73.

Renaut, Alain. *Un Humanisme de la diversité: Essai sur la décolonisation des identités*. Paris, France: Flammarion, 2009.

Renouvier, Charles. *Uchronie (L'Utopie dans l'histoire). Esquisse historique apocryphe du développement de la civilisation européenne tel qu'il n'a pas été, tel qu'il aurait pu être*. Paris, France: Bureau de la Critique Philosophique, 1876.

Ricardou, Jean, ed. *Claude Simon: analyse, théorie*. Paris: U.G.E., 1975.

Riding, Alan. "France Ties Africa Aid to Democracy." *The New York Times*, June 22, 1990. https://www.nytimes.com/1990/06/22/world/france-ties-africa-aid-to-democracy.html. Accessed December 9, 2018.

Riesz, János. "A propos des 'classiques africains': Quels modèles pour un canon des littératures africaines?" *Etudes Littéraires Africaines* 32 (2011): 147–56.

Robert, Marthe. *Origins of the Novel*. 1972. Translated by Sacha Rabinovitch. Bloomington, IN: Indiana University Press, 1980.

Robertson, Eric. *Writing Between the Lines: René Schickele, 'Citoyen français, deutscher Dichter'* 1883-1940. Amsterdam, Netherlands, and Atlanta, GA: Rodopi, 1995.

Robertson, Eric. *Yvan Goll–Claire Goll: Texts and Contexts*. Amsterdam, Netherlands, and Atlanta, GA: Rodopi, 1997.

Rocheleau, Alain-Michel. "Gay Theater in Quebec: The Search for an Identity." *Yale French Studies* 90 (1996): 11–36.

Roger, Geoffrey, and Julia DeBres. "Langues de France et Charte européenne des langues régionales et minoritaires: inventaire critiques des arguments anti-ratification." *Sociolinguistic Studies* 11, no. 1 (2017): 131–52.

Rosello, Mireille. *Postcolonial Hospitality: The Immigrant as Guest*. Stanford, CA: Stanford University Press, 2001.

Rosello, Mireille. "Unhoming Francophone Studies: A House in the Middle of the Current." *Yale French Studies* 103 (2001): 123–32.

Roy, Ananya. "Urban Informality: Toward an Epistemology of Planning." *Journal of the American Planning Association* 71, no. 2 (2005): 147–58.

Said, Edward. *Culture and Imperialism*. New York, NY: Vintage, 1994.

Said, Edward. *Representations of the Intellectual*. New York, NY: Vintage, 1996.

Salidu, Giuseppa. "'La Romania mi ha dato le radici, la Francia le ali.' Profilo biografico di Matei Visniec." *Prove di drammaturgia. Rivista di inchieste teatrali* 1 (April 2009): 6–12.

Sansal, Boualem. *2084: The End of the World*. Translated by Alison Anderson. New York, NY: Europa Editions. 2017.

Sansal, Boualem. *2084: La Fin du monde*. Paris, France: Gallimard. 2015.

Sansal, Boualem. "Boualem Sansal: '2015 marquera peut-être le début de la troisième guerre mondiale.'" Interview with Julien Bisson. *Lire*, December 1, 2015. http://www.lexpress.fr/culture/livre/boualem-sansal-2015-marquera-peut-etre-le-debut-de-la-troisieme-guerre-mondiale_1747284.html. Accessed November 20, 2018.

Sansal, Boualem. "Boualem Sansal: 'Le mauvais islam continue à avancer.'" Interview with Grégoire Leménager. *BiblioObs*, October 14, 2011. https://bibliobs.nouvelobs.com/romans/20111011.OBS2224/boualem-sansal-le-mauvais-islam-continue-a-avancer.html. Accessed November 20, 2018.

Sansal, Boualem. "A Rustle in History: Conversations with Boualem Sansal." Interview with Dinah Assouline Stillman. *World Literature Today*, September 2012. https://www.worldliteraturetoday.org/2012/september/rustle-history-conversations-boualem-sansal-dinah-assouline-stillman-0. Accessed November 20, 2018.

Santaki, Rachid. Interview with Pierre Labainville. "Quel statut pour le parler des banlieues?." *On parle média*, 4 July 2017. https://onparlemedia.wordpress.com/2017/07/04/quel-statut-pour-le-parler-des-banlieues/. Accessed July 13, 2018.

Sapiro, Gisèle. *Les contradictions de la globalisation éditoriale*. Paris, France: Éditions Nouveau Monde, 2009.

Sapiro, Gisèle. "Translation and Symbolic Capital in the Era of Globalization: French Literature in the United States." *Cultural Sociology* 9 (2015): 1–27.

Sarangi, Dhir. "L'inspiration spirituelle dans la poésie de Sri Aurobindo, de Nolini Kanta Gupta et de Prithwindra Mukherjee." In "Ecriture indienne d'expression française," edited by Vijaya Rao and Shantha Ramakrishna. Special issue, *Rencontre avec l'Inde* 29, no. 3 (2000): 18–35.

Sargent, Lyman Tower. "The Three Faces of Utopianism Revisited." *Utopian Studies* 5, no. 1 (1994): 1–37.

Sarkar, Ranajit. *Langue étrangère et autres poèmes*. Edited by Vijaya Rao. New Delhi, India: Daastaan, 2012.

Sarkozy, Nicolas. "Le discours de Dakar de Nicolas Sarkozy de 2007: L'intégralité du discours du président de la République, prononcé le 26 juillet 2007." *LeMonde.fr*, November 9, 2007. Last modified October 12, 2012. https://www.lemonde.fr/afrique/article/2007/11/09/le-discours-de-dakar-de-nicolas-sarkozy_1774758_3212.html. Accessed February 24, 2019.

Sartre, Jean-Paul. "Black Orpheus." Translated by John MacCombie. In *Race*, edited by Robert Bernasconi, 115–42. Oxford, UK: Blackwell, 2001.

Sassen, Saskia. *The Global City: New York, London, Tokyo*. Princeton, NJ: Princeton University Press, 2013.

Saussy, Haun. "Interplanetary Literature." *Comparative Literature* 63, no. 4 (2011): 438–47.

Schechner, Richard. "News, Sex, and Performance Theory." In *Innovation/Renovation: New Perspectives on the Humanities*, edited by Ihab Hassan and Sully Hassan, 191–208. Madison, WI, and London, UK: University of Wisconsin Press, 1983.

Schofield, Hugh. "Why Don't French Books Sell Abroad?" *BBC News Magazine*, December 9, 2013. https://www.bbc.com/news/magazine-25198154. Accessed November 20, 2018.

Schor, Naomi. "The Crisis of French Universalism." *Yale French Studies* 100 (2001): 43–64.

Scott, Joan Wallach. *The Politics of the Veil*. Princeton, NJ: Princeton University Press, 2007.

Schwartzwald, Robert. "'Chus t'un homme': Trois (re)mises en scène d'*Hosanna* de Michel Tremblay." *Globe* 11, no. 2 (2008): 43–60.

Schwartzwald, Robert. "From Authenticity to Ambivalence: Michel Tremblay's *Hosanna*." *American Review of Canadian Studies* 22, no. 4 (1992): 499–510.

Schwartzwald, Robert. "(Homo)sexualité et problématique identitaire." In *Fictions de l'identité au Québec*, by Sherry Simon, Pierre L'Hérault, Robert Schwartzwald, and Alexis Nouss, 115–50. Montreal: XYZ, 1991.

Seabrook, Jeremy. *In the Cities of the South: Scenes from a Developing World*. London, UK: Verso, 1996.

Selao, Ching. "Aimé Césaire: 'L'exécuteur de ces œuvres hautes' 1913-2008." *Spirale* 221 (2008): 48–9.

Senghor, Léopold Sédar. "De la négritude." In *Liberté V: Le Dialogue des cultures*, 14–26. Paris, France: Seuil, 1993.

Senghor, Léopold Sédar. *Liberté I: Négritude et Humanisme*. Paris, France: Seuil, 1964.

Senghor, Léopold Sédar. *Négritude, arabisme et francité: réflexions sur le problème de la culture*. Beirut, Lebanon: Éditions Dar al-Kitab Allubnani, 1967.

Serres, Michel. "La bataille idéologique." April 6, 2018. http://www.academie-francaise.fr/la-bataille-ideologique. Accessed June 2, 2019.

Smith, Blake. "Indian Literature Speaks French." *The Wire*, April 29, 2018.

Smith, Blake. "This Indian Author Wrote His Stories in French. Is that Why We Don't Remember Him?" *Scroll.in*, April 1, 2017. https://scroll.in/article/833389/this-indian-

author-wrote-his-stories-in-french-is-that-why-we-dont-remember-him. Accessed May 19, 2019.
Spivak, Gayatri Chakravorty. *An Aesthetic Education in the Era of Globalization*. Cambridge, MA: Harvard University Press, 2011.
Spivak, Gayatri Chakravorty. *Death of a Discipline*. New York, NY: Columbia University Press, 2003.
Spivak, Gayatri Chakravorty, and David Damrosch. "Comparative Literature/World Literature: A Discussion with Gayatri Chakravorty Spivak and David Damrosch." *Comparative Literature* 63, no. 4 (2011): 455–85.
Sri Aurobindo. "The Alexandrine." *The Future Poetry*. https://www.sriaurobindoashram.org/sriaurobindo/downloadpdf.php?id=39. Accessed January 16, 2019.
Sri Aurobindo. "Fragment d'un poème." In Rao, *Ecriture indienne d'expression française*, 3.
Statista: The Statistics Portal. "Book Titles Ranked by Unit Sales in France in 2017." March 2018. https://www.statista.com/statistics/420806/book-best-sellers-france/. Accessed November 20, 2018.
Strich, Fritz. *Goethe and World Literature*. Translated by C. A. M. Sym. London, UK: Routledge, 1949.
Sugnet, Charles J. "*Pour une littérature-monde en français*: Manifesto retro?" *International Journal of Francophone Studies* 12, nos. 2–3 (2009): 237–52.
Suleiman, Susan Rubin, and Christie McDonald. "Introduction: The National and the Global." In *French Global: A New Approach to Literary History*, edited by Christie McDonald and Susan Rubin Suleiman, ix–xxi. New York, NY: Columbia University Press, 2010.
Tagore, Rabrindranath. *Viswa Sahitya*. Translated by Rijula Das and Makarand R. Paranjape. In *Rabindranath Tagore in the 21st Century*, Sophia Studies in Cross-cultural Philosophy of Traditions and Cultures 7, edited by D. Banerji, 277–88. New Delhi, India: Springer India, 2015.
"Taubira accueille le mariage pour tous avec humour et poésie." *Le Monde*, February 12, 2013. http://www.lemonde.fr/politique/video/2013/02/12/taubira-accueille-le-mariage-pour-tous-avec-humour-et-poesie_1831484_823448.html. Accessed December 8, 2018.
Taubira, Christiane. "Le mariage civil est désormais universel." *Le Huffington Post*, April 23, 2013. http://www.huffingtonpost.fr/christiane-taubira/vote-mariage-gay_b_3137872.html. Accessed December 2, 2018.
Taubira, Christiane. *L'esclavage raconté à ma fille*. Paris, France: Bibliophane, 2002.
Taylor, Lucien. "Creolité Bites: A Conversation with Patrick Chamoiseau. Raphaël Confiant, and Jean Bernabé." *Transition* 74 (1997): 124–61.
Tchak, Sami. "Le Moi au miroir fragmenté du nous." In Mabanckou, *Penser et écrire l'Afrique aujourd'hui*, 203–5.
Thierry, Raphaël. *Le marché du livre africain et ses dynamiques littéraires: Le cas du Cameroun*. Pessac, France: Presses Universitaires de Bordeaux, 2015.
Thierry, Raphaël. "Quand l'édition africaine s'émancipe." *INA Global* (Institut National de l'Audiovisuel). April 20, 2016. http://www.inaglobal.fr/edition/article/quand-l-edition-africaine-s-emancipe-8944. Accessed August 9, 2017.
Toledo, Camille de. *Visiter le Flurkistan ou les illusions de la littérature monde*. Paris, France: PUF, 2008.
Toumson, Roger, and Simonne Henry-Valmore. *Aime Césaire: Le nègre inconsolé*. Paris, France: Syros, 1993.

Tremblay, Michel. *Théâtre I*. Montreal, Canada: Leméac, 1991.
Tremblay, Michel. *Thérèse et Pierrette à l'école des Saints-Anges*. Montreal, Canada: Bibliothèque Québécoise, 1991.
Trouillot, Evelyne. "Dans cette grande mouvance de lamentations n'oublions surtout pas les vrais perdants." Facebook, July 10, 2018.
Trouillot, Evelyne. *Le Rond Point*. Port-au-Prince, Haiti: L'Imprimeur, 2015.
Trouillot, Michel-Rolph. "The Odd and the Ordinary: Haiti, the Caribbean, and the World." *Cimarrón: New Perspectives on the Caribbean* 2, no. 3 (1990): 3–12.
United Nations Human Settlements Programme. *The Challenge of Slums: Global Report on Human Settlements 2003*. London, UK: Earthscan Publications, 2003.
United Nations Human Settlements Programme. *The Quito Papers and the New Urban Agenda*. New York, NY: Routledge, 2018.
Vakulovski, Mihail, ed. *Portret de grup cu "generația '80." Interviuri*. Bucharest, Romania: Tracus Arte, 2010.
Valdiguié, Laurent. "Taubira: 'Des terres pour les descendants d'esclaves.'" *Le Journal du Dimanche*, May 11, 2013. http://www.lejdd.fr/Societe/Justice/Actualite/Taubira-Des-terres-pour-les-descendants-d-esclaves-606801. Accessed December 3, 2018.
Valdman, Albert. "La Langue des faubourgs et des banlieues: De l'argot au français populaire." *The French Review* 73, no. 6 (May 2000): 1179–92.
Varghese, Annamma. "From Crisis to Comfort: Contemporary Bestsellers and the French Middlebrow's Narrative of Recovery." *Belphégor* 15, no. 2 (November 2017). http://journals.openedition.org/belphegor/965. Accessed November 20, 2018.
Veldwachter, Nadège. *Littérature francophone et mondialisation*. Paris, France: Karthala, 2012.
Verdery, Katherine. "Beyond the Nation in Eastern Europe." *Social Text* 38 (1994): 1–19.
Vertovec, Steven. "Conceiving and Researching Transnationalism." *Ethnic and Racial Studies* 22, no. 2 (1999): 447–62.
Victor, Gary. "Littérature-monde ou liberté d'être." In Le Bris and Rouaud, *Pour une littérature-monde*, 315–20.
Vignal, Daniel. "L'homophilie dans le roman négro-africain d'expression anglaise et française." *Peuples noirs, peuples africains* 33 (1983): 63–81.
Visniec, Matei. Author's statement in a dossier compiled by the company Pli Urgent for the play *Le dernier Godot*, 2. Avignon, France: Festival Off d'Avignon, 1996.
Visniec, Matei. *De la sensation d'élasticité lorsqu'on marche sur des cadavres*. Carnières-Morlanwelz, Belgium: Lansman, 2010.
Visniec, Matei. *Despre senzația de elasticitate când pășim peste cadavre*. With a "Note" by the Author: Pitești, Romania: Paralela 45, 2009.
Visniec, Matei. *Domnul K. eliberat*. With an introduction by the author. Bucharest, Romania: Cartea Românească, 2010.
Visniec, Matei. *Înțeleptul la ora de ceai*. Bucharest, Romania: Cartea Românească, 1984.
Visniec, Matei. *La femme comme champ de bataille ou Du sexe de la femme comme champ de bataille dans la guerre en Bosnie* and *Paparazzi ou La chronique d'un lever de soleil avorté*. Paris, France: Actes Sud-Papiers, 1997.
Visniec, Matei. *Le mot "progrès" dans la bouche de ma mère sonnait terriblement faux*. Carnières-Morlanwelz, Belgium: Lansman, 2007.
Visniec, Matei. *Le spectateur condamné à mort*. Translated by Claire Jéquier and M. V. Paris, France: Espace d'un Instant, 2006.
Visniec, Matei. '*Le spectateur condamné à mort*' *et autres pièces*. Translated by Claire Jéquier. Paris, France: L'Espace d'un Instant, 2013.

Visniec, Matei. *Le syndrome de panique dans la Ville Lumière*. Translated by Nicolas Cavaillès. Paris, France: Non Lieu, 2012.
Visniec, Matei. *Monsieur K. libéré*. Translated by Faustine Vega. Paris, France: Non Lieu, 2013.
Visniec, Matei. *Negustorul de începuturi de roman*. Bucharest, Romania: Cartea Românească, 2013.
Visniec, Matei. *Occidental Express*. With an introductory essay by Gerardo Guccini, translated and edited by Gianpiero Borgia. Corazzano, Italy: Titivillus, 2012.
Visniec, Matei. *Opera poetică*. Volumes I–II. Bucharest, Romania: Cartier, 2011.
Visniec, Matei. *Orașul cu un singur locuitor*. Bucharest, Romania: Cartea Românească, 1982.
Visniec, Matei. *Richard III n'aura pas lieu ou scènes de la vie de Meyerhold*. With a preface by the author, "Collection Nocturnes Théâtrales." Carnières-Morlanwelz, Belgium: Lansman, 2005.
Visniec, Matei. *Sindromul de panică în Orașul Luminilor*. Bucharest, Romania: Cartea Românească, 2009.
Visniec, Matei. *Teatru: Păianjenul în rană*. Vol. I. 2nd ed. With a preface by Mircea Ghițulescu. Bucharest, Romania: Cartea Românească, 2007.
Visniec, Matei. *Théâtre décomposé ou l'homme-poubelle*. Foreword by Georges Banu, "Matei Visniec ou de la Décomposition" and an "Avertissement" by Matei Visniec. Paris, France: L'Harmattan, 1996.
Voignac, Joseph. "Michel Houellebecq: Le Monde Anglophone réagit à *Soumission*," October 29, 2015. http://www.revuedesdeuxmondes.fr/michel-houellebecq-le-monde-anglophone-reagit-a-soumission/. Accessed November 20, 2018.
Volodine, Antoine. *Dondog*. Paris, France: Seuil, 2002.
Waberi, Abdourahman. "Ecrivains en position d'entraver." In Le Bris and Rouaud, *Pour une littérature-monde*, 67–75.
Waberi, Abdourahman. "'Les enfants de la postcolonie' précédé d'une note liminaire." In Mabanckou, *Penser et écrire l'Afrique aujourd'hui*, 148-61.
Walkowitz, Rebecca L. *Born Translated: The Contemporary Novel in an Age of World Literature*. New York, NY: Columbia University Press, 2015.
Warwick Research Collective. *Combined and Uneven Development: Towards a New Theory of World-Literature*. Liverpool, UK: Liverpool University Press, 2015.
Washbourne, Kelly. "Translation, *Littérisation*, and the Nobel Prize for Literature." *TranscUlturAl* 8, no. 1 (2016): 57–75. http://dx.doi.org/10.21992/T92H02. Accessed August 9, 2017.
Waters, Sarah. "The 2008 Economic Crisis and the French Narrative of National Decline: Une causalité diabolique." *Modern & Contemporary France* 21, no. 3 (2013): 335–54.
Watt, Ian. "*Robinson Crusoe* as a Myth." In Defoe, *Robinson Crusoe*, 288–306.
Weber, Raymond. "Culture et développement: vers un nouveau paradigme?" In *Cooperación cultural entre Europa y África. Actas del 1er Campus Euroafricano de Cooperación*, 99-138. Madrid, Spain: Agencia Española de Cooperación Internacional para el Desarrollo, 2010.
Weidhaas, Peter. *A History of the Frankfurt Book Fair*. Toronto, Canada: Dundurn, 2003.
Weidhaas, Peter. *See You in Frankfurt! Life at the Helm of the Largest Book Fair in the World*. New York, NY: Locus Publishing, 2010.
Weisman, Steven R. "Many Faces of the Mahabharata." *The New York Times*, October 27, 1987: C17, National edition.

Westphal, Bertrand. *Geocriticism: Real and Fictional Spaces.* Translated by Robert Tally. New York, NY: Palgrave Macmillan, 2011.

White, Duncan. "Patrick Modiano: The Nobel Prize Winner Nobody Had Read." *The Telegraph*, July 18, 2015. https://www.telegraph.co.uk/culture/books/11741343/Patrick-Modiano-the-Nobel-Prize-. Accessed November 20, 2018.

White, Michael V. "Reading and Rewriting: The Production of an Economic *Robinson Crusoe*." In Grapard and Hewitson, *Robinson Crusoe's Economic Man*, 15–41.

Wikipedia, "Abés." https://fr.wikipedia.org/wiki/Ab%C3%A9s. Accessed October 20, 2018.

Wiredu, Kwasi. *A Companion to African Philosophy*. Oxford, UK: Blackwell, 2003.

Wiredu, Kwasi. *Cultural Universals and Particulars: An African Perspective*. Bloomington, IN: Indiana University Press, 1996.

Woodward, Servanne. "French-Language Fiction." In *A History of Twentieth-Century African Literatures*, edited by Oyekan Owomoyela, 173–97. Lincoln, NE: University of Nebraska Press, 1993.

World Atlas. "The 10 Largest Cities in the World." Last updated November 2, 2018. https://www.worldatlas.com/articles/the-10-largest-cities-in-the-world.html. Accessed June 24, 2019.

Wynter, Sylvia. "Beyond the Word of Man: Glissant and the New Discourse of the Antilles." *World Literature Today* 63, no. 4 (1989): 637–48.

Yancy, George, and Judith Butler. "What's Wrong with 'All Lives Matter'?" *New York Times*, January 12, 2015.

Yoda, Lalbila Aristide. "Traduction et plurilinguisme au Burkina Faso." *Hermès, La Revue* 56, no. 1 (2010): 35–42. https://www.cairn.info/revue-hermes-la-revue-2010-1-page-35.htm. Accessed February 24, 2019.

Zabus, Chantal. *Out in Africa: Same-Sex Desire in Sub-Saharan Literatures and Cultures*. Woodbridge, UK: James Currey, 2013.

Zabus, Chantal. *Tempests after Shakespeare*. New York, NY: Palgrave, 2002.

Zaganiaris, Jean. *Queer Maroc: Sexualités, genres et (trans)identités dans la littérature marocaine*. N.pl.: Des ailes sur un tracteur, 2013.

Zell, Hans. "African Book Industry Data & the State of African National Bibliographies." *The African Book Publishing Record* 44, no. 4 (2018): 363–89.

Zell, Hans. *The African Book World & Press: A Directory*. Munich, Germany: K.G. Saur, 1980.

Zell, Hans. "A Sixteen-year Japanese Contribution to African Publishing." *Logos* 7, no. 2 (1996): 162–7.

Zell, Hans, and Raphaël Thierry. "Le don de livre, mais à quel prix, et en échange de quoi? Un regard sur le don de livre en Afrique francophone." *African Research & Documentation. Journal of SCOLMA (the UK Libraries and Archives Group on Africa)* 127 (2015). http://scolma.org/category/ard.

Žižek, Slavoj. *Event: Philosophy in Transit*. London, UK: Penguin Books, 2014.

Žižek, Slavoj. "A Leftist Plea for 'Eurocentrism.'" *Critical Inquiry* 24, no. 4 (1988): 988–1009.

Žižek, Slavoj. *Less than Nothing: Hegel and the Shadow of Dialectical Materialism*. New York, NY: Verso, 2012.

Žižek, Slavoj. *Violence: Six Sideways Reflections*. New York, NY: Picador, 2008.

Contributors

Christian Moraru is Class of 1949 Distinguished Professor in the Humanities and Professor of English at University of North Carolina, Greensboro. He specializes in contemporary fiction, critical theory, and comparative and world literature with emphasis on international postmodernism and its post–Cold War developments and successors, as well as on the relations between globalism and new writing in Anglophone and Romance-language traditions. His literary Francophonie scholarship has focused on writers of a range of backgrounds, from Michel Houellebecq, Frédéric Beigbeder, Sorj Chalandon, Dai Sijie, and Maryse Condé to authors of East European, especially Romanian, provenance such as Benjamin Fondane and E. M. Cioran. His recent publications include monographs such as *Cosmodernism: American Narrative, Late Globalization, and the New Cultural Imaginary* (2011) and *Reading for the Planet: Toward a Geomethodology* (2015). He is the editor of *Postcommunism, Postmodernism, and the Global Imagination* (2009) and the coeditor of *The Planetary Turn: Relationality and Geoaesthetics in the Twenty-First Century* (2015), *Romanian Literature as World Literature* (2018), and *The Bloomsbury Handbook of World Theory* (forthcoming 2021).

Nicole Simek is Cushing Eells Professor of Philosophy and Literature and Professor of French and Interdisciplinary Studies at Whitman College. She specializes in French-Caribbean literature, with research interests in the intersection of literature and politics, trauma theory, postcolonial critique, and sociological approaches to literature. Her publications include monographs such as *Hunger and Irony in the French Caribbean: Literature, Theory, and Public Life* (2016) and *Eating Well, Reading Well: Maryse Condé and the Ethics of Interpretation* (2008), as well as the coedited volumes *Feasting on Words: Maryse Condé, Cannibalism, and the Caribbean Text* (2006) and an issue of *Dalhousie French Studies* on "Representations of Trauma in French and Francophone Literature" (Winter 2007).

Bertrand Westphal is Professor of Comparative Literature at the University of Limoges, France, where he headed the research team "Human Spaces and Cultural Interactions" (1999–2019). Founder of geocriticism, Westphal also specializes in world literature, postmodernism, and the relationships between literature and contemporary art, with particular focus on literary cartographies and artistic maps. His recent publications include monographs such as *L'œil de la Méditerranée. Une odyssée littéraire* (2005), *Geocriticism: Real and Fictional Spaces* (translated into English by Robert Tally [2011]; also translated into Italian and Portuguese), *A Plausible World* (translated by Amy Wells [2013], with Spanish translation forthcoming), and *La cage des méridiens. Le roman et l'art contemporain face à la globalisation* (2016; Mandarin translation forthcoming). He is the coeditor of seven books on geocriticism, literature, the aftermath of the 1990s Yugoslav Wars, and other subjects.

Emilia David is Associate Professor and Researcher in Romanian Language and Literature at the University of Pisa, Italy. In 2006, she completed her PhD in Italian Literature at the University of Turin, and in 2015 she received her PhD in Philology from a joint doctoral program of the Universities of Bucharest, Romania, and Turin, Italy. She has written primarily on the European avant-gardes. Her main book publications in Italian are *Futurismo, dadaismo e avanguardia romena: contaminazioni fra culture europee (1909–1930)* (2006) and *Avanguardie, nazionalismi e interventismo nei primi decenni del XX secolo* (2nd ed., 2011), and she has translated into Romanian Filippo Tommaso Marinetti's manifestos (*Manifestele Futurismului* [The Futurist Manifestos], 2009). She is also the author of two monographs on contemporary Romanian literature: *Poezia generației '80: intertextualitate și "performance"* (The Poetry of the 1980s Generation: Intertextuality and "Performance" [2016]) and *Consecințele bilingvismului în teatrul lui Matei Vișniec* (The Consequences of Bilingualism in Matei Vișniec's Theater [2015]).

Bi Kacou Parfait Diandué was Professor of General and Comparative Literature at the Félix Houphouët-Boigny University in Abidjan, Côte d'Ivoire. He published numerous articles and several books, including *Rupture et continuité* (2004), *Topolectes I* (2005), *Une Géocritique de l'Afrique: Mutations et stabilité de la spatialité et de la temporalité dans le locus africain* (2009), *Topolectes 2* (2013), *Réflexions géocritiques sur l'œuvre d'Ahmadou Kourouma* (2013), and *Le pinceau-narrateur* (2017).

Jacqueline Dutton is Associate Professor in French Studies at the University of Melbourne. She has written widely on contemporary French and Francophone literatures and cultures, her publications ranging from a monograph in French on 2008 Nobel Laureate J. M. G. Le Clézio's utopian visions, *Le Chercheur d'or et d'ailleurs: L'Utopie de J. M. G. Le Clézio* (2003), to a major article for *French Studies* on "World Literature in French, *Littérature-monde*, and the Translingual Turn" (2016). Her work on comparative utopianism is included in the 2012 *Cambridge Companion to Utopian Literature*, and her writing on world literatures in French has appeared in many journals and edited books including David Damrosch's 2014 *World Literature in Theory*. Recent editing projects include special-topic journal issues on dark travel (*Postcolonial Studies*), counterculture (*M/C Journal*), time and travel writing (*Nottingham French Studies*), and the future of Francophonie (*Australian Journal of French Studies*). She is currently working on a cultural history of wine in Bordeaux, Burgundy, and Champagne and is coediting a book on wine, terroir, and utopia with Peter Howland.

Vincent Gélinas-Lemaire is Assistant Professor of French at the University of British Columbia, Canada. He received his PhD in Romance Languages and Literatures from Harvard University in 2015. His doctoral dissertation "La représentation de l'espace dans le récit" surveys the fundamental strategies of spatial invention in novels and will be published in revised form under the title *Le récit architecte: cinq aspects de l'espace*.

Jarrod Hayes is Professor of French and Francophone Studies at Monash University, Australia. His research focuses on the intersection between postcolonial studies and queer theory. He is the author of *Queer Nations: Marginal Sexualities in the Maghreb* (2000) and *Queer Roots for the Diaspora: Ghosts in the Family Tree* (2016). He coedited *Comparatively Queer: Interrogating Identities across Time and Cultures* (2010) with Margaret R. Higonnet and William J. Spurlin. He is currently working on a third book project, *Reading across the Color Line: Racialization in the French Americas*.

Jane Hiddleston is Professor of Literatures in French at University of Oxford and Official Fellow in French at Exeter College Oxford. She is the author of *Reinventing Community: Identity and Difference in Late Twentieth-Century Philosophy and Literature in French* (2005), *Assia Djebar: Out of Algeria* (2006), *Understanding Postcolonialism* (2009), *Poststructuralism and Postcoloniality: The Anxiety of Theory* (2010), *Decolonising the Intellectual: Politics, Culture, and Humanism at the End of the French Empire* (2014), and, most recently, *Writing after Postcolonialism: Francophone North African Literature in Transition* (2017).

Régine Michelle Jean-Charles is Associate Professor of Romance Languages and Literatures and African and African Diaspora Studies at Boston College. She teaches classes and does research on black feminisms, Caribbean and African women writers, African film, and Haitian studies. She is the author of *Conflict Bodies: The Politics of Rape Representation in the Francophone Imaginary* (2014). She has also published numerous articles that have appeared in *The Journal of Haitian Studies*, *American Quarterly*, *Callaloo*, *French Forum*, *Journal of Romance Studies*, *Research in African Literatures*, and *Small Axe*. She has also contributed essays to edited volumes including most recently "A Border between Geographies of Grief: Border Crossings and Crossroads between Haiti and the Dominican Republic" for *The Transnational Hispaniola Reader* (2018). She has received fellowships from the Ford Foundation, the Mellon Mays Foundation, and the Woodrow Wilson Foundation. Her current book project is on feminist ethics in contemporary Haitian literature.

Thérèse Migraine-George is Professor at the University of Cincinnati with a joint appointment in the Department of Romance Languages and Literatures and the Department of Women's, Gender, and Sexuality Studies. Her main areas of interest and research are African and Francophone literature, French and Francophone women writers, African queer studies, and creative writing. She is the author of *African Women and Representation: From Performance to Politics* (2008), *From Francophonie to World Literature in French: Ethics, Poetics, and Politics* (2013), a book of essays titled *Mes Etats-Unis: Portraits d'une Amérique que vous ne connaissez pas* (2009), and two novels: *Amour de travers* (2010) and *Envol* (2014). She has also published various book chapters and peer-reviewed articles in journals such as *Women in French Studies*, *Comparative Literature Studies*, *International Journal of Francophone Studies*, *Research in African Literatures*, and *GLQ: A Journal of Lesbian and Gay Studies*. She is currently working on a book that focuses on the politics of difference in a transatlantic perspective.

Eric Prieto is Professor of French and Comparative Literature at the University of California, Santa Barbara. He is the author of *Listening In: Music, Mind, and the Modernist Narrative* (2002), *Literature, Geography, and the Postmodern Poetics of Place* (2012), as well as of a number of articles in postcolonial studies, spatial studies, ecocritical studies, and music and literature. He is currently at work on a book on informal urbanism in the developing world.

Vijaya Rao is Professor at the Centre for French and Francophone Studies of Jawaharlal Nehru University in New Delhi. Her teaching and research focus on Québec literature, representations of India in French and Francophone literatures, and the literature of the Indian Ocean. Her major publications include *Écriture indienne d'expression française* (2008) and the edited volume *Reaching the Great Moghul: Francophone Travel Writing on India of the 17th & 18th Centuries* (2012). In 2008, she coedited a special issue for the journal *Synergies-Inde* on cross-readings and Francophone encounters between Québec and India. In February 2018, she was awarded the *Médaille du 50e anniversaire du Ministère des relations internationales et de la Francophonie* of the government of Québec for her contribution to the development of Québec studies.

Laura Reeck is Professor of French and Chair of International Studies at Allegheny College, Meadville, Pennsylvania. Her research interests include postcolonial literary categories, the *banlieue* cultural field, the *harkis* in literature, guerrilla filmmaking, and the extreme contemporary. She is the author of *Writerly Identities in Beur Fiction and Beyond* (2011). She has recently contributed to *A Practical Guide to French Harki Literature* (2014), *Souffles-Anfas* (2015), and *The Oxford Handbook of Arab Novelistic Traditions* (2017). She is a coeditor of the 2018 annual volume for the Society for Francophone Postcolonial Studies, *Post-Migratory Cultures in Postcolonial France*.

Raphaël Thierry is Postdoctoral Fellow and Lecturer at the University of Mannheim, Germany. Since 2008, his research and publications have focused on African publishing and literary developments in Africa, especially in the literatures of French-speaking African countries, as well as on world book market trends. He received his PhD in 2013 from the University of Lorraine, France, in a program developed in partnership with University of Yaounde 1, Cameroon. Appearing as a book in 2015, his dissertation, *Le marché du livre africain et ses dynamiques littéraires. Le cas du Cameroun*, focuses on the position of African publishing industry in the global book market. With Hans Zell, he has published an article titled "Book Donation Programmes for Africa: Time for a Reappraisal?" in a 2015 issue of *African Research & Documentation: Journal of SCOLMA*. He is currently working on a project on publishing in Francophone Africa. Thierry is also a researcher associated with "Les Afriques dans le monde" (LAM UMR 5115 CNRS/Sciences Po Bordeaux) and the Centre de recherche "Écritures" (EA 3943, Université de Lorraine).

Zahi Zalloua is Cushing Eells Professor of Philosophy and Literature and Professor of French and Interdisciplinary Studies at Whitman College and editor of *The Comparatist*. He has published *Montaigne and the Ethics of Skepticism* (2005), *Reading Unruly: Interpretation and its Ethical Demands* (2014), and *Continental Philosophy and the Palestinian Question: Beyond the Jew and the Greek* (2017). He has also edited volumes and special journal issues on globalization, literary theory, ethical criticism, and trauma studies. His articles have appeared in *symplokē*, *Montaigne Studies*, *Intertexts*, *SubStance*, *L'Esprit Créateur*, and *Symposium*, among other venues.

Index

Académie Française 19, 125, 213
Achebe, Chinua 52, 53, 59, 71, 72, 112
Adichie, Chimamanda 131
African literatures 49–50, 52–3, 56, 59–61, 66–73, 83, 90
    Francophone 32–3, 49, 75–6
Afro-pessimist 111–12
Alecsandri, Vasile 257
apocalyptic novel(s) 139, 141, 148
Appiah, Kwame Anthony 25, 175
Apter, Emily 26, 55, 167
assimilation 137
    colonial 174
    and literary canon 168
    resisting 170–2, 175, 240–1
Association for the Dissemination of French Thought (ADPF) 75
Auerbach, Erich 147
Aurobindo, Sri 33, 94–7

Bâ, Mariama 75–6
banlieue literature 34, 122–3, 124–7, 129–32, *see also* verlan
    langues de 125–6
bas-fonds literature 34, 109, 118–19
Bate, Jonathan 154, *see also* ecopoetry
Beckett, Samuel 53, 143, 256
Beecroft, Alexander 34, 123–4, 132
Bhattacharya, Baidik 169
Boisseron, Bénédicte 189
Bourdieu, Pierre 52, 129
Brossard, Nicole 36, 182, 191
Bush, Ruth 68

Camus, Albert 53, 60, 100, 210, 256
Caragiale, Ion Luca 257–9, *see also* Generation of the 1980s
Caribbean
    French Caribbean 101, 190, 227
    literature 53, 152, 240
Casanova, Pascale 26, 136, 168–9

center-periphery hierarchy 215
Césaire, Aimé 37, 53, 138, 153–5, 162, 173–4, 239–43
    i, laminaria... 156–9
    "Lost Body" 155
    A Tempest (*Une Tempête*) 243–6
Chamoiseau, Patrick 37, 189, 227–9, 240, 242
    individuation disease 234–5
Cheah, Pheng 34, 176, 227–8, 239, *see also* worlding
    What Is a World? 153
Chroniques d'une société annoncée 129
Cioran, E.M. 37, 147, 257
cities of the South 108
city writing 34, 107, 109, 111
class division 195–6, 198–204
Coetzee, J.M. 52, 230
collective memory 99, 101
colonization 9, 33, 56, 58, 60, 88, 101, 243
    French 83–4, 214, 217, 257
Condé, Maryse 17, 20, 122, 189, 241
Corvin, Michael 258
cosmic time (*le Grand Temps*) 154, 157
créolité 240, 242, 245, *see also* négritude

Damas, Léon-Gontran 171, 173–5
Damrosch, David 26, 93, 98, 100, 136, 168–9, *see also* world literature
Daunais, Isabelle 136, 148–9
    L'idylle 136–7, 148–9
declinism 210–12
Defoe, Daniel 37, 142, 227–30, 234
Derrida, Jacques 25, 153–4, 169–70, 175
    Monolingualism of the Other 167, 174
    on *Robinson Crusoe* 227, 230–1, 234–5
Diagne, Souleymane Bachir 10, 57
diaspora 188, 190, 214, *see also* transnational identity

Age of Diasporas   49
Francophone African   76, 182, 191
Haitian   195, 203
Indian   101
Romanian   257
Dickner, Nicolas   139
Diop, Cheikh Anta   6, 138
dire le monde   3, 6, 210, 212, 218
   prédire le monde   36, 212, 219
Djaïdani, Rachid   128–9
Djebar, Assia   12, 52
dystopia   130–1, 148, 212, 218–20
   critical   219, 222

ecology   157
   Francophonie's language   9–10, 13, 15, 24, 34
   global literary   34, 123–4, 131–2
   of literary production   152
   multilingual   3
   world   153, 162
ecopoetry   154
Ekotto, Frieda   36, 187, 191
Escarpit, Robert   70–1, 73–4
   and Ronald E. Barker   71, 74
Étonnants Voyageurs   17, 76–7, 210
exile   110, 114, 169, 190, 214

Fall, Aminata Sow   75
Fanon, Frantz   50, 174, 188–9, 243, 245–7, *see also* négritude
   Fanonian model   112, 119
First Congress of Black Writers and Artists   58, 68

Garnier, Xavier   118
Generation of the 1980s   253, *see also* Vișniec, Matei
geoaesthetic   27–8
geocriticism (*géocritique*)   26, 33, 84–6
geocultural assemblage   24–5, 28
Glissant, Édouard   1–2, 20, 29, 108, 119, 153–4, 158, 162
   Dream Country, Real Country   158–62
   geocultural imaginary   18
   Poetics of Relation   2, 158
   relation, *tout-monde*   21, 27, 110, 156
global cities   108, 119

globalization (*mondialisation*)   8, 23–4, 28–9, 34, 49, 52, 58, 77–8, 139, 168, 239, 253
   anti-   25
   and capitalism   145–6
   economic   108
   homoglobalization   35–6, 180–1
   and planetarity   26–7
   and publishing   211
Goethe, Johann Wolfgang von   21–2, 32, 52, 55, 57, 97, 100, 136, 151, 167, 170, *see also* Weltliteratur
Guay-Poliquin, Christian   34, 140–1, 143, 148
Gupta, Nolini Kanta   33, 96

Heidegger, Martin   27–8, 153–4, 242
   post-Heideggerian   34
Hexagon   5, 13, 20
   and Francophonie   24, 57
   prestige of   23, 211
   writing outside   18, 94, 209
Hollande, François   173
   In Dakar, October 2012   51
Homer   143
Houellebecq, Michel   36, 211–22, *see also* declinism; transnational identity
   "Je suis Charlie"   212
Hugo, Victor   56, 60, 109, 196
Huysmans, Joris-Karl   146–8, 213–14, 216
hybridity (*Métissage*)   21, 242–3

In Praise of Creoleness   242
intertextuality   36–7, 143, 214, 254–5, 259
   intertextual network   143
   restricted   254
Ionesco, Eugène (Eugen Ionescu)   37, 252, 256–61
Istrati, Panaït   37, 257
Ivănescu, Mircea   253–4
Iyengar, Aditya   98

Jelloun, Tahar Ben   12–13, 17, 57, 122, *see also* Pour une littérature-monde en français
joual   138, 182

Kafka, Franz 254–5
Kālidāsa 57
Kane, CheikhHamidou 59, 112–13
Kern, William S. 229
Khalfa, Jean 154–5
Kilito, Abdelfattah 12–13
Kourouma, Ahmadou 10, 33, 52, 59, 84, 87, 89–91

Laye, Camara 112
Le Bris, Michel 27, 31
 and Jean Rouard (see "Pour une littérature-monde en français" manifesto)
Le Clézio, J.M.G. 17, 60, 210
Lefebvre, Henri 107–8, 139, 146
Leftah, Mohamed 36, 184, 186, 188, 191
Lefter, Ion Bogdan 253–5
legalization of same-sex marriage (*mariage pour tous*) 167, 173–5
Lévinas, Emmanuel 173–4
l'idylle, see Daunais, Isabelle
Lionnet, Françoise 22–4
literary canon 50–1, 56, 58, 168
 African 61
 center and periphery 17, 20, 58, 168, 170, 215
 Francophone periphery 122, 127, 129
literary imagination 85, 131
literature of the everyday (*littérature-mondaine*) 36, 195, *see also* Munro, Martin
littérature-monde 2–3, 54, 68, 167, 180, *see also* "Pour une littérature-monde en français"
 Francophone 24, 28, 31
 movement 67, 76
 planetary 29–30
 politics of hospitality 35, 167
 relationship to world literature 21–2, 35–6, 61, 168–70, 176
 and sexuality studies 181

Mabanckou, Alain 16–18, 49, 57, 59, 76, 111, 122, 171
McCarthy, Cormac 139–40
Mahabharata
 Peter Brook's 97
 of Women by K. Madavane (*Mahabharata des Femmes*) 33, 98–100
Mahfouz, Naguib 52–3
Malcolm X 247
Manolescu, Nicolae 255
Martin, Mircea 253
Marx, Karl 52, 230–1, *see also* Weltliteratur, Marxian
Mavrikakis, Catherine 34, 140, 144–8
Mbari Artist and Writer's Club 71
Mbembe, Achille 24–6, 32, 49, 54, 169, 172, 175–6
 planetary condition 32
Mbue, Imbolo 11
Ménard, Nadève 204
Milcé, Jean-Euphèle 36, 189–91
mimesis 25, 85, 87, 89
 create language beyond 153
 cultural 257
Modiano, Patrick 210, 256
Mohanty, Satya 33, 93, 100
Moï, Anna 11, 17
Monénembo, Tierno 107, 110–19, *see also bas-fonds* literature; city writing
Moraru, Christian 27, 230
Moretti, Franco 26, 169
Mounsi, Mohand 127–8
Mudimbe, V.Y. 32
Mufti, Aamir R. 55, 57–8, 151–2, 169
Mukherjee, Prithwindra 33, 96
Mukundan, M. 100
Munro, Brenna M. 186–7
Munro, Martin 36, 195, *see also* literature of the everyday (*littérature-mondaine*)
Mzee, Said 72–3

Nandy, Ashish 96–7
négritude 37, 239–41, 243–5, *see also* Césaire, Aimé; *créolité*; Damas, Léon-Gontran; Fanon, Frantz; Senghor, Léopold Sédar
 movement 171, 174
 worlding 245–8
Nelligan, Émile 141, 147
Nganang, Patrice 111

shantytown novel (*le roman de bidonville*) 109
Niblett, Michael 34, 152–3, *see also* ecology, world
1980 Frankfurt Book Fair 73, 75
Nobel Prize for Literature 52, 56
nonhuman world (nonhuman environment) 152–5, 158–62

Okri, Ben 75
Organisation Internationale de la Francophonie (OIF) 3, 7–9, 67, 74, 77, 209, 257
Orwell, George 213–14, 218, 220
Oustinoff, Michaël 4

planetary problematics (*problématique-monde*) 1, 32, 34
Polet, Grégoire 21
postcolonial
 histories 169
 particularity 248
 period 4
 queering of theory 180
"Pour une littérature-monde en français" manifesto (*Manifeste pour une littérature-monde en français*) 1, 17, 24–7, 32, 36, 68, 122–3, 129, 152, 167–8, 210, 212, 215, *see also littérature-monde*
 context for 19–20
Présence Africaine 58, 68–71, 73, 75
Proust, Marcel 53, 147, 256
Provencher, Denis 184–5

Québec
 literature (*Lettres québécoises*) 34, 136–8
 queer studies 184
 studies 138, 182
queer
 desires 183–4, 186–7, 189, 192
 Queer Nations 181, 184
 queerness and/or MSM and WSW 180–2, 186, 189–90
 studies 52, 181
Quiet Revolution (*Révolution tranquille*) 138, 182
Qui fait la France? 123, 129

Ramayana 98, 101
Rancière, Jacques 247
Rao, Vijaya 11, 33
Raspail 213–14
Regional Centre for Book Promotion in Africa (CREPLA) 72–6, *see also* UNESCO
regional languages 94, 98, 101, 126
 French heritage 5
 minoritarian languages 125–6
Renaut, Alain 175
Rhizome 57, 118
Romanian literary history 252, 257
romans du terroir 138–9, 143

Said, Edward 50
 Orientalism 52, 56–8, 185, 217
Sansal, Boualem 17, 36, 212–14, 216–22
Santaki, Rachid 126, 130
Sapiro, Gisèle 67, 211
Sarkar, Ranajit 33, 96
Sartre, Jean-Paul 50, 100, 210, 242, 256
 Sartrean objection 245
Schizolinguistic state 89
Sembène, Ousmane 51
Senghor, Léopold Sédar 10, 53, 71, 75, 138, 169–70, 184
 black-being-in-the-world 242
 Nouvelles Editions Africaines (NEA) 75–6
Shakespeare, William 56
 The Tempest 37, 51, 239, 243–4
shantytown novel (*le roman de bidonville*), *see* Nganang, Patrice
Society of African Culture (SAC) 68
Soucy, Gaétan 139–40
Soyinka, Wole 52, 54, 71, 74–5
Spivak, Gayatri Chakravorty 25–6, 168

Tagore, Rabindranath 97
Tansi, Sony Labou 59, 112
Taubira, Christiane 35, 167–8, 171–6, *see also* legalization of same-sex marriage (*mariage pour tous*)
"think otherness" and Lévinas 174
Tchak, Sami 59, 61, 76, 111
Theater of the absurd 252, 256, 259, 261
Thierry, Raphaël 59–61
Thiong'o, Ngũgĩwa 151

topolect   84–8
  French as   84
Tournier, Michel   140, 227, 230, 256
transduction   107–8
  transductive poetics   110
translation
  contemporary French literature in   210–12, 215
  as cultural democracy   55
  international markets   10, 71, 122, 151, 210, 213–14
  and publishing opportunities   10, 70, 221
  and world literature   21, 31, 35, 56, 99–100, 167
transnational identity   36, 214–17, 222
  transcultural ideals   219–22
Tremblay, Michel   36, 182–3, 190
Trouillot, Evelyne   36, 194–200, 203–4
Tzara, Tristan   37, 147, 257

uchronia(s)   219, 221
uncanny (*unheimlich*)   228, 230–1, 237
UNESCO
  and publishing   61, 68, 70–2, 74, 76
universalism   52, 129, 175, 240
  anti-   159
  of blackness   242, 245–7 (*see also négritude*)
  cultural   138
  French   167, 172, 174–5

Varghese, Annamma   211
verlan   125–8, *see also banlieue* literature
Victor, Gary   54, 60

visibility
  of literature   60–1, 67, 77, 99
  logics of   201
Vişniec, Matei   37, 252–61, *see also* Generation of the 1980s
Volodine, Antoine   139–40, 144, 147

Waberi, Abdourahman   17, 59, 61, 76, 111
Weltliteratur, see also Goethe, Johann Wolfgang von
  Goethean   21–2, 32, 51–2, 55, 57, 97, 100, 151, 167, 170
  Marxian   5
world literature
  as discipline   52, 168
  in French   18, 20, 22, 36, 122, 129, 132, 167, 180, 212
  Norton Anthology of   52–4
  and sexuality studies   36, 180–1
world-making   152–3, 155, 159
  world-forming   228
  world remaking   227
worlding   9, 18, 27–8, 37, 153, 228
  act of   36, 239
  Francophone writing   32
  négritude   245–8
  re-world   227
Wynter, Sylvia
  Word of Man   158–9

Yacine, Kateb   12, 59

Žižek, Slavoj   245, 247
  adiaphora   245

www.ingramcontent.com/pod-product-compliance
Lightning Source LLC
Chambersburg PA
CBHW072123290426
44111CB00012B/1759